Personality-Guided Forensic Psychology

Personality-Guided
Forensic Psychology

Robert J. Craig

Series Editor Theodore Millon

AMERICAN PSYCHOLOGICAL ASSOCIATION
WASHINGTON, DC

Published by
American Psychological Association
750 First Street, NE
Washington, DC 20002
www.apa.org

To order
APA Order Department
P.O. Box 92984
Washington, DC 20090-2984
Tel: (800) 374-2721
Direct: (202) 336-5510
Fax: (202) 336-5502
TDD/TTY: (202) 336-6123
Online: www.apa.org/books/
E-mail: order@apa.org

In the U.K., Europe, Africa, and the Middle East, copies may be ordered from
American Psychological Association
3 Henrietta Street
Covent Garden, London
WC2E 8LU England

Typeset in Goudy by World Composition Services, Inc., Sterling, VA

Printer: Sheriden Books, Ann Arbor, MI
Cover Designer: Berg Design, Albany, NY
Technical/Production Editor: Gail B. Munroe

The opinions and statements published are the responsibility of the authors, and such opinions and statements do not necessarily represent the policies of the American Psychological Association.

Library of Congress Cataloging-in-Publication Data

Craig, Robert J., 1941-
    Personality-guided forensic psychology / Robert J. Craig.—1st ed.
        p. cm.—(Personality-guided psychology)
    Includes bibliographical references and index.
    ISBN 1-59147-151-6
    1. Forensic psychology. 2. Personality assessment. 3. Personality tests. 4. Personality disorders. I. Title.

    RA1148.C73 2004
    614'.15—dc22   2004000547

British Library Cataloguing-in-Publication Data
A CIP record is available from the British Library.

Printed in the United States of America
First Edition

This book is dedicated to Ted Millon, PhD, DSc. There can be no finer professional role model for a psychologist. His breadth of knowledge in a plethora of areas is remarkable. His general brilliance shines through the subspecialties of personology, clinical psychology, psychopathology, and theoretical analysis. I consider him to be one of the greatest men of his generation. The psychology profession is proud to have him as one of us.

CONTENTS

SERIES FOREWORD

The turn of the 20th century saw the emergence of psychological interest in the concept of individual differences, the recognition that the many realms of scientific study then in vogue displayed considerable variability among "laboratory subjects." Sir Francis Galton in Great Britain and many of his disciples, notably Charles Spearman in England, Alfred Binet in France, and James McKeen Cattell in the United States, laid the groundwork for recognizing that intelligence was a major element of import in what came to be called *differential psychology*. Largely through the influence of psychoanalytic thought, and then only indirectly, did this new field expand the topic of individual differences in the direction of character and personality.

And so here we are at the dawn of the 21st century, ready to focus our attentions ever more seriously on the subject of personality trait differences and their impact on a wide variety of psychological subjects—how they impinge on behavioral medicine outcomes, alter gerontological and adolescent treatment, regulate residential care programs, affect the management of depressive and PTSD patients, transform the style of cognitive–behavioral and interpersonal therapies, guide sophisticated forensic and correctional assessments—a whole bevy of important themes that typify where psychologists center their scientific and applied efforts today.

It is toward the end of alerting psychologists who work in diverse areas of study and practice that the present series, entitled *Personality-Guided Psychology*, has been developed for publication by the American Psychological Association. The originating concept underlying the series may be traced to Henry Murray's seminal proposal in his 1938 volume, *Explorations in Personality*, in which he advanced a new field of study termed *personology*.

It took its contemporary form in a work of mine, published in 1999 under the title *Personality-Guided Therapy*.

The utility and relevance of personality as a variable is spreading in all directions, and the series sets out to illustrate where things stand today. As will be evident as the series' publication progresses, the most prominent work at present is found with creative thinkers whose efforts are directed toward enhancing a more efficacious treatment of patients. We hope to demonstrate, further, some of the newer realms of application and research that lie just at the edge of scientific advances in our field. Thus, we trust that the volumes included in this series will help us look beyond the threshold of the present and toward the vast horizon that represents all of psychology. Fortunately, there is a growing awareness that personality variables can be a guiding factor in all spheres of study. We trust the series will provide a map of an open country that encourages innovative ventures and provides a foundation for investigators who wish to locate directions in which they themselves can assume leading roles.

Theodore Millon, PhD, DSc
Series Editor

PREFACE

Over the last half of the 20th century, three megatrends have affected the practice of clinical psychology. First, the growth of clinical psychology as an independent profession has resulted in psychologists engaging in assessment and treatment areas that, heretofore, were outside the realm of practice. The second trend is the resurgence of interest in personality evaluation and the diagnosis of personality disorders, stimulated by the development of Axis II in the official diagnostic nomenclature. Finally, there has been a spate of interest and opportunities in the area of forensic psychology—the interface between law and psychology.

Unfortunately, even though these trends developed at approximately the same time, they have not been integrated into theory and practice. For example, psychologists have tended to engage in personality assessment without a cohering theoretical foundation, which is quite different from their practice of psychotherapy, which historically has been practiced within a preferred theoretical orientation. And they have tended to practice forensic psychology as if the underlying personality had little effect on the Axis I syndromes that may be related to the ultimate question of innocence or guilt, risk of recidivism, or likely response to treatment.

This book attempts to bridge these bodies of scientific literature and practice by demonstrating the central role of personality and personality disorders in the assessment of patients within the context of court-related issues and problems. It illustrates how personality-guided assessment adds to what the psychometricians might call "incremental validity," what the social psychologists might call "ecological validity," and what triers of fact (judges and juries) might call "the truth."

Two threads connect the chapters of this book. First and foremost is the role of personality as it pertains to the issues addressed in each chapter.

Chapters have been structured to reflect the central role that personality variables play in the issues in question. Similarly, areas where personality factors seem to play a more diminished role, such as determining competency to stand trial, issues of civil commitment, evaluations of various insanity pleas, and so forth, are not addressed in this volume. Even though forensic psychologists have played a central role in these evaluations for the court, their final decision as to the "ultimate question" is more often based on psychopathology than on personality.

Psychology is becoming an empirical science with evidence-based assessment and evidence-based practice. This brings us to the second thread in this book—the role of base rate data in the assessment process (Ellwood, 1993). It cannot be stressed enough how important it is to compare the findings in an individual case with the findings of the population represented by that case. Wherever possible and feasible, I have applied what is known about available test findings to the issues at hand, sometimes presenting the data in tables and at other times referencing the sources of these data for interested readers. Test findings are especially important in forensic work, where depositions and testimony will be challenged on cross-examination. Buttressing a professional opinion with data is more persuasive to judges and juries and more difficult for the opposing attorney to undermine.

The material in this book concentrates on the assessment of adults. However, in a few sections, material related to the assessment of juvenile offenders is included, especially the assessment of psychopathy and violence risk assessments.

Chapter 1 introduces the field of personality-guided forensic assessment. I discuss preparation to become a forensic psychologist, rules of evidence, criminal defenses and levels of proofs, commonly used psychological assessment methods in forensic personality assessment, detection of impression management, assessment of psychopathy (probably the most frequent diagnosis among offenders), and issues in personality assessment of juvenile offenders, and I end with a discussion of ethics in forensic psychology.

Chapter 2 presents an overview of the personality theories that have been most influential in contemporary psychological practice and comments on their relevance and utility for forensic psychology. Millon's evolutionary biopsychosocial theory is stressed as the personality theory that has greatest applicability to forensic psychological assessment. Accordingly, applications of Millon's model are emphasized throughout the remaining chapters.

The organization of the remaining chapters is based on severity of the personality pathology likely to be manifested within the assessment situation, from relatively normal (assessment of police and law enforcement applicants) to the more severe forms of personality pathology (assessment of abuse, aggression, and lethal violence).

Chapter 3 addresses the important gatekeeping function of assessing law enforcement applicants. The chapter looks at the nature and job requirements of police officers, characteristics and personality traits that distinguish successful from unsuccessful officers, and the psychological instruments commonly used for this screening process (several tables provide applicable data and norms) and concludes with a discussion of issues of adverse impact on groups of employee selection methods and procedures.

Chapter 4 presents an overview of the field of child custody evaluations and highlights published guidelines and standards in this area. The chapter presents commonly used assessment measures, addresses child abuse assessment and false allegations of child abuse, discusses some ethical problems in conducting these evaluations and risk management activities to reduce potential liability, and concludes with a recommended strategy for custody evaluations.

Chapter 5 addresses personal injury assessments. It discusses workers' compensation programs; presents data on the psychological experience of pain, emphasizing orthopedic pain; and then presents Minnesota Multiphasic Personality Inventory (MMPI) studies with chronic pain patients (and provides supporting tables). Also discussed are assessments of medical and pain patients using the Rorschach and the Millon Clinical Multiaxial Inventory (MCMI). Finally, the treatment outcome literature with pain patients is referenced. The assessment of posttraumatic stress disorder (PTSD) with the MMPI and the MCMI is also included, as many litigants claim PTSD as a result of personal injury. The chapter concludes with a case example of a personal injury psychological assessment.

In chapter 6, I discuss the psychological evaluation of sexual harassment claimants. I review the legal definition of sexual harassment and the employer's responsibility to provide a safe working environment for employees. I also present examples of sexually harassing behaviors under the law and provide case examples of both sexual and nonsexual harassment behaviors.

Chapter 7 begins with some statistics on the extent of child abuse in America. I address the controversial issue of psychological profiling of sex offenders, which rests on the question of whether personality traits in this group can be reliably assessed with extant methods. This chapter discusses the forensic and psychological assessment of sex offenders and not only commonly used tools for their assessment (clinical interview, personality tests, deviant interest tests) but also additional assessment methods (i.e., statement analysis, phallometry). I discuss the question of risk of relapse, reoffense, and recidivism and conclude by presenting a case and its analysis through to conclusions.

Chapter 8 addresses the assessment of abuse, aggression, and lethal violence in both juveniles and adults. I discuss the issues of domestic violence and partner abuse, the battered spouse syndrome, and the assessment of lethal violence. The psychometric assessment of these behaviors emphasizes MMPI studies, but Rorschach and MCMI studies are also presented. I argue that Millon's subtypes of the antisocial, aggressive, and passive-aggressive prototypes appear to be particularly helpful in understanding the empirical data. Guidelines for the assessment of lethal violence are offered, and several cases are interspersed throughout the chapter.

Chapter 9 concludes the volume by suggesting some possible future directions in this field.

ACKNOWLEDGMENTS

Deepest appreciation is extended to Susan Koval for her extensive assistance in procuring many reference materials through interlibrary loan. I also thank the anonymous reviewers of drafts of this manuscript, whose incisive and critical comments and suggestions helped to improve the final product. A full measure of thanks also goes to the staff at the American Psychological Association who participated in the various phases of the production of this book.

Personality-Guided Forensic Psychology

1

INTRODUCTION TO FORENSIC PSYCHOLOGICAL PRACTICE

Forensic psychology may be defined as the interface between psychology and law. The word *forensic* is a Latin derivative of the word meaning *forum*, a place where trials were held in ancient Rome. The purview of forensic psychology continues to expand, demonstrating the breadth and differentiating scope of practice in this specialty field. Although initially practitioners in forensic psychology were generally clinical psychologists, now many forensic psychologists receive training and practical experience in this specialty as graduate students and in postgraduate fellowships in forensic settings. Today, more than 2,000 psychologists are members of the American Psychological Association's Division 41, the American Psychology–Law Society.

Hugo Munsterberg (1908) is generally credited with developing the field of forensic psychology. In a seminal book called *On the Witness Stand*, he reported, largely on the basis of his own experiences, how the knowledge base of psychology can be used to help the court in several defined areas (e.g., witness memory, the value of hypnosis in crime detection, and witness interrogation). The book contains no reference citations, and his claims were largely exaggerated and were not based on empirical evidence, but Munsterberg's book served as a beginning point for the empirical study of law and psychology.

Forensic psychology has two broad areas of application: research and practice. The research boundaries are porous and continue to expand. Some forensic research crosses over into other areas of psychological research, particularly social psychology. Research activities of forensic psychologists include the study of eyewitness memory and the conditions under which it deteriorates or maintains reliability, jury decision-making processes, whether the presence of an attorney is truly a safeguard for the defendant's rights at a lineup, legal definitions such as *reasonableness* in the "reasonable person" standard, criminal behavior, the variability of jury awards in sentences by race of defendant and by jury instructions, and privacy rights.

Most of forensic practice has occurred in one of three main functions: (a) friend of the court (amicus curiae) activities, (b) consultation, and (c) acting as an expert witness (Blau, 1998). Some areas of forensic practice overlap with areas of clinical psychology, particularly those pertaining to psychological evaluations necessitating psychological tests. Some of the activities that constitute forensic psychological practice include (but are not limited to)

- providing child custody evaluations,
- screening police applicants,
- screening applicants for public safety jobs, such as access to nuclear power plants,
- evaluating sex offenders,
- evaluating various insanity pleas,
- evaluating defendants in capital cases,
- providing services (treatment, intervention, prevention) to offenders and correctional staff, and
- providing courtroom testimony.

This book addresses only professional forensic practice and does not deal with forensic psychological research, except to describe the research that underpins this practice. This book also concentrates on the assessment of adults and on adult offenders, although material on the assessment of juvenile offenders is occasionally included as well.

PREPARATION FOR FORENSIC PSYCHOLOGICAL PRACTICE

Forensic psychological practice inevitably involves depositions and courtroom testimony. To best serve their clients, forensic psychologists normally require the following preparation:

1. A doctoral degree from a school of psychology accredited by the American Psychological Association must be completed.

2. State licensure or registration is required by all.
3. Direct and relevant experience in the matters before the court is mandatory. For example, if substance abuse is an issue in the court proceeding, then the psychologist must be able to demonstrate expertise in alcohol and drug abuse screening, evaluations, and treatment. If posttraumatic stress disorder (PTSD) is an issue, the psychologist must be able to demonstrate competence and knowledge in the full range of the disorder. Demonstrating that one has evaluated and treated a sufficient number of PTSD cases so as to be able to render a believable conclusion on demand might reflect this competence.
4. Attendance at continuing education workshops, seminars, symposia, and the like is evidence of continuing involvement in an area of expertise and is further evidence of competence.
5. Attainment of advanced specializations and certifications of competency, such as diplomate status (clinical or forensic) or fellow status granted by external bodies is additional evidence of expertise. For example, if the psychologist testifies as an expert in psychological testing, then fellow status in APA Division 5 (Evaluation, Measurement, and Statistics) or fellow status in the Society for Personality Assessment would be a recognized credential. Normally, fellow status in serious professional organizations requires that one have a national reputation in a body of knowledge, have significantly contributed to the advancement of that knowledge and skill, or have demonstrated competency in practice applications as attested to by one's peers.
6. Membership in relevant professional organizations (Otto & Heilbrun, 2002) is helpful as well as publication of relevant material, preferably in peer-reviewed journals, that adds to scientific discovery.

To function within the best practice parameters of the psychology profession, forensic psychologists must be aware of and knowledgeable about legal issues, legal standards, legal definitions and terms, and legal procedures. They must also be aware of the unique ethical issues that affect forensic practice. Various sources of information about applicable statutes and procedures are available (Van Der Velde, 1999), and a code of ethics for forensic practice has been developed (Committee on Ethical Guidelines for Forensic Psychologists, 1991). Also, there are journals that are specifically devoted to forensic issues; among the more frequently cited are the following:

- *American Journal of Forensic Psychology,*
- *Behavioral Sciences and the Law,*
- *Criminal Justice and Behavior,*
- *Law and Human Behavior,*
- *Journal of Forensic Psychology Practice,*
- *Psychology, Public Policy, and the Law,*
- *Journal of Psychiatry and Law,*
- *Journal of Threat Assessment,*
- *American Journal of Forensic Psychiatry,*
- *Journal of the American Academy of Psychiatry and Law,*
- *Journal of Forensic Psychiatry and Psychology,* and
- *Rules of Evidence.*

In *Jenkins v. United States* (1962), the court ruled that psychologists may testify as expert witnesses on mental disorders as long as they have appropriate training and expertise. Three psychologists had testified pertaining to a defendant's mental disease. The trial judge instructed the jury to disregard the testimony of the psychologists because they were not physicians. On appeal, both the American Psychological Association and the American Psychiatric Association filed amicus curiae briefs. The psychology association argued that psychologists were professionally qualified to diagnose mental illness, whereas the psychiatry association argued that although psychologists may be good testers, they function only as assistants to psychiatrists and are not qualified to diagnose or treat mental illness.

Judge David Bazelon ruled that it was not a medical degree that conferred expertise on the question of mental disease, but rather a person's training, skills, and knowledge. He ruled that psychologists did have these necessary requirements and therefore could serve as expert witnesses in the case, as long as they become familiar with rules of evidence that allow certain kinds of testimony to be admissible (or inadmissible) in court proceedings.

Rules of evidence vary across jurisdictions. State courts rely on either codified rules of evidence or extensive case law, and some use the federal rules of evidence as a model. In federal courts, the admissibility of scientific evidence may rely on one of three legal standards:

1. In the *Federal Rules of Evidence* (FRE, 1992), the evidence is admissible if it is relevant and helpful.
2. In the *Frye* standard (*United States v. Frye,* 1923), the court ruled that if a test, methodology, or procedure has general acceptance in the field to which it belongs (e.g., scientific community), then it can be admitted in court.
3. In 1993 the Supreme Court clarified that the *FRE* should be used in federal courts and then outlined the standards that the courts could use. In *Daubert v. Merrell Dow Pharmaceuticals*

(1993), the court ruled that the trier of fact (judge or jury) must make a preliminary assessment as to whether the expert's reasoning and methodology are scientifically valid and can be properly applied to the facts at issue in the court. This new standard now compels the forensic psychologist to pay far more attention to issues of reliability and validity and to other technical matters (e.g., operating characteristics and diagnostic power) of the psychometric instruments on which the testimony is based.

The U.S. Supreme Court has subsequently clarified and elaborated on the interpretation of the *Daubert* standard in *General Electric v. Joiner* (1997) and *Kumho Tire Company Ltd. et al. v. Carmichael et al.* (1999). In *General Electric*, the court ruled that a judge's determination on *Daubert* admissibility may not be overturned unless the judge has abused the discretionary authority. In *Kumho*, the court ruled that the requirements of *Daubert* do not have to be met in every case and that judges have wide discretion in determining a method's reliability. No doubt there will be increasing refinement, interpretation, and application of the *FRE* and *Daubert* in subsequent court reviews.

The *FRE* was modified as of December 1, 2000 but continues to rely on *Daubert*. This revision requires that the testimony be based on scientific facts or data and be the product of reliable principles and methods and that the expert witness have applied the principles and methods reliably to the facts of the case. These conditions continue to be modified by case law and subject to interpretation.

Daubert relies on scientific philosopher Karl Popper's criteria for the falsifiability of scientific theories. Popper's theorem states that a scientific theory should be so operationally (and concretely) defined that it can be tested and found false. The court also suggested additional criteria: Has the theory or technique been subjected to peer review and published in scientific journals? Is there general acceptance of the theory or technique in the scientific community? Does the theory or technique have a known error rate, and are there standards to control for this error rate? The court stated that these criteria were not meant to be exhaustive, but it did not rule that a test or theory had to meet all four elements of the criteria in order for the testimony to be admissible in court.

Professional standards also apply to this stricture. Psychologists practice according to specialty guidelines (American Psychological Association, 1981) and the American Psychological Association (2002a) *Ethical Principles of Psychologists and Code of Conduct* (Ethics Code), which prescribe general ethical psychological practices and address assessment practice. Heilbrun (1992) published recommended criteria to use in judging the adequacy of a psychological test for purposes of court testimony. Heilbrun's guidelines, which are increasingly being referenced in the professional literature and may become the standard in the future, are as follows:

- Is the test commercially available, with a manual and at least one independent review?
- Is the test's reliability (interrater and test–retest) at least .80?
- Is the test relevant to the legal issue or to a psychological construct underlying the legal issue?
- Does the test have a standard method of administration, and should it be administered as close as possible to this standard?
- Is the test applicable to the population and purpose for which it is being used?
- Does the test have objective scoring criteria, and does it have actuarial data that can combine scores, which is preferable?
- Does the test measure response styles?

It is advisable for the forensic psychologist to apply these criteria, as well as the *Daubert* standard, to each method used on which there may be court testimony. Forensic psychologists should also expect cross-examination on each of these criteria and on the methods used, and they should prepare rebuttal arguments to these challenges. Consultation with a competent attorney should be quite helpful with this rebuttal process, especially in depositions where an attorney's line of attack is revealed, thereby allowing the psychologist to prepare rebuttal arguments during actual court testimony.

The *FRE* governs the admissibility of expert testimony in federal courts. State courts have individual determinations for admissibility of evidence, although most rely on some or all aspects of the *FRE*, *Frye*, and *Daubert*. It is advisable for the psychologist to consult with an attorney to ascertain what may or may not be introduced into evidence on the basis of state law.

TESTIMONY ON THE ULTIMATE ISSUE

Controversy exists concerning the issue of testifying as to the ultimate (legal) issue in the case (e.g., Was the person legally insane? Was he or she able to maintain mens rea?). Some jurisdictions permit such testimony by experts, whereas others prohibit it, deferring such judgments to the triers of fact. Some psychologists argue that they should reject pressure to testify as to the ultimate issue, that their training generally does not provide sufficient competence training and development to offer conclusions in matters of law. However, there is some evidence that judges want expert opinion on ultimate issues (Melton, Petrila, Poythress, & Slobogin, 1997).

Psychologists should consult with the hiring attorney about the limits of their testimony.

CRIMINAL DEFENSES

Most criminal statutes include elements pertaining to conduct and mental state in terms of mens rea, or level of intent to commit a specific act, which includes knowledge and purpose. Some states also include the specific circumstance or result of the criminal act in their statutes.

Defendants have a limited number of possible pleas that can be entered in a criminal case, other than guilty. Psychologists working in the courts should have a rudimentary knowledge of these pleas and a more thorough knowledge regarding insanity pleas, if they conduct insanity evaluations. The reader is urged to consult more exhaustive sources for a thorough explanation of these defenses (e.g., Goldstein, Morse, & Shapiro, 2003). The following are the most common defenses entered into the court:

1. *Duress:* With a duress plea the defendant argues that he or she was threatened with death or serious bodily harm unless he or she engaged in the criminal behavior.
2. *Extreme mental or emotional disturbance:* With this plea, duress and extreme provocation result in the criminal act. Battered wife syndrome, addressed in chapter 8, is a good example of this type of plea.
3. *Involuntary intoxication:* Most statutes that allow involuntary intoxication as a plea (and excuse for the criminal act) also stipulate that it must have caused a mental abnormality that meets the legal definition of insanity for the defendant to avoid culpability.
4. *Provocation or pressure:* In this plea it is argued that the criminal behavior was the result of provocation that was so compelling that a reasonable person would act in a similar manner under similar circumstances.
5. *"Twinkie" defense:* The California Supreme Court allowed some mitigation of criminal responsibility after evidence was introduced that ingesting an excessive amount of junk food with high sugar content caused the defendant's behavior. (The California legislature later repealed this as a defense.)
6. *XYY defense:* This plea involves a chromosomal abnormality in men. The legal theory holds that the extra Y chromosome produces abnormal aggression with poor impulse control. It

is then argued that as a consequence of this defect, the accused is legally insane. Psychologists rarely become involved in this type of defense.

7. *M'Naughton rule (insanity plea)*: The M'Naughton rule holds that "The party accused was lacking under such a defect of reason, from disease of the mind, as not to know the nature and quality of the act he was doing; or if he did know, that he did not know what he was doing was wrong" (M'Naughton, 1843, p. 722). This rule is strictly a cognitive standard of insanity and is called a "right and wrong" test. It does not take into account the emotional aspects of behavior and affective states.

8. *Irresistible impulse (insanity plea)*: The irresistible impulse plea means that the "reasoning powers [of the accused] were so far dethroned by his diseased mental condition as to deprive him of will power to resist the insane impulse to perpetuate the deed, though knowing it would be wrong" (*Smith v. United States*, 1929, pp. 548, 549). This plea adds a volitional component to the cognitive component of the M'Naughton standard. Irresistible impulse is extremely difficult to prove. How does one differentiate between an irresistible impulse and an unresisted impulse? At what point does a person distinguish between choosing not to exert control versus being unable to exert control? The courts have ruled that the behavior falls under the definition of irresistible impulse if the presence of a police officer would not be sufficient to stop the behavior.

9. *Durham rule (insanity plea)*: *Durham v. United States* (1954) established that the accused is not criminally responsible if his or her criminal activity was the product of a mental disease or defect. Initially the word *product* was excessively vague. Psychodynamic theory can argue that virtually anything can cause anything else, and *mental disease and defect* was also undefined and left up to the practitioner to define. Subsequently, *mental disease and defect* was defined as "any abnormal condition of the mind which substantially affects mental and emotional processes or substantially impairs behavior controls" (*McDonald v. United States*, 1962). (This standard has now been replaced by the American Law Institute standard—see below.)

10. *Diminished capacity (insanity plea)*: Culpability requires one to deliberate, premeditate, maturely and meaningfully reflect upon one's act, harbor malice, and be able to form the neces-

sary intent (mens rea) to commit the crime. The diminished capacity standard exculpates a defendant if, as a result of mental disease or defect, a person lacks the requisite specific intent to commit the alleged crime.

11. *American Law Institute (ALI; insanity plea,* articulated in the *Model Penal Code;* ALI, 1962): "As a result of mental disease or defect [the accused] lacks substantial capacity either to appreciate the criminality [wrongfulness] of his conduct or to conform his conduct to the requirements of law" (Sect. 4.01, p. 23). This standard excludes antisocial and psychopathic abnormalities.

12. *Federal Insanity Defense Reform Act (1984) (insanity plea):* "The defendant, as a result of severe mental disease or defect, was unable to appreciate the nature and quality of the wrongfulness of the act" (as cited in American Bar Association, 1989, p. 20). Mental disease or defect and cognitive incapacity are components of insanity standards across all jurisdictions. Volitional incapacity and exclusion of antisocial personality disorders vary in each state's insanity standard. In most jurisdictions, personality disorders, substance abuse, and disorders of impulse control (e.g., pyromania, gambling) do not exculpate defendants.

13. *Guilty but mentally ill (insanity plea):* In this plea, defendants are committed to a psychiatric hospital for treatment until their mental illness is in remission. They are then transferred from the hospital to a correctional facility to complete their sentence. Their time in the hospital is credited toward their prison sentence.

LEVELS OF PROOF

Psychologists have been trained to rely on probability theory to ascribe a degree of certainty to a hypothesis. If the level of probability is .01, then it is 99% probable that the results can be attributed to the variables under investigation. In court, different standards of proof apply, depending on the jurisdiction and the legal issue in question. These levels of proof are "beyond a reasonable doubt," "clear and convincing evidence," and "preponderance of evidence." The psychologist will be asked to render an opinion "to a reasonable degree of certainty." This phrase does not apply to statistical probability or to legal definitions of proof; it means that the psychologist has ruled out other possible explanations and is reasonably confident that the explanation given is the most likely one.

DIFFERENCES BETWEEN CLINICAL AND FORENSIC PRACTICE

Forensic interviews differ from traditional clinical interviews in a number of significant ways. In treatment, psychologists usually adopt a supportive, accepting, and empathic stance toward the patient, but the forensic psychologist must adopt a more investigative role while searching for truth. In doing so, the forensic psychologist may act in a neutral, objective, and detached manner (Greenberg & Shuman, 1997). There is sufficient evidence to support the notion that litigating patients are prone to malinger, to overreport symptoms, and to answer questions in ways that affect psychological test scores. For example, patients injured in industrial accidents tend to heal at certain rates, but compensation-seeking patients with the same injuries may take longer to heal (see Williams, Lees-Haley, & Djanogly, 1999). Workplace injuries are more fully discussed in chapter 5.

The clinical psychologist's main goal is to help the client; the forensic psychologist's main goal is to help the court. Clinical psychologists often are required to make a psychiatric diagnosis, but the forensic psychologist makes only those diagnoses that are incidental to the main issue in the case. To the extent that the diagnosis is helpful to the court (i.e., psychotic disorders in insanity pleas), forensic psychologists make such diagnoses. In other cases (e.g., child custody evaluations, screening of law enforcement applicants), diagnoses may not be warranted.

Whereas clinical psychologists may see the patient for multiple sessions over an extended period of time and in less structured formats, the forensic psychologist may see the patient only for a few sessions and, in some cases, only once or twice and in highly structured formats. These different interview conditions require a different way of thinking by the psychologist. For example, if a patient has been deposed on several occasions about PTSD, then prior exposure to the evaluation and questioning may help the patient present a more realistic picture of the disorder to the next forensic psychologist at the next evaluation. Clinical psychologists rarely consider this, but a forensic psychologist would have to explore for this possibility. As a standard of proof for the veracity of a conclusion, clinical psychologists tend to trust their clinical judgment, research psychologists rely on alpha levels, and the forensic psychologist must follow the court dictates that require "beyond a reasonable doubt," a "preponderance of evidence," or "clear and convincing evidence."

Privilege is the right to protection of information given in the context of a professional relationship from discovery in evidentiary proceedings. Most work of the clinical psychologist is privileged information (unless the client waives his or her right of privilege), whereas most forensic evaluations have no such protection. In fact, forensic psychologists are ethically required to inform clients that the results of the inquiry, evaluation, and conclusions can and will be used against them in a court of law.

The clinical psychologist needs to be aware of only those areas of law that govern professional practice. The forensic psychologist, in a general way, also needs to be aware of the law that pertains to the case. (Packer & Borum, 2003, provided a partial list of case law relevant to many areas of forensic psychological practice.)

The consequences of forensic evaluations also differ from those of other types of clinical evaluations. In forensic practice, a client may lose custody of a child, be denied compensation (or perhaps awarded millions of dollars), or go to jail as a result, in part, of the forensic evaluation. (This is now called "high stakes" testing.)

Perhaps the real difference pertains to who the client is. For clinical psychologists the patient is the client; the forensic psychologist has dual roles, and in many cases the client is the court or the referring attorney.

ASSESSMENT INSTRUMENTS (ADULTS)

The forensic psychologist needs to be aware of commonly used assessment methods in forensic cases and of those methods that are able to withstand both scientific scrutiny and cross-examination as to admissibility and relevance. Assessment instruments can be classified as either *forensic assessment instruments*—those that "are directly relevant to a specific legal standard and reflect and focus on specific capabilities, abilities, or knowledge that are embodied by the law"—or *forensically relevant instruments*—those that "address constructs that are often pertinent to evaluating persons in the legal system" (Otto & Heilbrun, 2002, p. 5). In this section I review some frequently used methods in forensic evaluations with a focus on the objective and projective measures of personality that have been used in court testimony. Cognitive and neuropsychological measures are not discussed, even though these have relevance in many forensic evaluations.

The Minnesota Multiphasic Personality Inventory (MMPI; Hathaway & McKinley, 1943), usually in its revised version, the MMPI–2 (Butcher, Dahlstrom, Graham, Tellegen, & Kaemmer, 1989), is the most commonly used psychological test and, therefore, the most commonly used objective measure of personality. The Rorschach test (1942) is the most commonly used projective test measure of personality. The Wechsler scales (1997, 2004) are the most commonly used measures of intellectual functioning (Butcher & Rouse, 1996; Craig & Horowitz, 1990; Lubin, Larsen, & Matarazzo, 1984; Watkins, Campbell, Nieberding, & Hallmark, 1995).

Objective Personality Tests

The MMPI–2 is particularly useful because its validity scales have relevance to many aspects of forensic evaluations, such as malingering, exaggeration, and underreporting. Its clinical, content, and supplemental scales are well researched and well validated, and literature is available that recommends ways to use findings in court proceedings (Ben-Porath, Graham, Hall, Hirschman, & Zaragoza, 1995; Pope, Butcher, & Seelen, 1993). The MMPI–2 has rarely been excluded from legal proceedings, except when it is used in ways that are not supported by empirical results (Otto, 2002). However, there is generally a substantial literature relating this test to many forensic questions pertaining to competency, dangerousness, custody evaluations, capital offenses, posttraumatic stress conditions, and psychological consequences of various medical conditions, among others. There is also MMPI data that distinguishes forensic psychiatry patients from general inmate groups (Schmaltz, Fehr, & Dalby, 1989). Evidence from the MMPI–2 is admissible in court (Meloy, 1991); one can still expect strenuous cross-examination of one's testimony, but challenges to the test itself will not be upheld, on the basis of case law.

The forensic psychologist also needs to be aware of other tests, methods, and procedures commonly used in evaluations for specific purposes. In general, the MMPI–2 almost always is cited as a frequently used test (except in cases of mental retardation) and therefore appears on most published recommendations and in lists of frequently used tests. In fact, lists of frequently used tests in clinical evaluation turn out to be almost identical to those of frequently used tests in forensic evaluations (Borum & Grisso, 1995).

The Millon Clinical Multiaxial Inventory (MCMI; Millon, 1983, 1987, 1994a) is a test of personality that is increasingly used in psychological assessment (Butcher & Rouse, 1996) and that has a strong empirical literature (Craig, 1993a, 1997). The test seems particularly well suited to assess personality disorders or a person's underlying personality style, and there are several good sources to assist in the interpretation of this test (Choca & Van Denburg, 1996; Craig, 1993b, 1994, 1999a).

Researchers have argued that only the MCMI–II Avoidant, Schizotypal, and Borderline scales (Millon, 1987) meet the admissibility standards established by *Daubert* (R. Rogers, Salekin, & Sewell, 1999). R. Rogers et al. argued that these scales have reasonable convergent and discriminant validity, whereas the other scales of the MCMI do not. They also argued that many forensic issues, such as insanity, have not been studied with the MCMI, and they therefore cautioned against use of the MCMI in such proceedings. However, *People v. Stoll* (1989) was the precedent-setting case that upheld the admissibility of the MCMI in court testimony. McCann and Dyer (1996) found 22 cases through 1994 that recognized results from the MCMI–I and MCMI–II as part of psychological testimony. These issues pertained to the classification of sex offenders, domestic violence, assessment of malingering and deception, evaluation of criminal defendants, child custody evaluations, and termination of parental rights. Craig (1999b) presented commentary and recommended guidelines on preparing for and presenting MCMI-based testimony in court, and McCann (2002) reported additional commentary.

I have not found any situations where the courts have ruled that the MCMI was not admissible. Furthermore, the issue of the MCMI–III validity as it pertains to forensic cases remains under debate (Dyer & McCann, 2000; Retzlaff, 2000; R. Rogers, Salekin, & Sewell, 2000). As for the "general acceptance" requirement of the *Frye* standard, the MCMI meets that standard as evidenced by its frequent use in psychological practice based on test use surveys. Also, no rules of evidence mandate that a method or technique must be without controversy before material based on that technique is admissible. Still, the prudent psychologist would do well to read the arguments presented by R. Rogers et al. (1999) and to prepare potential testimony to refute attacks on the test's validity.

Projective Tests

Rorschach

The Rorschach is useful because it, too, is well researched; avoids the problems of conscious exaggeration, malingering (Perry & Kinder, 1990), and underreporting; and can tap unconscious processes and motivational determinants relevant to issues before the court. The Rorschach tends to bridge objective and projective measures, because although the test itself is a projective test, use of the Comprehensive System (CS) for scoring (Exner, 1993) results in objective scores with a solid research base and good evidence of both reliability and validity (Parker, 1983). The Rorschach has been judged to meet evidence from scientific scrutiny and rules of evidence and is, therefore, admissible in courts of law (McCann, 1998; Meloy, 1991; Meloy, Hansen, & Weiner, 1997). In fact, in a review of 7,943 federal and state court cases, there was only one case where Rorschach-based testimony was not admissible as evidence (Weiner, Exner, & Sciara, 1996).

A recent controversy has surfaced relative to the Rorschach norms used by most clinicians. Exner developed these norms for the CS, the scoring system used by almost all clinicians who score the Rorschach. However, recent data suggest that nonpatient adults tend to appear pathological when compared to the CS norms (Wood, Nezworski, Garb, & Lilienfeld, 2001). These data seem compelling, notwithstanding rebuttal arguments (G. J. Meyer, 2001), and psychologists may increasingly be challenged when CS norms are used. Challenge could be especially likely in contentious cases such as child custody and accident-related injury and disability assessments. One way to circumvent such challenges is to use multiple assessment methods. If many tests convey essentially the same conclusions, then the issues of norm reference and bias may not be quite as strong. Exner (2002) is developing a revised nonpatient standardization sample that hopefully will obviate such challenges and problems.

A large body of empirical evidence supports the reliability (G. J. Meyer et al., 2002), validity (Gacono, Loving, & Bodholt, 2001; Ganellen, 2001), and clinical utility of the Rorschach. The test shows no evidence of differential validity or test bias based on race (G. J. Meyer, 2002). Still, scholars have reached contradictory and even opposite conclusions concerning the scientific merits of the Rorschach (Garb, 1999; Garb, Wood, Nezworski, Grove, & Stejskal, 2001; Hunsley & Bailey, 1999; Viglione, 1999; Wood & Lilienfeld, 1999; Wood, Lilienfeld, Nezworski, & Garb, 2001; Wood, Nezworski, & Stejskal, 1996). Some have even called for a moratorium on the clinical and forensic use of the Rorschach (Garb, 1999). Similar arguments and controversies have been raised concerning projective techniques as an assessment class (S. Hibbard, 2003; Lilienfeld, Wood, & Garb, 2000).

Those who embrace the Rorschach have argued that the cited polemics ignore the full range of scientific evidence. Weiner (2001) considered the published attacks on the Rorschach as akin to legal briefs, which are introduced to present evidence and arguments to support opposing attorneys' arguments. On the other hand, the scientific literature is supposed to be an unbiased and objective presentation of the empirical evidence. Some of these challenges to expert testimony based on the Rorschach may be introduced in the courtroom, so forensic psychologists must be prepared to defend their assessment methods.

Other Tools

The Thematic Apperception Test (TAT; Murray, 1943) is a frequently used measure in forensic settings and has been successfully used in juvenile forensic settings as well (Haynes & Poltran, 1985). The TAT has been especially useful in matters related to sexual abuse; this use of the test is expanded on in chapter 4.

Figure drawings, such as the Draw-A-Person and the House–Tree–Person (Buck, 1992; Hammer, 1963, 1999; Koppitz, 1968; Machover, 1949), along with the Kinetic Family Drawing (KFD; Burns & Kaufman, 1972; Handler & Habenicht, 1999), are used in forensic cases, especially in child custody (Ackerman & Ackerman, 1997; Keilin & Bloom, 1986) and evaluations of child abuse (Goodwin, 1982; Heinze & Grisso, 1996; R. A. Hibbard & Hartman, 1990; R. A. Hibbard, Roghmann, & Hoekelman, 1987). The use of figure drawings in clinical assessments continues to be controversial

(Riethmiller & Handler, 1997). Research has failed to substantiate many of the alleged hypotheses or interpretations for many figure drawing signs (Kahill, 1984; Roback, 1968; Smith & Dumont, 1995; Swensen, 1957, 1968). Research suggests that the personality of the interpreter interacts with his or her skill level in interpreting figure drawings (Scribner & Handler, 1987), implying that some professionals are better than others in interpreting figure drawings. Psychologists who use figure drawings as part of the assessment process can expect challenges in cross-examination to their facility in interpreting these tests, along with basic challenges to the test itself.

Researchers continue to try to give figure drawing interpretation a more empirical foundation (Blain, Gerbner, Lewis, & Goldstein, 1981; Bovan & Craig, 2002; Naglieri, McNeish, & Baidos, 1991). A more global or holistic interpretation of the drawings may lead to a more accurate interpretation than the "sign" approach (Handler & Riethmiller, 1999; Tharinger & Stark, 1990). However, Lally (2001) applied both Heilbrun's (1992) criteria and the *Daubert* standard to figure drawings and found them not to meet admissibility standards. Lally concluded that although figure drawings may have a place in clinical practice, they have no place in the courtroom. However, there is often a confluence of clinical and forensic practice, and when figure drawings are part of an initial evaluation preceding clinical treatment, the findings from this evaluation may have relevance in a forensic case. I cite three case examples.

In the first case, a 7½-year-old biracial White and African American girl was brought to therapy by her mother with complaints of recurring nightmares, immature and aggressive behavior, extremely overdependent behavior, constant fright, apprehension, and even paniclike behavior. The child was given a routine battery of tests, which included the KFD. Her figure drawing consisted of a child being pulled on each arm by her mother and father, with the mother on the ground, the father somewhat off the ground, and the child well off the ground. The mother had a speech bubble pointing toward her mouth in which the child wrote, "Let her go." The arm being pulled by the father had an X marked through it, as if he were about to pull it off.

At the time of the evaluation, the parents were having marital problems and had separated. The overall picture and stance of the people would normally reflect that the child was being "pulled" (emotionally) between her parents. However, the X on the arm suggested possible physical abuse. Subsequent inquiry revealed that the father, during a recent visitation, told the girl to get him marijuana from a box on the table. When she refused, he beat her on the arm with a pipe. She further revealed that he had tried to abduct her after school and at a playground on several occasions. The KFD was included as a copy and attached to the report, which convinced the judge (even if it might not convince researchers).

In the second case, the patient was being evaluated for sexually abusing his 5-year-old son and denied the charge. Again, as part of the evaluation, the patient was given the House–Tree–Person test. He drew a happy family scene. It was during the holiday season, and he drew a Christmas tree. His wife was visible in the kitchen, and his children were in the living room watching TV, as was the alleged victim. The patient drew himself standing directly in front of the victim with his hand on his crotch, apparently about to expose his penis.

In a third case, an alleged perpetrator of child sexual abuse was given the House–Tree–Person, and he drew a small house (clinically reflecting inadequacy), an extremely large phallic-like tree, and himself, quite small (more inadequacy), holding a lawn mower in his hand (a phallic symbol). His drawing communicated his feelings of personal and sexual inadequacy, thereby compelling him to abuse children, with whom he could exert power and not feel inadequate. A psychologist would have a difficult time convincing a judge or jury as to the validity and forensic relevance of the drawing in Case 3, but the picture in Case 2 speaks for itself and would (and did) convince most triers of fact.

DETECTION OF MALINGERING AND MINIMIZATION

In many evaluation contexts, including custody evaluations and employment screening, minimization or underreporting of psychological problems can be expected. In other contexts, such as personal injury litigation and evaluations and insanity pleas, the patient may exaggerate, overreport, malinger, or feign a psychological disorder. Failure to detect the underreporting of problems could put children or the general public at risk, depending on the nature of the evaluation. Similarly, the detection of malingering overrides all other clinical issues. If the forensic psychologist determines that the patient is malingering or faking a disorder and has objective evidence to back up that conclusion, then this is likely to destroy the claimant's credibility as to the substantive issues in the case (R. Rogers & Bender, 2003).

Furthermore, attorneys may advise their clients on how to respond to psychological tests, and they may make suggestions about what to tell psychologists and what not to disclose and about what symptoms or traits to emphasize (Lees-Haley, 1997a; Wetter & Corrigan, 1995; Youngjohn, 1995). Researchers are moving away from studies that detect whether symptoms on a psychological test have been exaggerated. More recent studies are now investigating whether a test can discriminate the results of people coached on malingering strategies from those of psychiatric patients and a sample of uncoached respondents. Early results suggest that the MMPI–2 has been able to discriminate between these groups (Baer & Miller, 2002;

Storm & Graham, 2000). No research to date has applied such strategies to other personality tests.

ASSESSMENT OF UNDERREPORTING AND OVERREPORTING OF PROBLEMS

Clinical Interview

The forensic psychologist should never make a definitive conclusion as to minimization or malingering based solely on a clinical interview. Rather, interviews should be complemented with objective test data. To help objectify the clinical interview, R. Rogers, Bagby, and Dickens (1992) developed a structured interview that presents interviewing strategies for detecting respondents who are feigning psychopathology, including investigating the reported presence of rare symptoms, improbable symptoms (e.g., tingling that radiates from the middle of the arm and ends slightly above the ear), improbable symptom combinations (e.g., nightmares in the midst of manic episodes), symptom severity, indiscriminate symptom endorsements, obvious versus subtle symptoms, and reported versus observed symptoms. A recommended strategy is to conduct the usual clinical interview and to intersperse inquiries about each type of symptom listed (R. Rogers, 1987, 1995).

MMPI–2

The issue of respondents underreporting ("faking good") or overreporting ("faking bad," malingering, or feigning) symptoms and problems has occupied psychologists for some time. Certain forensic psychological evaluations are prone to underreporting (e.g., custody evaluations, employment screening, fitness for duty examinations, evaluations of the likelihood of recidivism among sexual offenders) and overreporting (e.g., insanity and competency evaluations, fitness to stand trial, fitness for duty evaluations, personal injury litigation). Accordingly, there has been extensive research on the question of whether psychological assessment methods can detect these response tendencies. Much of this research has derived from the MMPI, and meta-analyses have determined that several scales of the original MMPI have been able to detect the underreporting of psychopathology (Baer, Wetter, & Berry, 1992) and malingering (Berry, Baer, & Harris, 1991).

With the introduction of the MMPI–2, researchers have continued to study whether scales on this omnibus personality inventory are able to detect response distortions. The more recent research has explored whether the MMPI–2 can (a) detect respondents instructed to fake general psychopathology (either faking good or faking bad), (b) detect respondents instructed to fake specific psychopathology (e.g., PTSD, depression, or schizophrenia), and (c) the extent to which coaching respondents affects the ability of the MMPI to detect one of these response tendencies.

With respect to the detection of fake-good profiles, the literature suggests that the traditional MMPI–2 validity scales (L, K, S) as well as supplemental scales (subtle-obvious scales, Wiggins social desirability scale) are reasonably effective in detecting underreporting (Bagby et al., 1997; Timbrook, Graham, Keiller, & Watts, 1993) and that the supplemental scales add significantly to incremental validity over scales L and K in detecting underreporting (Baer, Wetter, Nicholson, Greene, & Berry, 1995). However, although still effective, these same scales show a somewhat reduced ability to detect underreporting under a variety of coaching instructions (Baer & Miller, 2002; Baer & Sikirnjah, 1997).

With respect to the detection of malingering, faking, or exaggerating general psychopathology, the literature suggests that scales F (unnamed), Backside F (FB), and Infrequent Psychopathology (F(p)) have been able to detect these response tendencies, with F(p) outperforming F and FB in this regard (Arfice & Ben-Porath, 1998; D. D. Blanchard, McGrath, Pogge, & Khadini, 2003; Lewis, Simcox, & Berry, 2002; Nicholson et al., 1997; Timbrook et al., 1993). The F(p) scale has good normative data with relevance for the forensic assessment of malingering (Rothke et al., 2000). Furthermore, although some research suggests that coaching participants may improve their ability to avoid detection of faking on the MMPI–2 (Viglione et al., 2001), most research has reported that a variety of coaching strategies had little effect on participants' ability to avoid detection of response exaggeration (Bagby, Nicholson, Bacchiochi, Rysler, & Bury, 2002; Bagby et al., 1997; Storm & Graham, 2000; Wetter, Baer, Berry, Robinson, & Sumpter, 1993).

Studies have also investigated whether participants can fake specific disorders. Two studies found that some coached participants were able to fake schizophrenia on the MMPI–2 (Bagby et al., 1997; R. Rogers, Bagby, & Chakraparty, 1993). Three studies reported that the MMPI–2 showed good ability to detect feigned depression (Bagby, Nicholson, Buis, & Bacchiochi, 2000; Bagby et al., 1997; Walters & Clopton, 2002), and two studies found that participants given information on depression were more successful at faking depression than uncoached participants (Bagby et al., 1997; Walters & Clopton, 2002). Six studies have found that participants were unable to successfully fake PTSD on the MMPI–2 (Berry et al., 1995; Bury & Bagby, 2002; Elhai, Gold, Freuh, & Gold, 2000; Elhai, Gold, Sellers, & Dorfman, 2001; Freuh & Kinder, 1994; Wetter & Deutsch, 1996). Also, the MMPI–2 scales were able to detect attempts to fake closed-head injury (Wetter & Deutsch, 1996; Berry et al., 1995).

Rorschach

Although a sample of sex offenders produced normal MMPI–2 profiles, they did show evidence of psychopathology on the Rorschach both in content and in perceptual distortions (Wasyliw, Zenn, Grossman, & Haywood, 1998). Commercial airline pilots, mandated to undergo a psychological evaluation after completing a substance abuse rehabilitation program, showed defensive responding on the MMPI–2 but showed evidence of psychopathology on the Rorschach, including emotional distress, self-critical ideation, and difficulties in interpersonal relationships—problems that were not reported on the MMPI–2 (Ganellen, 1994). However, participants given information about schizophrenia were capable of avoiding detection on the Rorschach (Netter & Viglione, 1994). Participants instructed to fake PTSD on the Rorschach produced certain signs that suggested faking (Freuh & Kinder, 1994).

MCMI

Although the MCMI Disclosure Index assesses minimization and the Debasement Index assesses exaggeration, the MCMI has a high tolerance for faking bad. In fact, the MMPI–2 F scale would have to reach T 120 before the MCMI Debasement Index reaches a high enough level to call the profile invalid (Morgan, Schoenberg, Dorr, & Burke, 2002). The computer algorithm makes adjustments for tendencies to minimize and exaggerate, so it is difficult to produce an MCMI profile that detects invalid responding.

Assessment of Underreporting or Overreporting in Juvenile Offenders

It may be comforting to know that the mean profile elevations previously reported for profile invalidity for the MMPI–2 continue to be useful and valid as measures of profile invalidity on the MMPI version for adolescents (MMPI–A; Butcher et al., 1992) . These scales have shown the ability to distinguish between fake-good profiles generated by adolescents in both correctional and noncorrectional sites (Stern & Graham, 1999).

In summary, evidence to date suggests that the tests forensic psychologists commonly use to detect faking good or faking bad do a credible job in this task, although some respondents may elude detection on a single instrument. However, the research evidence on the ability to detect overreporting is stronger than that for underreporting (Baer et al., 1992; Berry, 1995). Using sets of scales within a test and using tests in combination (particularly the combined use of the MMPI–2 and the Rorschach) should substantially increase the likelihood of detecting intentional response distortion.

ASSESSMENT OF PSYCHOPATHY

Assessment of psychopathy is important, because severity of psychopathy is linked to a number of outcome variables, such as prediction of violence, institutional adjustment and misconduct, recidivism, and treatment success (Gacono, Loving, Evans, & Jumes, 2002). Antisocial personality disorder, as *psychopathy* is called in the fourth edition of the *Diagnostic and Statistical Manual of Mental Disorders (DSM–IV*; American Psychiatric Association, 1994), has higher prevalence rates in most correctional settings than other personality disorders, is instrumentally related to many personality-based forensic evaluations, and is associated with high recidivism rates and lack of responsiveness to treatment. Accordingly, the assessment of psychopathy has occupied a central role in forensic psychology. The *DSM–IV* criteria for antisocial personality disorder emphasize overt delinquent and criminal behaviors, whereas a more broad definition of this construct would include personological, interpersonal, affective, and behavioral symptoms of the disorder that would bring it closer to the taxon originally conceived by Cleckley (1941).

Although most clinicians use the clinical interview to form diagnostic impressions (Westen, 1997), forensic psychologists rely on more objective evidence for their professional evaluations. The following sections review commonly used methods for assessing psychopathy. Testing methods for this population should require (a) minimal levels of cooperation due to issues of response distortion commonly seen among psychopaths, (b) minimal levels of insight, and (c) minimal literacy because patients with this disorder frequently have low levels of formal education (Hemphill & Hart, 2003).

Psychopathy Check List

The Psychopathy Check List—Revised (PCL–R; Hare, 1991) is the most commonly used assessment tool for the assessment of psychopathy. It is a 20-item scale that assesses behavioral, affective, and interpersonal features of this disorder and is scored after a semistructured clinical interview has been completed. This interview can take up to two hours. Each PCL–R item corresponds to one of the diagnostic criteria associated with psychopathy. The item is then rated on a 3-point scale (0–2) based on how well the patient meets the criteria for that item. Scores range from 0 to 40, with a cutoff score of more than 30 reflecting psychopathy.

The PCL–R was originally developed as a research tool for assessing psychopathy among incarcerated prisoners but now enjoys wider clinical application. It demonstrates good concurrent validity with the *DSM* antisocial personality disorder criteria. It shows no evidence of bias with African American compared with White respondents (Cooke, Kosson, & Michre, 2001) and has been translated into more than a dozen languages. Literally hundreds of studies have been published on the PCL and PCL–R demonstrating its very good psychometric properties. It meets the criteria for admissibility regardless of which legal standards are used (e.g., *FRE, Daubert*) and is able to judge the severity of psychopathy (Salekin, Rogers, & Sewell, 1996).

MMPI–2

The MMPI–2 has several useful scales to assess the psychopathic construct. These are the Psychopathic Deviate (Pd), the Antisocial Practices (ASP), and the Anger (ANG) content scales, as well as the substance abuse scales (the MacAndrews Alcoholism Scale—Revised, the Addiction Admission Scale [AAS], and the Addiction Potential Scale [APS]). However, the Pd scale contains several items that are irrelevant to the assessment of psychopathy, and elevations on this scale can be due to factors other than antisocial traits. The clinician needs to evaluate the Harris–Lingoes subscales of Pd to determine the source of the Pd elevation. The ASP demonstrates good concurrent and discriminant validity compared with self-report, interviews, family history, and observer measures of psychopathy (Lilienfeld, 1996). Elevations of Pd with concurrent elevations in ASP and ANG are good markers for antisocial personality traits.

MCMI–III

The MCMI–III has two clinical personality pattern scales and two clinical syndrome scales that are especially useful in the assessment of psychopathy. This test measures both antisocial personality disorder (ASPD) and the aggressive (sadistic) personality disorder (APD). Earlier versions of the MCMI (Millon, 1983, 1987) merged the antisocial personality traits with the criminal behaviors associated with this disorder. Both the MCMI–II and MCMI–III separate these two elements, with the APD scale assessing the more malignant and aggressive forms of the antisocial disorder. These two scales often covary among psychopaths. Also, the ASPD is often elevated among substance abusers who live a lifestyle associated with antisocial behaviors but who may not have an antisocial personality disorder (Craig, 1997); these behaviors often attenuate when the person enters recovery. The APD scale is elevated when the person either is overly controlling (i.e., verbally aggressive) or tends to be physically abusive or violent (see chap. 8).

Socialization Scale

Gough (1969, 1987, 1996) developed the Socialization scale of the California Psychological Inventory (CPI) as a measure of social deviance. Low scores on Socialization reflect immaturity, emotional maladjustment, immoral behavior, unreliability and a lack of conscientiousness, nonconformist behavior, disagreeableness, problematic interpersonal relations, aggressiveness, impulsive behavior, and hostility. Specific problems associated with low CPI Socialization scores include low academic achievement; drug abuse; tendencies toward violence, lying, and cheating; family history of child abuse and neglect; and antisocial and narcissistic personality disorder (Gough, 1994). The scale may be given apart from the CPI without loss of concurrent validity (Alterman et al., 2003).

Personality Assessment Inventory

The Antisocial Features (ANT) scale of the Personality Assessment Inventory (PAI) taps primarily behavioral symptoms of psychopathy instead of affective symptoms. It has low to moderate efficiency in diagnosing psychopathy and correlates in the mid-50s with the PCL (Edens, Hart, Johnson, Johnson, & Oliver, 2000). There are three facet scales associated with this parent scale. Antisocial Behaviors (ANT–A) taps a history of antisocial behaviors and criminality. Egocentricity (ANT–E) assesses self-centered and callous personality traits along with remorseless behavior. Stimulus Seeking (ANT–S) tests for such traits as excitement seeking and low boredom tolerance. The examiner should consult these facet scales to determine the source of the ANT parent scale results. For example, if a person enjoys bungee jumping, hang-gliding, and parasailing, then he or she may score high on ANT–E and ANT–S but not have psychopathic traits.

Rorschach

The Rorschach has been successfully used with a variety of forensic populations and assessment needs in both adolescents and adults (see Gacono, Evans, & Viglione, 2002, for extensive citations). Meloy (1988) has written an excellent treatise of the dynamics of psychopathy and has stipulated Rorschach indexes suggestive of this diagnosis, which appear in Table 1.1. These signs are reasonable Rorschach indexes given the nature of psychopathic psychological operations. Gacono and Meloy (1994) also stipulated Rorschach signs of adolescent psychopathy, and the interested reader is referred to this source for additional material on this subject.

The diagnosis of psychopathy and determination of its severity are usually made from a confluence of sources. In addition to test findings, clinical, contextual, and historical factors and interview and collateral information are required before rendering a final judgment and recommendations. Psychologists are also reminded to consider the standard error of the mean (SEM) statistic associated with test scores. Most scores are associated with measurement error, and the SEM indicates the likelihood that the individual will attain a particular score on retesting.

ETHICS IN FORENSIC PSYCHOLOGY

One may argue that all clinical and forensic decisions involve ethical components. However, in forensic practice, the psychologist's evaluations and testimony often have more serious repercussions than clinical practice for the defendant, who may experience loss of civil liberties, loss of child visitation rights, incarceration, or a denial of damages in civil cases. Thus, ethical decisions play a critical role in this specialty (Knapp & Vendercreek, 2001). The Ethics Code of the American Psychological Association (2002a) contains standards that apply to ethical practice in forensic cases. These standards do not directly address the myriad of dilemmas forensic psychologists encounter in their daily work, and many areas, such as child custody evaluations and personal injury cases, contain ambiguities and subjectivities. Thus, these ethical principles are aspirational standards and are to be used as a basis for ethical practice.

One particular ethical dilemma is encountered by the clinical psychologist who testifies on forensic issues on behalf of his or her patient. This dilemma most frequently occurs in cases of sexual abuse allegations, child custody evaluations, and civil litigation associated with personal injury. In such cases, the clinical psychologist may be called on to testify on behalf of a patient he or she has been seeing for psychotherapy. Greenberg and Shuman (1997) argued that therapists usually do not have the requisite database to testify appropriately about psycholegal issues of their patients and hence should avoid this kind of dual relationship. They argued that clinical psychologists are highly invested in the welfare of their patients and are generally unfamiliar with relevant law.

Ethical standards mandate that psychologists avoid potentially harmful or exploitative dual relationships, but there may be circumstances when a psychologist is court ordered to testify, so it is not always possible to avoid this dilemma. Furthermore, I am unaware of any legal standards that address the exclusion of a treating psychologist who served as a litigant's therapist.

TABLE 1.1
Rorschach Indexes Suggestive of Psychopathy

Area	Sign	Explanation
Test taking attitude	Low R (13–77)	Restricted and defensive attitude
	Elevated Lambda (> .85)	Uninvolved in test; restricted and defensive
	W responses uncorrelated with diagnosis	Lack of involvement with test
	DQ response configurations uncorrelated with diagnosis	Attenuated willingness to cooperate
	Blends infrequent (< 3)	Lack of commitment to the testing process
	Space responses elevated (> 2)	Oppositional and negativistic behavior; hostile and angry if autonomy is threatened
	Personalized responses frequent (> 2)	Defensive; a compensatory shoring up of the grandiose self structure in the face of perceived threat
Internal operations	Preferred problem solving EB = ambitent	Due to severity of object relation disturbance and probable borderline defensive structure; slight tendency toward extratensive
Adaptive style	$T = 0$	Absence of affectional bonding and dependency needs; may be a somatosensory analogue for lack of skin contact with mother
	$V = 0$	Same (unless clinically depressed)
	$C' > 0$	If facing a criminal charge
	$FC < CF + F$	Unwillingness to moderate affective displays
	$C > 1$	Ongoing difficulty with impulse control
Intrusiveness of internal operations	Elevated Lambda (> .85)	Narcissistic defenses that split off intense affect
	MOR = 0	If present, likely to appear with Aggressive Movement (Ag), suggesting identification with the aggressor rather than the victim within the morbid response
	As > 0	Increased likelihood of aggression and chronically negative, with hostile attitudes toward others
Content of operations	M < 3	Absence of bonding in the emotional life

PERSONALITY-GUIDED FORENSIC PSYCHOLOGY

Category	Criteria	Interpretation
Balance and quality of time spent in self-focus	Egocentric Index > .45	Suggests a grandiose self-structure
	MOR = 0	Same as explained earlier above
	RF or Fr > 1	Intensely self-focused, with grandiosity and entitlement
	V = 0	Unless there is a severe external stressor
	Fd = 0	Lack of internal reflection
External operations		
Efficiency of perceiving and processing data	X + % < 70	Suggests conventionality
	X − % < 15	Some impairment in the accurate perception of exteroceptive stimuli
	XSUM6 > 6	Cognitive dysfunction expected due to borderline personality organization
Efficiency of organization attempts	Zd < −.30	Impulsivity
Degree of need to identify with external world	X + % < 70	Disidentification with reality
	S > 2	Oppositional and negativistic
	P < 5	Unwillingness or difficulty in giving conventional responses
Degree of need to achieve	W:M > 3:1	Grandiose, unrealistic striving
Presence of affect	AFR < .55	Tendency to avoid emotionality
Modulation of affect when processed	M < 3	All these signs due to lack of affection and to predatory violence with impulsivity and problematic mediation of affect
	FC < CF + C'	
	FM > M	
	C' > 0	
Identifications	M	Malignant pseudoidentifications with aggressive content (usually minus form quality)
	H < 4	Due to narcissism and absence of affective bonding
	T = 0	Lack of emotional relatedness
	Fd = 0	Absence of oral neediness
	Isolation index: R > 33%	Strong tendency toward social isolation
	Ag > 0	Correlates with verbal and physical aggression in interpersonal relationships
	S > 2	Hostile and angry
Self as actor or acted upon	a > p	
	Ma > Mp	

Note. Source: Meloy (1988). W = whole; DQ = developmental quality; EB = experience balance; T = texture; V = vista; C' = achromatic color; FC = form color; CF = color form; MOR = morbid; M = human movement; RF = reflections; Fr = form reflections; Fd = food; Zd = organizational processing; S = space responses; P = populars; AFR = affective ratio; FM = animal movement; H = human context; Ag = aggression; Ma = human movement active; Mp = human movement passive; p = passive movement.

Instead, the courts seek issues of competence and relevance when it comes to expert testimony.

ASSESSMENT OF JUVENILE OFFENDERS

Although the number of specialty training programs in forensic psychology has increased in the past two decades, there are very few specialty training programs specializing in juvenile forensic psychology. Most forensic psychologists working with juvenile populations receive their training and practical experience during practicum, internship, and on-the-job exposure. Also, there are no specific standards for assessment, treatment, and ethical practice in juvenile forensic psychology, although the Ethics Code of the American Psychological Association (2002a) and forensic ethical standards (Committee on Ethical Guidelines for Forensic Psychologists, 1991) certainly apply to this specialty area.

The assessment of juvenile offenders requires a different knowledge base, use of different assessment tools, and a different set of clinical skills than adult offender assessment. For example, knowledge of human development is particularly and more saliently required in evaluating adolescents than in evaluating adult offenders. Also required is a strong knowledge of adolescent psychopathology. The forensic psychologist must be aware of the specific juvenile laws, delinquency laws in particular, and juvenile detention procedures. Juvenile courts tend to operate somewhat differently from adult courts. Finally, there are several areas in juvenile justice in which a forensic psychologist might be called on to assess the likelihood of future criminal activity; estimate the likelihood of committing a specific type of criminal activity, such as violence or sex offenses; and carry out evaluations concerning dispositions such as probation or custody dispositions, length of sentencing, and level of security involved when the decision is incarceration.

Grisso (2003) identified the following key issues and questions in juvenile forensic evaluations:

- Can youths understand their Miranda rights (*In re Gault,* 1967) and thus waive their constitutional rights against self-incrimination?
- Is there sufficient evidence of a youth's danger to the community to meet the legal standard for the deprivation of his or her liberty?
- What (psychological) evidence is required to determine if a youth meets the legal criteria for not being amenable to treatment and, hence, can be sent to adult criminal court for trial?
- Is the youth competent to stand trial?

Capacity to Waive Miranda Rights

In *In re Gault* (1967), the U.S. Supreme Court ruled that juveniles in delinquency cases have many of the same rights as adults in criminal cases. One of these is the right not to incriminate oneself. *Miranda v. Arizona* (1966) ruled that defendants must be read a statement of their rights (i.e., the "Miranda" warning), which includes the right to an attorney (Fourteenth Amendment), the right to avoid self-incrimination (Fifth Amendment), and the notification that anything said at interrogation may be used against them in court. This procedural requirement is now standard during arrests, and most police departments have Miranda rights printed on paper. The court subsequently ruled that confessions are considered voluntary as long as there is an absence of police coercion (*Colorado v. Connelly*, 1986). Any juvenile confession must also be preceded by a Miranda warning. Some states allow the presence of parents before an adolescent waives these rights, but the parents themselves cannot waive them.

For statements or confessions to be admissible as evidence, the person must knowingly, intelligently, and voluntarily waive his or her Miranda rights. Two essential features need to be evaluated in determining the capacity of a juvenile to waive his or her Miranda rights: (a) the totality of the situation in which the confession occurred and (b) the characteristics of the youth who made the confession. The first element is largely construed to mean the absence of police coercion, whereas the latter refers to potential diminished abilities to understand or appreciate the meaning of the warning, even if the youth has given consent to waive the rights. Regarding the characteristics of the youth, the psychologist has to consider such factors as the following:

1. *Age:* Youths under age 12 are usually considered by the courts to be too young to understand their Miranda rights. However, a psychologist might present test findings to challenge this assumption.
2. *Intelligence* as measured by IQ tests and tests of functional ability: Defendants who score in the range of mental retardation are usually considered to lack the requisite capacity to understand any waiver of rights.
3. *Education* (along with achievement test scores): Education level is sometimes considered, especially when there is evidence that the youth has been in special education classes for emotionally, behaviorally, or otherwise maladjusted youths.

Psychologists usually receive a referral after the youth has waived his or her Miranda rights and has confessed. The legal question is often whether the youth did so within the dictates of the laws and procedures related to evidence and its admissibility. Grisso (1998) proposed a model for the evaluation of a youth's capacity to waive Miranda rights; made suggestions for how to obtain academic, school, mental health, and police records; discussed the process of interviewing the youth and parents; and discussed several specific instruments that have been developed to measure a youth's functional abilities in waiving Miranda rights. The reader is urged to consult this source for additional suggestions.

The present debate among legal scholars is whether or not to require videotaping of police interrogations, which can help ensure the absence of coercion. However, police question youths in a variety of venues, such as in the home, on the street, and at the crime scene, so videotaping is not always practical. Miranda warnings are required only when a youth is in custody.

False confessions do occur. In addition to police coercion and bargaining, Ackerman (1999) listed the following reasons why a youth might confess to a crime that he or she did not commit:

- desire for notoriety,
- inability to distinguish fact from fiction,
- need to repent and atone for other crimes,
- desire for relief from the stress of police interrogation,
- internalization of the police's insistence on their guilt, and
- desire to protect someone else.

Research also suggests that tricky interrogation can lead to false confessions because of the suggestibility of younger persons (Redlick & Goodman, 2003; Trowbridge, 2003).

Assessment procedures for adolescent capacity to waive Miranda rights require investigation of circumstances surrounding the police questioning, a review of police records, an interview with the youth concerning the nature of the interrogation, and parental interviews. The forensic psychologist looks for any factor that might affect the youth's emotional capacity to offer an uncoerced confession. Such factors might include length of interrogation, time of occurrence of the interrogation, physical conditions where the confession occurred, provision of food and other necessities, opportunities to communicate with support systems, and any evidence that the police behaved in a manner that could be construed as fear inducing (Grisso, 1998). Psychological testing of juveniles also includes measures of cognition (IQ tests for cognitive capacity) and perhaps neuropsychological tests (to rule out organicity), as well as personality tests commonly given adolescents.

Assessment of Psychopathy and Juvenile Delinquency

Delinquency is not an event; it is a process that typically begins with early conduct problems, such as conflicts with school and parents and defiance of rules and authority, and progresses to aggressive behavior and antisocial acts. Prospective studies indicate that high scores on both reactive and instrumental measures of psychopathy predict aggressive behavior among adolescents. Also, elevated scores on the PCL–R had incremental validity over and above the contributions made by clinical diagnosis (Cornell, 2003). On the other hand, measures of adolescent psychopathy often show only modest agreement (Murrie & Cornell, 2002; Salekin, Larrea, & Ziegler, 2002), so multiple assessment tools are required for the accurate assessment of psychopathy. A thorough assessment would include clinical interviews, structured objective tests, and projective tests, along with collateral information and review of criminal records. Several psychological forensic assessment instruments developed for use with adult populations have been standardized for use with juvenile populations; the following sections address the more popular instruments used with juvenile offenders.

Psychopathy Check List—Youth Version (PCL–YV)

Hare's PCL–R has been successfully adapted to the assessment of juveniles (Forth, Kosson, & Hare, 2003). The PCL–YV consists of a 20-item checklist that is completed after a clinical interview. The examiner completes the checklist using information gleaned in the interview with the youth, an interview with the parents, and examination of criminal records. Although the instrument was designed to be used with children and adolescents, it is probably more appropriately used with adolescents ages 15 and older. Items pertain to lack of goals, extent of short-term relations, lack of guilt or remorse, parasitic lifestyle, and other examples of psychopathic behavior and traits. It yields a total score indicating the overall level of psychopathy and two subscores; one, called "callous/deceitful," pertains to psychopathic traits (e.g., lying, narcissism) and the other, called "conduct disorder," pertains to acts of antisocial behavior.

Psychopathy Check List—Youth Version scores predict antisocial behaviors as well as other indexes of childhood psychopathy, interpersonal behaviors associated with adult psychopathy, and attachment problems with parents (Kosson, Cyterski, Steuerwald, Neumann, & Walker-Matthews, 2002). It can reliably assess psychopathy in both Black and White male offenders (Brandt, Kennedy, Patrick, & Curtin, 1997). However, the extent of predictive validity using the PCL–YV is somewhat limited (Hoge, 2002), but given the increased attention to juveniles in the court system, it is likely that more research will be done using the PCL–YV.

MMPI and MMPI–A

Studies that have used the MMPI and MMPI–2 with delinquent male youths have usually reported code types consisting of elevations in Psychopathic Deviant (Pd), Schizophrenia (Sc), and Hypomania (Ma). These scales are typically also elevated in delinquent adolescent girls, along with Depression (Dep). Dep may reflect the effects of incarceration, however, and not actual clinical depression (Megargee & Carbonell, 1995).

Studies have shown that elevations on Psychopathic Deviance (Pd) and Paranoia (Pa) are reasonable markers for juvenile delinquency on the MMPI–A (Morton, Farras, & Brenowitz, 2002). The 13 MMPI–A scales and their supplemental scales show differences in scores between juvenile delinquent and nondelinquent adolescents that are clinically meaningful (Pena, Megargee, & Brody, 1996) and have good concurrent validity (Toyer & Weed, 1998). Also, a comprehensive list of clinical correlates for MMPI–A elevated scores in a large sample of male delinquent offenders is available, and the reader is urged to consult this source for additional references (Cashel, Rogers, Sewell, & Holliman, 1998).

A number of studies have found that the MMPI–A successfully distinguishes between delinquent and nondelinquent male juvenile offenders (Gallucci, 1997; Glaser, Calhoun, & Petrocelli, 2002; Hume, Kennedy, Patrick, & Partyka, 1996; Losada-Paisey, 1998; Moore, Thompson-Pope, & Whited, 1996). The scales of Psychopathic Deviate (Pd) and Paranoia (Pa), the MacAndrews Alcoholism Scale—Revised, and the Immaturity content scale are particularly useful in identifying male juvenile delinquents. In addition, Psychopathic Deviate, Schizophrenia, Alcohol or Drug Problem Proneness, Social Avoidance, and Adolescent Health Concerns content scales often appear in the discriminant function analyses that differentiate male juvenile offenders from nonoffending adolescents.

Millon Adolescent Clinical Inventory

The Millon Adolescent Clinical Inventory (MACI; Millon, 1993) is a useful tool to assess adolescents. It consists of Personality Pattern scales (Introversive, Inhibited, Doleful, Submissive, Dramatizing, Egotistic, Unruly, Forceful, Conforming, Oppositional, Self-Demeaning, and Borderline Tendency), Expressed Concerns scales (Identity Diffusion, Self-Devaluation, Body Disapproval, Sexual Discomfort, Peer Insecurity, Social Insensitivity, Family Discord, and Childhood Abuse), and Clinical Syndrome scales (Eating Dysfunctions, Substance Abuse Proneness, Delinquent Predisposition, Impulsive Propensity, Anxious Feelings, Depressive Affect, and Suicidal Tendency).

The basic Personality Pattern scale of Unruly and the Clinical Syndrome scales of Delinquent Predisposition and Substance Abuse Proneness (SAP) provide a tripartite core of scales that assess conduct disorders in adolescence. Furthermore, research shows that the Unruly and SAP scales significantly negatively correlate with the PCL–R and were able to correctly distinguish between adolescents rated high and low in psychopathy with 79% accuracy (Murrie & Cornell, 2002). Furthermore, elevated scores on the MCMI scales of Forceful, Unruly, Substance Abuse Proneness, Impulsive Propensity, and Family Discord, along with elevated scores on the MACI Psychopathy Content Scale, were associated with reduced empathy and guilt and self-reports of instrumental motivation for violence (Booker, Hoffschmidt, & Ash, 2001). Also, the MACI can identify significant levels of depression and anxiety, as well as personal problems such as feelings of inadequacy and peer insecurity, among adolescent offenders (Salekin et al., 2002).

A scale that measures psychopathy has been developed from MACI items, and preliminary data suggest that this scale has good criterion and predictive validity. Most of the items pertain to egocentric and callous traits (Salekin, Ziegler, Larrea, Anthony, & Bennet, 2003). The scale was shown to be able to predict violent reoffending among adolescents.

Socialization Scale From the California Psychological Inventory

The Socialization scale from the CPI is an excellent scale for the assessment of delinquency and has been reliably linked to a number of behaviors associated with conduct disorder problems in adolescents (Gough, 1994). It has previously been discussed in the section on the assessment of adult psychopathy.

Rorschach

Many juvenile offenders come to the assessment process with deficient reading skills that make the use of the more traditional assessment tools (e.g., MMPI–A, MACI) problematic. Use of the Rorschach obviates this problem. There is a growing database on the use of the Rorschach with juvenile offenders (Gacono & Meloy, 1994; Loving & Russell, 2000). Rorschach ratings of ego strength significantly improved the prediction of adolescent delinquency over parent ratings of mother–child relations and externalizing behaviors, thus demonstrating incremental validity of the Rorschach in the assessment of delinquency (Janson & Stattin, 2003). Reflection (i.e., narcissism) and Texture Responses (i.e., lack of capacity for genuine intimacy or attachment) and, to some extent, Vista (i.e., lack of guilt or remorse) and White Space (oppositional tendencies) differentiate levels of psychopathy (mild, moderate, severe) in juvenile offenders (Loving & Russell, 2000).

Other Tests

Achenbach's (1991) Child Behavior Check List (CBCL) is a well validated and well recognized screening measure for childhood behavior problems (both internalizing and externalizing problems). A substantial amount of research data is associated with its ability to assess delinquent youths from a variety of racial and ethnic backgrounds. The CBCL does not assess psychopathy directly but does identify externalizing behaviors often associated with delinquency. The test is completed by a knowledgeable informant, usually a parent or teacher. Also, the Family Environment Scale (Moos & Moos, 1986) is the most often used measure to assess a youth's social context.

The assessment of juvenile offenders may also require the assessment of cognitive and intellectual ability, achievement, and attitudes. The reader is referred to other sources for information on instruments appropriate for juvenile offenders (Hoge & Andrews, 1996).

Research has shown that the variables of low parental warmth, psychosocial problems in parents, inconsistent discipline, poor parental monitoring, parental neglect, and problematic parent–child relationships are associated with adolescent delinquency and conduct-disordered behavior (Janson & Stattin, 2003). These variables should also be explored in a clinical interview with the parents of the adolescent.

Ethics in Juvenile Assessment

There are no specific ethical standards for use in work with juvenile offenders, and the previously cited ethical provisions remain applicable (American Psychological Association, 2002a; Committee on Ethical Guidelines for Forensic Psychologists, 1991). In general, as with adults, psychologists have an obligation to report all data that are relevant to the legal issue in the case. They must consider and discuss the limitations of these data and must not suppress disconfirming data. They must consider and discuss reasonable alternative explanations and hypotheses for these results, and, if subpoenaed, they must release all data consistent with law and ethics. (Some states allow the nondisclosure of therapist personal notes and speculations with certain provisions, so it is incumbent on the psychologist to know these laws.)

Additional guidelines for use of psychological tests in forensic contexts have been published as well as detailed guidelines for the use of tests for classification, description, prediction, intervention planning, and tracking. There are also guidelines for training and supervision (Turner, DeMers, Fox, & Reed, 2001). I elaborate on only a few of these recommendations:

1. The forensic psychologist must understand the legal issues in a case and ensure that he or she has the competence to properly evaluate the issues and to testify about his or her findings in court.

2. The psychologist should inform the inquiring attorney about the limits of his or her expertise in a given area. Even though the psychologist might have been trained in forensic psychology and have a diplomate in it, he or she might not have any exposure to or experience with a particular issue and, thus, has no additional credibility over any other clinician.

3. Forensic psychologists should never work as a "hired gun." Attorneys are paid advocates for their clients, and they try to hire expert witnesses who will support their arguments and thus help them win the case. One can avoid this by remaining objective and relying on test findings, combined with empirical bases of test findings, so as not to be unduly swayed by attorney influences.

4. The forensic psychologist should separate the financial aspect of his or her relationship with the attorney and client from his or her professional judgment and evaluation. Contingency fees (i.e., getting paid contingent on the client winning the case) should never be accepted, as to do so could be an ethical violation. Whenever I do forensic work, I always insist on getting paid before I start the evaluation and before I ever see the client. A professional relationship is established when professional services are rendered, independent of getting paid for those services. In custody evaluations, some third party is often aggrieved, and they may retaliate against the psychologist by not paying the fee. Getting paid in advance of providing service can eliminate such repercussions. Once the psychologist initiates service, it may be considered unethical to withhold service, such as a report to an attorney, until the psychologist gets paid.

5. The forensic psychologist should discuss with the attorney whether or not he or she will be asked to testify as to the ultimate issue. Actually, triers of fact have this responsibility and expert witnesses do not, but attorneys will try and slip in

ultimate issue conclusions for a jury to hear. Even though the judge should instruct the jury to disregard that part of the testimony, the effect has been made.

6. If at all possible, forensic psychologists should try to avoid dual roles (i.e., therapist and subsequent patient witness), although this may be impossible in small communities.

7. Before the forensic psychologist begins the evaluation with the client, he or she should mention that the evaluation is not confidential and that anything the client says or does is subject to discovery in a court of law. The psychologist must tell the client that he or she is not obligated to tell the psychologist anything (a Fifth Amendment protection), but that the court will likely view such a refusal as noncooperation. Normally, I include all aspects of the evaluation, including its nonconfidential nature, in a "contract" that I have clients sign indicating that they have been told their rights and have understood them. (Incompetent clients are a special case; the psychologist should consult with an attorney about such cases.)

8. The forensic psychologist should not seek clinical information that is not relevant to the issue under evaluation.

9. One critical area that deserves further elaboration pertains to forensic evaluations involving psychometric and psychological measures. Specifically, the forensic psychologist needs to be critically aware of and appreciate base rate data as applied to the issue at hand. To provide the best evaluation possible, the psychologist must consider the effect of context on base rate scores; patients often are defensive during an evaluation (Bannatyne, Gacono, & Greene, 1999), and a given individual within a particular context may score differently on a given test in comparison to base rate scores for that population in that context (Stukenberg, Brady, & Klinetob, 2000).

Butcher and Pope (1993) identified seven ethical issues that emanated from the revised American Psychological Association ethical standards. These issues pertain to relevant graduate education and training, competence in the use of assessment procedures, selection of tests and methods that fit the task of the evaluation and the person being evaluated (regarding such issues as race and education), administration of tests in an appropriate manner, appropriate use of computerized assessments and reports, and assessment of factors that may affect the meaning of a particular test finding. These issues remain applicable to the 2002 ethical standards as well (American Psychological Association, 2002a). In addition, Weissman and DeBow

(2003) provided excellent examples of American Psychological Association ethical standards and their applicability to forensic ethical dilemmas.

In summary, in this chapter I have discussed the field of forensic psychology, education and training in forensic practice, rules of evidence that lay the groundwork for later testimony, various criminal defenses that the forensic psychologist is likely to encounter, levels of proof required in verdicts, the detection of malingering and underreporting, the assessment of psychopathy, and commonly used assessment methods in forensic practice, and the chapter ended with a commentary on ethical decision making in forensic practice. Before addressing specific issues of forensic practice and presenting the role of personality in them, I first review personality models that may have some relevance in forensic practice.

2

MODELS OF PERSONALITY

Forensic psychologists wishing to place personality at the center of their thinking and practice need to adopt a systematic and coherent theory of personality functioning that can serve as a guide to their conclusions. In this chapter I focus on those theoretical formulations that have produced the most debate and research and that have been most influential in the practice of clinical psychology and, to some extent, in psychiatry as well. These theories include Freud's psychoanalytic model, Jung's typological theory, Cattell's Sixteen Personality Factor classification, Cloninger's psychobiological model, the five-factor model, and Millon's bioevolutionary model. I also comment on the extent to which these theories are likely to be applicable and relevant to forensic psychological practice.

THEORETICAL MODELS OF PERSONALITY CLASSIFICATION

Efforts to classify personality date back at least to the four humoral patterns identified by Hippocrates. The workgroups for the fourth edition of the *Diagnostic and Statistical Manual of Mental Disorders* (*DSM–IV*; American Psychiatric Association, 1994) allegedly took an atheoretical approach to the classification of personality disorders and codified 11 such entities into three clusters. The Anxious-Fearful group is composed of the histrionic, narcissistic, antisocial, and borderline disorders. The Dramatic group consists of avoidant, dependent, compulsive, and passive-aggressive disorders. Finally, the Odd or Eccentric group is characterized by schizoid, schizotypal, and paranoid disorders.

There have been a myriad of complaints about the *DSM–IV* personality disorder section, especially that it lacks a dimensional approach to the understanding and classification of personality disorders; that there is extensive criteria overlap, resulting in patients meeting the diagnostic threshold for multiple disorders; and that there is possible gender bias in the criteria (Widiger, in press). Also, some have lamented that the classification system lacks a theoretical foundation.

Between the inelegant musings of Hippocrates and the atheoretical musings of official psychiatric classifications are many proposals to classify personality and personality disorders. And there are many scattered approaches to understanding human behavior. For example, there are psychodynamic theories, exemplified by the ego analysts and object relational approaches to studying personality. There are dispositional theories, such as trait approaches, typological approaches (Jung), and psychological need theories (Murray, Maslow, Gough). There are learning theory approaches, such as classical (Pavlov), operant (Skinner), and social learning foci (Bandura), that understand personality in terms of the rewards and punishments of behavior in certain environments. There are phenomenological theories of personality (Rogers, Kelly) and integrationists (Magnussen). There are only a few theory-driven models of personality classification that are dimensional in nature; Millon's bioevolutionary theory appears to have the best fit for understanding both personality and personality disorders and how these interact and help explain behavior that pertains to forensic assessment.

FREUD'S PSYCHOANALYTIC MODEL

Overview

Sigmund Freud became convinced that personality was formed from the interaction of biological needs with people and relationships at the earliest stages of development. This interaction normally involves the mother but can emanate from any consistent caregiver. Freud also became convinced that unconscious forces play a dominant role in helping to shape personality. He theorized that personality develops through successive stages of psychosexual activity, which he labeled *oral, anal, phallic,* and *genital,* associated with the "erogenous zones." Freud did not use the term *personality disorders* but rather referred to them as character types.

In classical Freudian theory, the oral stage is from birth to about two years of age. Children at this stage gratify their needs through sucking and biting, so he labeled this the *oral stage*. If a child's development becomes fixated at this stage, then he or she is said to have an oral personality. If the fixation occurs at the oral-incorporative stage, then the personality is overdependent and emotionally immature, with an exaggerated need for praise and undue reliance on dominant others to take care of them. People with an oral-incorporative personality tend to be submissive, subservient, and acquiescent and to have a weak self-image. This stage might apply to the depressive, dependent, and masochistic personality disorders. If the fixation occurs at the oral-aggressive stage, the person's behavior is character-ized by oral aggression expressed through verbal hostility, sarcasm, and petulance; feelings of deprivation; and gullibility. Children fixated at this later stage are considered to be oral-sadistic.

The anal stage is generally from two to three years of age, when the anus becomes the focus of attention, particularly through toilet training practices. If fixation occurs in the anal-expulsive stage, then the person is negative and disorderly but ambitious. If parents are strict or harsh in their training methods, the child may hold back feces. Children who become fixated at this stage are anal-retentive and develop personalities that are overly concerned with cleanliness or perhaps excessive saving and hoarding. They develop a cluster of behavior patterns associated with compulsive behaviors. They act in an excessively dutiful and obedient manner, focusing on productivity, reliability, meticulousness, efficiency, and rigid adherence to societal rules and regulations so as to not displease a feared significant other, who unconsciously represents the harsh toilet-training caregiver dur-ing the anal phase. The personality disorder of obsessive–compulsive is theorized to occur from fixations at this stage.

During the fourth and fifth years of age, the *oedipus complex* (for boys) and the *electra complex* (for girls) begin to develop. The child feels an unconscious sexual attraction toward the parent of the opposite gender and wants to possess him or her. Castration anxiety in boys and penis envy in girls may result in problems arising from phallic fixations. The child may experience rejection, disappointment, and depression, which can affect his or her sense of self and even sexual identity and lead to impaired interpersonal relationships as adults.

The genital stage occurs with the onset of puberty and continues into adulthood. (The ages between six years and puberty are called the *latency period* because of a lack of sexual development in the analytic sense.) With adolescence comes the need to develop mature relationships, select a voca-tion, become socialized, and select a mate. This model of psychosexual development is portrayed in Table 2.1.

TABLE 2.1
Classical Freudian Theory on Stages of Psychosexual Development

Stage of psychosexual development	Erogenous zone	Main activity	Personality development
Oral	Mouth	Sucking, biting	Oral-incorporative (dependent) Oral-aggressive (sadistic)
Anal	Anus	Withholding	Anal-retentive or anal-expulsive (compulsive)
Phallic	Genital organs	Masturbation, autoeroticism	Oedipal behaviors, over- or undersexualized
Genital	Genitals	Sexual desire, sexual relations	Mature adult behavior

Unfortunately for theory, classification, and model building, Freud had no interest in using his theories to develop a typology of character structures and spent most of his efforts at developing his method of personality change—psychoanalysis.

Applicability to Forensic Assessment

Although it is possible to maintain a psychodynamic orientation to understand the motivation of offenders, it is more problematic to use this formulation to diagnose a given individual. We can discuss patient behaviors in terms of such concepts as oral deprivation and oral fixation, but it is far more difficult to use these traits in a diagnostic sense. They represent theoretical constructs that remain problematic in terms of jury testimony, and they do not lead to categorical diagnoses consistent with current nosology (e.g., the *DSM–IV*). These terms remain popular within the fields of psychiatry and psychology, but they are used more as shorthand references that subsume a wide array of behaviors and traits in a terse label.

JUNG'S TYPOLOGICAL THEORY

Overview

Jung (1990) diverged from Freud's thinking in several dimensions. He believed that sexual and aggressive forces are instrumentally related to early personality development and that past childhood trauma is substantially less significant in shaping subsequent personality. Instead, he stressed present problems and conflicts and argued that individuation (psychological maturation) is a continuing and lifelong process. Although he believed in an unconscious, he also believed that there is a "collective unconscious" that consists of ancient cultural memories that form archetypes. Archetypes are master patterns, such as "mother," "father," "hero," and so forth that are transmitted from generation to generation. To understand the meaning of these archetypes within an individual, Jung used both psychoanalysis and dream interpretation. (He also tried word association tests but later abandoned them.)

Jung believed that personality is a dynamically interactive construct. He developed a personality typology according to how people "prefer" to use their minds. Of course, some of these preferences can be outside of consciousness. Fundamental to personality are the concepts of Extroversion (E) and Introversion (I), and one or the other assumes a dominant function in behavior. He also argued that there are four psychic functions: thought, feelings, sensation, and intuition. These psychic functions interact with extroversion–introversion and refer to how a person is energized. The two modes of perceiving, Sensation (S) and Intuition (N), pertain to what a person pays attention to. The Thinking (T)–Feeling (F) dichotomy reflects two different ways of judging and making decisions. Finally, the Judgment (J) and Perception (P) types reflect the preference for judging or perceiving in how people tend to live their lives.

Extroverted people focus their attention on external objects and are concerned with relations with other people. They get their psychic energy from the outside world. They are very involved with people, enjoy interacting with them, and tend to be very action oriented and become impatient with slow jobs and slow-working people. They seem energetic and enthusiastic. They like to express ideas and seek opportunities to make an impact. The introverted type is more concerned about inner psychological processes. They get their psychic energy more from solitary activities. They like to work through ideas with much concentration and reflection. They do not mind working alone on a project and can tolerate long periods without interruptions. They like to think before expressing their ideas and tend to restrain expressions of enthusiasm.

The Sensation (or Sensing) type prefers direct observation through the five senses. People with this personality type are very practical and rely on facts and established procedures. They tend to prefer a step-by-step approach and to rely on what they already know to be true. They like evidence and depend on insights as well as on their own experience. The Intuition (or Intuitive) type prefers to go beyond the senses to look for meaning, innovation, change, and potentialities. They like novelty and enjoy theoretical possibilities. They rely on a "sixth sense." Jung theorized that those in creative and imaginative professions mostly preferred the Intuitive type of perceiving.

The Thinking type arrives at judgments through rational and logical methods. Such people rely on justice, principles, reason, objectivity, and rationality. They may not pay enough attention to the feelings of others. Although fair-minded, they tend to be critical. The Feeling type seeks information through activities characterized by warmth, harmony, compassion, and affiliation with others. They reason from the heart and are sympathetic. They avoid criticizing others. Usually they have good people skills.

People who are high on the Judgment preference, which addresses how people come to conclusions, want things to be planned and orderly. They tend to be settled and controlled. They are organized and decisive. Their lives seem quite regulated. They want to get things done and seem to want structure and schedules. They dislike surprises. Those who prefer the Perception (or Perceiving) function—which addresses how people take in ideas and how they become aware of people and events—prefer flexibility and to keep their lives open to other possibilities. They adapt easily and let life happen. They seem to enjoy last-minute changes and surprise turns of events. They dislike deadlines.

Jung's psychological or personality types have been operationalized in the Myers–Briggs Type Indicator (MBTI; Myers & McCaulley, 1992). According to theory, then, and as exemplified by the MBTI, one pole of a pair is preferred over the other pole, resulting in 16 possible combinations or "types." One's preference in each of the four functions is given an alphabetical code. For example, an ENTJ is an extrovert who uses intuition with thinking and judgment. Such people would be characterized as logical, organized, objective, and decisive; provide structure to themselves and to others; tend to be leaders; and are action oriented, efficient, structured, and tough. They may, however, overlook people's needs and may act in a domineering manner. Jung's typology of characterological types is detailed in Exhibit 2.1.

Applicability to Forensic Practice

Jung's typology and its operational measure, the MBTI, would seem to have limited applicability in forensic practice. The MBTI is immensely popular in business, education, and to some extent marital counseling, but it has not been used in forensic assessment and is not likely to be used in the future. Its main applicability has been in nonforensic settings.

EXHIBIT 2.1
Jung's Typology of Characterological Types

(E) Extroversion Focuses on outer world; draws energy from external sources and people	**(I)** Introversion Prefers inner world of ideas and impressions; draws energy from own internal world
(S) Sensing Prefers to gain information primarily through the senses and what is actual	**(N)** Intuition Prefers to think about patterns and possibilities; considers what "might be"
(T) Thinking Bases decisions on logic, rationality, cause-and-effect relationships, objectivity; prefers to organize and structure information	**(F)** Feeling Bases decisions on evaluation
(J) Judgment Likes planned and organized approaches to life; seeks closure	**(P)** Perception Prefers spontaneity and flexibility

CATTELL'S SIXTEEN PERSONALITY FACTOR MODEL

Overview

Trait theorist Raymond B. Cattell studied, dimensionalized, and tested his system for personality classification for more than 40 years (see R. B. Cattell, 1989). He used the method of factor analysis to refine more than 4,000 adjectives into what he considered the most meaningful, nonredundant descriptions of personality, which he labeled *factors* (Craig, 1999a) and operationalized in the Sixteen Personality Factor Questionnaire (16PF; R. B. Cattell, Eber, & Tatsuoka, 1970a; Russell, Karol, Cattell, Cattell, & Cattell, 1994). Cattell argued that there are 16 primary factors, sometimes referred to as *source traits*, on which to align personality. Cattell believed that these source traits underlie surface traits. These source dimensions then are alleged to parsimoniously represent all possible types of personalities.

Although Cattell believed that these factors represent the primary descriptors for categorizing and describing people, subsequent investigators have found a way to further refine these 16 factors into the global or second-order factors of Extroversion, Anxiety, Tough-Mindedness, Independence, and Self-Control (Karson, Karson, & O'Dell, 1997). These factors are quite similar to the five-factor model discussed later in this chapter and are independent and bipolar dimensions. Cattell's factors and source traits are presented in Table 2.2.

TABLE 2.2
Cattell's Source Traits

Factor		Source trait extremes	
		Low	High
A	Warmth	Reserved	Warm
B	Reasoning	Concrete thinking	Abstract thinking
C	Emotional Stability	Affected by feelings	Emotionally stable
E	Dominance[a]	Submissive	Dominant
F	Liveliness	Serious	Enthusiastic
G	Rule-Consciousness	Expedient	Conscientious
H	Social Boldness	Shy	Bold
I	Sensitivity[a]	Tough-minded	Sensitive
L	Vigilance	Trusting	Suspicious
M	Abstractedness	Practical	Imaginative
N	Privateness	Forthright	Private
O	Apprehension	Self-assured	Apprehensive
Q1	Openness to Change	Conservative	Experimenting
Q2	Self-Reliance	Group-oriented	Self-sufficient
Q3	Perfectionism	Tolerates disorder	Perfectionistic
Q4	Tension	Relaxed	Tense

[a]Factors D, J, and K did not replicate in adults.

Applicability to Forensic Assessments

The 16PF test has some use in forensic assessments, particularly in assessing more normal clients such as police force applicants and some fitness-for-duty examinations. It has also occasionally been used for custody evaluations (see chap. 4, this volume). The test has rarely been used in assessment of forensic clinical populations, such as sexual abusers, pain patients, or abuse victims, nor has it been used in capital cases, and it has never been used for other common forensic assessments (dangerousness, insanity pleas). The test has evolved into more industrial applications and to some extent for use in marital counseling and is likely to experience a diminished role in forensic use in the future. Although the test has been somewhat popular in selected settings, Cattell's model of personality factors is rarely invoked as an explanatory construct.

CLONINGER'S PSYCHOBIOLOGICAL MODEL

Overview

Cloninger (1987b; Cloninger, Svrakic, & Przybeck, 1993) developed his theories from family studies, psychometric studies of personality, neuro-pharmacologic and neuroanatomical studies, and studies of behavioral conditioning and learning in humans and animals. He proposed a biosocial theory of personality that seeks to integrate both genetic and environmental influences on personality.

He originally proposed a three-dimensional model, which theorized that three fundamental dimensions of personality (Novelty Seeking, Harm Avoidance, and Reward Dependence) are associated with three brain activities (behavioral activation, inhibition, and maintenance) and with three neurotransmitters (dopamine, serotonin, and norepinephrine). He believed that these are genetically independent dimensions of personality. He argued that these basic factors apply to both normal and deviant traits and are heritable personality traits.

He now has developed a seven-factor model that consists of the three original factors plus four new ones (Persistence, Self-Directedness, Cooperativeness, and Self-Transcendence). The first three factors are believed to be biologically and genetically based, whereas the last four are said to develop from one's self-concept (Cloninger & Svrakic, 1994). The first three are personality traits and are assessed using the Tridimensional Personality Questionnaire (Cloninger, 1987c; Cloninger, Przybeck, & Svrakic, 1991). The last four are character traits and are assessed by the Temperament and Character Inventory (Cloninger, Przybeck, Svrakic, & Wetzel, 1997).

According to this model, novelty seeking is an inherited tendency toward activation (e.g., exploratory activity) in response to novelty. It is the tendency to be attracted to unfamiliar stimuli and is associated with impulsive decision making, quick loss of temper, and extravagance in one's approaches to the cues of rewards. It is theorized to be associated with low basal activity in the dopaminergic system. The person high in novelty seeking avoids monotony and routine, shows frequent exploratory behavior, and is disposed to exhilaration and excitement. Such people are excitable, distractible, impulsive, and extravagant.

Harm avoidance is theorized as an inherited tendency to escape situations that may be associated with punishment and leads the person to inhibit behaviors to avoid punishment and frustrations. It is theorized to be associated with high basal activity in the serotonergic system. These personality types tend to be shy, passive, and easily fatigued and tend to worry and to be pessimistic and fearful.

Reward dependence is characterized by strong reaction to reward, including social approval, and greater resistance to the extinction of reward. It is theorized to be associated with low basal activity in the noradrenergic system. Personality traits include sentimentality, persistence, dependence, and strong attachment to others and their approval. Again, it is presumed to be inherited. These three dimensions interact with one another in everyday behavior.

Cloninger's model can be applied to understanding personality disorders. For example, someone with antisocial personality disorder would be described as low in harm avoidance and high in novelty seeking. The schizoid and schizotypal personality disorders would be described as low in harm avoidance, low in novelty seeking, and low in reward dependence (Cloninger, 2000). The model can also be applied to clinical syndromes. In his highly referenced theory of alcoholism, Cloninger (1987a) proposed that low novelty seeking, high harm avoidance, and high reward dependence characterize Type I alcoholism. Type II alcoholism is characterized by high novelty seeking, low harm avoidance, and low reward dependence. This model has been more often used in psychiatric than in psychological research.

Research to date suggests that the dimensions of harm avoidance and novelty seeking are psychometrically sound, but reward dependence seems to comprise two other factors and is psychometrically weaker than the other dimensions (Chen, Chen, Chen, Yu, & Chen, 2002). Also, factor analytic studies often show that these hypothesized personality traits do not often load on their underlying trait factor. The personality disorders generated by the model conform only loosely to the *DSM–IV* types, and a number are not represented at all (Millon, Meagher, & Grossman, 2001).

Applicability to Forensic Practice

Cloninger's theory has had influence in psychiatric research but has had little influence in forensic issues. However, there is some evidence of its utility in the assessment of violent and nonviolent offenders and of sexual offenders, especially in assessing impulsivity and empathy (Nussbaum et al., 2002). Cloninger's theory of genetic and inheritable traits may eventually enter into attorney arguments and psychiatric expert testimony, but to date little use has been made of either the theory or its operational measures in forensic settings. This could change in the future (see chaps. 7 and 8, this volume).

THE FIVE-FACTOR MODEL

Overview

The most influential personality classification model in terms of research, debate, and range of applicability has been termed the five-factor model (Digman, 1990). This theory holds that all personality dimensions can be subsumed under five basic dimensions: *Neuroticism, Extroversion, Openness to Experience* (sometimes called *Intelligence* or *Culture*), *Agreeableness,* and *Conscientiousness.* This personality model has been operationalized by the Neuroticism, Extroversion, Openness to Experience Personality Inventory—Revised (NEO–PI–R; Costa & McCrae, 1992). (Harkness & McNulty, 1994, found a different set of factors, which they labeled *Aggressiveness, Psychoticism, Constraint, Negative Emotionality/Neuroticism,* and *Positive Emotionality/Extroversion.* They termed this set the Psychopathology Five, or the *Psy-5.*) The consistency with which this model has appeared in personality trait research has led researchers to nickname this model the Big Five.

Proponents argue that the usefulness of the five-factor model has been demonstrated across instruments, populations, and cultures (Goldberg, 1981). Opponents of this model argue that the model is incomplete, superficial, and problematic when it comes to predicting external criteria other than the testing situation itself (Block, 1995; McAdams, 1992). Another problem with the five-factor model is that its description places more emphasis on normal personality than disordered personality. Although the model recently has been applied to describing personality disorders (Costa & Widiger, 2000; McCrae, 1991), proponents of this model would argue that it does so rather awkwardly. For example, a psychopath might be described as a person low in Agreeableness and Conscientiousness and high in Extroversion and Openness to Experience, but this profile could also apply to someone who enjoys bungee jumping, parasailing, and hang gliding and who is not in any way psychopathic.

Applicability to Forensic Assessment

To date the five-factor model has been used in forensic assessments of law enforcement applicants (especially relevant is the Conscientiousness factor) and in child custody evaluations (see chaps. 3 and 4, this volume). Researchers who prefer this model have been demonstrating its applicability to the assessment of personality disorders with some success (Costa & Widiger, 2000). Given that personality disorders are a critical fact in many forensic matters, the use of the theoretical model's operational measures, such as the NEO–PI–R, is likely to increase in forensic applications in the future. However, the theoretical model itself is not likely to be invoked in testimony.

MILLON'S BIOEVOLUTIONARY MODEL

Overview

Cattell was interested in developing personality taxonomies of traits rather than personality styles and did not describe how these personality traits evolve into personality disorders (Strack & Lorr, 1997). Millon (1990), on the other hand, developed a parsimonious model of personality development, anchored by both evolutionary and ecological theory, that offers a taxonomy of both normal and disordered personality types.

Millon argued that there are four "polarities" that are central to evolutionary and ecological theory; these are existence, adaptation, replication, and abstraction. Millon used the first three spheres to develop a theoretical model of personality development and personality classification, but his model continues to develop and individuate, and he presently is beginning to explore ways to integrate the Abstraction sphere into his model.

He persuasively argued that the first task of evolution in a species is to maintain Existence. At the biological level organisms do this by making efforts to enhance their lives, thereby increasing survivability and countering entropic disintegration, or merely to preserve their lives by avoiding events that might terminate life. At the psychological level humans can enhance their lives by seeking pleasurable experiences that are rewarding and avoiding experiences that are punishing.

After one's existence has been ensured, the next evolutionary task is that of Adaptation—the second polarity. Organisms can merely accommodate to their surroundings and fit in, or they can modify the environment, thereby increasing their chances of survival. At the psychological level, the latter strategy represents an active versus a passive way of adapting.

Once existence has been ensured and the organism has adapted to its environment, the third task of an organism is Replication—the third polarity. Replication ensures the continued existence of a species. By reproducing, a biological strategy that is focused on oneself, the organism produces offspring, which require nurturance for continued existence, a strategy that focuses on others. Thus, at the psychological level, a person can focus only on the self, or the person can focus on helping others. Millon believed that these three polarities are the foundation for personality development. (He recently added Abstraction as a fourth polarity but has yet to develop it further in terms of personality schema.)

He proposed three axes—pleasure–pain, active–passive, and self–other—as the basic building blocks of both normal personality styles and personality disorders. The model crosses the active–passive axis with five reinforcement strategies, leading to basic personality styles of detached, dependent, independent, ambivalent, and discordant. This results in a 5×2 matrix of 10 theoretically derived personality types plus three severe personality disorders, as presented in Table 2.3. Normal personalities have a good balance of the three polarities, whereas disordered personalities are imbalanced in one or more of the polarities. His theory, then, derives personality disordered types but also is able to characterize normal personality styles, as presented in Table 2.3. He argued that personality disorders are mere

TABLE 2.3
Millon's Theory-Derived Personality Classification

Instrumental behavior patterns	Sources of reinforcement				
	Independent	Dependent	Ambivalent	Discordant	Detached
Active					
Normal	Unruly	Sociable	Sensitive	Forceful	Inhibited
Disordered	Antisocial	Histrionic	Negativistic	Aggressive	Avoidant
Passive					
Normal	Confident	Cooperative	Respectful	Defeatist	Introversive
Disordered	Narcissistic	Dependent depressive	Compulsive	Self-defeating	Schizoid
Severe variants	Paranoid or borderline	Borderline or paranoid	Borderline or paranoid	Borderline	Schizotypal or paranoid

extensions of the basic personality types that decompensate in the presence of environmental stress or compromised biology.

Millon's theory of personality pathology can thus be applied both to the official nosology of personality disorders and to those personality disorders generated by the model but not contained in the *DSM–IV*. The model description is explicated by using the term *dominant* to mean fixated in an analytic sense or reinforced in the behavioral sense. Although the meaning of *dominant* is not exactly conveyed by such words as *fixated* and *reinforced*, it does convey a sense of the term's meaning for personality function and is closer to the meaning of *dominant function* developed by Jung, as described in the MBTI test.

Millon's model, as applied to *DSM–IV* categories as well as to those generated by the model itself, is presented in Table 2.4. The dominant function of the polarity is presented in bold type, and deficits appear in italics. If a personality is dominant in one part of the axis (e.g., passive), then it is deficient in the other part of the axis (e.g., active).

The structurally deficient personality disorders are schizotypal, borderline, and paranoid. They can be classified as active or passive. The schizotypal is deficient or weak on all polarities. The borderline is conflicted on all polarities. The paranoid is average on all polarities and is intractable and largely unalterable.

Millon also developed a descriptive model for understanding personality pathology using structural and functional domain criteria in the behavior, phenomenological, intrapsychic, and biophysical categories. Across these two planes are the functional domains of expressive acts, interpersonal conduct, cognitive style, and regulatory mechanisms and the structural domains of object representations, self-image, morphologic organization, and

TABLE 2.4
Millon's Schematic of Personality Pathology According to the
Bioevolutionary Polarity Model

Personality disorder	Survival aims		Adaptive modes		Replication strategies	
	Pain	Pleasure	Passive	Active	Self	Other
Schizoid	*Deficit*	*Deficit*	**Dominant**	*Deficit*	**Dominant**	Average
Avoidant	**Dominant**	*Deficit*	Weak	**Dominant**	Weak	Weak
Depressive	*Deficit*	**Dominant**	**Dominant**	Weak	Weak	Weak
Dependent	Average	Average	**Dominant**	Weak	*Deficit*	**Dominant**
Histrionic	Average	Average	*Deficit*	**Dominant**	Average	**Dominant**
Narcissistic	Average	Weak	**Dominant**	Weak	**Dominant**	*Deficit*
Antisocial	Average	Weak	Weak	**Dominant**	**Dominant**	*Deficit*
Aggressive/ Sadistic	Average	**Dominant**	Weak	**Dominant**	Average	Weak
Compulsive	*Deficit*	Average	**Dominant**	Weak	Weak	Average
Passive- Aggressive (negativistic)	*Deficit*	Average	Average	**Dominant**	Average	Weak
Self-Defeating	Weak	**Dominant**	**Dominant**	Average	*Deficit*	Average
Schizotypal	*Deficit*	*Deficit*	*Deficit*	*Deficit*	*Deficit*	*Deficit*
Borderline	Average	Average	Average	Average	Average	Average
Paranoid	Weak	Weak	Weak	Weak	Weak	Weak

Note. Dominant on polarity in bold type, weak on polarity underlined, average on polarity in normal type, and deficit on polarity in italics.

mood or temperament. Each personality disorder can thus be described using these categories for explication.

Millon's approach is called a "prototype" approach whose categories represent the "pure" case of the disorder. Of course, pure cases exist only in theory and in textbooks, whereas, in nature, various blends result in slight variations of the prototype. (For further information regarding Millon's model of personality disorder, the reader is referred to his most recent thoughts on the matter; Millon & Davis, 1997.)

Millon developed instrumentation to assess his theorized types for both clinical and nonclinical populations. This theoretical model and its operational measures have generated a substantial amount of research (Craig, 1997; Millon, 1997) and continue to play an influential role in present-day clinical psychology. Millon's theory, in fact, was the proximate cause of having the avoidant personality disorder included in the third edition of the *DSM* (American Psychiatric Association, 1987) and in subsequent revisions and in introducing the multiaxial system.

Applicability to Forensic Practice

The tools Millon developed as operational measures of his theoretical types—especially the MCMI–III (and prior versions), styles, and disorders—

are increasingly being used by forensic psychologists. Much of this application is presented in later chapters of this book. The MCMI in particular has generated a substantial amount of research and has demonstrated much validity across a variety of populations and clinical applications (Millon, 1997). Among self-report measures, it has become the instrument of choice when evaluating for personality disorders.

Models of personality configurations and classifications are beginning to be tested empirically, and psychologists can look forward to increasingly sophisticated analyses to test the models' basic postulates (O'Connor & Dyce, 1998). Whether or not one adopts a particular model of personality development and personality pathology, the categories of personality type and the instruments to assess them will be extremely valuable in forensic work. Nevertheless, throughout the remaining chapters of this volume, Millon's theory of personality pathology is used as the permeating theory in which to understand behavior (personality) disorders.

3

POLICE PSYCHOLOGY

This chapter explores the psychological screening of law enforcement personnel with an emphasis on the screening of police officers. (Additional law enforcement personnel who may experience psychological screening include security personnel, particularly, more recently, airport security personnel.) I consider the legal basis for such screening and then review the literature on police psychology, which provides a job work analysis and reviews personality characteristics of successful and unsuccessful police officers. I review the process of evaluating such personnel and assessment tools commonly used for this purpose. The chapter concludes with an overview of possible adverse impacts on groups of assessment tools and, finally, the implications of race norming for instruments and the selection ratio.

SCREENING OF LAW ENFORCEMENT PERSONNEL

It is now widely recognized that the screening of police officers and other law enforcement personnel is desirable to assess their emotional stability and to aid in the prediction, control, and prevention of police corruption and abuse. Such screening was initially endorsed by the 1967 President's Commission on Law and the Administration of Justice and by the 1968 National Advisory Commission on Civil Disorder (Scrivner, 1994). The courts have upheld the right of law enforcement agencies to require psychological testing of police officer candidates (*Conte v. Horcher*, 1977; *McCabe v. Hoberman*, 1969; *McKenna v. Fargo*, 1978). They have also ruled that testing is the responsibility of agencies when it results in increased protection to the community, and failure to provide psychological screening of police officer candidates has been construed by the courts as negligence (*Bonsignore v. City of New York*, 1981). Today, over 80% of police districts require the psychological screening of applicants to the police force. This screening usually entails psychological testing and a clinical interview. Reliance on psychological test findings alone is insufficient for a competent psychological evaluation (Hartman, 1987). Instead, the forensic psychologist needs to examine all sources of data relevant to the assessment question.

The Minnesota Multiphasic Personality Inventory (MMPI; Burnstein, 1980; Hiatt & Hargrave, 1988), the 16 Personality Factor Questionnaire (16PF; Cattell, Eber, & Tatsuoka, 1970b; H. M. Snibbe, Fabricatore, & Azen, 1975), the California Psychological Inventory (CPI; Hargrave & Hiatt, 1989), and the Inwald Personality Inventory (IPI; Inwald, Knatz, & Shusman, 1983) have been used to screen law enforcement personnel. Other tests that have been used for this purpose include the Rokeach Value Survey, the Eysenck Personality Inventory, the Myers–Briggs Type Indicator, the Rorschach test, the Draw-A-Person test, the Edwards Personal Preference Test, and the Strong Vocational Interest Blank (see Burbeck & Furnham, 1985).

The Personality Assessment Inventory (PAI; Morey, 1991) is a broad-band personality test for psychopathology and clinical syndromes. This test has normative data on more than 17,000 public safety applicants (Roberts, Thompson, & Johnson, 1999) and is likely to be used to screen law enforcement applicants with greater frequency in the future. However, the MMPI is the most widely used psychological test to screen police officers. Some measures used by psychologists may not tap the skills and traits necessary to become successful police officers. Psychologists bear the responsibility of demonstrating that atypical assessment methods have adequate predictive validity when used for personnel selection.

The MMPI–2 is a 567-item true–false questionnaire yielding up to 7 validity scales and 10 clinical scales, along with multiple content and supplemental scales. The CPI, as revised (Gough, 1969, 1996), is a 434-item true–false questionnaire that yields 20 separate scales. The 16PF, as revised (Conn & Rieke, 1994), is a 185-item true–false personality inventory that yields 16 primary factors and five global or second-order factors.

These tests were developed as broad measures of personality or psychopathology and have been applied to the selection of police officers. In contrast to this approach, the IPI is a 310-item true–false questionnaire that was empirically developed in law enforcement settings expressly for the purpose of screening police applicants for their psychological suitability. It yields 26 scores related to police functioning, including validity scales, acting-out behaviors (drugs, alcohol, antisocial attitudes), coping methods (Type A behavior), interpersonal difficulties (family conflict, spouse or mate conflict), and internalized conflict measures (anxiety, depression, illness concerns). Initial studies with the IPI have been encouraging (Ostrov, 1985; Shusman, 1987; Shusman, Inwald, & Knatz, 1987; Shusman, Inwald, & Landa, 1984). Scales from the IPI and the MMPI correlate from .01 to .64, suggesting that although they are not completely independent, each makes some unique contributions to the assessment process (Shusman, 1987). Also, the IPI was found to be more susceptible than the MMPI to faking good. Both were effective in identifying problems when the respondents produced a normal MMPI profile, but although the MMPI identified 100% of the cases subsequently determined to be unfit for police duty, the IPI identified 75% of such cases (Muller & Bruno, 1986).

To validate assessment measures with law enforcement personnel, re-searchers have engaged in one of two experimental strategies. First, they try to link variables—most commonly test scores—with performance criteria on the job, a predictive validity research design. In a concurrent validity design, researchers sample police officers on the job using a psychological test and then correlate these scores with current job ratings or with other evidence of job success. In the second strategy, researchers use police officer applicants, and the scores of their initial screening are then compared with an "intermediate" criterion, such as some training goal that is proximally related to future on-the-job success. Examples would include training and classroom performance while at the police academy. The problem with the latter validity strategy is that variables associated with intermediate criteria may not be the ones that lead to success on the job as a functioning police officer. Researchers in this area have also studied mental tests and biographical information, but the discussion in this chapter addresses only those studies that have investigated the role of personality variables in police officer selection.

Guidelines for the screening of law enforcement personnel revised by the International Association of Chiefs of Police (Curren, 1998) present 22 recommendations for a comprehensive framework for pre-employment psychological evaluations. These recommendations include (a) objective assessment instruments that have been validated for use with public safety applicants, (b) the requirement of a semistructured clinical interview, and (c) the need to continually validate the criteria used to determine applicant suitability. These guidelines are consistent with the American Psychological Association (APA; 2002a) *Ethical Principles of Psychologists and Code of Conduct* (Ethics Code).

What role does personality theory play in the personality assessment of law enforcement applicants and in fitness-for-duty evaluations? What does the extant research tell us about the personality of police officers? The data available to date demonstrate that successful police officers are well adjusted and emotionally stable. In Millon's theory, they have a good balance between the three polarities of existence, adaptation, and replication and tend toward enhancing, modifying, and other-focused reinforcement strategies. On the other hand, problematic police officers are imbalanced in one or more of these polarities.

There are two main facets of the accurate psychological assessment of police officers. First, the assessment can identify aspects of the job (e.g., work analysis) and identify those traits necessary for the successful performance of this job. Second, the assessment can identify personality traits that have been associated with success as a police officer.

Job Work Analysis of Successful Police Officers

There is general agreement that the following traits are necessary to successfully perform the typical functions required of police officers:

- thoroughness and attention to detail,
- a strong work ethic evidenced by dependability and reliability and little absenteeism,
- sensitivity and flexibility in a broad array of situations,
- good decision-making skills, and
- emotional stability.

Police officers must show good judgment and discretion in stressful situations, have high stress tolerance, have a professional appearance, show proper initiative and a positive work attitude, and be cooperative. They also need a degree of suspiciousness and need to be in a state of continual preparedness to respond appropriately. They must show compliance with the authoritarian nature of police administration, yet be aggressive toward perpetrators. An unwritten quality is the willingness to follow the informal code of conduct that requires loyalty to their peers. The forensic psychologist screening police officer candidates must use assessment tools that address these qualities.

Millon (1994b) reported on a structured job analysis for personality traits deemed desirable for entry-level police officers using consensus ratings from field officer trainers. He found that adherence to a work ethic, thoroughness and attentiveness to details, sensitivity to the interests of others, and emotional stability were considered essential to effective performance.

Some undesirable qualities for a police officer, besides serious psychopathology, include a lack of objectivity, difficulty in performing under pressure, selfishness, oversensitivity, extreme introversion, immaturity, low levels of drive or ambition, excessive security consciousness, poor health, lack of enthusiasm, egotism, lack of career direction, lack of respect, overemotionality, reluctance to exercise authority, poor temper control, excessive aggressiveness, a tendency to be too autocratic or too dependent, impulsivity, anxiety, nervousness, excessive rigidity, and a tendency to try to please others too much (Burbeck & Furnham, 1985).

The positive traits reflect people who are well adjusted and have good coping skills, given the many contradictory roles required of this profession. For example, police officers must adapt to unique demands that can expose them to dangerous situations. They must balance the need to comply with supervisory demands on the one hand and the need to resist offenders' efforts to escape on the other. They must be tough and aggressive in one situation and interpersonally sensitive in the other.

Thus, the screening of police applicants does not merely require confirmation of the absence of general psychopathology. Rather, it requires the assessment of a unique set of traits that set police officers apart from the general population.

The motivation to become a police officer may include such factors as security, social esteem, and, of course, salary. Most tend to come from a working-class environment and espouse traditional values and attitudes. They tend to prefer traditional, rigid, and directional leadership with external controls, yet they want discretionary authority as required of the situation. This dual preference is sometimes problematic; the most common offense of police officers is absence without leave, and the most common complaint against them is abuse or brutality while exercising their discretionary powers (Crosby, 1979; Lefkowitz, 1977).

Police have two main functions. Traits required for the former may be different than traits required for the latter. They have to enforce the law and maintain the peace. Frequently they have to function as quasi–social workers when intervening in domestic violence disputes, crises, and a variety of human problems.

Personality Traits of Police Officers

This section reviews research that has addressed the personality traits of police officers using objective personality tests. Because the overwhelming majority of studies have used the MMPI, the presentation and discussion necessarily concentrates on this instrument.

MMPI Studies

By and large, police applicants and effective police officers have been found to be psychologically healthy. Early studies found them to be somewhat defensive and slightly impulsive (e.g., preferring action to contemplation), free from pretense, "masculine" in style and demeanor, socially appropriate, and exhibitionistic. They tended to stay out of trouble, despite some tendencies to overindulge in sex and alcohol use, and had higher than average needs in aggression and autonomy (Borum & Stock, 1993; Matarazzo, Allen, Saslow, & Wiens, 1964). This profile may suggest that police officers have personal traits that are conducive to seeking out and adapting to the needs of the job (Holland, Heim, & Holt, 1976). Most would be characterized as active, conscientious, forceful and assertive, straightforward, and dependable.

More recent studies have reported that successful police officers (sheriff's deputies, $N = 249$, and highway patrolmen, $N = 442$) are more socially outgoing and gregarious and have a greater capacity for socially rewarding relationships. Urban police officers were found to be more assertive, less anxious and depressed, and more socially outgoing and tended to present a good impression (B. Carpenter & Raza, 1987).

Among 359 correctional officers, MMPI scores reflected mild defensiveness (the K validity scale) with primary elevations (at subclinical levels) on Psychopathic Deviate (Pd) and Hypomania (Ma) and low on Social Introversion (Si). This pattern suggests outgoing, talkative, energetic, and ambitious traits with an action-oriented interpersonal style. These officers may have had difficulty generating concern for the feelings and needs of others. Secondary elevations on Hysteria (Hy) suggest an inhibitory effect making truly impulsive behavior unlikely. Because these were functioning correctional officers who worked in a highly charged and dangerous environment, the effects of this working environment on the personality of the respondents remains unknown (Holland et al., 1976). For both the MMPI and MMPI–2, peace officers had low-level elevations on K and Pd (Hargrave, Hiatt, Ogard, & Karr, 1994).

Correlates of Problematic Police Behavior

The MMPI scales have been shown to correlate with problematic behaviors of police officers (i.e., absences, lateness, disciplinary interviews) across racial groups (Knatz, Inwald, Brockwell, & Tran, 1993). Elevations on the Psychopathic Deviate (Pd) scale were directly related to incidence of auto accidents among 95 police officers, whereas scores on the Depression (Dep) scale were inversely related to problematic behaviors (Azen, Snibbe, & Montgomery, 1973; Marsh, 1962). Elevations on Pd correlated with poor work histories, inappropriate use of force, complaints of petty thievery, excessive use of alcohol or drugs, and charges of sexual misconduct (Blau,

Super, & Brady, 1993). Elevations on Psychasthenia (Pt) and Schizophrenia (Sc) were highly correlated with serious misconduct charges, such as absenteeism and disciplinary charges (Blum, 1964). Officers with elevated scores on Hypochondriasis (Hs) and Hysteria (Hy) and on the MacAndrew Alcoholism Scale (MAC) showed increasing levels of psychopathology over time (Costello, Schoenfeld, & Kobos, 1982). Elevated scores on the F validity scale have been associated with academy attrition, poor academy performance, lower supervisory ratings, and aggression. Higher scores on Hypomania (Ma) have been associated with low performance ratings, automobile accidents, unsatisfactory job performance, and inappropriate aggression. Higher scores on Paranoia (Pa) have also been associated with lower supervisor ratings (Hiatt & Hargrave, 1988).

Successful Versus Unsuccessful Officers

Gottlieb and Baker (1974) reported that after three years on the job, higher rated police officers, compared with lower rated officers, had somewhat higher scores on the K validity scale, whereas the lower rated officers had higher scores on L and F, suggesting that the latter were more prone to act on aggressive feelings and to have deficient self-control and that they tried to fake answers on the test. Higher K scores in this case probably suggest healthy self-esteem. The lower rated officers were somewhat higher on Paranoia (Pa), suggesting that they were more egocentric and resentful (of nonstereotypical citizens), whereas the higher-rated officers were less rebellious. The results of this study suggest that higher rated police officers were characterized by a sense of independence, some defensiveness, self-acceptance, and self-control under stress. Lower rated officers appeared to be childish, immature, and dependent under stress. They appeared motivated by excitement and adventure.

Successful policemen in Los Angeles scored higher on the L and K validity scales, Hysteria (Hy), and Paranoia (Pa), but still at normal-range levels. Applicants who were subsequently rejected for police training scored higher on the F validity scale, Hypochondriasis (Hs), Psychopathic Deviant (Pd), and Schizophrenia (Sc). Police officers who were selected but who left the department within three years scored higher on Psychasthenia (Pt; Saxe & Reiser, 1976). The Goldberg Index (T scores on L + Pa + Sc − Hy + Pt) was able to distinguish between successful and unsuccessful applicants (N = 424; Costello et al., 1982). Scores on the K validity scale, Pd, Masculinity/Femininity (Mf), and Hypomania (Ma) were able to successfully predict negative performance criteria, such as supervisory ratings, among 146 law enforcement cadets (Hargrave, 1985). Social Introversion (Si) and the Harris–Lingoes subscale D4 (Mental Dullness) differentiated high- from low-performing officers (Hargrave, Hiatt, & Gaffney, 1986). The MMPI was able to differentiate small town police officers who were successful on the job from those who were not (N = 102).

An immaturity index composed of the L validity scale, Psychopathic Deviant (Pd), and Hypomania (Ma) was a strong predictor of termination (Bartol, 1982). An aggression index composed of the F validity scale, Pd, and Ma predicted disciplinary suspensions among 107 police officers three years later (Costello, Schneider, & Schoenfeld, 1981).

The MMPI successfully predicted later job performance among 307 newly hired government security personnel (Inwald & Brockwell, 1991). These researchers used discriminant function analysis to determine results and did not report individual scale differences. Higher classification accuracy rates were achieved with the IPI, and the best overall rates of accurate classification were achieved using both tests in combination.

Similarly, both the MMPI and the IPI were given to 69 police officer recruits in Alabama, and their on-the-job performance was studied one year later. Criterion variables included verbal and written reprimands, vehicular reprimands, citizen complaints, and positive recognitions. Results indicated that Psychopathic Deviate (Pd), Psychasthenia (Pt), Masculinity/Femininity (Mf), Hypochondriasis (Hs), and Hysteria (Hy) demonstrated significant predictive validity. A substantial number of IPI scales successfully predicted many of the criterion variables and did so at stronger levels than the MMPI scales (72% compared with 64% classification accuracy). This study suggests that both the MMPI and the IPI were able to significantly predict short-term law enforcement job behavior (Scogin, Schumaker, Gardner, & Chaplin, 1995).

Supervisor ratings may not be the best criterion for judging the adequacy of the MMPI with police screening, because such ratings can reflect friendship patterns instead of job-related factors. For example, candidates who were more dysphoric (e.g., high scores on Depression; Dep) received higher supervisory ratings, but these scores were negatively correlated with more objective criteria, such as reprimands for use of excessive force, suspensions, negative reports for a variety of reasons, and workshops attended (Beutler, Storm, Kirkish, Scogin, & Gaines, 1985). On the other hand, no significant differences were found on MMPI scales between police officers judged acceptable and those judged unacceptable among 424 applicants (Schoenfeld, Kobos, & Phinney, 1980), but the MMPI was able to reliably classify police academy recruits into successful, marginal, and unsuccessful at police training (Hargrave, 1985).

Evidence also exists that the role of the police officer can take a psychological toll. One study found that at the end of two years of service, and later after four years of service, Arizona officers eventually terminated from service showed higher amounts of somatic symptoms, anxiety, and alcohol use. Most likely job stress accounted for these findings (Beutler, Nussbaum, & Meredith, 1988).

Mandatory fitness-for-duty or return-to-duty evaluations almost always involve a dispute about the facts of the case, and the truthfulness of the respondent in such cases always needs to be evaluated. Most psychologists have used the MMPI or IPI for both initial police selection and for fitness for duty evaluations. The MMPI validity scales (F, K, L) are particularly useful here. One study involved officers who wanted to return to duty, officers who did not want to return to duty, and a control group. Officers wanting to return to duty minimized their psychological difficulties significantly more than the other groups and scored higher on four of six validity measures, including F and an F–K index (Grossman, Haywood, Ostrov, Wasyliw, & Cavanaugh, 1990).

The normative scores for police officer positions are based largely on data from the original MMPI. One question is the extent to which prior MMPI-based knowledge of law enforcement personnel would transfer to the MMPI–2. To address this question, researchers administered both the MMPI and MMPI–2 to 166 peace officers. These two tests are highly correlated, with an overall concordance rate of 78% when normal limit profiles and high-point and two-point code types are grouped together. The so-called well-defined code types resulted in a 90% concordance rate. When individual profiles were inspected, about 50% produced the same high-point code type, about 33% produced the same two-point code type, and 70% produced a normal limit profile on both tests. However, on the MMPI–2, both men and women police applicants scored lower on Depression (Dep); on Masculinity/Femininity (Mf), women scored higher and men scored lower (Hargrave et al., 1994).

Kornfeld (1995) gave the MMPI–2 to 84 police officer applicants in Connecticut. Both White and minority applicants had similar MMPI–2 profiles, although White applicants scored significantly higher than Black applicants on Hypochondriasis (Hs), with both within normal ranges. All applicants showed a defensive response style and low scores on Depression (Dep), Masculinity/Femininity (Mf), and Social Introversion (Si), although female applicants scored higher on Mf. Low scores on Dep suggest a generally positive mood and less tendency to worry, be indecisive, and have one's feelings easily bruised. Low scores on Mf suggest adherence to traditional sex roles and interest patterns, whereas higher scores on Mf suggest rebellion from these stereotyped roles, aggressiveness, self-confidence, and assertive behavior. Low scores on Si suggest a generally extroverted, outgoing, and socially gregarious nature.

Kornfeld (2000) gave the MMPI–2 to 111 male law enforcement applicants. He was interested in exploring how these recruits responded to the Harris–Lingoes Psychopathic Deviate (Pd) subscales. They had significantly lower scores, compared to the MMPI–2 normative sample, on Pd1 (Familial Discord), Pd4 (Social Alienation), and Pd5 (Self-Alienation) and significantly higher scores on Pd2 (Authority Problems) and Pd3 (Social Imperturbability). These results suggest that applicants reported more self-confidence and resistance to authority and less social alienation and personal unhappiness than the normative sample. Pd2 was the best predictor of Pd scores on the parent scale. Pd2 has also correlated with job satisfaction and performance of police officers (Weiss & Buehler, 1995).

A total of 467 police applicants in Missouri were given the MMPI–2 and the IPI as part of a normative data collection for police officer candidates. High scores on the L and K validity scales characterized the MMPI–2 profiles of applicants and did not vary by race or gender. Minority men scored higher than White men on the F validity scale and Depression (Dep), but all scores were in the average range. Women scored higher on Masculinity/Femininity (Mf). Police veterans scored higher on Hysteria (Hy) and lower on Hypomania (Ma) than recruits, perhaps reflecting more vulnerability to the stress of the job and also lower energy levels. A number of MMPI–2 scales were positive and negatively related to IPI scales. The interested reader is referred to the original study for discussion of the exact nature and direction of these correlations (Detrick, Chibnall, & Rosso, 2001). On the other hand, Bartol (1982) found that higher scores on Hy were predictive of better job performance ratings and may suggest increased optimism and self-confidence.

EVALUATION PROCESS FOR POLICE FORCE CANDIDATES

Police applicants undergo often extensive prepsychological evaluations. They take (and must pass) written or oral exams or both, undergo background checks, have a physical exam, take other tests such as general intelligence and agility tests, have a medical history and evaluation, and submit to a personal interview (Devan, Hungersford, Wood, & Greene, 2001). Several background variables tend to be associated with poor subsequent performance as police officers, including multiple prior vehicle code violations, multiple convictions for minor offenses, frequent job changes, and employment of short duration (Devan et al., 2001; Pallone, 1992).

Usually this preselection process has been completed before the psychologist meets the applicant, allowing the psychologist to ask follow-up questions pertaining to both the background information and the psychological test results. Usually psychological evaluations occur after the applicant has met all other requirements of the job and has passed a background check. Thus, the clinical evaluation is usually the last step in the process.

Applicants who make it to this point and then fail to be selected probably assume that they did not pass the psychological evaluation. Thus, a nonselection recommendation puts the psychologist at risk for civil suits on a variety of charges (e.g., discrimination, incompetence). It is therefore critical that such decisions are based on sound and defensible criteria.

Psychological evaluations may also be required for promotions and for fitness-for-duty evaluations, in addition to pre-employment screening. In these instances, both psychological testing and a clinical interview are standard procedure.

The first step in the psychological evaluation process is to determine the psychological factors that relate to successful performance on the job. It is advisable for the forensic psychologist to develop a list of behaviors and factors to use in assessing the applicant. Such a list will help to objectify the process. However, the psychologist must be able to cite evidence that the traits and factors on the list have predictive validity for the specific job being evaluated (Pallone, 1992).

Clinical interviews may lack reliability. That is, two interviewers may not come to the same conclusions or make the same recommendations about the same applicant. Although there is some research on what makes an effective police officer, there is little research literature that the psychologist can use to demonstrate the reliability of his or her conclusions based solely on a clinical interview, despite efforts to make these interviews more objective (Varela, Scogin, & Vipperman, 1999). Hargrave (1985) reported on good agreement between two clinicians regarding the likelihood of acceptable, marginal, and unsuccessful academy training experiences based on MMPI and California Psychological Inventory (CPI) data. However, generally psychologists must rely on their expertise and reputation and general competence in evidentiary proceedings on this matter.

On the other hand, there is a fair body of data on the psychological testing of recruits and functioning police officers. Reliance on this data, much of which is presented in this chapter, will lend credibility to one's interpretations. Crosby (1979) reported that the overall rejection rates following psychological evaluations ranged from 5% to 25%, with a median of 15%. Forensic psychologists need to monitor their recommendations and their rejection rates and look for any problem in this area.

Evaluating psychologists should bear in mind that most recruits have never seen a psychologist before and are likely to be apprehensive about being "psychoanalyzed." Many do not realize that such screening is routine. It is recommended that the forensic psychologist tell applicants that they have not been singled out, but rather that all applicants are required to undergo psychological screening.

Table 3.1 presents MMPI *T* score data on studies that have used the MMPI for male police officer selection, Table 3.2 presents MMPI–2 *T* score

TABLE 3.1
Minnesota Multiphasic Personality Inventory *T* Scores of Male Law Enforcement Applicants and Officers

Study	N	L	F	K	Hs	Dep	Hy	Pd	Mf	Pa	Pt	Sc	Ma	Si
1	35	54	48	67	52	53	56	65	54	53	52	52	52	46
2	203	50	48	62	49	51	56	60	51	49	51	51	56	45
3	34	48	46	48	48	52	55	57	54	49	52	50	55	47
	36	47	51	51	48	50	54	59	54	52	53	52	58	47
4	100	56	49	66	51	51	58	57	52	53	53	55	57	43
	100	53	50	64	53	52	56	62	52	52	52	54	56	44
	100	54	49	62	50	53	56	57	53	50	52	52	56	44
5	359	54	50	60	50	52	56	59	55	51	52	53	59	45
6	424	49	50	58	50	52	48	60	54	50	53	52	60	50
7	1,119	52	52	56	47	52	54	57	53	51	52	52	57	47
8	102	50	50	59	50	51	55	56	59	56	54	55	58	46
	36	50	50	57	49	50	51	53	57	56	53	53	50	47
9	65	48	49	60	51	51	58	58	—	55	52	53	54	45
10	316	53	52	58	50	52	54	56	57	55	54	54	54	50
	128	52	50	61	50	50	55	57	55	53	53	54	58	46
	137	52	52	59	50	52	54	56	58	56	54	54	58	49
	23	57	54	57	52	54	54	57	54	55	55	56	58	54
	51	51	50	62	50	49	56	58	55	52	53	55	60	44
	12	53	50	61	51	56	54	59	56	54	57	57	60	50
11	37	54	45	55	48	48	51	54	48	49	48	50	54	44
	86	53	46	54	50	49	51	54	48	49	48	48	53	46
	23	56	43	55	46	46	49	53	48	47	49	49	50	45
	126	53	44	57	48	46	51	54	48	49	48	51	55	43
12	5	50	51	61	51	50	57	60	—	55	51	52	59	45
	11	52	53	63	57	54	63	64	—	62	55	55	55	42
13	143	53	49	62	51	54	56	58	54	51	53	52	57	43
	332	54	47	63	50	47	55	56	55	49	52	52	56	43
	384	54	48	64	50	49	57	58	54	52	52	54	56	42
	404	55	49	64	51	51	57	59	55	53	52	54	56	43
	127	60	53	64	49	53	56	60	49	56	50	52	60	48
	129	62	55	59	52	55	60	58	46	57	53	55	62	43
	39	54	47	62	49	43	57	57	55	54	52	51	59	41
14	267	53	53	57	49	53	53	53	53	50	52	55	60	49
	40	50	58	53	49	56	51	57	57	56	56	61	65	50
	25	50	50	57	49	47	52	49	48	49	50	51	60	47
15	7	50	51	62	53	53	57	58	57	67	54	54	57	47
16	47	51	48	64	50	53	56	60	53	51	53	54	55	46
Mean		53	50	59	50	51	55	57	53	53	52	53	57	46

Note. Dashes indicate no score for that variable on scale. Study 1 (Matarazzo, Allen, Saslow, & Wiens, 1964) examined urban officers. Study 2 (Gottsman, 1969) examined urban officers. Study 3 (Gottlieb & Baker, 1974) examined police officers with 3 years of service who received high efficiency ratings (row 1) and low efficiency ratings (row 2). Study 4 (Saxe & Reiser, 1976) examined successful applicants (row 1), rejected applicants (row 2), and applicants who were selected but dropped out during first 3 years. Study 5 (Holland, Heim, & Holt, 1976) examined urban correctional officer recruits. Study 6 (Schoenfeld, Kobos, & Phinney, 1980) examined urban police officers. Study 7 (Costello, Schneider, & Schoenfeld, 1981) examined police academy recruits. Study 8 (Bartol, 1982) examined small town police officers (row 1) and those rated above average by supervisors (row 2). Study 9 (Beutler, Storm, Kirkish, Scogin, & Gaines, 1985) examined newly selected law enforcement officers. Study 10 (Hargrave, Hiatt, & Gaffney, 1986) examined traffic officers (row 1), sheriff's deputies (row 2), traffic officers rated high by supervisors (row 3), traffic officers rated low by supervisors (row 4), sheriff's deputies rated high by supervisors (row 5), and sheriff's deputies rated low by supervisors (row 6). Study 11 (Carpenter & Raza, 1987) examined urban police officers (row 1), small town police officers (row 2), medium town police applicants (row 3), and large town police applicants (row 4). Study 12 (Beutler, Nussbaum, & Meredith, 1988) examined White police officers after 2 years on the job (row 1) and White police officers after 4 years on the job (row 2). Study 13 (Muller, 1990) examined four samples of White police applicants (rows 1–4), Black police applicants (row 5), Hispanic police applicants (row 6), and later-career officers (row 7). Study 14 (Inwald & Brockwell, 1991) examined security officers with satisfactory ratings (row 1), unsatisfactory ratings (row 2), and exceptional ratings (row 3). Study 15 (Hargrave, Hiatt, Ogard, & Karr, 1994) examined peace officers. Study 16 (Millon, 1994b) examined police candidates.

TABLE 3.2
Minnesota Multiphasic Personality Inventory (Revised) *T* Scores of Male Law Enforcement Applicants and Officers

Study	N	L	F	K	Hs	Dep	Hy	Pd	Mf	Pa	Pt	Sc	Ma	Si
1	100	56	42	58	45	42	50	50	42	49	47	47	51	41
2	96	51	45	57	50	46	49	49	44	50	47	47	50	45
3	61	57	40	62	48	42	49	49	39	48	46	45	46	38
	11	53	38	59	40	40	47	46	43	50	47	45	47	36
4	395	61	41	64	49	46	51	51	40	48	48	47	48	40
	35	65	44	63	51	49	50	51	44	45	49	48	48	44
	193	61	42	65	50	47	52	52	41	48	48	48	46	40
	232	62	41	63	49	46	50	51	41	47	48	47	49	41
	247	62	42	64	50	47	51	52	40	47	48	48	48	40
	183	60	41	63	49	45	51	51	41	48	48	47	47	40
Mean		59	42	62	48	45	50	50	41	48	48	47	48	40

Note. Study 1 (Muller, 1990) examined police officer applicants. Study 2 (Hargrave, Hiatt, Ogard, & Karr, 1994) examined peace officers. Study 3 (Kornfeld, 1995) examined White police officer candidates (row 1) and minority police officer candidates (row 2). Study 4 (Detrick, Chibnall, & Rosso, 2001) examined White police officer applicants (row 1), minority police officer applicants (row 2), veteran police officers (row 3), police officer recruits (row 4), county officers (row 5), and municipal officers (row 6).

data for male police law enforcement applicants, and Table 3.3 presents MMPI and MMPI–2 *T* score data for female police applicants. These tables can be used as guides for "normative" data on modal profiles of these selected groups (Ellwood, 1993). The tables suggest that the mean MMPI profiles of successful police officers are similar to those of unsuccessful police officers and that there seem to be few MMPI profile differences between male and female police officers (Devan et al., 2001).

In summary, the research to date suggests that elevated scores on the F validity profile, Depression (Dep), Psychopathic Deviate (Pd), Psychasthenia (Pt), Schizophrenia (Sc), Hypomania (Ma), and Social Introversion (Si) tend to be correlated with subsequent negative performance in role behaviors specific to police officers. In addition, the voluminous research on behavioral correlates associated with these scales has found that they are invariably negative, suggesting maladjustment. Pallone (1992) concluded based on his review of the literature that the K validity scale and Hysteria (Hy), which can measure defensiveness, positively correlate with ratings of performance. Scales that measure social undesirability, including the L validity scale, Psychopathic Deviate (Pd), Paranoia (Pa), and Hypomania (Ma), tend to be negatively correlated with supervisor ratings of performance.

California Psychological Inventory

The CPI manual (Gough, 1969) listed scores of over 400 police officers and found them to be above average on the traits of self-acceptance,

TABLE 3.3
Minnesota Multiphasic Personality Inventory (MMPI) *T* Scores of
Female Law Enforcement Applicants and Officers

Scale	MMPI–1				MMPI–2			MMPI–2
	1	2		3	4	5	6	mean scores
N	20	70	108	32	70	12	34	
L	54	48	53	60	48	60	60	57
F	45	52	44	50	48	39	43	45
K	56	59	59	66	56	65	63	62
Hs	50	50	47	50	48	45	47	47
Dep	55	52	45	46	46	38	43	43
Hy	48	54	50	55	50	46	48	50
Pd	59	59	56	62	51	49	52	53
Mf	55	51	55	60	54	64	61	60
Pa	48	56	52	54	50	41	47	48
Pt	51	52	49	53	48	44	47	48
Sc	53	53	49	52	48	45	48	48
Ma	59	55	60	59	50	46	48	51
Si	44	50	45	48	45	39	41	43

Note. Study 1 (Carpenter & Raza, 1987) examined urban police officers. Study 2 (Hargrave, Hiatt, Ogard, & Karr, 1994) examined peace officers. Study 3 (Muller, 1990) examined White police officer applicants (column 1) and Black police officer applicants (column 2). Study 4 (Hargrave, Hiatt, Ogard, & Karr, 1994) examined peace officers. Study 5 (Kornfeld, 1995) examined White police officer applicants. Study 6 (Detrick, Chibnall, & Rosso, 2001) examined White applicants.

sociability, responsibility, empathy, poise, confidence, and intellectual efficiency. CPI studies also demonstrate that police officers tend to be self-confident, well adjusted, and dependable and not overly touchy, suspicious, or sensitive. Hogan (1971) looked at classes of police cadets in Maryland and compared their scores on the CPI with those of state police officers. Supervisory ratings served as the criterion. Scores on the CPI scales of Intellectual Efficiency (Ie), Well-Being (Wb), and Achievement via Independence (AI) were particularly related to the positive traits described in the manual. These three scales are referred to in the CPI literature as the Class III scales and should be a focus of attention among psychologists who use the CPI to screen police.

Pugh (1985) examined the supervisory ratings of police officers followed over a two-year period. The CPI scales Capacity for Status (Cs), Intellectual Efficiency (Ie), Tolerance (To), Achievement via Independence (Ai), Well-Being (Wb), and Socialization (So) discriminated high from low performers. The CPI has also been shown to successfully and reliably classify recruits in terms of acceptable performance (Hargrave, 1985).

Both the MMPI–2 and the CPI–R have computer-generated interpretive reports specific to law enforcement personnel (Gough, 1996). Although they provide convenience and often comprehensive analysis, computer-generated reports can be problematic in forensic work. To the extent that such reports may be inaccurate, or when the psychologist arrives at interpretations and conclusions that differ from the computer report, then the psychologist faces the potential task of convincing a judge or jury that the computer "experts" are wrong. Also, keep in mind that a computer narrative report is not a report on an individual client, but rather a summary of the most appropriate test descriptors for a set of test scores.

Sixteen Personality Factor Questionnaire

Overall psychological adjustment on the 16PF is characterized as high on Emotional Stability (C); lower on Vigilance (L), Apprehension (O), Tension (Q4), and Boldness (H); and higher in Perfectionism (Q3) (Conn & Rieke, 1994). This profile applies to the general public; a police officer may need traits that vary from this general description and yet would reflect positive qualities for this profession.

The 16PF was given to 461 Los Angeles patrolmen and revealed that they had common traits of self-assurance and conservatism. They were bright and alert (B, reasoning), though somewhat interpersonally cool and detached (A, Warmth). This profile has a positive value in that police officers often have to deal with passionate and emotionally charged situations and people. They were assertive (E, Dominance) and self-assured (O, Apprehension), well grounded in reality (M, Abstractness), and tough-minded (I, Sensitivity). They were concerned about self-image and reputation (Q1, Openness to Change) and maintained self-discipline (Q2, Self-Reliance). Compared to White officers, Mexican American officers appeared more conservative and relaxed, whereas Black officers appeared more experimental, analytical, and group oriented (H. M. Snibbe et al., 1975).

Eber (1991) reported on what was considered a distinctive police personality profile based on 15,000 candidates for positions in various law enforcement agencies nationwide. Using the second-order factors, Eber reported that police applicants tended to score high on Extroversion (A, F, H, and Q2), low on Anxiety (−C, L, O, −Q3, and Q4), high on Tough Poise (−A, −I, and −M), slightly high on Independence (E, L, M, Q1, and Q2), and high on Control (G and Q3). Eber's results suggest that the average police candidate is high in control, tough-minded, slightly independent, and low in anxiety and is oriented toward extroversion.

Lorr and Strack (1994) gave the 16PF to 275 police applicants in several states. Group profiles showed police applicants to be higher in Extroversion, Control, Independence, and Tough Poise and very low in Anxiety. They conducted a cluster analysis and found three distinct subgroups. Cluster I ($n = 77$) were described as primarily tough and independent and low in anxiety. Cluster II ($n = 100$) were very controlled, independent, and extroverted and very low in anxiety. This cluster was quite similar to Eber's

(1991) prototype 16PF police applicant. Cluster III applicants ($n = 98$) were highly controlled and tough and low in anxiety; these applicants appeared self-disciplined, socially bold, extroverted, and emotionally tough and reported less anxiety.

Zeidhlach (2003) gave the 16PF to 246 applicants from several states. He then compared the mean factor scores with the means of the normative sample using the omega squared statistic, which provides a measure of association that is independent of sample size and hence is the preferred statistic for these purposes (Sheshkin, 2000). (Omega squared generally falls between 0 and 1 but can appear as a negative number. The closer it is to 1, the stronger the association, and the closer it is to 0, the weaker the association. Cohen's [1988, 1992] values for interpreting effect sizes were used.) Zeidhlach found that these applicants scored higher than the standardization sample on Social Boldness (H) and Perfectionism (Q3) and lower on Liveliness (F), Apprehension (O), and Tension (Q4), with a medium effect size, meaning that the behaviors would be obvious to an untrained observer. They also scored higher on Reasoning (B), Dominance (E), Rule-Consciousness (G), and Vigilance (L) and lower on Openness to Change (Q1) and Self-Reliance (Q2), with a small effect size (i.e., behaviors not visible to the naked eye). These applicants scored lower (large effect size) on the global factors of Anxiety, Neuroticism, and Superego Control (medium effect size) and lower on Extroversion (small effect size).

Table 3.4 presents 16PF scores from published studies with law enforcement personnel. These data suggest that police applicants, compared with the 16PF standardization sample, tend to be average in warmth, rule-consciousness, vigilance, impulsivity, and shrewdness; slightly above average in intelligence, reasoning ability, perfectionism and organization; emotional stability, and dominance; and a bit below average in sensitivity and anxiety and tension.

Inwald Personality Inventory

Over the past 20 years a substantial number of research studies have examined the use of the IPI in the screening of law enforcement officers. This research has established that IPI scores are related to outcome criteria. In this section I report on only a small amount of this research.

The IPI validity scales have been shown to be able to differentiate police applicant respondents who were deceptively responding (i.e., defensive) from nondefensive responders (Borum & Stock, 1993). This finding is important, as psychologists can expect that applicants in pre-employment screening will minimize any existing problems. The IPI also shows greater accuracy in the prediction of successful performance than honesty or integrity tests (Inwald, Hurwitz, & Kaufman, 1991).

TABLE 3.4
Sixteen Personality Factor Questionnaire Scores for Policemen

Factor	Study 1				Study 2	Study 3
	A	B	C	D		
N	461	399	29	33	106	246
A	4.3	4.2	5.3	5.0	6.0	6.1
B	6.6	6.7	6.0	6.7	5.0	6.6
C	5.7	5.8	5.7	5.6	6.0	7.7
E	6.2	6.2	6.6	6.0	6.5	6.2
F	5.3	5.3	5.7	5.6	5.1	7.2
G	5.9	5.9	6.5	5.8	5.7	6.3
H	5.2	5.1	6.0	5.8	5.5	7.6
I	4.4	4.2	5.7	5.0	3.9	4.9
L	5.4	5.4	5.8	5.2	5.2	4.2
M	5.0	5.0	4.8	5.3	4.4	4.99
N	5.7	5.7	5.7	5.6	5.3	5.6
O	5.0	5.1	5.0	4.2	5.0	3.7
Q1	5.0	5.0	6.1	4.8	4.7	4.2
Q2	6.0	6.1	4.9	5.2	4.8	4.6
Q3	6.0	6.0	6.4	6.4	5.9	7.6
Q4	5.3	5.4	5.2	4.3	5.5	3.1

Note. Study 1 (H. M. Snibbe, Fabricatore, & Azen, 1975) examined total patrolmen (A), White patrolmen (B), Black patrolmen (C), and Mexican American patrolmen (D). Study 2 (Cattell, Eber, & Tatsuoka, 1970b) examined *N* (sample size) not specified, police applicants. Study 3 (Zeidhlach, 2003) examined 246 police applicants. Factors A (Warmth), B (Reasoning), C (Emotional Stability), E (Dominance), F (Liveliness), G (Rule-Consciousness), H (Social Boldness), I (Sensitivity), L (Vigilance), M (Abstractedness), N (Privateness), O (Apprehension), Q1 (Openness to Change), Q2 (Self-Reliance), Q3 (Perfectionism), Q4 (Tension).

In addition, IPI scores correlate with successful and unsuccessful outcome criteria. For example, the IPI was given to 138 male applicants for the police force, and the IPI scores were used to predict applicant performance one year later. The IPI scores significantly predicted family conflicts, guardedness, and driving violations, suggesting that the IPI has good predictive validity at the pre-employment screening level (Detrick & Chibnall, 2003). The IPI scores were subsequently related to on-the-job performance after one year, and the relationships between test scores and outcome variables were stronger for the IPI than for the MMPI–2 (Scogin et al., 1995). The IPI scores also were related to absences, lateness, and disciplinary interviews across racial groups of police applicants one year later (Knatz et al., 1993). The IPI scores (i.e., elevations on Driving Violations and Lack of Assertiveness and low scores on Type A and Rigid Type) were significantly related to supervisors' performance ratings after one year on the job and were positively correlated with poor ratings or termination (Mufson & Mufson, 1997). The IPI scores had higher hit rates than the MMPI or behavioral and biographical data in classifying police applicants after six months of training at the police academy (Shusman et al., 1987).

In summary, the IPI has good predictive validity in police candidate selection one year following training. Outcome measures such as tardiness, absenteeism, substance abuse, poor supervisory ratings, and disciplinary reviews and other measures of poor outcome have been related to IPI scores (Inwald, 1988). Using the IPI in conjunction with other screening measures improves predictive accuracy.

Arrigo and Claussen (2003) recommended using the MMPI–2 and the IPI to screen for psychopathology, especially for antisocial personality disorder, and the NEO–PI–R to assess for normal personality traits (e.g., conscientiousness). Indeed, there are rational and empirical justifications for this suggestion (Cortina, Doherty, Schmitt, & Kaufman, 1992). In fact, research indicates that the combined use of the MMPI and the IPI results in greater predictive efficiency than use of either test alone (Inwald & Brockwell, 1991), because absence of psychopathology alone is insufficient in identifying high-risk police candidates (Shusman, 1987). Also, psychologists can administer the Rorschach when they suspect the existence of psychopathology, personality disorder, or traits not tapped by objective self-report instruments (Zacker, 1997). The Rorschach can test for capacity for control and stress tolerance (Adj. D, ES; and Coping Deficit Index), self-perception (Egocentricity Index), Information Processing (Lambda), and many other variables that may not be captured by self-report inventories.

Millon Index of Personality Styles

The Millon Index of Personality Styles (MIPS; Millon, 1994b) may also be considered for use with police force applicants. The test is an operational measure of Millon's bioevolutionary theory to be used with a normal population. The test consists of scales that measure motivating aims (enhancing–pleasure, preserving–pain, modifying–active, accommodating–passive, individuating–self, nurturing–others), cognitive modes (constructs of personality types from Jung's theory), and interpersonal behavior (retiring–aloof, outgoing–gregarious, hesitating–insecurity, asserting–confident, dissenting–unconventional, conforming–duty-bound, yielding–submissive, controlling–dominant, complaining–discontented, and agreeing–congenial).

Preliminary data on the use of the MIPS with police officer candidates indicate that they have a relatively moderate elevation on Controlling and are well balanced on Individuating and Nurturing scales and scored highest on the Thinking cognitive scale and on the Asserting and Enhancing scales. They also scored about one standard deviation above the MIPS male standardization sample on the Adjustment Index. They scored lowest on the Dissenting, Preserving, and Complaining scales. The MIPS scales were shown to significantly correlate with cadet performance in training exercises at the academy as well as with performance in the field. Of note is the fact that high scores on the Controlling scale (a normal variant of the clinical personality disorder of Aggressive) were associated with poorer ratings during supervised training (Millon, 1994b). Also, the MIPS scales correlated negatively with the MMPI Pd scale among male police candidates, suggesting they measure different entities.

Using psychological tests for personnel screening invariably results in range restriction that makes it difficult to detect differences between groups. Agencies are reluctant to hire recruits who have abnormal test findings, resulting in police officers whose test results represent little variation. This "regression to the mean" and the truncated criterion variable distribution effect attenuate predictive relationships and place an additional burden on researchers to find meaningful differences between groups. Even so, psychological tests have been able to discern group differences on some scales. The question facing the psychologist is whether the few scale score differences that may exist between groups represent true clinical significance, such that the psychologist can make valid recommendations on that basis.

Another issue is the question of predictive validity. Only a handful of studies have addressed the predictive validity of scale scores regarding objective, performance-based criteria. Results of these studies reveal only modest relations between predictor and criterion variables.

ADVERSE IMPACT

Definitions

The *Uniform Guidelines* (U.S. Equal Employment Opportunity Commission [EEOC] et al., 1978) defined *adverse impact* as a substantially different rate of selection in hiring, promotion, or other employment decision which works to the disadvantage of members of a race, sex, or ethnic group. The criterion established for the appearance of adverse impact is the "80/20" or "four-fifths" rule. That is, adverse impact may be established if the selection rate for any referenced group is less than 80% of the selection rate for the group with the highest selection rate. Any selection procedure, including psychological testing or clinical interviewing, that has an adverse impact is said to be discriminatory. However, some courts have rejected the 80/20 rule and have outlined specific procedures that would identify discriminatory practices (Campos, 1989), so the forensic psychologist is advised to learn of the stipulations in their states that define adverse impact.

The *Uniform Guidelines* define *unfairness* as when members of one (ethnic) group characteristically obtain lower scores on a selection procedure than members of another group, and the difference in scores is not reflected in differences in a measure of job performance (U.S. EEOC, 1978). The *Uniform Guidelines* do not provide a definition for *bias*. However, a selection device such as a test may be biased if it discriminates persons differently than does the criterion measure of satisfactory job performance, if it correlates more with one ethnic group than with the job criterion it intends to predict, or if it differentially predicts job success in one ethnic group than another (Campos, 1989). Differences in test means between two groups do not necessarily establish test bias. An equal hypothesis is that the measure is accurately reflecting true differences in the population. I use an absurd example to demonstrate this concept.

Suppose that a job requires an individual to stand on a precipice, unaided by any equipment, and place a bar over a crevice. Through a job analysis it has been determined that individuals of certain heights are required to do this task. The researcher then takes a ruler and measures the height of all job applicants. When looking at the data, the researcher notices that White applicants have a higher selection rate than Asian American applicants. The researcher then goes back and learns that, according to the ruler, Whites, on average, are taller than Asian Americans. Hence the difference in test means. However, the researcher would not discard the ruler because of these differences. Instead, he or she would assume that the ruler is accurately measuring true differences between groups as to height.

Thus, it is incumbent on forensic psychologists to review the selection tools and make certain that those they use do not produce a disadvantage of one group over another. When group differences appear, psychologists must ensure that the measures are related to the job criterion and that the methods assess all groups equally.

Another consideration is that of cultural bias. It is true that the most commonly used measures for the selection of police officers were designed from a European American perspective, which emphasizes individuality over collectivism, and were not designed to measure ethnic differences per se. However, psychological tests might be sensitive to such differences, and this is a researchable question. Also, even when test developers included minorities and culturally diverse participants in their standardization sample, this does not ensure against either conceptual or content bias in the test. Even when behaviors are consistently identified as commonly expressed across cultural groups, these behaviors may have varying meanings as a function of a specific culture. Even when research has established there is no evidence of test bias, there may be important ethnic-specific characteristics that the test does not identify. Finally, unless the psychologist understands culture, he or she can accurately administer a given test and still make interpretive errors because he or she failed to understand how culture affected the individual's response to a test item (Dana, 1995; G. C. Hall & Phung, 2001).

Adverse Impact and Psychological Tests

Most of the research in the literature has been on race, and not ethnicity or culture. The bulk of this literature has dealt with Black–White differences, and there is a relative paucity of research on Latinos, Asian Americans, and Native Americans. Also, the overwhelming majority of studies used the MMPI.

Initially, Gynther (1972) reported that Black respondents scored higher on the MMPI scales of the F validity scale, Psychopathic Deviate (Pd), Schizophrenia (Sc), and Hypomania (Ma). Because these respondents were being compared with White norms (all patients in the original MMPI standardization sample were White), Gynther concluded that normal Blacks and Blacks with psychopathology would be ascribed as having more psychopathology than normal Whites and Whites with psychopathology. He believed that this showed evidence of test bias toward Blacks. Later, Pritchard and Rosenblatt (1980) reviewed this same data as well as more recent research, and although they documented the same findings as Gynther, they reached different conclusions. They argued that differences in means do not in and of themselves establish test bias, because the test may be detecting true differences between groups. They further said that to demonstrate test bias, these groups have to first be equated in degree of psychopathology. Then, if there were a difference in means based on race, that difference would establish test bias. They were unable to find any study that did so.

Greene (1987), reporting on these same differences, found that, on average, Blacks scored ½ standardization higher than Whites on these scales based on 54 studies with 81 Black–White comparisons. However, he argued that a statistical difference in five T scores between groups did not result in a clinical significance between groups on these scales. In a major compendium on this subject, researchers demonstrated that when significant subject moderator variables were controlled for—such as age, IQ, socioeconomic differences, and diagnosis—these initial differences between Blacks and Whites disappeared (Dahlstrom, Lachar, & Dahlstrom, 1986).

The MMPI–2 included African Americans, Hispanics, Asian Americans, and Native Americans in the standardization sample. Research to date suggests that the earlier differences on the F validity scale, Psychopathic Deviate (Pd), Schizophrenia (Sc), and Hypomania (Ma) between Blacks and Whites are not applicable to the revised MMPI. Current research comparing the validity of scores on the MMPI–2 for Whites and African Americans has reported little or no evidence of test bias (Timbrook & Graham, 1994).

Although Black men at a community mental health center scored higher on MMPI–2 validity scale L and on the Fears content scale than did White counterparts, and although Black women scored higher on the low self-esteem content scale than did White counterparts, the correlations between their MMPI–2 scores and the criterion showed no racial effects. Muller and Bruno (1990) found no MMPI scale differences between 300 entry-level public safety officers (police, firefighters) on the basis of race. African American women tended to score higher on Masculinity/Femininity (Mf) and Hypomania (Ma), suggesting more action-oriented, assertive coping styles yet also a passive style with dependency as a way of coping with stress (Reed, Walker, Williams, McLeod, & Jones, 1996). In other words, the MMPI–2 predicted the criterion equally well for Blacks and for Whites (McNulty, Graham, Ben-Porath, & Stein, 1997).

Furthermore, a meta-analysis of 25 studies using either the MMPI or MMPI–2 with African American and European American men found that any ethnic differences between the groups were not substantive. It was concluded that the MMPI and MMPI–2 did not unfairly portray African Americans and Latinos as pathological and that any statistical differences were trivial (G. C. Hall, Bansal, & Lopez, 1999). There were no significant differences on the validity or clinical MMPI–2 scales between Black and White veteran patients, but Black patients scored higher on the content scales of Fears, Bizarre Mentation, Cynicism, and Antisocial Practices (Munley, Morris, McMurray, & Baines, 2001).

Relatively fewer studies have compared Hispanics with Whites, but there are a sufficient number to generate some tentative conclusions (Zalewski & Greene, 1996). First, Hispanic population groups are aggregated in research as "Latino." However, there may be important within-group differences—for example, between Mexican Americans, Cuban Americans, Puerto Rican Americans, and South Americans—that would warrant individual study. Furthermore, the influence of language, acculturation, ethnic identification, discrimination experiences, and perceived minority status also needs to be considered (G. C. Hall & Phung, 2001).

Hispanics were slightly underrepresented in the MMPI–2 standardization sample compared to the 1980 census by almost 3%. So far, Mexican Americans tend to score higher on the L and K validity scales, Hysteria (Hy), and Psychopathic Deviate (Pd) on the MMPI–2. In general, Mexican American college students who were recent immigrants scored higher on the L validity scale, Hypochondriasis (Hs), Masculinity/Femininity (Mf), Schizophrenia (Sc), and Social Introversion (Si). The translation and adaptation of the MMPI–2 yielded similar results for Mexican college students and American college students. College men in general tended to score higher than recent immigrants on L, Depression (Dep), and Mf (Lucio, Reyes-Lagunes, & Scott, 1994), but in comparison the Hispanic men tended to score lower on Mf and higher on L. One interpretation of this finding has been the machismo ethic in Hispanic cultures that tends to emphasize manifestations of masculinity and sex-stereotyped behaviors and portrayals to others of a good impression or a positive image. On the other hand, these results may also reflect men's desire to take care of their families within a patriarchal culture.

Even after controlling for participant variables, there were MMPI–2 differences between Hispanic and White male psychiatric patients with a diagnosis of schizophrenia and depression but no differences in those diagnosed with antisocial personality disorder (Geisinger, 1992; Velasquez, Callahan, & Young, 1993). However, after reviewing the relevant literature, Campos (1989) concluded that after controlling for test scores that covary with participant variables, such as socioeconomic status, age, education, income, occupational level, psychiatric status, and level of acculturation, differences between Hispanics and Whites tend to shrink or disappear. The one exception to this conclusion is the L validity score, which remains high even after these variables have been controlled. It is possible that the previously observed differences between racial groups were due to the effects of poverty and social deprivation, not ethnicity (Dahlstrom, Lachar, & Dahlstrom, 1986).

Asian Americans have tended to score higher on Depression (Dep), Paranoia (Pa), Psychasthenia (Pt), Schizophrenia (Sc), and Social Introversion (Si), except those who are well acculturated, who tend to score similar to European Americans (Zalewski & Greene, 1996). One interpretation of these findings is that Asian Americans have more somatization, depression, anxiety, and feelings of alienation. An alternative hypothesis is that they are more modest, restrained, and imperturbable. Degree of acculturation can also affect test scores. Tsai and Pike (2000) gave the MMPI–2 to a sample of Asian American students, who were assigned to groups on the basis of their level of acculturation. Compared with a matched group of White students, low-acculturated Asian American students scored higher on Hypomania (Ma) and bicultural Asian Americans scored higher on six scales. Highly acculturated Asian Americans did not differ from their White counterparts.

Native Americans score higher on most MMPI scales (Zalewski & Greene, 1996). Dana (1993) summarized this literature to date as follows: Northern Ontario Ojibwa and Cree were elevated on all scales, resulting in a 50% misclassification rate. Plains Indians had elevations on Depression (Dep), Paranoia (Pa), and Social Introversion (Si), and an item analysis on endorsed F validity scale items indicated that these endorsements were consistent with the Lakota culture, which was associated with higher rates of alcoholism, unemployment, poverty, and illness.

Matching subjects on relevant participant variables attenuates most within-group differences (Zalewski & Greene, 1996). However, there may be significant group differences on other unknown or unmatched demographic variables. Although most major psychological tests have been translated into other languages, there could be problems with the translation and difficulty in translating subjective emotional responses.

On the CPI, Hispanic correctional officers scored lower on Dominance (Do), Capacity for Status (Cs), Tolerance (To), Communality (Com), and Intellectual Efficiency (Ie). These findings are from only one study (Campos, 1989).

Finding no evidence of ethnic group differences is not sufficient proof that the test is not biased, because test scores may or may not be correlated with the same extratest behavior across ethnic groups (G. C. Hall et al., 1999). That is a researchable question. One practical suggestion that emanates from these studies is to administer a test of acculturation to any immigrant being evaluated for personnel selection decisions.

RACE NORMING

The EEOC stated that it is unlawful to adjust scores of, use different cutoff scores for or otherwise alter the results of employment-related tests on the basis of race, color, religion, or national origin (U.S. EEOC, 1978). This provision was enacted by Congress to prevent misuse of tests with possible or proved racial bias. The initial concern was over the U.S. Department of Labor's use of the General Aptitude Test Battery (GATB). The GATB was developed by the U.S. Employment Service, Department of Labor, to assess the strengths and weaknesses of job applicants to see if they can perform certain job-related tasks. The government uses this test to assess applicants for certain civil service jobs and occupations. Minority groups criticized the validity of this test as it applied to them, and others complained of the Department's policy of lowering scores on this test for minorities so that more of them would qualify; White applicants had to obtain higher scores than minority applicants to quality for the same job. This practice constituted race norming.

Personality tests commonly publish separate test norms based on gender, and some (e.g., the MCMI) provide separate norms based on race, placing the developers of these tests in possible violation of the EEOC rules. However, many argue that separate norms are needed because these groups score differently on psychological tests. The CPI–R now is available with unisex norms. The only scale on the MMPI–2 that is scored differently based on gender is Masculinity/Femininity (Mf).

The Americans With Disabilities Act (ADA; 1990)—a federal statute—bars employers from administering medical tests or asking questions about alcohol and drug use and past psychiatric conditions before offering an applicant a job. The ADA includes psychological and personality tests in the definition of a "medical test." These tests may be given to detect a substance abuse or psychiatric problem that cannot reasonably be accommodated once the applicant has been conditionally offered a position. (See Foote, 2003, for a list of disorders excluded by the ADA.) Prior to the enactment of the ADA, pre-employment psychological evaluations were characteristically done early in the hiring process to screen out applicants with problems that would negatively affect job performance. Now, these evaluations are typically given near the end of the process, placing the evaluating psychologist at risk for suit.

An aggrieved applicant who has been denied a job may retain an attorney, who will learn of any company policies that stipulate a psychological evaluation after the applicant has met all other requirements of the job. The suit will attest to the multiple phases the applicant has successfully proceeded through and will report that the applicant saw the psychologist and then was denied the position. The inference will be that it was because of the psychological report that the applicant was denied employment. Then the psychologist will have to defend the methods, findings, and conclusions at trial. It is understandable that many psychologists feel that these new procedures place an undue burden on the results of the psychological evaluation.

Some psychological tests, including those used to screen police, are given during the preoffer stage and also place psychologists in jeopardy for subsequent litigation in defiance of the ADA. The CPI deleted several questions that might have posed problems. The courts will eventually produce a body of case law that will give greater clarification concerning these practices.

Because the psychological tests referenced in this chapter appear to predict job performance of police applicants equally well for Whites and for Blacks and Hispanics, their continued use for these purposes is justified. There is little data on criterion validity with other racial groups (e.g., Asian Americans, Native Americans, Pacific Islanders).

Testing (and denial in hiring) a non-White applicant can lead to litigation. Psychologists should keep in mind that adverse impact and race norming apply not only to the screening and selection of law enforcement personnel but also to any employee selection and to any selection instrument. The forensic psychologist may expect challenges in this area and needs to be cognizant of the prevailing data and alternative interpretations.

Although we have presented data concerning base rates of scores on objective personality tests for men and women public safety applicants without external validity of data, the Civil Rights Act of 1991 stipulates that gender differences can no longer be considered in employment testing. Some legal advisors even require that gender and ethnic background information be excluded from data generated for research, including the Department of Justice's "Hiring in the Spirit of Service" project. Although academics may see this as unfortunate because gender differences do make prediction equations weaker when both genders are considered together, it is an increasing trend based on the law.

4

CHILD CUSTODY EVALUATIONS

In the Old Testament, King Solomon had to decide to whom he would award "custody" of an infant between two contesting claimants, both alleging to be the infant's mother. To "satisfy" both claimants, Solomon suggested that the infant be cut in two. He eventually awarded the infant to the woman who was willing to relinquish her claim to the infant to avoid harming the child (Roseby, 1995). Few of us possess the wisdom and competence of King Solomon, and so we must rely on guidelines, standards, training, experience, ethics, and judgment in rendering an opinion to the court on child custody matters.

OVERVIEW

The forensic psychologist is often called on to render an opinion in matters of child custody. Most states follow or parallel the Uniform Marriage and Divorce Act (1987). Section 402 of that act specifies that custody decisions be made in the "best interest of the child." The court is directed to consider the following relevant facts in rendering a decision:

- the wishes of the child,
- the wishes of the parents,
- the interaction of the child with parents and siblings,
- the child's adjustment to home, school, and community, and
- the mental and physical health of all persons involved.

Custody evaluations are somewhat different than most psychological evaluations, where the psychologist usually evaluates one person—the patient. In custody evaluations, the psychologist is required to interview and evaluate both parents, the affected child or children, and perhaps others as well.

Custody evaluations carry with them a high risk for malpractice suits and ethical complaints (American Psychological Association [APA], 2002b; Kirkland & Kirkland, 2001), because the aggrieved party—the parent who is denied custody—may retaliate by filing suit. Therefore, it is critical that the psychologist maintain the utmost professional objectivity, ethical standards, and risk management activities in these cases (as in all cases).

GUIDELINES AND STANDARDS

The APA has published guidelines for child custody evaluations (APA, 1994). The psychologist is advised to obtain a copy of these guidelines for individual review. Also, these guidelines are "aspirational" and not prescriptive, and the psychologist needs to diverge from them when it is appropriate to the individual case (Gindes, 1995). Highlights of these recommendations are as follows:

- The primary purpose of these evaluations is to assess what is in the best (psychological) interest of the child.
- The focus of the evaluation is to determine the parenting capacity of competing parties, to assess the psychological and developmental needs of the child, and then to determine the functional ability of the parents to meet these needs. The wishes of the child also should be considered.
- The psychologist needs to maintain objectivity, acting neither as an advocate nor a judge, but rather as an impartial evaluator.
- To competently perform this role, the psychologist needs expertise in child and family development, psychopathology, the effects of divorce on children, and training and supervision in custody evaluations.
- The psychologist needs to have insight into his or her own biases and should not discriminate with respect to the evaluation recommendations.
- As in all other areas of practice, the psychologist must try to avoid multiple or dual relationships (i.e., testifying in custody evaluations when one of the parents or the child is a client of the psychologist).
- The psychologist should determine the scope of the evaluation, though the court may have special requirements. A comprehen-

sive evaluation requires evaluation of the parents and guardians as well as the child, including observations of the interactions of both parents with the child. However, in certain cases, the evaluation may be limited to the child. The psychologist should never evaluate only one of the parents without evaluating the other parent, unless that is impossible.

- Informed consent needs to be obtained from adult (i.e., "of age") parents (see APA, 1994, for specific requirements). The psychologist also must explain to the child the purpose of the evaluation.
- The psychologist explains limits of confidentiality and disclosure of information and obtains a waiver of confidentiality, where applicable, from the parties allowing disclosure to the court or to authorized legal representatives.
- The evaluation must include multiple assessment methods and make recommendations based on the data.
- The psychologist does not give an opinion about the psychological functioning of someone that he or she has not personally evaluated.
- Financial arrangements are agreed to prior to the evaluation.
- Written records are maintained according to APA (1993) recordkeeping guidelines.

The American Academy of Family Mediators has also published *Standards of Practice for Family and Divorce Mediation* (1998), and the American Professional Society on the Abuse of Children has published *Guidelines for Psychological Evaluation of Suspected Sexual Abuse in Young Children* (1997), which are also relevant to custody evaluations (Ackerman, 1995). Additional practice guidelines and standards have been published by other interested groups (American Academy of Child and Adolescent Psychiatry, 1997a, 1997b; Association of Family and Conciliation Courts, n.d.), and readers may want to incorporate some of these recommendations into their evaluation process.

Philosophically, the courts try to maintain the integrity of the family while preserving individual liberty, and they call on the doctrine of *parens patriae* to determine the best interests of the child. *Parens patriae* literally means "parent of the country" and refers to the role of the state as sovereign and guardian of persons under legal age. The so-called tender years doctrine assumes that children below certain ages cannot fully determine what is in their best interests, and courts call on experts to advise them on this question. In domestic issues psychologists can be called on to (a) assess the emotional atmosphere in the home; (b) assess the competency of a minor; (c) evaluate the legitimacy of religious beliefs of a parent who is refusing medical treatment for a child; (d) determine the suitability of adoption in foster placement; (e) evaluate the question of termination of parental rights; (f) make treatment recommendations; (g) determine if a couple is so incapable of reconciliation because of personality conflicts that reconciliation in divorce proceedings is improbable; and (h) assess the ability of parents to act in the best interest of the child in custody suits. They may also testify as to basic custody arrangements, an unwed father's contesting of adoption, and cases of alleged child abuse (Hess & Brinson, 1999).

Child custody evaluations are among the most difficult for the forensic psychologist because of the conflict and animosity that often exist between the parties, the emotional charge existing in even the simplest of issues, ethical dilemmas inherent in these evaluations, and issues pertaining to possible child sexual and physical abuse and domestic violence. The psychologist needs expertise in such diverse but interrelated areas as child development, child psychopathology, adult adjustment and psychopathology, and family systems and a knowledge of legal procedures (Bow & Quinnell, 2001).

ASSESSMENT MEASURES

One way to avoid, reduce, or defend against allegations of malpractice is to use standard and commonly used assessment measures for custody evaluations. Several surveys (Ackerman & Ackerman, 1997; Bow & Quinnell, 2001; Hagen & Castagna, 2001) have highlighted measures that have been frequently used in custody evaluations.

For cognitive evaluations, an IQ test, usually the Wechsler scales, is used. The Rorschach; the Thematic Apperception Test (TAT); figure drawings, especially the Kinetic Family Drawing; and sentence completion tests are the most frequently used projective methods of personality assessment in child custody evaluations. Surveys continue to show that projective tests are a mainstay among psychologists in custody evaluations (Ackerman & Ackerman, 1997; Hagen & Castagna, 2001; Keilin & Bloom, 1986).

There is a special need to use projective techniques when the possibility of sexual abuse is an issue. Recent research has suggested that projective techniques have shown an ability to discriminate between sexually abused and nonsexually abused children with a very large effect size ($d = .81$; West, 1998), although the use of projective tests for the detection of child abuse remains controversial (Garb, Wood, & Nezworski, 2000). The effect size is reduced somewhat when researchers use a control group of children in distress but without evidence of abuse. Westen et al.'s scoring of object relations from TAT stories has shown a particularly good ability to discriminate abused from nonabused but distressed girls (Westen, Lohr, Silk, Kerber, & Goodrich, 1985; see also Stovall & Craig, 1990). Keep in mind, however, that these tests generally do not determine whether a child has been abused. Rather, they assess the psychological state, current symptom picture, and object relations of the child. The issue of using tests to determine whether the child has been sexually abused is discussed in greater detail later in this chapter.

A number of objective personality tests are used in child custody evaluations, and these are discussed in the following sections.

Minnesota Multiphasic Personality Inventory

The Minnesota Multiphasic Personality Inventory (MMPI) is the assessment test used most frequently by psychologists in evaluating child custody issues (Ackerman & Ackerman, 1997; Hagen & Castagna, 2001; Keilin & Bloom, 1986). The MMPI is able to screen for issues that are particularly important in custody evaluations, including the ability of family members to relate in an appropriate manner, parenting capacity, and in particular the degree of emotional adjustment or maladjustment. In addition, the test can detect impression management and the degree to which it may mask underlying problems (Baer & Miller, 2002; Baer, Wetter, & Berry, 1992).

We should also comment on the difference between impression management and self-deception. *Impression management* may be defined as consciously presenting a picture of virtue, denial of even minor faults, and claims of behavior control. Self-deception, on the other hand, is largely unconscious; the respondent conceals symptoms and any signs of maladjustment but seems unaware that this concealment is occurring. Because child custody evaluations are often contentious, the respondents are likely to answer self-report questionnaires to make themselves look good to persuade the psychologist that they deserve a recommendation of custody. The MMPI–2 has scales and procedures that can detect these response styles, even among child custody litigants (Posthuma & Harper, 1998; Siegel, 1996; Strong, Greene, Hoppe, Johnston, & Olesin, 1999).

Also, MMPI normative data are available for this population (Bathhurst, Gottfried, & Gottfried, 1997; Posthuma & Harper, 1998). The data suggest that 11% responded with defensive underreporting and 21% with a self-favorable response set, and 31% had elevated Over-Controlled hostility (OH) scores. Higher than average scale scores were obtained on Hysteria (Hy), Paranoia (Pa), and Psychopathic Deviant (Pd), but they were generally within normal limit scores (Podrygula, 1997). Clinically, psychologists can generally expect a valid but defensive response set (J. Segal, 1996). Subspikes on Pd are generally due to Harris–Lingoes subscale elevations on family problems. Also, the OH scale is often elevated in disputed custody evaluations. Elevations on Hy are also common among women and probably reflect the stress of custody litigation. Ben-Porath (1995) reported that parents with high scores on Depression (Dep) and Pa tended to lose legal custody of their children; moderately elevated scores on Social Introversion (Si), Anxiety, Low Self Esteem, and Family Problems were also associated with loss of custody.

However, there is a debate as to whether these statistically observed differences, especially as they pertain to the validity scale scores suggesting defensiveness (L and K) among child custody litigants, have any clinical significance. Elevations on L and K typically do not invalidate MMPI–2 profiles in this population and may not even suppress scores on the clinical scales. Such elevations, it has been argued, may reflect not only defensiveness but also personality traits such as rigidity of thought, self-control, strong reliance on denial, lack of insight, or an unrealistic self-image (Medoff, 1999). As with any other test sign, psychologists need to corroborate their interpretations using multiple assessment tools.

Siegel and Langford (1998) produced evidence that parents who attempt to alienate their child from the other parent score higher on the K and lower on the F validity scales than nonalienating parents involved in custody evaluations. Evidence of such alienation would include such behavior as complaining about the other parent in front of the child, telling the child that the other parent does not love him or her, making false allegations about the other parent, lying, unreasonably obstructing parental visitation rights and participation in child-rearing activities such as school functions and extracurricular activities, violating court orders, engaging in excessive litigation to limit a parent's access to the child, greatly exaggerating a parent's faults, and so forth. Parents who engage in such behaviors were found to produce excessively defensive MMPI–2 profiles that may appear to reflect psychological health. Such parents probably would not admit to any personal responsibility for the difficulties they had in the prior relationship. Psychologists conducting custody evaluations should explore for such alienating behaviors as part of the workup.

Research suggests that custodial parents of both genders scored significantly lower on the F validity scale, Psychopathic Deviant (Pd), Masculinity/Femininity (Mf), Paranoia (Pa), and Hypomania (Ma) and lower on the MacAndrew Alcoholism Scale (MAC) and higher on the K validity scale. All fathers scored significantly higher than mothers on Depression (Dep), Mf, Psychasthenia (Pt), and Ma and also on the MAC, perhaps suggesting the stress and tension of expecting the courts to award custody to the mother. In any event, these results suggest that custodial parents appeared healthier, coped better with feelings of anger (probably induced by the custody litigation), were less impulsive, were more trusting and open with others, and had lower substance abuse scores (Ollendick & Otto, 1984).

Hackney and Ribordy (1980) found that parents in marriage counseling and parents who were in the process of divorce scored significantly higher on Hypochondriasis (Hs), Depression (Dep), Psychopathic Deviate (Pd), Psychasthenia (Pt), Schizophrenia (Sc), and Paranoia (Pa) compared with happily married parents and parents who had already been divorced 6 to 12 months. Using a cross-sectional research design, researchers found that feelings of anxiety, depression, and hostility were prominent but had abated by the 12th month postdivorce in most cases. Other researchers found results consistent with this thesis (Ollendick, Otto, & Heider, 1983).

Ackerman (1995) offered a series of speculative hypotheses concerning MMPI scale elevations and their meaning as related to parenting skills. Although these hypotheses are based on clinical judgment and without a basis in evidentiary research, they are nevertheless interesting, and the reader may want to consult this reference for further details.

Millon Clinical Multiaxial Inventory

Many psychologists use the Millon Clinical Multiaxial Inventory (MCMI), as revised (Millon, 1983, 1987, 1994a) to assess either basic personality styles of parents or personality disorders. Although some have argued that the MCMI should not be used in custody evaluations because it does not provide norms for differentiating clinical from nonclinical respondents (Butcher & Miller, 1999), the MCMI is being used in custody evaluations with increased frequency (Ackerman & Ackerman, 1997; Hagen & Castagna, 2001). The MCMI–III test manual indicates that the MCMI–III is suitable for use with custody litigants because the standardization sample included many such cases. The MCMI–III also has scales that test for a desirability response set and amount of self-disclosure.

Furthermore, the test's base rate (BR) score at 30 represents the raw score mean of all nonclinical participants in the standardization sample, whereas a BR of 85 is the raw score mean of all patients in the standardization sample with the disorder at a diagnosable level. So it is incorrect to argue that the test does not differentiate nonclinical from clinical respondents, because BR scores lower than 75 suggest no problems in the areas assessed by the scale, and the standardization procedures included scores from nonclinical respondents. MCMI norms in custody evaluations have recently been published (McCann et al., 2001).

Lampel (1999) gave the MCMI–III to 50 custody litigants and reported that, as a group, they scored highest on Obsessive-Compulsive, Histrionic, and Narcissistic scales and had a defensive response set. Previous reviews of how the MCMI scales operate in clinical practice have reported that elevations on these scales are most often obtained by respondents in nonclinical settings and correlate with measures of psychological well-being rather than with measures of maladjustment (Craig, 1997). Hence, caution is suggested when interpreting these scales in the context of custody evaluations.

One question pertains to whether the observed results reflect actual personality style and traits or whether respondents endorse items on the test to be seen as conscientious, self-confident, extroverted, and sociable. On the other hand, Halon (2001) argued that custody evaluation litigants are necessarily "clinical," and hence elevations on these scales may, in fact, represent the more pathological personality characteristics associated, in theory, with these scales. Convergence of other sources of evidence is necessary to make such determinations.

Use of the MCMI–III with litigants continues to be controversial, especially in the context of testing "normal" parents with a test designed mostly for psychiatric patients. There is little published research on the use of the MCMI in custody evaluations, but MCMI norms in custody evaluations have recently appeared in the literature (McCann et al., 2001), and a growing database on the use of this instrument in custody evaluations can be expected. Still, the testifying psychologist who reports conclusions based in part on MCMI test findings should expect a rigorous challenge by attorneys concerning the use of this test with their clients. Craig (1999b), Schutte (2001), and McCann (2002) reported on the kinds of difficulties that forensic psychologists may encounter and suggested responses to challenges that address the standardization sample of the MCMI–III, the question of possible overpathologizing, difficulties in understanding base rate scores, diagnostic efficiency statistics (too low), sparse research on MCMI–III and especially its validity scales; and other concerns.

Other Measures

Adolescent psychiatric inpatients who reported a history of childhood abuse scored higher than nonabused control participants in measures of dependency, suicidality, violence, impulsivity, substance abuse problems, and borderline personality traits on the Millon Adolescent Clinical Inventory (Grilo, Sanislow, Fehon, Martino, & McGlashan, 1999). The Ackerman–Schoendorf Scales for Parent Evaluation of Custody (ASPECT; Ackerman & Schoendorf, 1992), the Bricklin Perceptual Scales (Bricklin, 1984), the Parent–Child Relationship Inventory (Gerard, 1994), and the Parenting Stress Index (Abidin, 1990) are also commonly used in custody evaluations (Heinze & Grisso, 1996). These scales, and others like them, are attempts to provide more quantitative assessment approaches in the assessment of custody and visitation disputes.

The ASPECT is not a test at all but rather a way of quantifying the results from other assessments—including psychological testing, interviews, and records—regarding suitability for parenting. The ASPECT is done after all these assessments have been completed. The psychologist uses the data to respond to 56 forced-choice questions on three subscales—Observational, Social, and Cognitive/Emotional. The Observational scale has 9 items and addresses such issues as parent effectiveness in hygiene and grooming, cooperation with the evaluation, and insight. The Social scale has 28 items that address such matters as the social environment provided by the parent, parental interactions with the child, and aspects of the community. The Cognitive/Emotional scale has 19 items that assess the parent's cognitive and emotional capacity to raise a child. The parent with the higher score is considered the preferred custodial parent.

The Bricklin Perceptual Scales consist of 64 questions that try to measure a child's perception of each parent. Half of the questions pertain to the child's perception of the mother, and half pertain to perceptions of the father. Content areas deal with issues of parental competence, support, consistency, and desirable traits. The child rates the parent on a scale ranging from 1 to 60. The parent who scores highest is deemed the parent of choice in a custody recommendation.

The 78-item Parent–Child Relationship Inventory assesses parent attitudes in the areas of parental support, satisfaction with parenting, involvement with the child, communication, limit setting, autonomy, and role. High scores suggest good parenting skills.

The Parenting Stress Index assesses the extent to which a parent experiences stress in the role of parent. The test has 101 items with two stress domain scales, Child Domain and Parent Domain. The Child Domain yields scores in child adaptability, acceptability, demandingness, mood, hyperactivity and distractibility, and reinforcement. The Parent Domain includes scales on depression, attachment, restriction of role, competence, social isolation, relationship with spouse, and parental health. Responses are separately scored for each domain, and a Total Stress Score is calculated, with higher scores suggestive of increased risk of dysfunctional parenting.

More detailed information is available on these tests and scales, including their development and standardization, psychometric qualities, and strengths and weaknesses. The interested reader is referred to more authoritative sources (Heinze & Grisso, 1996).

An increasing number of psychologists are using computer-assisted psychological assessments as part of the custody evaluation procedures. It is argued that computer-assisted interpretation minimizes errors in test scoring, increases the objectivity of test interpretation, promotes the establishment of databases, and takes advantage of the actuarial approach to testing. There are disadvantages as well, and these include increased risk of test use by unqualified professionals, increased risk of inappropriate use of tests, encouragement of passive test interpretation, and promotion of an aura of scientific predictability that does not exist (Otto & Butcher, 1995).

Brodzinsky (1993) argued that psychologists often misuse psychological test data in child custody and visitation disputes and cited a number of examples to buttress this argument. He argued that the problem is not so much with the test, per se, as with the way the psychologist uses the test or misinterprets the test data. Psychologists are cautioned to consider Heilbrun's (1992) criteria for selection assessment methods in custody evaluations.

ASSESSING ALLEGATIONS OF CHILD ABUSE

The evaluation of child sexual abuse allegations may occur with or without the nexus of a child custody evaluation. These evaluations are fraught with difficulty because usually there are no witnesses, medical evidence is usually absent, the alleged perpetrator almost always denies the allegation, and the signs and symptoms of abuse can be caused by nonabuse factors. Researchers have not established a cluster of signs and symptoms that invariably can be attributed to child sexual abuse. Abused children maintain secrecy associated with the abuse, may retract the initial allegation, live in fear of the potential consequences of discovery, and may suffer long-term sequelae as a result, and some may not have developed the necessary language and memory to understand or realize that abuse has occurred. As a result, courts may request expert opinion on the question of child abuse.

Psychologists rely on clinical interviews, psychological tests, and record reviews to conduct custody evaluations. On the basis of this evaluation, the psychologist may render an opinion as to the current psychological state of the child and whether the child has been abused and recommend disposition as to custody and treatment. This procedure involves what has been called "backward reasoning," because the expert is called on to review signs and symptoms of the child (and the family) and then postdict the cause of these signs and symptoms. Because no clear-cut and invariable syndrome or symptoms exist associated with child abuse, many argue that it is unscientific and unethical to render this kind of backward reasoning (Sbraga & O'Donohue, 2003).

One useful distinction is between a psychological marker and a probability for identifying a particular disorder. A marker is a trait or characteristic that is always present in a given condition and never present in the absence of the condition. If such a marker existed for child abuse on tests, then psychologists would be justified in concluding that the child has been abused.

In fact, there are no such markers. In contrast, a probability is a degree of certainty (<100%) that a given condition is present, given the presence of a sign or signs. Furthermore, these signs are consistent with the known facts (Weiner, 2003). With this distinction, then, psychologists can render conclusions as stipulated by the court.

Clinical Interview

In addition to psychological tests—especially projective tests—the clinical interview remains the essential assessment tool to evaluate allegations of child sexual abuse. Kuehnle (2003) recommended a structure for interviewing a child suspected of being a victim of abuse. Other structured children's interviews have been reviewed by Logan (in press). The recommended interview format is to (a) build rapport, (b) assess the child's ability to answer questions and provide details, (c) provide ground rules for the interview, (d) do a practice interview that pertains to nonabuse questions, and (e) introduce the topic of sexual abuse using open-ended questions. In practicing nonabuse questions, the psychologist may ask the child, "Tell me what you did at school yesterday. Tell me everything that happened" and then probes for details. Then the psychologist has the child report what he or she did after school and later that night. The psychologist may do this a few times with selected events to evaluate the child's capacity and competency in providing important details surrounding an event.

The psychologist then transitions to the topic of sexual abuse using open-ended questions. For example, the psychologist may tell the child, "I would like to talk about the reason we are here today." The psychologist may ask the child if he or she knows the difference between good touches and bad touches or if anyone has ever touched his or her private parts. If the answer is affirmative, the psychologist asks about the circumstances and surrounding details, such as the color of the walls in the room where the abuse occurred, the color of the clothes of the perpetrator, and so forth, up to and including details of the sexual event or events themselves.

The use of anatomically correct dolls in the interview remains controversial, as does the issue of child abuse interviewing as a whole. Because of children's suggestibility, the concern is that an interviewer will unconsciously ask leading questions that result in a child admitting to behaviors that did not occur. The best way to counter such allegations is to audiotape or videotape the interview after obtaining parental informed consent.

Within the past 15 years, a number of structured instruments have been developed for the assessment of childhood trauma. These are displayed in Table 4.1. Some are specific to violence exposure (Praver, 1994), some have items related to sexual abuse as a separate subscale (Briere, 1996), some assess sexual abuse with norms for both abused and nonabused children

TABLE 4.1
Screening Instruments for the Assessment of Childhood Trauma

Instrument	Authors	Year
Child Dissociation Checklist	Putnam	1990
Children's Impact of Traumatic Events Scale	Wolfe, Wolfe, Gentile, and Larose	1986
Child PTSD Reaction Index	Frederich, Pynoos, and Nader	1992
Child Rating Scales: Exposure to Interpersonal Abuse	Praver	1994
Child's Reaction to Traumatic Events Scale	Jones	1994
Child Sexual Behavior Interests	Freidrich	1997
Children's PTSD Inventory	Saigh	1997
Clinician-Administered PTSD Scale: Child and Adolescent version	Nader, Kriegler, Blake, and Pynoos	1994
Kiddie Posttraumatic Symptomatology Scale	March	1999
Trauma Symptom Checklist for Children	Briere	1996
When Bad Things Happen Scale	Fletcher	1991

Note. PTSD = posttraumatic stress disorder.

(Friedrich, 1992, 1998), and many assess symptoms related to posttraumatic stress disorder and their impact on the child's functioning. The reader is urged to consult more authoritative sources for the psychometric properties of these instruments and scales before selecting one of them for clinical use (Kuehnle, 1996; Nader, 1997; Sparta, 2003).

Psychological testing is a critical part of child abuse allegations. Although researchers differ as to the value and role of projective techniques (Kuehnle, 1996; West, 1998), three projective tests are recommended: figure drawings, an apperceptive method, and the Rorschach.

Figure Drawings

Figure drawings have resulted in some of the strongest suggestions for the validity of sexual abuse allegations (Goodwin, 1982; Waldman, Silber, Holmstrom, & Karp, 1994). The American Academy of Child and Adolescent Psychiatry (1997b) endorsed the use of figure drawings in the assessment of child sexual abuse, especially when drawings depict nude genitalia. Although this is a low-frequency behavior, its appearance in figure drawings among sexually abused children has been substantiated by preliminary research (R. A. Hibbard, Roghmann, & Hoekelman, 1987) and warrants further investigation. Additional "indicators" of sexual abuse in figure drawings may include legs pressed together, big hands as well as genitalia, and more indicators of anxiety compared with drawings of non–sexually abused children (R. A. Hibbard & Hartman, 1990). Additional figure drawing indexes have been reported for children who have been physically abused (Blain, Gerbner, Lewis, & Goldstein, 1981). However, the research on the use of figure drawings to establish or confirm child abuse has not always been substantiated (Palmer, Farrar, Valle, Ghahary, Panella, & DeGraw, 2000; Sidun & Rosenthal, 1987).

Thematic Apperception Test

Westen developed a scoring method for analyzing narrative stories generated using the Thematic Apperception Test (TAT) in terms of their object relations and social cognitions (H. G. Segal, Westen, Lohr, & Silk, 1993; Westen, 1991; Westen et al., 1985). The method produces six scales: Episode Integration, Accuracy of Casual Attributions, Affect-Tone of Relationship Paradigms, Capacity for Emotional Investment in Relationships and Moral Standards, Complexity of Representations, and Accuracy of Character Ascriptions. The method has been subsequently refined using four scales to assess object relations from TAT stories. The scales showing good validity are Complexities of Representations of People, Affect-Tone of Relationship Paradigms (from malevolent to benevolent), Capacity for Emotional Investment in Relationships and Moral Standards, and Understanding of Social Causality. Each of these elements is assessed on a 5-point scale representing various levels of these dimensions.

The TAT has been successfully used to differentiate between the object relations of physically and sexually abused latency-age girls (Stovall & Craig, 1990). Other TAT scoring methods have also demonstrated an ability to distinguish between sexually abused and nonabused girls (Pistole & Ornduff, 1994), but the Westen scoring of TAT protocols for sexual abuse appears to be the most promising (Ornduff, Freedenfeld, Kelsey, & Critelli, 1994). However, none of these scoring systems has demonstrated validity at the level of the individual case, and only group discrimination has been reported in the literature.

Rorschach

There are limited empirical data on the use of the Rorschach in the evaluation of child sexual abuse. There is some evidence that sexually abused girls score higher on the DEPI index, suggesting depression or dysphoria. An analysis of the individual signs that make up this index suggested that abused girls gave more achromatic color responses, suggesting more constrained affect; more morbid responses, suggesting perceptions of a damaged self; and more color shading blends, suggesting more painful ambivalent feelings. The other signs in the index did not differentiate groups. Also, the abused group demonstrated a positive relationship between depression and the variables of Zf (organization activity) and access to adaptive resources (EA) (Shapiro, Leifer, Martone, & Kassem, 1990). African American abused girls showed more disturbed thinking on the Rorschach (WSUMSPC6; X–%) and higher levels of stress (DEPI, Sum Shading) relative to their adaptive ability (D, ES), described human relationships in more negative terms (Elizer's Content Hostility Scale), and had more preoccupation with sexuality (sexual percepts; Leifer, Shapiro, Martone, & Kassem, 1991). These results have not been replicated.

Zivney, Nash, and Hulsey (1988) studied 37 girls who were sexually abused before the age of nine years, 43 who were sexually abused after the age of nine years, and 72 control patients with no history of abuse. Over half of the early abuse victims showed disturbed cognition (index consisting of M-, deviant verbalizations, and FABCOMs [fabulized combination]), a damaged sense of self (Morbid and Personal responses; Y [pure shading] + YF [shading form] = FY [form shading]), and preoccupation with themes of primitive supplies and transitional relatedness (low X% with high M-; sum of Food and Clothes + X Ray + Abstract responses higher).

Respondents with a history of sexual abuse scored higher on the Temperament and Character Inventory measures and on Rorschach aggression indexes, particularly Aggressive Movement (Ag), that were seen as violent or sadistic (Kamphus, Kirgeares, & Finn, 2000). Furthermore, the occurrence of Cooperative Movement (COP) and Ag captured the malevolence directed at sexually abused girls, who scored higher on COP–Ag than nonabused girls (Ornduff, Centeno, & Kelsey, 1999).

Projective tests to establish or confirm allegations of child abuse remain controversial. The best conclusion that appears to be consistent with the empirical data at this time is that projective tests cannot definitively distinguish between abused and nonabused groups, but they seem to distinguish between distressed and nondistressed respondents (Palmer, Farrar, Valle, Ghahary, Panella, & DeGraw, 2000). The source of this stress could be the abuse, but it could also be the allegations and evaluations associated with the legal process or the emotions within the home associated with these allegations.

FALSE ALLEGATIONS OF ABUSE

One area of concern is a parent who alleges sexual abuse in the context of the custody dispute. There are limited data on the extent to which allegations of child sexual abuse arise in the context of custody disputes. The available data suggest that child abuse allegations occur in anywhere from 1% to 10% of custody disputes, and 20% to 80% of those claims have been determined to be false (Wakefield & Underwager, 1991). Groups of falsely accusing parents and falsely accused parents were compared to a control group of parents in custody litigation involving no allegations of abuse. The falsely accusing parents were more likely to have a personality disorder of histrionic, borderline, passive-aggressive, or paranoid. Although most of the custody-only group was assessed as normal, only 25% of the falsely accusing parents were assessed as normal (Wakefield & Underwager, 1990).

Personality and False Abuse Allegations

The dynamics of the reasons behind false accusations of child abuse seem to vary by the nature of the associated personality disorder. For example, the person with a histrionic personality who alleges that his or her child has been sexually abused may, in fact, make such allegations on the basis of his or her own (unconscious) sexualized feelings. Accordingly, he or she may spend an inordinate amount of time examining the child's genitals or quizzing the child regarding sexual activity to gratify his or her own needs. The person with a borderline personality may report bizarre events in his or her history, which often include a history of sexual abuse. With the stress of divorce, such a person could easily experience a kind of transient psychotic state, lose contact with reality, and engage in false accusations.

The mother or father with underlying paranoia could easily project his or her own feelings onto those of an estranged spouse and engage in accusations that have little or no basis in reality. The charges stem from his or her own psychopathology. The passive-aggressive parent—in the traditional sense of the term—may make false accusations after years of bottling up his or her emotions and acting in a deferent, compliant, and passive way in the marital relationship. When the spouse leaves, this causes the passive-aggressive parent to vent his or her emotions and to use the opportunity to express years of restrained hostility through false accusations. A parent with a narcissistic personality disorder may construe the divorce proceedings as a narcissistic injury to a fragile sense of self and retaliate by making false charges to (unconsciously) reconstitute his or her grandiose sense of self. A person with an antisocial personality disorder may use the custody proceedings as yet another means to maintain dominance and control over another person, with little empathic regard, guilt, or remorse for making false accusations. Thus, a person's personality pathology can interact with environmental circumstances to influence interpersonal behavior.

On the basis of their clinical experience, Wakefield and Underwager (1990) proposed a typology of personalities who make false sexual abuse allegations. One type is the severely disturbed personality who has lost contact with reality and is unable to differentiate fact from fiction. This type probably represents an atypical personality among the total population of custody litigants. A second type, they proposed, is the person with an intense hatred of his or her spouse who becomes obsessed with venting hostility toward the spouse. The child is a pawn in an ongoing vitriol against the spouse. A third type is a variant of the second type; the person, who may have a history of sexual abuse, becomes hypervigilant, looking for signs of sexual abuse and questioning the child repeatedly after returns from parental visitations. The following case examples represent an amalgam of these last two types and illustrate how these dynamics are expressed in two disputing couples.

Case Examples

The patient entered private psychotherapy to deal with a divorce and continuing disputes with his ex-wife pertaining to visitation of his daughter. While married and on vacation, they left their two-year-old daughter in the care of a male babysitter to go sightseeing. When they returned, the child was screaming uncontrollably, and the baby-sitter was unable to calm her down. The mother accused the baby-sitter of trying to sexually abuse her daughter, although there was no evidence of this. Some time later, while giving his daughter a bath, the father noticed some red marks on her buttocks and asked his wife about them. On seeing the marks, she began screaming, accused him of sexually abusing their daughter, and called the police. He was asked to leave the house, and the wife filed a restraining order of protection against him. He continued to assert his innocence, and an investigation resulted in no charges being filed against him. The couple eventually divorced. Later it was learned that the wife had been sexually abused as a child.

In another example, a patient entered psychotherapy to deal with the continuing resistance and problems he was having with his ex-wife around visitation with his two-year-old daughter. Each parent repeatedly brought the other parent into court on charges of violating the divorce decree. The patient became involved with a woman he eventually married. She had a four-year-old boy. On one occasion his ex-wife accused him of child neglect, alleging that on one visitation his new wife's son inserted a candy bar into the rectum of her daughter. This was alleged to have occurred three months previously. He told his therapist about it, saying that he planned to take his daughter to a physician for an examination, even though his therapist told him that, after this length of time, any possible evidence would have healed. The patient did not know what else to do to refute this charge. He did take her to the doctor, and the results were negative. Subsequent evaluation by the state authority resulted in no formal charges against him.

Other Considerations

Although the psychological and emotional consequences of child abuse are well known (Finkelhor, 1990; Kendall-Tackitt, Williams, & Finkelhor, 1993), there are no hard-and-fast behavioral signs that invariably suggest that a child has been sexually abused. Perhaps the most significant signs are sexual knowledge that seems to be beyond that expected of a child at that age and age-inappropriate sexual play. Also, spontaneous allegations from a child, depending on his or her age, may be more valid than those made after discussion with a parent (or even a therapist).

The motivations behind a parent making a false accusation of child sexual abuse do not always include the simple motives of gaining custody and alienating a child from the alleged abuser. In fact, in some cases, the accusing parent may actually believe that the abuse has occurred. Some parents have a history of sexual victimization as a child and are hypervigilant for such signs in their own children. Other parents have been flooded with media reports of "behavioral signs" of abused children, "recognize" these signs in their child, and file a report.

There are few legal consequences for making a false report. Generally, the investigating state authority will require that the alleged abuser leave the house and prohibit child visitation (unless supervised by an accompanying adult) until the charges have been validated or invalidated. Psychologists who, as part of custody evaluations, encounter a parental charge of sexual abuse need to weigh their findings very carefully because of the possible lifelong consequences for the accused parent of their conclusions.

Just as there are no invariant behavioral signs of childhood sexual abuse, there are also no invariant signs that indicate a false accusation of child sexual abuse. Wakefield and Underwager (1991) reviewed the literature on this matter, the highlights of which appear in Table 4.2.

One Final Caveat

Although observations of parent–child interactions are commonly used during custody evaluations, conjoint interviews with a child and a parent who has (or has been alleged to have) sexually abused the child may be particularly problematic, despite APA guidelines to the contrary. The emotional charge around such interactions could be considerable and even unnatural. Children are unlikely to report or discuss the abuse with the perpetrator, and the parent is likely to manipulate the child in such a way as to present favorable impressions of the child's feelings toward the parent. Although some writers advocate the use of conjoint interviews under such circumstances for the purpose of observing parent–child interactions (Faller,

TABLE 4.2

Differentiating True From False Accusations of Child Sexual Abuse
Allegations Arising in Child Custody Disputes

Factor	Accusation possibly false	Accusation possibly true
Origin of allegation	Parent initiates disclosure	Child initiates disclosure
Timing of allegation	Occurs after divorce	Occurs before divorce
Age of child	Child under age 5	Child over age 5
Behavior of accusing parent	Parent tells everyone	Parent is secretive, upset, and embarrassed
	Parent accepts explanation	Parent is willing to consider alternative explanations
	Parent is unwilling to allow child to be interviewed alone	Parent is willing to allow child to be interviewed alone
	Parent may shop for experts who agree with accusation	Parent is willing to accept expert opinion
Nature of allegations	Vague, not easily open to refutation	Specific complaints, open to verification
Child statements	Inconsistent and unrealistic Vague details Incongruent emotions	Consistent and realistic Specific details Congruent emotions
Personality	Accuser often has personality disorder or psychiatric problems; may have a history of childhood abuse	Accuser is usually normal

Note. Source: Wakefield and Underwager (1991).

Froning, & Lipovsky, 1991), even this practice may be problematic and may not add any incremental validity to the assessment that can be obtained through other means. The recommendation to avoid conjoint interviews with the alleged perpetrator and the victim is not always easy to follow. For example, what if the alleged perpetrator has supervised visits? There is still contact under such circumstances. What if the allegations are untrue? These kinds of cases can be extremely complex, and psychologists need to use their best professional judgment as to what is in the best interest of the child under the circumstances.

CUSTODY STANDARDS

Although either parent may privately retain the psychologist, most psychologists prefer to be retained by the court or jointly by the attorneys of both sides, if feasible (Ackerman & Ackerman, 1997). In testifying in child custody cases, psychologists consider the age and individual preferences of the child, the interactions of the child with each parent alone and as a family, the child's adjustment to the home and school, the mental and physical health and stress level of the parents, and the child abuse potential of a parent (Hess & Brinson, 1999).

There is little empirical research on psychometric test signs of parents at risk for child abuse. One study reported that such a population had elevations on the F validity scale, Psychopathic Deviate (Pd), and Schizophrenia (Sc; Egeland, Erickson, Butcher, & Ben-Porath, 1991). However, their sample would not be representative of the typical child custody case because it included high-risk, multiproblem women.

Milner (1990) developed the Child Abuse Potential Inventory to assess a parent's risk for physical (but not sexual) child abuse. It is a 160-item self-report inventory that measures personal and interpersonal characteristics said to be similar to those of parents who have abused their children. Higher scores reflect an increased risk of physical abuse.

Recommendations of Custody

There are four types of custody arrangements. In sole custody, one parent is given both legal and physical custody of the child, with visitation rights generally allowed to the noncustodial parent. In divided custody, both parents have legal and physical custody of the child. The child alternates living with each parent for a period of time that is specified in the divorce decree. Each parent has full control of decision making and child rearing when the child is living with him or her. The noncustodial parent at this time is allowed visitation rights. Psychologists generally do not like this arrangement because it may cause confusion in the child with regard to authority, discipline issues, and values and seems to promote an unstable environment for the child. In split custody one parent is awarded one or more children and the other parent is also awarded one or more children. Finally, in joint custody, both parents share the legal and physical custody of the child, although one of the parents is generally awarded physical custody. Both parents must agree to any matters pertaining to important decisions involving the child, such as medical care and school-related matters.

Exhibit 4.1 presents an overview of survey research that has identified the negative behaviors significantly affecting a recommendation regarding sole custody and behaviors that have been identified as significantly contributing to a recommendation by psychologists of joint custody based on surveys of research. Perhaps the best indicator is the ability of the parents to separate out their interpersonal and emotional issues for the benefit of the child.

EXHIBIT 4.1
Variables Associated With Recommendations for Sole or Joint Custody

Variables to consider in custody evaluations:
  The quality of the relationship between parents and child
  Absence of substance abuse
  Psychological stability of the parents
  Amount of anger and bitterness between parents
  Parental willingness to accept joint custody
  The wishes of the child (depending on the age)
  Cooperation with previous court stipulations
  Absence of problems with the law
  Parent's previous involvement in child-rearing responsibilities

Additional factors that may come into play:
  Capacity of each parent for attachment and separation
  Emotional availability of the parent as well as the capacity to restrain and
    appropriately control emotions
  Ability to set reasonable expectations and to set limits
  Ability to promote a child's social relationships
  Flexibility in child-rearing practices
  Lack of hostility and suspiciousness, unless deemed appropriate under the
    circumstances
  Ability to cooperate with the other parent

Variables negatively associated with recommendations of sole custody:
  Active substance abuse (being in recovery is not a negative finding)
  Attempts to alienate the child from the other parent
    Poorer parenting skills
    Lower emotional bond with one parent
    Parent is less psychologically stable
    Parent has not been cooperative with previous court orders
    Intolerance of a parent toward visitation rights
    Lack of active participation in child's education
    Extreme anger or bitterness toward the divorce
    Allegations of physical or sexual abuse
    History of psychiatric hospitalizations
    Criminal history

Note. Sources: Ackerman and Ackerman (1997); and Keilin and Bloom (1986).

General Considerations

The psychologist should keep in mind that custody disputes occur within the context of a particularly stressful time for all parties. The behavior observed during this period may not be representative of the typical behavior of the participants. This fact argues for personality measures that tap long-standing behavioral patterns as a necessary requirement in these evaluations.

Many psychologists who engage in child custody evaluations conduct

  ▪ a clinical interview with each parent that includes a psychological history of children and parents;

- a clinical interview with the child;
- a review of relevant documents, such as custody reports;
- parent–child observations in office or playroom;
- psychological testing of parents and children;
- contact with teachers, attorneys, and therapists; and
- a clinical interview with any partner currently living with either parent (Bow & Quinnell, 2001).

Custody evaluations, as one can see, are quite extensive. The average number of hours per case has ranged from 18 to 28 in published studies, with fees ranging over $3,000 on the average, excluding court testimony time (Bow & Quinnell, 2001).

Ethical Problems

A number of ethical problems are particularly extant in custody evaluations. Some of the more frequent are failing to obtain written informed consent, failing to address issues of confidentiality and its limits, evaluating the child without proper authorization, focusing exclusively on individual psychopathology rather than on parenting skills, failing to maintain objectivity and impartiality, failing to avoid multiple relationships (if possible), overinterpreting or misinterpreting test data, working on a contingency fee basis, giving opinions about persons not evaluated, and using certain tests inappropriately (Podrygula, 1997).

Risk Management

The following risk management suggestions are offered to avoid problems associated with custody evaluations. The psychologist should try to secure the cooperation of all critical participants, obtain written informed consent, follow all professional standards and ethical codes pertaining to this function, use state-of-the-art and standard policies and procedures, inform all parties in advance of these policies and procedures and then follow them, be prepared to justify any deviation from these policies and procedures, use multiple methods of data gathering with appropriate tests, provide objective information to the court, and clarify in advance all financial arrangements. Costs should not limit the extent of the evaluation to be done; if cost is a factor, the psychologist should do a pro bono evaluation or refuse the case. The psychologist should also keep excellent records, maintain evidence of training and competence in these evaluations (e.g., attendance at workshops), and conduct these evaluations only as a court-mandated, neutral expert (APA, 1993b; Podrygula, 1997).

Some have proposed that written agreements between all parties (both parents, attorneys, and psychologist) be executed prior to the evaluation.

This agreement would include such items as what specific questions will be addressed in the evaluation, how they will be assessed, and to whom the final report will be sent. A signed agreement might contain a clause that allows the parties to read the report but not to receive a copy of the report, which is sent only to the court. This practice protects client confidentiality and may prevent an aggrieved party from using the contents of the report against the other parent (Roseby, 1995). However, once this report is entered into evidence, it becomes a public document and hence is accessible to those who want to see it. Also, each attorney receives this document and may give a copy of it to his or her client, so the psychologist is cautioned to say only what is necessary in the context of the evaluation. Finally, the psychologist should assume that both parents will eventually see the report.

RECOMMENDED STRUCTURE OF CUSTODY EVALUATIONS

Preparation

All states have operationalized the meaning of *best interests of the child*, so the first step in preparing for custody evaluations is to determine the applicable laws in the jurisdiction in which the custody evaluation will occur (Otto, Buffington-Vollum, & Edens, 2003). Psychologists should also take the following steps:

- Speak with both attorneys before the evaluation and get a letter of understanding from both attorneys. Find out what is being requested and by whom.
- Make financial arrangements in advance.
- Obtain relevant court documents before the evaluation.
- Use identical procedures with each adult.
- Schedule enough time to do a thorough examination and for the parties to discuss whatever is on their mind.
- Use quotes as much as possible in note taking.

Structure of the Evaluation

The following are guidelines for structuring the evaluation:

- Interview each parent individually.
- Get written informed consent first.
- Discuss issues of confidentiality.
- Thoroughly explain the forthcoming procedures.
- In the clinical interview with the parents, look especially for insight, flexibility, responsibility, empathy, and parenting capacity.

Determine what efforts have been made to resolve the dispute and why this is still unsettled.

No standard set of questions is applicable to all situations. Some specific questions might include the following:

- What has been the history of the parental relationship?
- What will your partner or spouse say about you?
- What are your current living arrangements?
- What is the parent's evaluation of the child and of the other partner or spouse?
- What is the parent's developmental history?
- How does the parent discipline the child?
- Has any family member had prior psychiatric treatment? For what problem?
- Are there any problems with temper in the parent?
- Is any parent excessively narcissistic?
- What does the child want?
- Have there been any problems with visitation?
- What will the parent do if the court decides in favor of the other parent?
- What is the parent's current mental status?
- What is the strength of the parent–child bond?
- Who has control over decision making?
- What were the reasons for separation or divorce?
- Why would you make the best custodial parent?
- Why wouldn't the other parent make a good custodial parent?

Evaluation of the Child

The following steps are recommended when evaluating the child:

- Ensure comfortable accommodations for the child.
- Find out what the child knows about the evaluation and why it is being conducted.
- Explain confidentiality to the child.
- Determine how the child sees his or her role in the final decision.
- Get the child's opinion of the current situation, and assess what he or she understands about divorce, custody, and visitations.
- Learn what the child's reaction is to each parent and what his or her interaction has been with each parent during any visitations during parental separation.
- Ask about a typical day with each parent.
- Ask who the child talks to when he or she feels happy or sad.

- Ask what the child likes and dislikes about each parent.
- Find out which parent the child would prefer to be with.
- Ask if the child has been coached (by a parent, attorney, or anyone else) in answering interview questions.
- Explore the child's developmental history.
- For younger children, play therapy may have to be included as part of the evaluation.
- Observe for and explore the current impact of parental separation on the psychological functioning of the child.
- When testing a young child, start with figure drawings. These are nonthreatening and are often done in school, so the child will not feel uncomfortable when doing this task. The Rorschach is likely to be similarly seen as engaging and nonthreatening.

Criteria to assess what the best interest of the child is include the love and emotional bond between child and parent, the willingness and ability (if appropriate) of the custodial parent to allow a continuing relationship with the noncustodial parent, evidence of domestic violence, the ability to provide the child with continuing religious education if appropriate, the mental and physical health of the involved parties, the ability to provide the child with basic needs (food, clothing, shelter, medical care), the length of time the child has lived in a stable and satisfactory home environment, the preferences of the child if he or she is old enough to make a reasoned preference, the permanence of the family in the custodial home, the records of the child (e.g., school, medical, therapy), and the moral fitness of the parties.

In making such evaluations, the psychologist's understanding of the dynamics and probable outcome of personality disorders can contribute to the final recommendations. A parent with a personality disorder of schizoid would be unlikely to meet the emotional demands of a child due to an inability to express affectivity. The general style of interpersonal withdrawal would provide inappropriate modeling for future interpersonal relationships. Parents with an antisocial or aggressive–sadistic (negativistic) personality disorder expose a child to potential physical abuse and an amoral lifestyle and model a lack of empathy. Borderline personalities provide inconsistent parenting because of erratic emotionality. Paranoid parents are likely to become embroiled in undue suspiciousness regarding the child's interactions with others and to project these malevolent ideations onto the child. Finally, a parent with a schizotypal personality disorder is so mentally disturbed as to be unable to properly care for a child. These disorders are likely to contraindicate effective parenting. Parents with other personality disorders, such as avoidant, dependent, narcissistic, or compulsive, may have issues of their own, but these tend not to be so severe as to interfere with effective child rearing.

Psychological Testing

When engaging in psychological testing, the psychologist should choose appropriate tests, use tests that he or she feels confident enough will provide the information needed, draw conclusions that are defensible in court, and base all conclusions on objective data. As much as possible, the psychologist must avoid inferences and speculations.

Report to the Court

The psychologist should assume that all attorneys will read the report with a fine-tooth comb. Everything negative about a party will be subject to cross-examination designed to reduce the credibility of the psychologist's expertise and conclusions. The report should avoid jargon, demonstrate balance, cite positive and negative aspects where indicated, give clear recommendations, consider the short- and long-term consequences of those recommendations if implemented, and focus on what is in the best interest of the child.

Depositions and Testimony

When preparing to be deposed or to testify, the psychologist should testify only in areas of his or her expertise, making certain that this expertise can be validated by credentials. The psychologist should testify more as an expert witness than as a factual witness, avoid arguing with an attorney, and make his or her point and stand behind it. The psychologist can rely on the other attorney to allow him or her to rebut and redress any misunderstandings or any areas that need clarification. The psychologist should state that an assertion is fact when he or she knows it to be true, state when it is speculation, and say, "I don't know" if that is true. Finally, the psychologist must look and behave like an expert.

A psychologist lamented to a judge in chambers that he really disliked being put in the role of evaluating and then making a recommendation as to custody. The judge responded by saying, "If not you, then who?" Who has the requisite knowledge, training, empirical footing, ethical standards, and overall competence equivalent to those of psychologists to conduct these evaluations and make their recommendations based on facts? Of all the evaluations conducted by forensic psychologists, custody evaluations are perhaps the most central, critical, and consequential to all involved parties.

Forensic psychologists are well prepared for this task, and they must do it with humility and honor.

This chapter has presented an overview of the field of custody evaluations, highlighted published guidelines and standards for custody evaluations, specified commonly used assessment measures, addressed the child abuse assessment and false allegations of child abuse, discussed some ethical problems in conducting these evaluations as well as risk management efforts for reducing potential liability, and concluded with a recommended strategy for custody evaluations.

5

PERSONAL INJURY

Personal injury suits are filed under tort laws. A *tort* is a civil rather than a legal wrong that one person commits against another person. For a tort claim to be legally valid, there must be some type of duty owed by the defendant to the plaintiff, there must be a violation or breach of that duty, and there must be damage to the plaintiff as a result of that breach. The legal basis for this is the dictum of *respondent superior*—the employer is responsible for the actions of subordinates. Workers' compensation claims are the most common claims under tort laws and have been a rich source of psychological referrals and court testimony. Workers' compensation is the United States's oldest social insurance program. Each state's workers' compensation law is unique and contains differences in statutes, case law, and administrative practices. However, there are common threads in all workers' compensation programs:

- Workers' compensation is a no-fault insurance program. The affected employee need not prove negligence on the part of the employer to win compensation, the levels of which are limited by the program.
- All require that the employer provide medical benefits. Psychologists and psychological services are defined as medical benefits in these plans.

- Disabled employees are compensated with two thirds of their lost wages, subject to maximum benefits.

Workers' compensation cases are classified in three somewhat distinct categories. Each has different legal, administrative, and economic implications. The first category is called "physical–mental." The physical component refers to an actual occupational injury or disease that is compensable. As a consequence of this physical problem, the employee develops a psychological overlay that further disables the employee. For example, if an employee is working on a machine and receives an electric shock of a relatively severe nature requiring medical attention, and then he or she develops a conditioned-fear response and is afraid to return to that machine, this would qualify as a physical–mental claim.

The second kind of claim is called "mental–physical." The distinction between this type of claim and the physical–mental claim is one of etiology. In a mental–physical claim, the impairment results primarily from the mental component of the job (i.e., stress), which then results in a physical problem. A good example of this type of claim is an employee who develops ulcers because of constant exposure to customer complaints.

The third type of claim is more controversial and is called a "mental–mental" claim. Mental–mental claims can be further categorized into three differing sets of conditions:

1. A sudden and unusual event triggers a reaction. For example, a plane crash causes the death of close friends of a flight attendant, who develops fear of flying because of this trauma. Another example is an employee who witnesses workplace violence and then refuses to return to work because of disabling anticipatory anxiety.
2. Circumstances of the job require continued exposure to stressful conditions that are not sudden or unusual. For example, an air traffic controller works under conditions of chronic stress because of understaffing, increased air traffic, concerns about outdated equipment, and a growing risk of error that could lead to fatalities.
3. Workers allege a nervous breakdown, even in the absence of sudden or chronic stress or trauma. The disability is claimed on the basis of some type of chronic mental condition that leads to a disability. For example, an accountant is forced under threat of dismissal to falsify the books quarter after quarter in such a way as to avoid criminal behavior but to present a better picture of the firm than is truly the case. This pressure could serve as a basis of a mental–mental claim.

For more information on these categories of claims, the interested reader is referred to Barth (1990), who explains these details and their nuances in greater detail.

A substantial amount of time elapses from the date of injury to the onset of the trial. The forensic psychologist is likely to be called on to evaluate the litigant months or even years after the accident or injury occurred. One issue is the extent to which personality evaluation is a reliable reflection of personality changes and stability during this interim period. It is clear that personality changes have been documented following chronic pain (Sternbach & Timmermans, 1975). In one study, Colotla, Bowman, and Shercliffe (2001) evaluated 94 workers injured in an accident or crime. Workers were tested with the revised Minnesota Multiphasic Personality Inventory (MMPI–2) and then retested after an average of 21 months. The correlations ranged from .61 to .73 for the clinical scales, .52 to .82 for the supplemental scales, and .65 to .78 for the content scales. Catala et al. concluded that the MMPI–2 was moderately stable across almost two years for injured workers.

The MMPI has been the instrument of choice in evaluating patients with medical conditions. The MMPI has been used to explore personality patterns associated with almost any given disease, but the literature tends to concentrate on the emotional correlates associated with the following diseases: chronic pain, especially low back pain and headache; chronic hemodialysis; epilepsy; multiple sclerosis; rheumatoid arthritis; penile implants; impotence and other sexual dysfunctions; bronchial asthma; and ulcerative colitis. However, most workers' compensation claims are related to (a) industrial accidents, especially to the head and back and closed head injury, and (b) psychological trauma and claims of emotional disability associated with anxiety, depression, and posttraumatic stress disorder. Therefore, this chapter concentrates on the findings in workplace-related areas.

The findings from any psychological test, including the MMPI, are confounded with the patient's reaction to the illness or injury and to its treatment. Also, the patient may have had preexisting medical and psychological disorders, which may also confound the clinical picture. Psychologists performing workers' compensation and personal injury evaluations need to know how these other disorders tend to be manifested on evaluation instruments. They then need to determine what particular effects an accident had on the patient's personality over and above any preexisting condition. For example, if the patient had a history of migraine headaches and then experienced a head injury on the job, to what extent are present scores on a test due to the effects of the migraines compared to the effects of the recent accident? To know this, psychologists need an empirically derived test database that compares test findings of this group with another test database on this same population postinjury. Then they could compare how the individual patient stands in relation to these two population norms. This is the logic behind the material to be discussed in this chapter.

Because litigants often either consciously or unconsciously exaggerate their reported symptoms in terms of both number and severity, tests that assess for exaggeration are particularly useful in personal injury evaluations. Just because the litigant shows signs of malingering or exaggeration, however, does not mean that the damage has been entirely invented, nor does it mean that the injury did not occur as claimed.

The MMPI has received the most attention, both in analogue studies and from data based on actual workers' compensation studies. This research has established that both the MMPI (Berry, Baer, & Harris, 1991; Schretland, 1988; Storm & Graham, 2000) and the MMPI–2 are quite good at detecting malingering. The F validity scale, the Infrequent Psychopathology (Fp) scale, and to a lesser extent the Dissimulation (Ds) scale have been particularly useful in detecting malingering. Also, a fake-bad scale (Lees-Haley, English, & Glenn, 1991) has been found to be effective with personal injury litigants (Larrabee, 1998), probably because the scale contains many items from the Hypochondriasis (Hs) and Hysteria (Hy) scales (Tsushima & Tsushima, 2001).

The psychologist's tasks in personal injury claims are to (a) establish a baseline of the plaintiff's psychological functioning before the injury; (b) evaluate the nature, extent, and severity of the injury; (c) determine the probable cause of the psychological injury, if any; and (d) consider whether psychological intervention could restore the individual to preinjury functioning levels. The legal standard for the triers of fact is known as the "preponderance of evidence." An operational definition of this term would be whether the amount of evidence that favors the plaintiff is more convincing than the evidence that refutes the plaintiff's claim.

Three areas have been given prominence in the psychological literature regarding personal injury cases and personality function. These are orthopedic injuries, especially low back pain and chronic pain resulting from accidents or injuries; closed head injury as it pertains to personality changes; and posttraumatic stress disorder. This chapter addresses each of these areas separately.

THE PSYCHOLOGICAL EXPERIENCE OF PAIN

The International Association for the Study of Pain (1986) has defined *pain* as "an unpleasant sensory and emotional experience associated with actual or potential tissue damage" (p. 217). This definition separates tissue damage from the pain experience and suggests that pain is also a subjective psychological experience. Many clinical pain specialists have observed that a patient's experience or report of pain did not always correspond to the actual extent of tissue damage. Hence, pain specialists now recognize there are emotional, cognitive, behavioral, and social components to the development of pain reports (Keller & Butcher, 1991). Although medicine has traditionally viewed pain as the result of some underlying pathological process and disorder, this model does not necessarily explain patients' differing pain responses to similar injuries. And it does not account for patients' reports of pain without apparent or detectable physical injury.

Historically, clinicians operating from a psychoanalytic or psychodynamic perspective attempted to analyze the behavior of chronic pain patients using the construct of hypochondriasis—a condition in which patients report pain in the absence of known physical causation or negative physical findings. These analysts theorized that when an infant experiences rejection, emotional deprivation, or lack of love or nurturance and hence a narcissistic injury at the preoedipal stage of development, the emotional reactions to this infantile trauma are attached to the soma, because the sense of self has not yet developed. Rather than having the maturity to say, "I am angry and depressed," the infant is saying, "My body is in sadness." Later in life, through injury, threat, or other emotional trauma, a hypochondriacal reaction develops, causing the person to become whining, complaining, pessimistic, depressed, helpless, and defeatist. Such people go from one doctor to the next seeking medical explanations for their problems, to no avail. They also reject any psychological explanation of their behavior. These analysts argue that such patients make those around them miserable, because they are unconsciously demonstrating their anger indirectly over a preoedipal injury.

The other component of personality invoked by traditional analysis is that of hysteria. In this personality disorder, the patient is prone to somaticize under stress and to develop so-called conversion reactions, or the appearance of medical disorders in the absence of pathology. This led to the concept of organic versus functional disorders, and much of the early psychological research on pain was motivated from this etiological epistemology.

The organic–functional dichotomy is no longer predominant, and the traditional way of thinking about pain has been mitigated by the "gate control" theory of pain (Melzak & Wall, 1965). In this complicated physiological theory, pain is viewed as multidimensional and as being the result of interactions between biological, psychological, and social variables. Pain pathways are "gated" to transmit pain to the cerebral cortex by these processes. This theory essentially negates the old dichotomy of organic versus functional.

Learning theory approaches to the understanding of pain have long been recognized as applicable to pain patients and are consistent with the gate control theory. Using concepts from both classical and operant conditioning, psychologists now recognize that patients may have learned to emit pain behaviors associated with a variety of reinforcements. Comprehensive pain management programs now often include the behavioral treatment of pain as one component of the treatment regimen. The reader is referred to previous literature reviews on the use of the MMPI and MMPI–2 in assessing chronic pain patients for a more in-depth discussion of these issues (Adams, Heilbronn, Silk, Reider, & Blumer, 1981; Keller & Butcher, 1991; Love & Peck, 1987; Murray, 1982; Vendrig, 2000).

The bulk of this chapter focuses on psychological testing of personal injury litigants. However, psychological testing is only one step in the entire evaluation process, which includes clinical interviews, record reviews (including previous depositions, if any), collateral information, and medical reports. (A review of checkbook entries and credit card statements is one way to establish a patient's level of preinjury functioning and activities.)

ORTHOPEDIC DISORDERS

Chronic pain is defined as a disorder lasting six or more months with biological, psychological, affective, cognitive, motivational, and somatic components. The MMPI has been the instrument most often used to assess the personality factors contributing to the experience of chronic pain, dating from Hanvik's (1951) study of low back pain patients. Hanvik compared the MMPI findings of 30 patients with low back pain of known organic etiology and 30 cases of low back pain of unknown origin but with no clear-cut organic etiology—a "functional" pain group. The groups differed on several scale dimensions, and expert judges were able to sort these profiles into correct categories at a level better than chance. The functional pain group had the "Conversion V" configuration of elevations on the "neurotic triad"—Hypochondriasis (Hs), Hysteria (Hy), and Depression (Dep)— whereas the organic group had a relatively straight-line configuration on these scales with T scores in the normal range.

Since then, many studies have used the MMPI to investigate chronic pain patients. The early MMPI studies were conducted in an era that classified chronic pain as organic or functional, and substantial efforts were made to develop scales and find profiles that differentiated groups along these two dimensions. The organic–functional distinction no longer drives these studies.

The assessment of MMPI findings in personal injury cases is not a simple process. Profile scores have been found to differ for patients with pending litigation versus those without pending litigation on both the MMPI (Sternbach, Wolf, Murphy, & Akeson, 1973) and the MMPI–2 (Fow, Dorris,

Sittig, & Smith-Seemiller, 2002; Hoffman, Scott, Emrick, & Adams, 1999), for differing sites of pain (Beals & Hickman, 1972), for patients with multiple surgeries versus those without multiple surgeries (Wilfling, Klonoff, & Kokan, 1973), and for those who were satisfied with their surgery versus those who were not (Swanson, Swensen, Maruto, & Floreen, 1978). Pain profiles also differ based on the duration of pain (acute vs. chronic; Beals & Hickman, 1972; Cox, Chapman, & Black, 1978; Sternbach et al., 1973).

Low back pain patients in acute pain (i.e., less than six months duration) have shown a subclinical evaluation in the neurotic triad reflecting physiological symptoms without much depression. Low back pain patients with chronic pain (i.e., longer than six months duration) have shown elevations with the characteristic psychosomatic Conversion V configuration reflecting somatic preoccupation with depression. As the duration of pain prolongs, symptoms of neuroticism increase (Beals & Hickman, 1972; Cox et al., 1978; Sternbach et al., 1973).

Patients with pending litigation tend to have scale elevations on the neurotic triad and also on Psychopathic Deviate (Pd). Pd usually indicates anger, resentment toward authority, and rebelliousness. When these four scales are elevated, the prospects for improvement tend to be poor until the litigation is settled (Sternbach et al., 1973).

Scale elevations on Hypochondriasis (Hs) and Hysteria (Hy) are common in chronic pain patients, probably because of pain, parathesia, and malaise. It would be an interpretive error to view the Conversion V configuration as evidence of strong psychological components to chronic pain symptoms. Hy consists of two classes of items, admission of physical problems and denial of psychological problems.

One study asked chronic pain patients to answer the items on the K validity scale, Hypochondriasis (Hs), Depression (Dep), and Hysteria (Hy) as they would have answered when they were pain free and again as they currently feel with their pain. Hs and Hy were slightly elevated for the pain-free state, and those elevations were due to endorsement of the pain-specific items in the scale. At low to moderate elevations, the Conversion V configuration may not be associated with psychological components of pain behaviors, whereas at higher elevations, strong psychological factors associated with chronic pain may be suspected (Sherman, Camfield, & Arena, 1995). When K is also elevated, the psychologist might conclude that denial of psychological factors is associated with a physiological disorder (McGrath & O'Malley, 1986).

MMPI Studies With Chronic Pain Patients

This section presents the available MMPI and MMPI–2 studies on patients with chronic pain, emphasizing orthopedic pain and low back pain. One value of the tables (and others in this chapter and throughout this book) is that they represent the database with which to compare an individual claimant's test findings against expectations for patients with that condition. These data also may be presented to the court as part of briefs or in testimony.

Studies of chronic pain patients are quite heterogeneous. Some report on only male or female patients, whereas many others present the results of mixed samples of male and female patients. Table 5.1 summarizes MMPI studies with chronic pain patients. Table 5.2 gives an overview of studies emphasizing orthopedic and back pain. Table 5.3 presents T scores related to litigation for these same samples. Table 5.4 presents MMPI–2 studies for all cases of chronic pain. MMPI–2 studies have been far less frequent, but the initial findings based on more than 1,700 patients are substantially the same as findings using the original MMPI with more than 7,200 patients.

The data clearly reflect that chronic pain patients usually have elevations on the neurotic triad (Hypochondriasis, Hs; Depression, Dep; Hysteria, Hy) in various combinations of the 132' code type (e.g., 13'2, 132', 31'2, '312), although elevations vary across groups. This finding has been replicated so many times that any variation from this code type would be considered atypical and an aberration. This profile reflects somatic symptoms and excessive worry about physical problems to the extent that it dominates patients' lives.

Patients who endorse only actual physical problems on Hypochondriasis (Hs) will get a subspike on this scale. However, a T score greater than 70 on the MMPI or 65 on the MMPI–2 suggests that the patient is coping poorly with diagnosed physical problems or is exaggerating the extent or severity of the physical problems compared to an objective review of symptoms. With higher elevations on Hysteria (Hy), the probability of conversion disorders may be more likely, though conversion reactions seem to be less frequent in current psychiatric patients. Elevations on Depression (Dep) may reflect affective dysphoria associated with living with chronic pain or may be independent of it, or they may reflect anger at the medical establishment for not curing the pain.

MMPI–2 and Chronic Pain Profiles

With the revision of the MMPI, one question pertains to the degree to which information gleaned from MMPI-based research is transferable to the MMPI–2. The initial MMPI–2 study with chronic pain patients was conducted by Keller and Butcher (1991). They studied 268 men and 234 women in a treatment program for chronic pain. The mean profile for men was 132' and for women 312' (see Table 5.4). This study was also the initial one that presented data for content and supplementary scales. Both men and women scored in clinically significant ranges on Anxiety, Depression,

TABLE 5.1
Minnesota Multiphasic Personality Inventory Studies on Patients With Chronic Pain

Scale	Study 1		Study 2		Study 3		Study 4				
	Organic	Functional	Low back	Miscellaneous chronic	Men	Women	Poor	Fair	Good	Single	Multiple
L	50	51	52	52	53	56	57	56	57	57	57
F	52	52	51	51	55	53	58	56	57	58	58
K	58	54	53	53	54	55	56	55	56	57	57
Hs	58	73	73	60	80	74	74	78	55	66	78
Dep	58	63	70	64	76	69	78	69	57	63	76
Hy	57	69	72	65	73	74	70	70	55	62	73
Pd	49	58	60	57	60	56	56	60	60	58	58
Mf	48	49	55	55	54	52	58	57	50	55	58
Pa	47	51	54	54	54	56	56	54	50	52	55
Pt	48	56	57	51	63	59	61	58	58	58	60
Sc	47	55	54	51	61	59	60	59	59	60	57
Ma	47	53	53	52	54	53	56	56	56	57	57
Si	49	47	53	52	56	56	55	56	56	55	55
Code	a	1'3	132'	a	132'	13'2	213'	13'2	a	'1	123'

(continued)

TABLE 5.1
Minnesota Multiphasic Personality Inventory Studies on Patients With Chronic Pain (Continued)

Scale	Study 5							Study 6	
	Men	Women	Both	Acute	Chronic	Litigating	Not Litigating	Men	Women
L	50	54	51	52	52	52	52	52	51
F	58	55	57	59	57	58	57	52	49
K	54	54	55	50	56	54	54	61	59
Hs	72	70	70	67	73	78	70	75	70
Dep	71	66	68	59	70	74	66	71	66
Hy	69	70	71	65	72	75	69	73	71
Pd	67	60	62	64	64	69	62	69	62
Mf	58	48	57	52	52	53	52	54	46
Pa	49	57	69	63	58	60	59	54	50
Pt	63	58	60	60	60	64	59	66	54
Sc	64	59	61	61	62	64	63	57	55
Ma	59	57	58	67	57	64	59	54	54
Si	59	62	61	50	53	54	51	50	49
Code	12'34	13'2	31'2	'13	132'	132'4	'132	132'47	13'2
									(continued)

TABLE 5.1
Minnesota Multiphasic Personality Inventory Studies on Patients With Chronic Pain (Continued)

Scale	Study 7		Study 8			Study 9		Study 10	
	Yes	No	Organic	Functional	Mixed	Organic	Mixed	No	Yes
L	50	50	50	51	51	49	54	56	55
F	59	59	52	58	62	59	63	54	54
K	51	53	55	53	53	55	53	58	57
Hs	73	81	67	87	83	67	85	78	69
Dep	74	77	63	77	73	63	75	72	64
Hy	71	77	67	82	77	67	77	77	69
Pd	62	66	57	66	64	62	63	64	61
Mf	58	58	58	60	58	61	57	50	50
Pa	57	59	51	59	58	55	58	55	56
Pt	62	65	54	67	68	60	67	60	58
Sc	61	67	56	70	67	64	69	60	59
Ma	60	60	53	61	60	56	61	60	60
Si	52	52	50	54	53	51	52	49	49
Code	213'	123'8	'13	132'	132'	'13	132'8	132'	'13

(continued)

TABLE 5.1

Minnesota Multiphasic Personality Inventory Studies on Patients With Chronic Pain *(Continued)*

Scale	Study 11			Study 12				Study 13	Study 14
	Acute	Chronic I	Chronic II	I	II	III	IV		
L	51	50	54	53	54	54	49	53	50
F	56	54	55	51	54	50	54	62	58
K	56	56	61	60	57	57	49	54	53
Hs	62	73	75	74	78	63	78	82	71
Dep	60	70	73	61	72	57	79	82	67
Hy	60	75	75	75	78	66	79	80	71
Pd	58	58	60	61	62	51	66	80	63
Mf	50	48	51	48	47	48	47	53	—
Pa	55	58	56	54	58	53	71	65	60
Pt	57	60	61	56	64	51	73	73	—
Sc	58	60	61	59	62	52	75	81	63
Ma	51	53	50	57	55	52	58	60	61
Si	61	54	55	48	56	51	66	53	54
Code	a	312'	132'	13'	132'	'3	2138+	1283+	13'2 *(continued)*

TABLE 5.1
Minnesota Multiphasic Personality Inventory Studies on Patients With Chronic Pain (Continued)

| | Study 15 | | | | | Study 16 | | | | | | |
| | Men | | | Women | | | | | | | | |
Scale	I	II	III	I	II	Men	Women	Single	Multiple	Head	Back	Head and back
L	50	51	55	54	52	47	50	51	49	49	51	47
F	59	50	51	55	51	55	56	57	56	56	54	58
K	50	53	60	57	58	56	55	55	56	54	58	53
Hs	73	59	74	82	60	74	72	68	76	73	74	73
Dep	72	58	64	77	60	68	71	67	72	71	67	70
Hy	75	62	74	78	60	69	74	70	73	74	72	72
Pd	68	50	58	54	60	60	60	60	60	60	60	60
Mf	43	49	50	56	55	60	45	51	52	51	48	51
Pa	65	52	54	52	50	55	57	55	56	57	55	56
Pt	65	51	59	67	53	63	63	63	63	64	58	64
Sc	68	50	60	67	52	60	62	59	62	63	59	63
Ma	60	50	51	58	52	56	53	53	55	53	55	56
Si	60	50	49	57	49	53	57	55	55	57	56	67
Code	312'	a	13'	132'	a	1'32	312'	3'12	132'	312'	132	132'

(continued)

TABLE 5.1
Minnesota Multiphasic Personality Inventory Studies on Patients With Chronic Pain (Continued)

Scale	Study 17		Study 18					Study 19			Study 20		
	Good	Poor	I	II	III	IV	V	I	II	III	I	II	III
L	54	55	50	56	47	52	53	52	52	50	52	53	52
F	51	52	49	49	50	50	49	53	56	71	53	54	57
K	58	56	51	62	54	48	57	51	55	49	57	58	54
Hs	68	75	68	57	60	57	51	68	89	92	65	70	72
Dep	63	63	65	49	57	60	47	62	78	100	60	63	66
Hy	69	72	69	63	62	60	53	64	80	85	66	71	71
Pd	58	60	65	54	60	43	45	53	63	70	58	59	62
Mf	61	51	65	50	43	48	51	52	57	59	54	52	54
Pa	55	54	47	50	57	47	46	50	56	70	54	57	55
Pt	52	57	48	52	56	49	41	55	67	83	55	59	59
Sc	54	58	47	52	57	45	44	52	66	90	58	60	62
Ma	53	57	68	49	60	50	44	57	55	64	57	58	59
Si	50	50	49	48	50	54	48	53	56	63	52	51	52
Code	13'	13'	'31	a	a	a	a	'1	132'	2183+	'31	13'	13'

(continued)

TABLE 5.1
Minnesota Multiphasic Personality Inventory Studies on Patients With Chronic Pain (Continued)

| Scale | Study 21 | | | | | | | | Study 22 | | | | | | |
| | | | | | | | | | | | | | Months | | |
	I	II	III	IV	I	II	III	IV	I	II	III	IV	0–6	6–24	>24
L	56	50	47	54	52	52	51	54	55	53	47	51	53	53	52
F	60	49	76	55	59	49	78	55	57	51	71	52	53	53	56
K	51	55	46	58	55	54	48	58	46	57	44	54	58	58	55
Hs	85	61	80	75	85	62	85	76	75	66	78	81	65	70	70
Dep	84	62	82	66	85	60	89	65	77	61	74	67	58	61	66
Hy	79	60	74	74	77	58	79	73	72	66	74	85	65	70	71
Pd	63	53	76	63	65	51	78	63	59	56	80	77	57	61	60
Mf	68	49	61	54	56	48	65	58	56	50	55	48	54	52	53
Pa	59	52	77	59	53	50	78	54	63	52	76	63	52	52	58
Pt	73	54	85	59	73	54	87	59	68	56	77	58	54	57	59
Sc	72	51	94	60	70	51	98	59	62	55	88	66	57	59	61
Ma	52	53	74	59	54	53	74	61	51	55	71	70	54	59	60
Si	66	54	59	47	61	55	61	44	67	49	67	44	50	49	52
Code	1237+	a	8721	13'2	123'	a	8271	13'	213'	'3	8412+	3149	13'	13'	13'2

(continued)

TABLE 5.1
Minnesota Multiphasic Personality Inventory Studies on Patients With Chronic Pain (Continued)

| | Study 23 | | | | Study 24 | | | | | | | |
| | | | | | Men | | | | Women | | | |
Scale	I	II	III	IV	I	II	III	IV	I	II	III	IV
L	50	50	50	67	50	53	59	53	49	63	50	55
F	56	50	58	50	70	62	53	53	69	59	57	52
K	52	51	48	67	43	53	59	57	47	65	49	56
Hs	75	55	69	72	67	80	66	57	73	80	61	57
Dep	71	54	72	58	84	74	67	59	73	71	68	53
Hy	80	59	69	78	62	74	64	60	73	80	60	59
Pd	70	50	50	57	72	62	52	61	72	69	59	56
Mf	48	43	49	52	68	69	59	63	50	53	48	50
Pa	67	50	52	54	69	61	50	53	65	61	56	52
Pt	68	48	60	53	74	70	55	53	68	65	61	50
Sc	68	49	60	59	81	73	54	55	74	67	58	57
Ma	62	55	50	49	63	67	47	61	68	53	50	57
Si	52	51	68	48	67	53	53	48	58	54	64	48
Code	312	a	2'13	31'	2476	1238	'21	a	8123	132'	'2	a

(continued)

TABLE 5.1
Minnesota Multiphasic Personality Inventory Studies on Patients With Chronic Pain (Continued)

| Scale | Study 25 | | | | Study 26 | | | | Study 27 | Study 28 | | | | |
| | | | | | Private | | State | | | | | | | |
	I	II	III	IV	Men	Women	Men	Women		I	II	III	IV	V
L	53	48	49	56	57	52	53	55	50	50	51	56	55	46
F	60	57	73	50	57	52	80	77	60	55	51	54	62	69
K	54	48	49	59	58	55	53	53	53	57	55	60	53	45
Hs	92	68	92	79	77	67	91	62	72	55	56	75	80	74
Dep	81	58	99	64	67	59	80	66	70	55	57	66	83	68
Hy	85	63	82	73	71	68	80	65	72	61	60	73	79	71
Pd	62	59	77	56	41	64	77	69	63	61	53	61	67	73
Mf	58	57	64	53	53	52	59	53	52	62	48	54	55	60
Pa	56	55	69	51	54	55	71	71	64	59	53	55	64	72
Pt	65	56	84	53	62	58	79	62	64	55	51	56	68	70
Sc	64	57	92	55	66	58	85	74	67	58	51	57	67	76
Ma	56	61	64	58	59	56	60	65	63	64	50	53	51	74
Si	57	53	65	47	51	53	59	60	56	46	52	50	62	57
Code	132'	a	2187+	13'	13'	'31	1823+	86'4	12'8	a	a	13'2	23'78	8132

(continued)

TABLE 5.1
Minnesota Multiphasic Personality Inventory Studies on Patients With Chronic Pain (Continued)

Scale	Study 29				Study 30	Study 31 Years				Study 32			
	I	II	III	IV		< 1	1–2	> 2	Mean	I	II	III	IV
L	56	50	50	51	49	53	54	54	54	53	54	58	55
F	51	57	70	50	62	54	57	55	56	51	52	55	61
K	61	52	45	53	53	55	55	55	55	57	60	54	58
Hs	65	72	72	62	62	73	78	80	78	57	75	65	76
Dep	62	66	77	60	61	68	71	75	72	62	64	80	82
Hy	69	75	70	61	61	72	75	76	75	58	74	65	77
Pd	56	65	72	53	63	61	62	60	61	54	52	56	67
Mf	—	—	—	—	55	55	55	56	55	54	52	56	67
Pa	55	58	69	52	62	56	56	56	56	52	54	56	63
Pt	54	59	72	53	63	60	60	57	60	52	57	57	71
Sc	56	64	76	52	68	59	62	62	62	52	57	56	71
Ma	52	71	61	53	62	59	60	58	59	55	52	54	56
Si	51	48	71	50	56	51	52	51	52	50	50	55	56
Code	'31	319'	2814	a	'8	13'2	13'	132'	1'32'	a	13'	2'	2317+

(continued)

TABLE 5.1
Minnesota Multiphasic Personality Inventory Studies on Patients With Chronic Pain (Continued)

Scale	Study 33	Study 34	Study 35				Study 36						
			I	II	III	IV	I	II	III	IV	V	VI	VII
L	70	51	52	48	55	50	52	52	51	52	51	50	53
F	60	56	58	62	60	79	59	55	51	51	52	72	60
K	68	53	57	49	55	55	52	54	53	61	54	48	62
Hs	53	72	90	82	94	82	92	73	61	84	82	72	71
Dep	51	69	73	93	88	88	88	87	57	62	72	78	72
Hy	54	71	84	76	82	80	82	73	64	82	78	71	73
Pd	53	60	69	65	69	83	67	60	51	64	60	72	74
Mf	51	—	58	62	59	66	57	52	50	50	50	50	58
Pa	54	55	56	59	57	79	58	53	54	55	57	78	57
Pt	53	60	70	73	68	76	70	67	50	56	60	79	64
Sc	53	62	75	73	76	90	69	66	52	64	58	89	62
Ma	50	59	63	55	60	66	52	52	53	62	52	62	58
Si	52	52	51	64	54	54	58	60	51	47	51	61	52
Code	1'3	13'2	1382'	2138	1237	8213	1237	213	a	13'	132'	8764	4321

(continued)

TABLE 5.1
Minnesota Multiphasic Personality Inventory Studies on Patients With Chronic Pain (Continued)

| | Study 37 | | | | | | | | | | | | | | Study 38 | |
| | Men | | | | | | Women | | | | | | | | | |
Scale	I	II	III	IV	V	VI	I	II	III	IV	V	VI	VII	VIII	Miscellaneous	Litigating
L	51	52	50	54	54	55	49	51	52	54	53	54	53	54	53	53
F	55	60	79	56	65	80	63	52	68	54	58	52	74	54	59	59
K	54	51	44	52	49	46	53	57	43	55	50	55	51	55	54	53
Hs	73	79	93	74	90	71	82	63	70	72	75	65	86	72	77	78
Dep	65	83	88	64	91	69	80	53	84	70	77	58	89	57	77	77
Hy	69	76	83	68	80	67	83	64	70	72	75	66	85	73	76	76
Pd	62	67	79	57	70	74	74	57	70	58	63	54	88	63	66	67
Mf	60	60	62	57	62	67	44	54	44	46	45	45	50	54	53	55
Pa	56	60	80	54	66	90	69	55	69	58	63	52	84	54	61	62
Pt	59	68	88	56	76	79	74	56	77	61	68	53	90	59	67	68
Sc	61	67	100	59	79	110	79	61	80	60	69	55	102	67	68	69
Ma	64	56	75	60	61	85	67	67	61	49	57	55	70	69	59	61
Si	49	57	62	50	60	61	57	44	73	58	62	50	65	47	56	55
Code	13'2	2137	1237	13'2	2138	8694	3128	9'3	2871	132'	2138	31'	8724	3198	123'	123'87

Note. Dashes indicate no data for that variable on scale. Study 1 (Hanvik, 1951) examined the profiles of men and women with organic (*n* = 30) and functional (*n* = 30) low back pain. Study 2 (Beals & Hickman, 1972) examined the profiles of men and women with low back pain (*n* = 35) and miscellaneous chronic pain (*n* = 155). Study 3 (Shaffer, Nussbaum, & Little, 1972) examined the profiles of men (*n* = 766) and women (*n* = 298) with chronic pain. Study 4 (Wilfling, Klonoff, & Kokan, 1973) examined the profiles of orthopedic pain patients by outcome (poor, *n* = 7; fair, *n* = 12; good, *n* = 7) and number of surgeries (single, *n* = 15; multiple, *n* = 11). Study 5 (Sternbach, Wolf, Murphy, & Akeson, 1973) examined the profiles of men (*n* = 57) and women (*n* = 60) with low back pain by acute (*n* = 19) or chronic (*n* = 98) duration and presence of litigation (yes, *n* = 36; no, *n* = 81). Study 6 (Gentry, Shaw, & Thomas, 1974) examined the profiles of men (*n* = 31) and women (*n* = 25) with low back pain. Study 7 (Sternbach & Timmermans, 1975) examined the profiles of men and women by presence of chronic pain following surgery (yes, *n* = 29; no, *n* = 84). Study 8 (Freeman, Calsyn, & Louks, 1976) examined the profiles of men with organic (*n* = 31) and mixed (*n* = 12), functional (*n* = 12), and mixed (*n* = 12) low back pain. Study 9 (Calsyn, Louks, & Freeman, 1976) examined the profiles of women with chronic pain by satisfaction (no, *n* = 56; yes, *n* = 55). Study 11 (Cox, Chapman, & Black, 1978) examined the profiles of men and women with miscellaneous acute (*n* = 24) and chronic (I, *n* = 13; II, *n* = 20) pain. Study 12 (Bradley, Prokop, Margolis, & Gentry, 1978) examined the profiles of women with low back pain (I, II, III, IV; *N* = 315). Study 13 (J. R. Snibbe, Peterson, & Sosner, 1980) examined the profiles of 6 men and women with low back pain. Study 14 (McCreary, Turner, & Dawson, 1980) examined the profiles of 102 men and women with low back pain. Study 15 (Prokop, Bradley, Margolis, & Gentry, 1980) examined the profiles of men (I, *n* = 44; II, *n* = 61; III, *n* = 50) and women (I, *n* = 30; II, *n* = 30) with low back pain. Study 16 (Strassberg, Reimherr, Ward, Russell, & Cole, 1981) examined the profiles of men (*n* = 38) and women (*n* = 74) with chronic pain by presence of single (*n* = 33) or multiple (*n* = 12) pain sources and presence of head (*n* = 33), back (*n* = 33), or head and back (*n* = 34) pain. Study 17 (C. J. Long, 1981) examined the profiles of men and women with low back pain by outcome (good, $n = 22$; poor, $n = 22$). Study 18 (Snyder & Power, 1981) examined the profiles of men and women with chronic pain (I, $n = 46$; II, $n = 38$; III, $n = 27$; IV, $n = 18$; V, $n = 12$). Study 19 (D. P. Armentrout, Moore, Parker, Hewett, & Feltz, 1982) examined the profiles of men with chronic pain (I, $n = 61$; II, $n = 139$; III, $n = 38$). Study 20 (Leavitt & Garron, 1982) examined the profiles of men and women with low back pain (I, II, III; $N = 131$). Study 21 (McGill, Lawlis, Selby, Mooney, & McCoy, 1983) examined the profiles of men and women with low back pain (I, $n = 18$; II, $n = 25$; III, $n = 9$; IV, $n = 40$) and of four subgroups each of men ($N = 46$) and women ($N = 46$). Study 22 (Garron & Leavitt, 1983) examined the profiles of men and women with chronic low back pain of 0–6 months ($n = 39$), 6–24 months ($n = 35$), and more than 24 months ($n = 74$) duration. Study 23 (Bernstein & Garbin, 1983) examined the profiles of women with chronic low back pain (I, $n = 25$; II, $n = 12$; III, $n = 25$, IV, $n = 10$). Study 24 (Bradley, Hopson, & Ven der Heide, 1984) examined the profiles of men (I, II, III, IV; $N = 90$) and women (I, II, III, IV; $N = 218$) with low back pain. Study 25 (R. Hart, 1984) examined the profiles of men with chronic pain (I, $n = 23$; II, $n = 15$; III, $n = 17$; IV, $n = 15$). Study 26 (Pollach & Grainey, 1984) examined the profiles of patients with chronic pain in private (men, $n = 13$; women, $n = 13$) and state (men, $n = 13$; women, $n = 13$) hospitals. Study 27 (Repko & Cooper, 1985) examined the profiles of 43 patients with orthopedic pain. Study 28 (Rosen, Grubman, Bevins, & Frymoyer, 1987) examined the profiles of men and women with low back pain (I, $n = 69$; II, $n = 157$; III, $n = 75$; IV, $n = 38$; V, $n = 23$). Study 29 (Costello, Hulsey, Schoenfeld, & Ramamurthy, 1987) examined the profiles of women with chronic pain (I, II, III, IV; $N = 170$). Study 30 (Diamond, Barth, & Zillmer, 1988) examined the profiles of men and women with miscellaneous pain of less than 1 year ($n = 57$), 1–2 years ($n = 70$), and more than 2 years ($n = 71$) duration and provided means ($n = 198$). Study 31 (Levenson, Glenn, & Hirshfield, 1988) examined the profiles of 50 men and women with minor head injury. Study 32 (Adams, Heilbronn, & Blumer, 1986) examined the profiles of 45 patients with low back pain. Study 33 (Franz, Paul, Bautz, Choroba, & Hildebrandt, 1986) examined the profiles of 45 patients with low back pain. Study 34 (Naliboff, Cohen, & Yellen, 1982) examined the profiles of men and women with chronic pain (I, $n = 21$; II, $n = 24$; III, $n = 10$; IV, $n = 16$). Study 35 (Atkinson, Ingram, Kremer, & Saccuzzo, 1986) examined the profiles of men with miscellaneous orthopedic pain (I, $n = 17$; II, $n = 14$; III, $n = 12$; IV, $n = 10$). Study 36 (Heaton et al., 1982) examined the profiles of men and women with miscellaneous orthopedic pain (I, $n = 10$; II, $n = 29$; III, $n = 17$; IV, $n = 30$; V, $n = 15$, VI, $n = 15$; VII, $n = 9$). Study 37 (Guck, Meilman, Skultety, & Poloni, 1988) examined the profiles of men (I, $n = 73$; II, $n = 52$; III, $n = 14$; IV, $n = 119$; V, $n = 42$; VI, $n = 5$) and women (I, $n = 27$; II, $n = 21$; III, $n = 18$; IV, $n = 27$; II, $n = 62$; V, $n = 93$; VI, $n = 74$; VII, $n = 5$; VIII, $n = 29$) with chronic pain. Study 38 (Fow, Dorris, Sittig, & Smith-Seemiller, 2002) examined the profiles of miscellaneous ($n = 821$) and litigating ($n = 318$) chronic pain patients.

[a]Within normal limits.

TABLE 5.2
Overview of Studies on Patients With Chronic Pain (Orthopedic and Back)

	All studies	Low back pain				Miscellaneous chronic pain			
		Men	Women	Men and women	All cases	Men	Women	Men and women	All cases
No. studies	38	9	5	12	26	9	9	9	25
No. data sets	129	21	13	24	58	26	27	25	74
Total subjects	7,268	699	773	1,124	2,596	1,130	1,067	1,722	3,920
Scale									
L	55	53	53	55	53	52	53	52	52
F	57	56	57	56	56	62	59	56	59
K	54	55	55	54	54	53	53	55	54
Hs	72	72	70	70	71	81	71	71	74
Dep	68	70	66	67	68	77	67	69	72
Hy	71	70	71	69	70	75	72	71	72
Pd	62	62	61	58	60	66	63	61	63
Mf	54	58	48	53	54	59	49	53	53
Pa	58	55	57	57	57	61	60	57	59
Pt	62	62	60	58	60	68	62	60	63
Sc	63	62	65	60	60	72	65	61	65
Ma	59	58	55	56	57	61	60	56	59
Si	54	54	54	54	53	56	55	53	55
Code	13'2	123'	31'2	1'32	13'2	1238	31'2	13'2	123'

TABLE 5.3
Minnesota Multiphasic Personality Inventory *T* Scores of Litigating and Nonlitigating Chronic Pain (Orthopedic and Back) Patients

	Litigating patients	Nonlitigating patients
No. studies	7	31
No. data sets	15	94
Total subjects	2,367	3,384
Scale		
L	55	52
F	60	56
K	54	55
Hs	77	71
Dep	73	67
Hy	74	70
Pd	63	61
Mf	54	52
Pa	60	56
Pt	65	59
Sc	67	61
Ma	57	59
Si	55	54
Code	132'8	13'2

and Health Concerns. It is interesting that they did not score in elevated ranges on Anger or Family Problems. Both genders scored low on Ego Strength, suggesting that they are not psychologically minded and tend to behave in passive and dependent ways.

On the Harris–Lingoes subscales, these pain patients scored high on Subjective Depression (D1) and Mental Dullness (D4) and on Lassitude–Malaise (Hy3) and Somatic Items (Hy4). However, 120 patients in a four-week multimodal pain treatment program scored in the average range on the MMPI–2 content scales of Anxiety, Obsessive Thinking, and Depression and scored an average of only *T* 60 on Health Concerns (Vendrig, Deckson, & Meg, 1999). Clinically, elevated scores on the Work Interference Scale would suggest that the patient believes that he or she is unable to productively function in a work environment. This might suggest an unwillingness to return to work after an injury.

A visual picture of MMPI profiles is shown in Figure 5.1, which presents the modal profile of chronic pain patients for both the MMPI and the MMPI–2. The overall shape of the average chronic pain patient profile was maintained from the MMPI to the MMPI–2, indicating that the interpretations from MMPI research could be applied to MMPI–2 pain patient profiles. There were some differences, however. Whereas previous research had suggested that average pain patient profiles may differ based on chronicity or

TABLE 5.4
Minnesota Multiphasic Personality Inventory—2 Studies on Patients With Chronic Pain

Scale	Study 1		Study 2			Study 3			Study 4		Study 5	Study 6				Study 7	Study 8	Study 9	Average (N = 1,701)
	Men	Women	I	II	III	I	II	III	I	II		I	II	III	IV				
L	54	55	59	56	—	57	60	58	57	57	58	56	57	54	54	—	58	61	57
F	55	53	52	66	—	60	59	63	65	59	58	57	57	65	58	—	63	59	59
K	48	50	53	46	—	49	47	48	48	51	47	48	51	44	47	—	53	50	49
Hs	74	74	64	74	72	52	66	75	72	67	77	58	65	71	75	72	81	77	70
Dep	68	69	64	73	69	61	63	78	73	68	71	59	71	78	71	69	76	69	69
Hy	74	77	64	74	72	52	63	77	72	70	77	57	68	72	78	72	84	77	71
Pd	59	58	53	59	58	59	56	62	59	57	56	59	64	62	56	58	61	58	59
Mf	46	56	—	—	50	47	56	51	48	54	51	49	50	46	48	50	52	50	52
Pa	58	62	51	59	59	57	60	67	64	59	58	54	67	62	60	59	62	57	59
Pt	62	62	57	70	62	57	62	74	69	62	63	57	71	71	69	62	68	63	65
Sc	60	51	60	71	64	56	68	74	69	62	64	60	66	69	68	64	72	63	65
Ma	52	51	53	53	53	51	60	55	52	50	52	58	50	55	54	53	53	53	53
Si	53	52	50	60	53	55	54	56	57	53	55	53	57	59	56	53	54	53	55
Code	3'2	31'2	'123	1328'	132'	a	8'237	2317+	2137+	321'	312'	321'	132'	132'	312'	132'	3128	132'	321

Note. Dashes indicate no data for that scale on variable. Study 1 (Keller & Butcher, 1991) examined the profiles of 268 men and 234 women. Study 2 (Berry et al., 1995) examined the profiles of men and women (I, *n* = 31; II, *n* = 30; III, *n* = 120). Study 3 (Youngjohn, Davis, & Wolf, 1997) examined the profiles of men and women (I, *n* = 12; II, *n* = 18; III, *n* = 30). Study 4 (Lees-Haley, 1997b) examined the profiles of men and women (I, *n* = 230; II, *n* = 262). Study 5 (McGrath, Sweeney, O'Malley, & Carelton, 1998) examined the profiles of 125 men and women. Study 6 (Hoffman, Scott, Emrick, & Adams, 1999) examined the profiles of men and women (I, *n* = 44; II, *n* = 13; III, *n* = 18). Study 7 (Tsushima & Tsushima, 2001) examined the profiles of 37 men and women. Study 8 (Greiffenstein & Baker, 2001) examined the profiles of 23 men and women. Study 9 (Slesinger, Archer, & Duane, 2002) examined the profiles of 206 men and women.
aWithin normal limits.

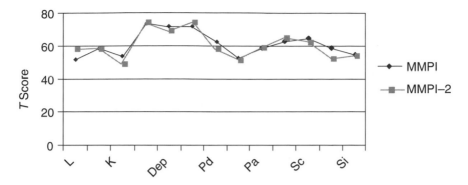

Figure 5.1. Modal profile for chronic pain patients on the Minnesota Multiphasic Personality Inventory (MMPI).

severity of pain or both, there were no such differences found in the MMPI–2 results. Similarly, litigating and compensation-seeking patients also did not differ from appropriate control groups; Figure 5.2 presents MMPI modal chronic pain patient profiles for litigating and nonlitigating patients. However, in small sample sizes ranging from 12 to 30, mildly head-injured patients who were litigating had paradoxically higher mean elevation profiles than severely head-injured nonlitigating patients (Youngjohn, Davis, & Wolf, 1997), and the fake-bad scale did differ among 120 litigating and 208 nonlitigating personal injury patients (Tsushima & Tsushima, 2001).

The commonly observed neurotic profile consisting of variants of the 132' code type was also found in 230 men and 262 women on the MMPI–2. However, scores on Psychasthenia (Pt) and Schizophrenia (Sc) were elevated in men (Lees-Haley, 1997b). This sample differed from that of Keller and Butcher (1991) in that they were all traumatically injured. The mean chronic

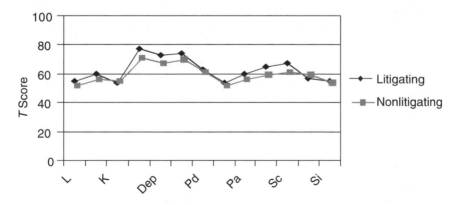

Figure 5.2. Effect of litigating on Minnesota Multiphasic Personality Inventory scores.

pain patient profile among 125 patients on the MMPI–2 was also 312'
(McGrath, Sweeney, O'Malley, & Carelton, 1998). Higher K validity scores
were associated with higher clinical ratings by staff regarding the role of
psychological features in the chronic pain. The 132' profile was also reported
among a group of heterogeneous pain patients (Slesinger, Archer, & Duane,
2002) and among litigating personal injury patients (Tsushima &
Tsushima, 2001).

Malingering among personal injury litigants was detectable among 289
pain patients, particularly through their inconsistent responding (TRIN and
VRIN inconsistency scales), perhaps due to problems with attention (Fox,
Gerson, & Lees-Haley, 1995). Various MMPI–2 scales were significantly
related to the prediction of treatment outcome, depending on the different
outcome measures used (Vendrig et al., 1999), but it is beyond the purpose
of this book to address that material, and the interested reader is referred
to that body of literature.

It is also comforting to know that recent large-scale research using the
MMPI–2 has reaffirmed that the external correlates associated with the 13/
31 code types for the MMPI continue to be essentially the same for the
MMPI–2 (Arbisi, Ben-Porath, & McNulty, 2003; Graham, Ben-Porath, &
McNulty, 1999). Thus, the interpretive statements generated for those code
types stem from replicated empirical findings.

Profile Interpretation

Patients with elevated scores on Hypochondriasis (Hs) are described
as bitter, whining, complaining, and pessimistic, with shifting and chronic
multiple physical complaints. They overreact to actual physical problems,
are very egocentric and selfish, and tend to defeat medical interventions or
at least are recalcitrant and refractory to care. They also resist psychological
explanations of their symptoms. Patients with elevations on Depression
(Dep) have descriptors that vary by scale elevation. T scores over 75 indicate
the vegetative signs of depression, and such patients would probably meet
the criteria for major depression, assuming valid profiles. At ranges T 65 to
74, patients have been described as retiring, dysphoric, shy, and remote; as
feeling inferior and inadequate and hopeless and helpless; as possibly having
problems with concentration, sleep, and energy; and as possibly having
physical complaints. Patients with clinical elevations on Hysteria (Hy) have
been described as using denial and repression as major defenses; they are
psychologically naive, uninsightful, flirtatious, gregarious, exhibitionistic,
demanding, and seductive and tend to decompensate into physical complaints when psychically stressed. The addition of elevated scores on Schizophrenia (Sc) often implies a psychiatric diagnosis along with a chronic
pain disorder.

In summary, studies using modal profile types or cluster analysis have been fairly consistent with each other, although there have been some differences. Most studies find some chronic pain patients whose MMPI profiles are normal. These patients seem to be coping well with their pain and do not have problematic psychological reactions to their pain or its treatment. Most studies find a group with a Conversion V profile, suggesting an underlying personality structure characterized by denial and repression as major defenses, along with depression and hypochondriacal reactions and foci. Some of these patients may be channeling emotional problems into somatic reactions, though it may be a reaction to living with pain rather than a cause of it (Vendrig, 2000).

Most studies find a group with an elevated neurotic triad, which is usually associated with greater functional disturbance, more severe pain intensity, and poor response to various types of interventions (Keller & Butcher, 1991). Finally, many studies, depending on the sample type, find a profile of chronic pain patients with a coexisting psychiatric disorder, which severely complicates treatment and intervention. Cluster analysis studies further document many relevant extratest behavioral correlates (e.g., degree of disability, number of prior surgeries, reports of pain intensity, depression, coping skills, treatment outcome; Love & Peck, 1987). Litigation is a strong mediating variable on MMPI (and probably other psychological test) scores (Fow et al., 2002; Rohling, Binder, & Langhinrichsen-Rohling, 1995). Litigating patients tend to score higher on the neurotic triad by ½ standard deviation (i.e., 5 T scores; see Table 5.2).

One problem with the modal profile approach is that it obscures possibly meaningful differences within a heterogeneous population. It is even possible (however improbable) that no patient in the sample has the modal profile. Researchers rarely report the percentages of patients with the modal profile. In fact, they rarely report content scale or Harris–Lingoes subscale information (Keller & Butcher, 1991). Also, although variants of the 132' profile seem to characterize the low back pain patient population, this configuration is not specific to low back pain and is observed in patients with chronic headaches (Franz, Paul, Bautz, Choroba, & Hildebrandt, 1986) and a number of other medical conditions (Keller & Butcher, 1991; Naliboff & Cohen, 1983). For these reasons, researchers have more recently used multivariate techniques, especially cluster and topological analysis, to discern more definitive subgroup types. The next sections discuss these studies.

Cluster Analysis

Rather than assess pain patients using aggregate modal profiles, cluster analysis is used to find common prototypes among a pain population that is considered to be heterogeneous. Several studies have used cluster analysis with groups of either men or women chronic pain patients (Armentrout, Moore, Parker, Hewett, & Feltz, 1982; Atkinson, Ingram, Kremer, & Saccuzzo, 1986; Bernstein & Garbin, 1983; Bradley, Hopson, & Ven der Heide, 1984; Bradley, Prokop, Margolis, & Gentry, 1978; Costello, Hulsey, Schoenfeld, & Ramamurthy, 1987; Guck, Meilman, Skultety, & Poloni, 1988; R. Hart, 1984; McGill, Lawlis, Selby, Mooney, & McCoy, 1983; Prokop, Bradley, Margolis, & Gentry, 1980) and with mixed samples of men and women patients (Adams, Heilbronn, & Blumer, 1986; Leavitt & Garron, 1982; Rosen, Grubman, Bevins, & Frymoyer, 1987). These studies have reported the following MMPI profile types:

- within normal limits profile,
- 132' (Hypochondriasis, Hysteria, and Depression) code type,
- 13' Conversion V code type, and
- 218 or 2183 (Depression, Hypochondriasis, Schizophrenia, and Hysteria) code type.

Psychologists should consult the many MMPI interpretive guidebooks for additional details on the psychological characteristics of these patients.

Rorschach Assessment

The Rorschach has rarely been used with chronic pain patients in published studies. Leavitt and Garron (1982) issued a report based on 131 chronic low back pain patients. Sixty of these patients had definitive organic findings, whereas 71 did not and were labeled "nonorganic." The patients with organic low back pain produced significantly lower F+%, suggesting tension and constraint; a lower SUM C, suggesting suppressed emotions; and higher F%, suggesting defensiveness and good reality testing.

CLOSED HEAD INJURY

As with other potentially actionable and compensable injuries, the clinical evaluation of closed head injury cases must take into account the effects of pending litigation on symptom report and expression. Binder and Willis (1991) found that patients with financially compensable minor head trauma performed more poorly on a forced-choice recognition memory procedure than did patients with brain dysfunction who were not applying for financial compensation. A meta-analysis of 18 studies and more than 2,500 cases concluded that clinicians should consider the effects of secondary gain and litigation, especially in cases of mild head injury where there is little or no abnormality in posttraumatic level of consciousness and normal results from brain neuroimaging. In this review, there was a moderate effect size

(.47) for patients with more reports of abnormality and symptoms of disability and in patients with financial incentives (Binder & Rohling, 1996).

Next, the clinician needs to evaluate the premorbid functioning and status of the patient to determine the extent and severity of postinjury symptoms and functioning. Greiffenstein and Baker (2001) reported on 23 patients with mild cranial or cervical injuries who were alleging major personality changes resulting from their injuries. These authors were able to obtain premorbid MMPI profiles for these claims from outpatient mental health clinics, inpatient or outpatient medical or surgical programs, or previous court contacts. It is interesting that only one of the 23 claimants had a higher postinjury MMPI–2 mean profile. Postinjury MMPI–2 profiles were characterized by increased defensiveness and decreased reports of antisocial behaviors and a decrease in behaviors resulting from hypomania. The mean preinjury code type was 3128+, suggesting substantial pre-injury psychopathology. The postinjury MMPI–2 profile was also a 3128+ code type. Few had the classic Conversion V profile premorbidly, suggesting significant somatization aspects to their personality. The postinjury decrease in psychopathology was interpreted as suggesting that the claimants may have been trying to minimize past problems in the context of their pending litigation.

This study, though small in sample size and without a relevant control group, is provocative and has both clinical and legal implications. Clinically, it suggests that examiners probably need to explore for premorbid psychopathology indirectly by examining for risk factors that often accompany psychopathology. These might include early parental separation, family psychopathology and especially psychopathy, unstable school and work histories, and work-related problems such as excessive sick leave or frequent job changes. Legally, it suggests that an MMPI–2 profile is likely to reflect premorbid personality traits and behaviors. Often psychologists lack a relevant premorbid standard to which to compare postinjury results. This study may provide a step toward meeting that lack (Greiffenstein & Baker, 2001).

Mild head trauma is considered a self-limiting event with only transitory and even negligible symptoms. The posttraumatic or postconcussion syndrome may include headache, difficulty in concentration, dizziness, memory impairment, emotional lability, anxiety, and hypochondriacal complaints. However, a person's psychological response to injury may include a persistence of these symptoms and disability. This emotional response can complicate recovery. In mild cases, MMPI–2 scales are sensitive to exaggeration and fabrication of symptoms (Berry et al., 1995), especially in the context of litigation (Hoffman et al., 1999; Youngjohn et al., 1997).

Table 5.5 presents the results of MMPI–2 studies for head-injured claimants with mild injuries. The mean profile is a 21387 code type, reflecting substantial somatization, anxiety, and cognitive psychological symptoms. In fact, there is general consistency across studies reflecting mean clinical

TABLE 5.5

Minnesota Multiphasic Personality Inventory—2
Studies on Patients With Closed Head Injuries and Other Trauma

Scale	Study 1		Study 2			Study 3		Study 4				Study 5	Study 6
	I	II	I	II	III	Men	Women	I	II	III	IV		
L	59	56	57	60	58	57	57	56	57	54	54	—	58
F	52	66	60	59	63	65	59	57	57	65	58	—	63
K	53	46	49	47	48	48	51	48	51	44	47	—	53
Hs	64	74	52	66	75	72	67	58	65	71	75	72	81
Dep	64	73	61	63	78	73	68	59	71	78	71	69	76
Hy	64	74	52	63	77	72	70	57	68	72	78	72	84
Pd	54	59	59	56	62	59	57	59	64	62	56	58	61
Mf	—	—	47	50	51	48	54	49	50	46	48	50	52
Pa	51	59	57	60	67	64	59	54	67	62	60	59	62
Pt	57	70	57	62	74	69	62	57	71	71	69	62	68
Sc	60	71	56	68	74	69	62	60	66	69	68	64	72
Ma	53	53	51	67	55	52	50	58	50	55	54	53	53
Si	50	60	55	54	56	57	53	53	57	59	56	53	54
Code	'123	1328+	a	81'2	2317	2137	321'	a	231'	3127	3127	132'	3128

Note. Dashes indicate no data for that scale on variable. Study 1 (Berry et al., 1995) examined the profiles of men and women with closed head injuries (I, n = 31; II, n = 30). Study 2 (Youngjohn, Davis, & Wolf, 1997) examined the profiles of men and women with closed head injuries (I, n = 12; II, n = 18; III, n = 30). Study 3 (Lees-Haley, 1997b) examined the profiles of 230 men and 262 women with miscellaneous traumas. Study 4 (Hoffman, Scott, Emrick, & Adams, 1999) examined the profiles of men and women with closed head injuries (I, n = 44; II, n = 13; III, n = 18; IV, n = 37). Study 5 (Tsushima & Tsushima, 2001) examined the profiles of 120 subjects with closed head trauma. Study 6 (Greiffenstein & Baker, 2001).
[a]Within normal limits.

elevations in these scales, although elevations and order of scale appearance in the code type vary. These patients also had higher scores on the Health Concerns content scale (Youngjohn et al., 1997). This finding is consistent with a previous literature review of 29 studies with brain-damaged psychiatric patients, which found that the Schizophrenia (Sc) scale, despite some inconsistencies, was the best indicator for separating brain-damaged from non-brain-damaged psychiatric patients. Low scores on Sc suggest an absence of psychiatric complications associated with the brain damage (Buchholz, 1984).

Of course, in cases of closed head injury, cognitive (intellectual) and neuropsychological tests are usually given as part of the test battery. The role of these tests in the evaluation process is outside the scope of this book.

Use of the MCMI

The MCMI was normed essentially on psychiatric patients or with patients who were in the process of being evaluated or treated in mental health settings. It was not designed for use with nonclinical (i.e., normal) populations, nor was it intended for general use with medical patients. In fact, the Millon Behavioral Medicine Diagnostic (MBMD; Millon, Antoni, Millon, Meagher, & Grossman, 2001) was developed for use with patients in medical settings. Although the MBMD was developed from the same biopsychosocial theory as the other Millon instruments (Millon, 1997), it was normed on medical patients and not on psychiatric patients. Hence, its use in medical settings may be more legitimate. The test has personality style scales (called "coping styles" on the MBMD) that correspond to Millon's theory, but it also has scales that assess negative habits (i.e., alcohol use, drug use, overeating, excessive caffeine intake, inactivity, and smoking), scales for possible psychiatric indications (i.e., anxiety, depression, cognitive dysfunction, emotional lability, and guardedness), scales that assess stress moderators (i.e., illness apprehension, functional deficits, pain sensitivity, social isolation, future pessimism, and spiritual absence), and scales that assess for treatment outcome prediction (i.e., intervention fragility, medication abuse, information discomfort, utilization excess, and problematic compliance). Finally, there are two scales that address problems that may call for behavioral interventions, termed "management guides" (i.e., adjustment difficulties and psych referral). The MBMD could be fruitfully applied in settings that assess for personal injury and deserves further consideration.

The MCMI has been used with medical patients, despite Millon's cautions to the contrary. In fact, according to my count, it has been used with about 4,000 medical patients in the published literature. The research use of the MCMI might be justified because the MCMI has scales that are relevant to psychological factors involved with medical disorders, including anxiety (A), depression (Dep, CC), somatoform disorders (H), and complaint tendencies (Z). There are also medical symptoms that might have a psychiatric etiology (e.g., sleep disorders, pain, appetite disturbance) that suggest psychopathology. The MMPI was also developed on psychiatric patients, but research over time has established its utility with medical patients and with nonclinical groups.

Reasons for Using the MCMI in Medical Settings

Psychological researchers have not been blind to the issues of using the MCMI in a medical setting. They often go to some length to justify the selection of this instrument. They cite the following reasons for using the MCMI in medical contexts:

- to psychologically evaluate or assess a specific population,
- to identify patterns or profiles that may characterize a defined medical patient group,
- to assess the psychological adjustment of patients with a defined medical disorder,
- to determine the extent and types of personality disorders that may be associated with a defined medical population,
- to determine psychological factors influencing the choice of medical treatment when various options are available,
- to use test scales deemed relevant to the specific disorder under investigation, and
- to replicate previous findings.

These reasons appear legitimate in a research environment. However, the most valid reason for using the MCMI in a medical setting may be to evaluate the extent and severity of personality disorders within this population, because there is considerable literature suggesting that psychiatric disorders are prevalent in medical populations. Other reasons to use the MCMI in a medical setting may include to explore whether expressed symptoms are a manifestation of psychopathology and to evaluate clinical syndromes using the syndromal scales.

The MCMI has been used with many different types of medical patients and with patients undergoing a variety of procedures and conditions, including amputation (M. Marshall, Helmes, & Deathe, 1992), breast cancer (Malec, Wolberg, Romsaas, Trump, & Tanner, 1988), head and neck cancer (Baile, Gibertini, Scott, & Endicott, 1993), testicular cancer (Malec, Romsaas, & Trump, 1985), choreoacanthocytosis (Medalia, Merriam, & Sandberg, 1989), chronic fatigue syndrome (C. Millon et al., 1989), chronic pain (M. Marshall et al., 1992; Papciak & Feurerstein, 1991), coronary artery disease and coronary bypass surgery (Chandarana, Cooper, Goldbach,

Coles, & Vesely, 1988), gastric stapling (Chandarana, Conlon, Holliday, Deslippe, & Field, 1990; Guisado et al., 2002), headache (Jay, Grove, & Grove, 1987), head injury (Tuoko, Vernon-Wilkinson, & Robinson, 1991), keratoconus (Mannis, Morrison, Holland, & Krachmer, 1987), lumbar laminectomy (Herron, Turner, & Weiner, 1986), magnesium toxicity (Barrington, Angle, Willcockson, Padula, & Korn, 1998), menstrual irregularities (Parry, Ehlers, Mostofi, & Phillips, 1996), neck sprain injury (Borchgrevink, Stiles, Borchgrevink, & Lereins, 1997), morbid obesity (Chandarana, Holliday, Conlon, & Deslippe, 1988), psoriasis (Rubino, Sornino, Pezzarossa, Ciani, & Bassi, 1995), psychosomatic symptoms (Organista & Miranda, 1991), sleep disorders (Dagan, Sela, Omer, Haller, & Dar, 1996), tinnitus (Briner, Risey, Guth, & Norris, 1990), and workers' compensation claimants (Boone et al., 1995; Repko & Cooper, 1985; J. R. Snibbe, Peterson, & Sosner, 1980).

The data show that except for patients with psoriasis, patients with medical disorders usually score within the normal range on both the MCMI–I and MCMI–II. (The psoriasis sample was Italian and used the Italian translation of the MCMI for purposes of this research, and there are no data indicating comparability between the English and Italian versions of the MCMI.)

Given these findings, it is incumbent on the investigator to provide an explicit argument for why the MCMI was chosen as the assessment instrument when evaluating medically related complaints. The most appropriate reason to use this instrument would be to evaluate the extent and severity of personality disorders within a defined population. A second legitimate reason might also be to determine if any scales might predict treatment outcome. The psychologist would have to provide a logical argument in advance as to why the particular scales are relevant to the assessment.

The Anxiety (A) and Dysthymia (D) scales are often elevated in the MCMI results of patients with a variety of medical disorders. (It should also be mentioned that research studies that did not report base rate [BR] scores for the entire test often did report BR scores for scales A and D that were clinically elevated or mentioned that scores on these scales were often elevated in clinically significant ranges.) The BR scores from the published studies suggest that reports of anxiety and depression from these patients were generally of mild to moderate intensity. The diagnostic and forensic question is whether these signs of psychological distress are the result of the medical disorder or are causally or instrumentally related to its development.

The Somatoform Disorder scale (H) would potentially be relevant for patients with medical disorders, especially those with chronic pain. BRs of greater than 74 on this scale would suggest that patients are not coping very well with their disorder, are making others around them miserable with their constant whining and complaining (as an unconscious means to cope with a primary childhood injury, according to psychoanalytic theory), and tend to be nonresponsive to medical interventions. Of the several published data sets for H with medical patients, only two report mean BR scores in the 70s, and no study reports mean BR scores greater than 74. In fact, most medical patients score around BR 60 on this test, which is the average score for all patients who took the test in the standardization sample. There are two possible interpretations for these findings: that medical patients in these studies were not somaticizing, at least with any greater frequency than other patients, or that the scale's sensitivity—the ability to detect a condition on the test if the patient has the problem—is poor. Although the MCMI manuals (Millon, 1983, 1987, 1994a) report good sensitivity values for H, the studies reported here do not describe the methodology well enough to evaluate the validity of this scale.

Treatment Outcome

Sometimes the forensic evaluation requires the psychologist to make a prediction or recommendation as to the likelihood of restoration of function, return to work, or continuing disability. The treatment outcome literature with the MCMI and medical patients is small enough to be addressed here. The treatment outcome literature with medical patients using the MMPI and MMPI–2 is too vast, and interested readers should consult the many literature reviews on this topic (Adams et al., 1981; Keller & Butcher, 1991; Love & Peck, 1987; Murray, 1982; Vendrig, 2000).

A few studies report that MCMI scores are lower in the expected direction following medical intervention. Selected MCMI scales predicted good outcome following lumbar laminectomy using the criteria of return to work, relief from pain, and use of analgesic medications (Uomoto, Turner, & Herron, 1988). Morbidly obese patients experienced significant reductions in MCMI scales Schizotypal (S) and Thought Disorder (SS) following gastric stapling (Chandarana et al., 1988), and there was significant improvement in Anxiety (A), Dysthymia (D), and Somatoform Disorder (H) at follow-up (Chandarana et al., 1990). Significant reductions in schizotypy and thought disorder would not be expected or predicted from any theory used in health psychology or related research. The most logical explanation of these findings is that they are a statistical artifact and not veridical. However, these findings await replication.

On the other hand, premorbid personality characteristics did not predict recovery from accident-induced neck sprain (Borchgrevnik et al., 1997) or recovery from disc disease (Herron et al., 1986). The data are too meager and the findings have not been replicated, and thus psychologists cannot offer any generalizations as to the predictive validity of the MCMI with medical patients. In fact, some of the studies in this literature are of dubious quality and have not been replicated.

TABLE 5.6

Minnesota Multiphasic Personality Inventory Studies on Patients Applying
for Disability Based on Emotional or Psychological Factors

Scale	Study 1	Study 2	Study 3
L	50	50	56
F	74	66	63
K	54	46	47
Hs	77	68	73
Dep	87	80	72
Hy	79	70	72
Pd	73	71	58
Mf	67	58	52
Pa	78	70	69
Pt	81	70	65
Sc	90	74	65
Ma	67	58	53
Si	63	61	56
Code	8273+	2846+	1236

Note. Study 1 (J. R. Snibbe, Peterson, & Sosner, 1980) examined 11 subjects. Study 2 (Repko & Cooper, 1985) examined 43 subjects. Study 3 (Gandolfo, 1995) examined 47 subjects using the MMPI–2.

With respect to issues of psychopathology in medical patients, some constructs in health psychology, such as those measured by scales assessing the impact of illness, quality of life measures, and various coping behavior inventories, emanate from theoretical concepts in clinical psychology and psychiatry and may not be the most appropriate fit for medical patients. In fact, coping styles in medical patients might easily be misconstrued as personality disordered behavior and appear as such on tests like the MCMI. This may be more the fault of the administrator of the instrument than of the instrument itself. Psychologists need to avoid transposing mental health models to medical populations.

Table 5.6 presents MMPI studies of patients applying for disability based on emotional factors, and Table 5.7 presents MCMI BR scores for patients applying for workers' compensation. The MMPI data suggest that these patients report substantial psychic distress or depression, or both, as well as cognitive dysfunction (Scale 8). Scales 1, 2, 3, 6, and 8, in various code types, are often elevated with emotional disability clients (Hersch & Alexander, 1990), in contrast to modal MMPI characteristics with personal injury litigants without emotional disability complaints. The available MCMI data show that medical patients, as a group, score in normal ranges on this test, and there would be no reason to believe otherwise, given the uniformity in the published research. Workers' compensation claimants also score in the normal range on the MCMI scales, except for the Anxiety scale, which, understandably, is moderately elevated. Continued research

TABLE 5.7

Millon Clinical Multiaxial Inventory Base Rate Scores for Workers' Compensation Claims

| Scale | Study 1 | | | | | Study 2 | | | Study 3 |
	Head injury	Psychological	Low back	Total	Orthopedic pain	Psychological	Total		Study 3
Schizoid	56	54	47	50	51	57	53	55
Avoidant	73	63	55	58	49	63	28	55
Dependent	73	65	60	68	59	57	59	61
Histrionic	48	54	63	50	56	46	52	52
Narcissistic	48	43	57	50	65	51	58	60
Antisocial	56	56	55	56	61	57	58	58
Compulsive	57	57	50	57	60	59	60	64
Passive-Aggressive	63	60	60	62	56	68	59	62
Schizotypal	65	64	60	64	49	51	49	48
Borderline	75	79	65	71	64	65	64	64
Paranoid	70	65	65	69	64	58	60	62
Anxiety	82	86	95	83	83	89	86	87
Somatoform	60	68	60	68	75	67	71	72
Bipolar	37	37	57	42	49	35	41	38
Dysthymic	76	85	77	79	71	83	77	80
Alcohol	65	62	75	66	53	56	53	54
Drug	58	57	62	59	57	51	52	53
Thought Disorder	62	57	53	57	52	57	53	56
Major Depression	60	58	56	56	50	59	53	57
Delusional Disorder	58	54	55	55	62	57	59	63

Note. Study 1 (J. R. Snibbe, Peterson, & Sosner, 1980) examined the profiles of 23 head injury, 11 psychological, and 6 low back pain patients and a total claimant sample of 50. Study 2 (Repko & Cooper, 1985) examined the profiles of 43 orthopedic pain and 43 psychological claimants and of a total claimant sample of 100. Study 3 (Boone et al., 1995) examined the profiles of 135 claimants.

with the MCMI in medical settings may eventually yield important information that would warrant the use of this instrument in such settings. To date, this promise remains unfulfilled.

POSTTRAUMATIC STRESS DISORDER

The majority of forensic psychologists advise against giving PTSD symptom checklists to patients, because these lists can suggest to the litigant what symptoms to report in subsequent evaluations, depositions, and testimony as part of their clinical picture. Rather, it is advised to give tests, like the MMPI–2 or the MCMI–III, that have scales that assess for PTSD. In clinical interviews, it is also recommended that the psychologist ask indirect rather than direct questions to assess for PTSD symptoms. For example, instead of asking, "Since the accident, have you had nightmares?" ask, instead, "Tell me what your dreams have been like over the past several months."

MMPI Assessment

Watson (1990) identified 12 different techniques to assess PTSD, including psychological tests and scales, rating scales, questionnaires, and structured interviews. However, the MMPI has been the instrument most frequently used to assess for PTSD, and a substantial amount of research has been devoted to the psychological profiling of patients exposed to major trauma (Wise, 1996). This literature is too vast to be discussed here. However, MMPI scores for patients applying for disability based on emotional and psychological factors are presented in Table 5.6. Although scores of articles have been published on MMPI scale scores with claimants alleging PTSD, the bulk of this research is related to war trauma and combat stress associated with Vietnam (Penk et al., 1988).

There are two main ways to look for PTSD on the MMPI. The first way is to explore for common profile types using the average or modal code type approach. The second is to develop supplemental scales to assess for PTSD. With respect to the first method, the literature has often reported that PTSD combat-stressed veterans often attain MMPI profiles in the high range but usually have elevation scales on Schizophrenia and Depression (82'/82+'codes; Penk et al., 1988; Wilson & Walker, 1990; Wise, 1996). However, because there are so many comorbidities associated with PTSD among combat veterans (Penk et al., 1989), it is too simplistic to assume that most patients will attain the 82' code type in the absence of other clinically elevated scales. The data seem to suggest the following (confusing) conclusions:

- If a patient alleges PTSD and achieves an 82' code type, the test results may be consistent with a PTSD diagnosis.
- If the patient's two highest scales have the 82 configuration in a high-ranging code type, then the patient may have PTSD with comorbidity.
- If the patient has an 82' code type, which has been associated with neurological disorders, especially epilepsy, such disorders should be ruled out.

Another way to assess for PTSD on the MMPI is to develop special scales derived from the MMPI item pool. Two such scales have achieved prominence in this regard—the Pk (posttraumatic stress disorder—Keane) scale (Keane, Malloy, & Fairbank, 1984) and the Ps (posttraumatic stress disorder—Schlenger) scale (Schlenger & Kulka, 1987). Pk is a 46-item scale derived from the scores of 100 male combat veterans in VA psychiatric clinics with and without PTSD. The major content theme of this scale is general distress. The scale has average sensitivity levels of 70% to 75% and is equally effective across racially diverse groups. Ps is a 60-item scale developed by contrasting emotionally healthy Vietnam-era veterans with PTSD veterans without comorbidities. Its major theme is also general distress.

These two scales have many items in common and hence are highly correlated (in the .90s). Perhaps because Pk is shorter and has a more substantial literature base, it has become the more commonly scored PTSD scale. The following conclusions are warranted:

- Because both Pk and Ps share much first-factor variance (variously called "general distress," "lack of ego resiliency," or "psychopathology"), low scores on Pk or Ps are not expected in most clinical patients.
- These scales are often elevated when the patient is in distress, regardless of whether the patient has been traumatized.
- To the extent that elevated scores on the Pk and Ps scales are also associated with the 82' code (or its variations), this adds possible incremental validity to the possibility of a PTSD diagnosis.

Most relevant is the finding that Pk is also elevated in civilian trauma (Gaston, Brunet, Koszycki, & Bradwejn, 1996; Koretsky & Peck, 1990; McCaffrey, Kirkling, & Marrazo, 1989; Noblitt, 1995; Perrin, Van Hasselt, & Hersen, 1997; Scheibe, Bagby, Miller, & Dorian, 2001) and hence is not restricted to men or to combat-related PTSD.

MCMI Assessment

There is a substantial MCMI-based literature on the assessment of PTSD (Craig, 1997; Hyer, Brandsma, & Boyd, 1997). As with the MMPI, this literature pertains almost exclusively to men with Vietnam-era combat stress. There have been no MCMI-based studies related to civilian trauma. The BR scores for all MCMI studies pertaining to PTSD appear in Craig (1997). This and additional data indicate that combat-traumatized men consistently attain group profiles with elevated scores on Passive-Aggressive (Negativistic) and Avoidant (8A2 code type). Cluster studies also replicate this profile, among a few others, as the prototype PTSD code type.

Personality traits associated with this style indicate that the patient's personality style is negativistic, erratically emotional, quarrelsome, demanding, oppositional, disruptive, petulant, disputatious, and argumentative at one moment and apologetic, contrite, and withdrawn at the next moment (Craig, 1993b). Again, although some researchers have concluded that the 8A2 code type is a "traumatogenic profile" and is unique to PTSD patients, the code type also appears in many other populations and is not specific to PTSD (Craig, 1995). However, a study by Craig and Olson (1997) among 32 substance-abusing patients with PTSD reported that, compared with 228 substance abusers without PTSD, the modal code type of the PTSD sample was not 8A2, but rather 16A (schizoid and antisocial). The schizoid component was interpreted not as problems in forming and maintaining relationships, but rather as a manifestation of social withdrawal, loner behavior, privateness, and emotional constriction.

The MCMI–III has a new 16-item scale (R) that assesses for PTSD. Its item content pertains to flashbacks, intrusive thoughts, nightmares, insomnia, moodiness, feelings of terror, absence of pleasure, depression, and prior suicide attempts. The MCMI–III manual (Millon, 1994a) reports that R has a sensitivity level (the ability to detect the disorder if it is present) of only .37 and a specificity level (the ability to rule out the disorder if it is not present) of .84. Craig and Olson (1997) found that the PTSD scale successfully differentiated between PTSD and non-PTSD groups and was the best predictor of PTSD in a multiple regression equation. In addition, the scale's sensitivity was above that provided by chance alone and even higher than the values reported in the test manual (i.e., .68), whereas its specificity (.83) was consistent with the values in the scale's standardization sample. As with the Pk scale, R on the MCMI–III is associated with a moderate degree of first-factor variance (general maladjustment; Craig & Bivens, 1998); hence, caution is needed when interpreting this scale because the scale's elevation could reflect general distress and not trauma-related symptoms. This scale deserves further research and should be evaluated with civilian trauma.

Malingering, or the production, exaggeration, or falsification of symptoms for personal gain, is a potential problem in forensic assessment. Because there are often substantial monetary rewards associated with malingering among litigants, the forensic psychologist must be vigilant to ensure that the patient's report of symptoms is an honest portrayal of his or her current functional status. Structured interviews for detecting malingering are available (R. Rogers, 1987), and the MMPI–2 has shown good ability to detect malingering (Baer & Miller, 2002; Baer, Wetter, & Berry, 1992; Lewis, Simcox, & Berry, 2002), especially the F validity scale and the Infrequent Psychopathology (Fp) scale. Also, the Structured Inventory of Malingered Symptomatology (SIMS; R. Rogers, Bagby, & Dickens, 1992) has shown good ability to detect malingering (G. P. Smith & Burger, 1997). The SIMS is a 75-item questionnaire with five scales—Low Intelligence, Affective Disorders, Neurological Impairment, Psychosis, and Amnesia.

In summary, this chapter addressed personal injury assessments and discussed workers' compensation programs, presented data on the psychological experience of pain with an emphasis on orthopedic pain, then presented MMPI and MMPI–2 studies with chronic pain patients. Also discussed were Rorschach and MCMI assessment of medical and pain patients and, briefly, the treatment outcome literature with pain patients. The assessment of PTSD with the MMPI and MCMI was also included.

I conclude this chapter by presenting, in detail, a case example of personal injury litigation and assessment from the perspective of both the litigant's psychologist and the defense psychologist. This case provides an example of how similar data can be interpreted differently and can help prepare psychologists for possible cross-examination and rebuttal based on the "opposition's" testimony. The case involves a personal injury litigant who invoked psychological trauma following an industrial accident. Raw score test data appear in Exhibit 5.1.

CASE STUDY

Background

The litigant was a 49-year-old, divorced, White man with 11 years of education who had been unemployed since he reported experiencing an industrial accident about three years ago following exposure to sulfur dioxide. He was referred for a psychological evaluation by the defense, who represented the company, to determine whether he had PTSD and depression, as claimed, or whether he was malingering.

EXHIBIT 5.1
Litigant's MMPI–2 Scores

TRIN	F50		Ma	49		WRK	76
VRIN	F57		Si	85		TRT	56
F(b)	100		ANX	72		MAC–R	R22 (T53)
L	R10 (T78)		FRS	87		APS	44
F	R22 (T104)		OBS	59		AAS	R2 (T46)
K	R15 (T49)		HEA	101		PK	82
Hs	105		BIZ	84		OH	62
Dep	95		ANG	56		A	68
Hy	96		CYN	52		R	78
Pd	67		ASP	44		Es	30
Mf	50		TPA	56		Do	41
Pa	85		LSE	57		Re	50
Pt	85		SOD	86		Ps	89
Sc	91		FAM	55			

He was divorced from his second wife and had two teenage children. His wife had left him for another man. He lived alone. He was in the U.S. Army for a regular two-year tour of duty, during which he drove a truck. He was in combat for 10 months, where he was injured in an accident and shipped stateside. He had driven a truck his entire career. He received a 100% VA disability pension and had received workers' compensation in the past.

There were several depositions given in this case (the file was eight inches thick), including the litigant's. On reviewing this voluminous material, the psychologist noted a discrepancy in the litigant's testimony about the amount of time he was exposed to the irritant. In one record, he testified that he was exposed for 30 to 40 minutes; in another record, he testified that he was exposed for 3 to 4 hours. When he was asked again, he said, "I can't remember." (It was probable that his attorney had noticed the discrepancy in the litigant's testimony and had instructed him to claim memory problems when asked this question again.)

Because the company had permission from the Environmental Protection Agency to periodically release sulfur dioxide into the air, the company kept close records of the amount, dates, and times of release and produced documents attesting to the fact that on the day of the litigant's exposure, sulfur dioxide was released for two minutes. These records were monitored and verified by the Environmental Protection Agency.

Following the exposure, the litigant alleged breathing difficulties, dizziness, light-headedness, disorientation (when the defense psychologist later asked him to explain the meaning of this symptom, the litigant said he did not become disoriented), and a taste of sulfur in his mouth; his face began to hurt, and his sinuses bothered him. He said that he frequently vomited or experienced dry heaves, had rubbery legs, felt cold and shivered, and had swollen eyes. He went to a physician, he said, who released him as "able to return to work" and prescribed Motrin. He alleged that his symptoms subsequently intensified, and he was hospitalized at a VA hospital, where he stayed for 31 days.

He said he had heart damage and a "valve that is messed up" and that he had reduced oxygen in his lungs, further adding to his "heart problems." He said his liver was enlarged because of the poisoning. He had shrapnel in his leg from his war injury and said that his leg hurt all the time since the accident. He thought he had three herniated discs in his back, so he could no longer bend, stoop, or lift. He said that riding, sitting, walking, or standing hurt. His hands, arms, and legs would "go numb." He underwent physical therapy and used hot packs on his back. He complained of a constant ringing in his ears. He developed jaundice, and it was later discovered that he had pulmonary fibrosis of disputed etiology.

He had had a stomach operation at the VA hospital. He claimed that the operation was necessitated by the exposure to sulfur dioxide, but the defense produced medical testimony from credible witnesses that his alleged symptoms and subsequent diagnosis could not have been due to this chemical, especially with such a brief exposure. Following the presentation of the evidence, the litigant changed his claim from a medical trauma to a psychological trauma, alleging PTSD and depression.

Records from the VA hospital indicated that he was in treatment for those conditions and received antidepressants and counseling from a mental health worker. He further alleged that he sought treatment for these conditions voluntarily and not on the advice of his attorney.

Behavioral Observations

During the testing, the litigant was very polite and thoughtful in answering the questions. He seemed even deliberate, perhaps thinking ahead to possible questions at a later deposition. A test that should have taken him about 1½ hours to complete (MMPI–2) took 4 hours. He seemed to be concentrating and thoughtfully answering the questions. He tried to present an appearance of honesty and morality combined with distress over what had happened to his life following the accident. He was quite pleasant, and later he and the psychologist talked about hunting and fishing and the patient was able to recall pleasant associations with these activities.

Mental Status Examination

Litigant's Psychologist

The patient was a well-developed, somewhat heavy man, casually but adequately dressed and groomed. He was appropriately and quite talkative; rapport was easily established. He appeared to be trying diligently on the test items. The results were reliable and valid.

His affect was constricted, and his mood was consistently dysphoric. He was oriented in all spheres. There was no evidence of hallucinations, delusions, or paranoia. His thought content and organization were somewhat impoverished but not confused. All mental functions, including fund of information, judgment, abstract reasoning, ability to perform calculations, and attention and concentration, were somewhat depressed. All memory functions, including immediate, recent, and remote, were also depressed (these findings were obtained from Wechsler Adult Intelligence System [WAIS] testing [Wechsler, 1997]).

Defense Psychologist

The litigant did not seem depressed during the interview. His mood seemed good. He was appropriately dressed and had good hygiene. He did not appear tense. In fact, he seemed rather relaxed. He showed no unusual mannerisms. His speech was articulate, logical, coherent, and relevant to directed associations. His hearing appeared unimpaired. He was able to concentrate well enough to take the test without assistance, to focus on the examiner's questions, and to read the newspaper during test breaks. No delusions or hallucinations were noted. He was not suicidal or homicidal. There was no reported violence in his history. He seemed to be a mild-mannered individual. His affect was appropriate and without evidence of sadness. His capacity to relate in a normal manner was intact. He was able to carry on a conversation without distraction. He did complain of some memory problems and was unable to answer some questions, alleging that he could not remember. He reported feelings of distrust and suspiciousness, which again were not observed during the evaluation. The psychologist concluded that there were no psychiatric symptoms seen during the clinical interview.

Patient Self-Report

To Litigant's Psychologist

The litigant claimed he was nervous all the time. Children screaming and large crowds made him nervous. He felt all worn out after long trips. He would get irritable but not violent. He said his memory and concentration were poor and getting worse. He was depressed all the time and had suicidal thoughts but had not tried suicide because he did not want to go to hell. He had difficulty going to sleep and slept about two hours a night. He was up and down all night. Pain, worry, and aggravation kept him from sleeping well. He did not feel rested in the morning. His appetite was better some days than others, but it was usually not good. He cried at times. He felt useless and worthless because of the shape he was in. He had heard someone talking to him when no one was there, and he would see things that were not there at times. He was not delusional, but he was paranoid. He took prescribed Effexor (muscle relaxant), trazodone (for sleep), and Naprosyn and Ultram (for pain). He did not drink or use drugs.

He spent most of the time watching TV and sleeping. He had no hobbies currently. He used to hunt and fish but no longer had the stamina to do these activities. He visited only his mother and one friend. He did not get many visitors. He belonged to no clubs but did go to church. He did not really want to see anyone, because he was anxious around people.

After returning from Vietnam, he had PTSD symptoms for about six months, then they stopped. As long as he was working, he had no symptoms. Now that he was disabled, his PTSD symptoms had returned. He said that screaming children reminded him of when he was in Vietnam. When he heard an explosion, he would try to get under his car, and his mother told him that he would run through the house at night in a rage. If she tried to get near him in this condition he would hit her, so she would not wake him. He said that he did not have these symptoms anymore until the sulfur dioxide exposure and that now they had returned.

On the day of the exposure, he was delivering chemicals to a chemical plant out of state. He unloaded his cargo and was doing paperwork in his truck when a man came out and told him that there was a sulfur dioxide leak. The man testified, "He states [after being told] he couldn't breathe through his nose and all his wind was shut off. . . . He needed to get water and medical attention." He felt he was going to die. He hurt all over. The "guys at the shop" made fun of him because he asked for an ambulance. The plant safety officer told him he did not need a doctor.

He then called a taxi and went to the emergency room, where he was given Motrin and nasal spray. The following weekend his symptoms intensified. He then "checked himself into a VA hospital," where "he was told he could have died."

To Defense Psychologist

The patient said that his mental health symptoms followed his industrial accident. He alleged depression, exemplified by a poor appetite (although he was substantially overweight), variable sleep, reduced energy, loss of interest, mild suicidal ideation, difficulties in concentration (although he was able to concentrate during the entire evaluation), and thought content primarily focused on the accident. He said his mother and sister did his housekeeping and cooking. He drove short distances to go to church or to see friends. He watched TV occasionally but said he spent most of his time dwelling on the accident. He said he was sexually active before the accident but no longer felt any desire for intimate relations. When the defense psychologist explained that the normal reaction to exposure to noxious chemicals—for example, ammonia—would have been to "get out of there," the litigant was unable to provide a satisfactory explanation as to why he sat in his truck and continued to be exposed to sulfur dioxide. Thus, the litigant reported symptoms of major depression, but none of these symptoms were observed during the defense psychologist's exam.

The litigant also reported symptoms of PTSD. He alleged flashbacks of the accident scene. However, the defense psychologist concluded these were not true flashbacks, but rather visual images upon voluntary recall, as opposed to involuntary images expressed in consciousness. The litigant said he had nightmares about the accident in which he felt he was about to die and then woke up in a cold sweat gasping for air.

He said he had not spoken to anyone about these matters, except his mother, sister, and brother. He had not told his pastor or his children or friends (and they did not appear in any of his mental health records). When asked why he did not tell his counselor or doctor about these matters, he said that he did not want them to think he was crazy. The defense psychologist concluded that this was not evidence of psychic numbing.

The patient did report diminished activities and some restricted range of affect, but the defense psychologist concluded that this was part of his personality prior to the accident. He said he avoided people and was basically a loner. (His occupational choice as a long-distance truck driver is consistent with this conclusion as well.) He reported difficulty staying asleep because of nightmares and recurrent and distressing thoughts surrounding the accident. He denied feeling symptomatic when seeing large semitrailers, which might, in theory, have triggered PTSD symptoms in some people. He was able to recall almost all aspects of the reported trauma except for the length of exposure.

Startle response, survivor guilt, and foreshortened future, also possible PTSD symptoms, were not relevant in this case. The symptoms of PTSD that he reported that could not be explained by other aspects of his personality, then, were nightmares, recurrent thoughts of the trauma, and diminished interest in social participation.

He further claimed visual and auditory hallucinations. Specifically, he alleged hearing what appeared to be vague voices, or, more specifically, a voice that he could not make out but that he thought was a voice. There was no content to this voice; he said it was occasionally "around." He also alleged seeing some type of movement in his house, which he thought was an image. It was indistinct and occasionally there. He said he worried about these things, but they did not disturb him, and he was not frightened by them. The defense psychologist concluded that these were not hallucinations, but rather voluntary products of an imagination–perceptual disturbance that was misattributed to hallucinations.

During the review of symptoms, the defense psychologist periodically interspersed incongruous and impossible symptoms, testing for possible malingering. For the most part, the litigant endorsed having these symptoms. For example, when asked whether he had pain that started in his lower neck and radiated to the midway point of his left ear and then stopped (having been told that this is a classic symptom of sulfur dioxide exposure), he replied, "Yes, I have that." When asked if his neck often had red spots and whether he had skin eruptions, ear tingling, and excessive warmth in the toes on the right side of his foot, he replied yes to all of these symptoms. When asked if he had painful calluses or whether his toes often became red, again he said yes.

Test Results

Both psychologists independently administered the Minnesota Multiphasic Personality Inventory—2 and the Millon Clinical Multiaxial Inventory—III.

Findings by Litigant's Psychologist

Strong self-deprecating judgments and feelings of inadequacy play a central role in his major depression. He exhibits a cluster of symptoms that not only fit his characterological structure but also may be an intrinsic and enduring part of his psychological makeup. Feelings of emptiness, deep self-doubts, diminished energy, guilt preoccupations, and a pessimistic and hopeless outlook on the future play an integral role in his everyday life. Unfortunately, he appears to tolerate this decreased functioning. He feels aggrieved and mistreated. He seems to habitually create conditions that foster his misfortunes, as if suffering were preferable to moments of good fortune.

Variable in mood and action, he is depressed and has a clinical anxiety disorder. He is indecisive, distractible, restless, and edgy and has signs of muscle weakness, headaches, and fatigue. He is unsure of himself and views the world as undermining his security. He may vent these feelings on the people he depends on. His traumatic experience precipitated intense fear, which resembled the fear of losing his life in the war. So he seeks to avoid such recollections. Where they cannot be avoided are in his dreams and nightmares, during which he becomes terrified.

Findings by Defense Psychologist

Both psychological tests demonstrated a pattern of symptom exaggeration consistent with his endorsement of impossible symptoms in the clinical interview. The MMPI–2 demonstrates consistent responding rather than random responding. Both tests also suggest symptoms associated with an anxiety disorder and a depressive disorder that are probably seen by the patient as incapacitating. He is generally passive and withdrawn, feels inadequate, and lives a life filled with anxiety, despite a generally calm and relaxed demeanor. Those who know him best would probably describe him as whining, demanding, complaining, fretful, and dissatisfied. He has a defeatist attitude toward treatment and resists psychological explanations of his symptoms and behavior. He has many personality features associated with his status as a chronic pain patient.

Diagnoses

The litigant's psychologist gave the following diagnoses: Axis I: Major Depression, recurrent, severe; Generalized Anxiety Disorder; and Posttraumatic Stress Disorder. The defense psychologist gave the following diagnoses: Generalized Anxiety Disorder; Major Depression, recurrent, moderate; and Malingering.

Conclusions

By Litigant's Psychologist

The litigant has severe anxiety, depression, and emotional conditions consistent with symptoms of chronic pain syndrome and PTSD. His accident exacerbated his Vietnam combat experiences, resulting in near panic. These combinations have resulted in his being unable to work. His prognosis is guarded. He is capable of managing his own funds.

By Defense Psychologist

The litigant meets the criteria for anxiety and depressive disorders and shows a pattern of personality traits often seen in chronic pain patients. The source of these problems are unclear, but it appears that most of them coincided with his lung disorder and operation at the VA medical center, after which he seems to have become dysfunctional and disabled. His reactions to the sulfur dioxide release seem exaggerated and lack authenticity.

In Vietnam he was never in combat, and his fear of death from sulfur dioxide also seems problematic and nonpersuasive.

Outcome

Following the testimony by the defense psychologist, the case was settled out of court.

6

HARASSMENT

Psychologists are increasingly being called on to assess allegations of sexual harassment as it applies to litigation for damages (Bureau of National Affairs, 1994). This assessment often includes a psychological evaluation of the litigant. The claims typically occur against large corporations and seek substantial damages, so there is likely to be a vigorous defense against these claims. This chapter discusses the legal definition of sexual harassment and the employer's responsibility to provide a safe working environment for its employees. I will provide examples of sexually harassing behaviors in the workplace under the law and discuss the role of the psychologist in sexual harassment cases, along with common assessment tools for this purpose. Case examples are provided for both sexual and nonsexual harassment behaviors.

DEFINITION

Sexual harassment is now widely recognized as a form of employment discrimination that is prohibited by civil rights laws. Public scandals, such as the Navy Tailhook incident and the Clarence Thomas–Anita Hill hearings, brought sexual harassment allegations to the forefront of public consciousness. The Equal Employment Opportunity Commission (EEOC) has determined that sexual harassment is a form of sex discrimination and is prohibited by Title VII of the Civil Rights Act of 1964, which prohibits discrimination in employment on the basis of race, sex, or other specific factors. The EEOC defined sexual harassment as "unwelcomed sexual advances, requests for sexual favors, and other verbal or physical conduct of a sexual nature" when (a) submission to such conduct is made either explicitly or implicitly a term or condition of an individual's employment, (b) submission to or rejection of such conduct by an individual is "used as the basis for employment decisions affecting such individuals," or (c) such conduct "has the purpose or effect of unreasonably interfering with an individual's work performance or creating an intimidating, hostile or offensive working environment" (EEOC, 1987).

Most legal definitions are vague enough to require subsequent case law to determine their legal meaning and boundaries. Courts have ruled that the harassment must be sufficiently severe or pervasive to affect the conditions of a person's employment and thereby create an abusive working environment. The psychologist's role in this process is usually to determine if the alleged harassment has occurred and if the alleged psychological injury resulted from the harassment.

The EEOC definition has two elements. First, it contains a quid pro quo element (*Meritor Savings Bank v. Vinson*, 1986). In this situation, there is either an explicit or implicit understanding that the person would not be promoted or given a raise or would be demoted or terminated unless sexual favors were granted. For example, a woman's claim that she was not hired because she refused the sexual advances of a selecting official who allegedly implied that such behavior would lead to a job falls under the quid pro quo definition of the EEOC guidelines. A single episode of a threat to fire an employee unless he or she agrees to provide sexual favors is sufficient to establish quid pro quo harassment.

The second part of the definition pertains to a hostile working environment and usually requires a pattern of behavior over time. A single incident is usually not sufficient to establish a hostile working environment. This is by far the most often-used part of the definition in claims. It is the most difficult to define and the most difficult to prove. Examples include sexual propositions, the repeated telling of dirty jokes, and visual displays that produce psychological distress in the worker. Employers who allow subordinates to continue these practices are also legally culpable.

The courts have struggled and debated whether or not some specific result is required for the behavior to be actionable. Some courts require that the litigant have been fired or denied a promotion or that the behavior have had some other impact on employment opportunities, and not merely social or personal consequences, before the suit can go forward. Some courts have ruled that even if one employee objects to a certain behavior that is not considered objectionable by other employees in the same "class," if this behavior is serious enough to affect that employee's work performance, then it can fall under the rubric of a hostile work environment.

An example of the type of behavior that causes a hostile working environment was brought to my attention by an employee who was not my supervisee, but who worked in a program under which I had authority and control. The setting was an inpatient mental health ward, and a female employee complained that male patients were openly reading *Playboy* magazines on the ward and leaving them on tables and bookshelves in open view, and she found this offensive (the other female employees on the unit found it amusing and not offensive). She demanded that I order the patients not to have these magazines on the unit, citing the EEOC guidelines and implying a threat of litigation if I did not comply with her demand. Of course, the patients strongly objected to this assertion and wanted to continue this behavior unchanged. I believed that the complaint fell within the provisions of the EEOC guidelines concerning a hostile work environment and that I was responsible for correcting this situation. I ordered that patients not bring these magazines into public areas but allowed them to retain them in their bedrooms, and so everyone was satisfied.

The quid pro quo and hostile work environment specifications are theoretically distinct claims. Nevertheless, the lines between them are blurred, and these two forms of harassment often occur together.

EMPLOYER RESPONSIBILITIES

In applying the general principles of Title VII, an employer or organization is responsible for the behavior of its employees and of its agents and supervisory employees concerning sexual harassment. This is true whether or not the specific acts were authorized or even forbidden by the employer and regardless whether the employer knew or should have known of their occurrence. This is referred to as the *constructive knowledge* standard. Concerning conduct between fellow employees (not between supervisors and employees), the employer is responsible for acts of sexual harassment in the workplace when the employer knows or should have known about such conduct, unless it can be proved that the employer took immediate and appropriate action to correct the situation. An employer may also be responsible for nonemployees with respect to sexual harassment in the workplace when the employer knew or should have known about the conduct and failed to take immediate and appropriate corrective action. Finally, when employment opportunities or other benefits have accrued because of a person's submission to the employer's advances and requests for sexual favors, the employer may be held liable for unlawful sexual discrimination against other persons who were qualified but who were denied that employment opportunity or benefit.

The two aspects of the definition of employer responsibility deal with *welcomeness* and the *reasonable person standard*. Concerning welcomeness, if the plaintiff does not object to the behavior or does not subjectively view the work environment as abusive, and if the conduct has not actually altered the conditions of employment, then no violation has occurred under the law. The reasonable person standard adds case law clarification to the definition. In *Harris v. Forklift Systems, Inc.* (1993), the courts ruled that (a) the behavior must be viewed through the eyes of a "reasonable person" and (b) the perspective of the plaintiff must be considered. The reasonable person standard is important, because what may be obnoxious and offensive to one person may be deemed a serious assault on the work environment by another person and merely a sign of immaturity by a third person. In evaluating the perspective of the plaintiff, the psychologist should explore, in detail, the characteristics of the event and the plaintiff's preincident mental state.

EXAMPLES OF HARASSMENT BEHAVIORS

The courts have not defined clear-cut standards of behavior that would always be a violation. The critical factor seems to be whether the employee's participation in sexual activity was voluntary or involuntary. Sexually related conduct becomes sexual harassment when the sexual behavior affects a term, condition, or privilege of employment and is so severe that it alters the conditions of the claimant's employment or creates an abusive work environment. Regarding the hostile work environment provision, the courts have required more than a single incident before finding a violation. The courts require that the action have been repeated and severe. Interestingly, the courts have not ruled that sexual orientation is protected under the law, but many courts have found same-sex harassment to be a violation under Title VII of the 1964 Civil Rights Act.

To harass one does not have to engage in the more obvious forms of sexual behavior, such as hugging, kissing, patting, stroking, or rubbing oneself sexually against a person or even more blatant attempts at sexual acts. Examples of harassment can be verbal and nonverbal. Exhibit 6.1 lists behaviors that come under the provisions of sexual harassment. Many of these behaviors seem quite innocuous, and others are clearly out of bounds. The issue of welcomeness is a strong determinant of whether or not these behaviors fall under the definition of harassment. In determining whether or not an individual act or a constellation of behaviors constitutes harassment, the court will look at the record as a whole and on a case-by-case basis.

EXHIBIT 6.1
Examples of Sexually Harassing Behaviors

Massaging another person's neck or shoulders
Asking personal questions about the person's social or sexual life
Touching the person's clothing, hair, or body, especially in a provocative manner
Hanging around the person
Giving personal gifts
Habitually discussing sexual topics
Habitually putting one's hand on the person's shoulder when talking
Calling the person "babe," "girl," "doll," "honey," "dear," or "hunk"
Prolonged staring or looking up and down at the person (i.e., "elevator eyes")
Telling lies or spreading rumors about the person's sex life
Repeatedly asking out the person after he or she expresses a lack of interest
Making sexual gestures with the hands or body movements
Following the person
Making sexual comments about the person's body
Blocking the person's path with one's body
Making various facial expressions, such as winking, licking one's lips, or throwing kisses
Whistling and making catcalls
Telling sexual jokes or stories
Making any sexual comments or innuendos
Promising preferential treatment in return for sex
Threatening to affect the person's employment status or future opportunities unless sexual favors are granted

Damages that may be awarded to an employee include reinstatement, immediate or retroactive promotion, restoration of withheld pay increases, back pay (possibly with interest), changes in performance ratings, reassignment, and training. The compensatory damages, in addition to actual damages, often make this area a source of litigation: Claimants may be paid for future emotional pain and suffering, mental anguish, loss of enjoyment of life, inconvenience, and future pecuniary or nonpecuniary losses. The employer's total number of employees determines the amount of the award during 20 or more calendar weeks in the current or preceding calendar year. The maximum amount, for employers with more than 500 employees, is $300,000 per complainant. Each member in the class action suit would be entitled to pursue an award of up to this amount. Punitive damages are in addition to actual and compensatory damage awards and can be pursued if it can be proved that the employer engaged in discriminating practices with malice and indifference.

SEXUAL HARASSMENT EXAMINATIONS

The psychologist may be called on in these cases to determine (a) whether the plaintiff has been damaged, (b) the extent of the psychological damage, (c) any current psychiatric diagnosis, (d) the prognosis, (e) whether the psychological damage was sustained as a result of the sexual harassment, (f) whether or not treatment will aid the process of recovery, and (g) whether the plaintiff is able to return to work. When interviewing plaintiffs in sexual harassment cases, the psychologist needs to get an exact description of the behavior in as much detail as possible (Rosman & McDonald, 1999). There is a strong investigative role to this process, and the psychologist functions very much as a detective. The plaintiff's predisposing psychological factors, such as history and functioning, need to be established. The psychologist has to determine the person's functioning at all levels before, during, and after the incidents. The psychologist must determine the impact of the trauma on the person's life.

I also recommend that psychologists explore any signs of childhood sexual abuse history. This is critically important, because many plaintiffs have a history of being sexually abused as a child. They may be acutely aware and still traumatized from these early experiences and may possibly misperceive behavior as sexualized when it is not. That is not to say that victims of childhood sexual abuse are never sexually harassed as adults. It is important to determine the facts of the case in all its elements, and the well-reported history of repetition compulsion among still-traumatized victims of childhood sexual abuse needs to be realized. The psychologist also has to evaluate for the presence of personality disorders and personality traits that may evoke sexual taunting, comments, or abuse. For example, people with histrionic personality disorder tend to be seductive, exhibitionistic, and provocative, and this is often outside their consciousness.

Certain psychiatric diagnoses most frequently appear among sexual harassment plaintiffs. The mood disorders of dysthymia, major depression, and bipolar disorders are most frequent. The anxiety disorders of posttraumatic stress disorder (PTSD), generalized anxiety disorder, and panic disorder are most frequent. Among personality disorders, the antisocial, borderline, dependent, and histrionic disorders are most frequent. Adjustment disorders, nonschizophrenic psychosis, and malingering are also quite frequent. Among psychologists testifying for the plaintiff, the most common diagnosis given is PTSD; among psychologists testifying for the defense, malingering is the most common diagnosis. Except for malingering, if one were to take a random sample of any psychiatric population, these diagnoses would be the most frequently appearing psychiatric diagnoses for that population, too (B. I. Long, 1994).

Omnibus objective personality measures, such as the Minnesota Multiphasic Personality Inventory—2 (MMPI–2; Butcher, Dahlstrom, Graham, Tellegen, & Kaemmer, 1989) or the Personality Assessment Inventory (Morey, 1991), are good tests that sample an array of symptoms and behaviors, and these measures have been used extensively in emotional injury cases (Boccaccini & Brodsky, 1999). If more nonclinical measures are required, one can use the 16 Personality Factor Questionnaire (Russell, Karol, Cattell, Cattell, & Cattell, 1994), the California Psychological Inventory (Gough, 1996), the Neuroticism, Extroversion, Openness to Experience Personality Inventory—Revised (Costa & McCrae, 1992), or the Millon Index of Personality Styles (Millon, Weiss, Millon, & Davis, 1994). The Rorschach (1942) may also be used as a general projective measure of personality. If personality disorders are an issue, the Millon Clinical Multiaxial Inventory (Millon, 1994a) or perhaps the Structured Clinical Interview for DSM Disorders (Spitzer, Williams, Gibbon, & First, 1994), in combination, are good choices. If one needs a specific symptom measure, there are several that are quite acceptable, such as the Trauma Symptom Inventory (Briere, 2004) and the Post Traumatic Diagnostic Scale for PTSD (Foa, 2003). Instruments such as the Beck Anxiety Inventory (Beck & Steen, 1993a), the Beck Depression Inventory (Beck & Steen, 1993b), or the Hamilton Depression Inventory are not recommended because of their susceptibility to malingering due to their obvious item content. If the psychologist suspects malingering, there are also several good assessment instruments to choose from, such as the Malingering Probability Scale and the Structured Interview of Reported Symptoms (Rogers, Bagby, & Dickens, 1992).

Psychologists are human and may succumb to the seemingly sincere descriptions of the plaintiff. Among psychologists who are employed by the plaintiff, the dangers include the assumption of the validity of what is claimed and a tendency to overidentify with the claimant. For psychologists who are employed by the defense, the danger is to assume malingering and dishonesty, and when the allegations are determined to be true, the danger is to believe that the plaintiff is exaggerating. The psychologist's job is to determine the validity of the sexual harassment claim and the validity of the claim of psychological damage.

People can and do exaggerate, especially when there is potential for financial reward (Feldman-Schorrig, 1996). They can appear convincing but still be lying. The motivation of the plaintiff should always be considered. Why has he or she filed a claim? out of revenge? for financial gain? as a displacement over some other issue? (Goodman-Delahunty & Foote, 1995). The psychologist needs to determine whether the plaintiff has some mental disorder that would lead him or her to be more hypersensitive than a "reasonable person" (Harris v. Forklift Systems, Inc., 1993; Reynolds & Kobak, 1995). Psychologists have to do a complete history and to examine the role of the events in the plaintiff's life. They need to determine the facts of the length and severity of the alleged harassment and to solicit clear evidence that this behavior was unwelcomed by the plaintiff and that he or she took steps to stop the behavior.

The essential procedure is to evaluate the plaintiff's "preclaim personality," the specific incidents that occurred, the plaintiff's behavior associated with the incidents, the nature of the harassment, whether psychological injury has occurred, and what damage resulted from the behavior. It should be the attorney's responsibility to determine the facts of the case, but the psychologist should not assume that this has been adequately done. The psychologist must try and find out what other claims have been filed against the employer before, what the litigant knows about sexual harassment law, what influence the litigant's attorney had in filing the suit, and whether the litigant was in psychotherapy after the incident and what influence the therapist had on the claim. The psychologist should not assume that just because the person went into psychotherapy, there has been psychological injury. Lawyers will instruct litigants to see a counselor to establish their subsequent claim, and some may even instruct their client (unethically) to lie to the counselor.

It is a good idea to review as much collateral material as possible. The psychologist should prepare a detailed chronology of the events and cross-check this with collateral data and evidence. Reported symptoms should be checked against the historical record; there will be affidavits and depositions from both the litigant and witnesses.

The psychologist must find out the nature of the incidents and the psychological state of the claimant before, during, and after the incidents. Are the reported symptoms consistent with the alleged diagnosis? Does objective and projective psychological testing agree with the reported symptoms and diagnosis? Would these symptoms result in temporary or permanent damage? Particularly important is to learn if the report of symptoms has changed over time across multiple depositions. Such changes can be especially relevant in PTSD cases, because claimants learn the symptoms of the diagnosis in the course of evaluation, especially when symptoms appear on objective (and transparent) PTSD checklists, and report them back to the psychologist. As in any diagnosis, the psychologist evaluates consistency across all materials—clinical history, collateral material, psychological testing, and personal observations, along with clinical interviews.

The following are examples of defenses that might be used to support the idea that there was no sexual harassment; the psychologist will have to explore the individual defense with the litigant as part of the evaluation:

- The allegation is a lie or misrepresentation. (Part of the investigation is to determine the truthfulness of the evaluation.)
- The incidents may have happened, but both parties consented. (One critical issue here is the question of consent. If the employee felt intimidated, then the "consent" may not have been voluntary. In *Meritor Savings Bank v. Vinson* (1986), the court

ruled that the question was not whether the sexual conduct was voluntary, but whether it was unwelcomed.)

- The complaint is invalid because the complainant did not object when employees other than the alleged harasser engaged in the same behavior. (This may or may not be a relevant defense for the court. Because the law states that unwelcomeness is a critical part of the law, the fact that the employee professed a dislike for the behavior may be sufficient enough notification that the behavior was offensive and hence compensable.)

- The complainant and alleged harasser had a prior relationship during which the complainant never said a word to the harasser that he or she found the behavior unwelcomed. (Here the credibility of both parties is at issue. The psychologist must determine whether or not the alleged harasser had some reason to believe that the advances would be welcomed and whether or not the victim clearly communicated that the behavior was no longer welcomed.)

- The incidents did occur, but the employer cannot be held responsible for it because the employer took immediate corrective action to stop it. (The court might not automatically judge the action sufficiently strong enough to stop the behavior.)

- No one else was offended. (Here the reasonable person standard would be invoked. Psychologists might ask themselves whether they would be offended by the behavior and whether they would permit this behavior to occur with their partner, spouse, brother, or sister.)

- A person should expect this sort of thing if working in a place like this. (The fact that an employee chooses to work in a particular environment does not abrogate the right to work in an environment free from sexual harassment.)

- The way he or she was dressed, he or she was just asking for it. (Sexually provocative speech or dress of a complainant is relevant in determining whether or not the litigant found the advances unwelcomed. Even so, the complaint may be valid and moved forward based on other facts of the case.)

- The employer would have done something about it but didn't know that anything was going on. (The EEOC guidelines hold the employer responsible for a hostile work environment when the employer should have known that sexual misconduct was occurring.)

- It only happened once. (The issue is the nature and severity of occurrence. For example, a single incident of an offensive remark does not constitute a hostile working environment, whereas a single incident of rape is unlawful. The EEOC presumes that a single episode of touching intimate body parts is sufficiently offensive to be a violation.)

OTHER TYPES OF HARASSMENT

This chapter has focused on sexual harassment, but there are other bases for filing workers' compensation claims based on harassment. Claims may be filed for a variety of job-related stress problems, and it is more difficult to assess the credibility of purely stress-related claims than for claims made on other bases. Gandolfo (1995) presented MMPI–2 data on 47 claimants who filed harassment charges for such allegations as excessive criticism, threats to job or physical harm, or discriminative practices, and for 82 claimants without harassment charges. Those alleging harassment scored higher on Paranoia (Pa), suggesting oversensitivity, anger and resentment, rationalization and externalization of blame, and undue suspicion. The real question is this: Do employees with underlying paranoid traits or personalities file more harassment claims, or does workplace harassment (or perceived maltreatment) result in elevated scores on Pa?

One type of nonsexual harassment case involves alleged racial harassment. For example, a psychologist received a referral from an attorney representing a Fortune 500 company being sued for harassment. The complainant, a White man, alleged that Black men at work were harassing him. He said that he complained to his supervisor about this, but "he did nothing about it." One day at lunchtime in the parking lot, the complainant got into a fight with one of the Black male employees, and both were fired. The complainant filed a reverse discrimination suit and alleged racial harassment.

His private psychologist had assessed the litigant psychologically, and the referring attorney asked an independent psychologist to review the psychological report. The independent psychologist read the report and had access to the raw test scores, and she advised the attorney that the private psychologist had accurately interpreted the test results but had included material in the report that did not emanate from the test results. She suggested that the material may have come from their private therapy sessions, but reiterated that it did not come from the psychological testing. The referring attorney then obtained a court order from the judge mandating that the litigant have another psychological evaluation and hired this independent psychologist.

The psychologist attempted to get as much information as possible about the case from the referring attorney, who seemed pleasant and engaging and willing to discuss the case—at least from his perspective. The psychologist asked what the referral questions were and was told to determine whether the litigant was lying and whether he had any personality disorder, especially a narcissistic disorder.

Although it was not explicitly stated, the psychologist suspected that although the initial referral question (i.e., lying) might be relevant in this case, it appeared probable that the attorney was on a fishing expedition, hoping that the psychologist would find something to help his case. She further suspected that the hunt for a narcissistic personality disorder was part of this fishing expedition and that the attorney sought such evidence to reduce any subsequent judgment.

There is a principle in law termed *contributory negligence*. For example, a person is running late and decides to take a shortcut home by hopping over a fence, which is the most direct route. However, the electric company owns this property. There are clearly posted signs on the fence reading "Warning! Keep Out! High Voltage!" But the person disregards this warning and hops the fence. While cutting across the electrical company's yard, the person steps on an exposed wire and receives a severe electric shock. He recovers, but with residual and permanent damage, and then sues the electric company for negligence in leaving the charged wire exposed.

One might reason that no damages should be awarded, because the injured party violated private property and sufficient warnings of the danger were in public view. However, the law says otherwise. Despite these postings and warnings, the electric company should not have had a live wire exposed for possible injuries.

The litigant sues for $1 million, and the jury finds the company at fault. However, there was a contributing fact here—the litigant violated private property, and there were sufficient warnings of the danger. So the jury might say there was contributing negligence of, say, 30%. This means that the company is 70% at fault and the injured party is 30% at fault. Hence, the final award is not $1 million, but rather $700,000.

The psychologist suspected that the attorney was looking for some quality in the litigant that might reduce any future judgment as a contributing factor. The attorney probably would argue to the jury at the penalty phase of the trial that the litigant had certain personality traits that evoked the behavior in others, which was the cause of the discrimination and harassment.

The second, independent evaluation essentially corroborated the conclusions of the initial psychologist and, hence, favored the litigant more than the defense. The psychologist's report said that the patient did not have a narcissistic personality, but rather was obsessive. Subsequently, the psychologist was called for a "taping," which she assumed to be a deposition. Upon arriving at the attorney's office, she was asked to listen to a tape of the litigant, who described harassing his former girlfriend by breaking into her basement-level apartment and leaving her notes professing his love, and calling her repeatedly begging for a reconciliation. The attorney asked the psychologist what she thought about this behavior. The psychologist replied that it verified the conclusion of the obsessive personality of the litigant. Tests do not reveal the nature of the obsession—one may be obsessed with winning the Nobel Prize or with winning back a girlfriend— but the complainant's behavior was consistent with the final evaluation. When the attorney was asked what this had to do with the harassment and discrimination case, he replied "Nothing," but that he was looking for a way of introducing this into testimony. This answer seemed to confirm the psychologist's original suspicions.

This case illustrates two important points. First, harassment cases need not pertain only to sexual harassment if the harassing behavior falls within the laws, statutes, and regulations governing harassment in general, and second, attorneys may not always tell the psychologist about their defense, lest they prejudice the evaluation.

CASE EXAMPLE

The plaintiff was a computer technician at a large technology firm. She had had excellent performance evaluations during the time she had worked for the company. When the director of her department resigned, the department was reorganized and restructured, which created a new supervisory position.

One evening another director was working late and found the plaintiff working late also. He invited her out to dinner, which she accepted. At dinner, the director encouraged her to apply for this new supervisory position, and the following morning he sent her flowers at her work station, along with a note thanking her for their "special evening." The next day he called her at work and asked her out to dinner. This time, she declined the invitation. Later that day, he offered her a ride home, which she also refused. That night he called her at home and asked her for a date, which she also refused.

She heard no more from him for a time, and she formally applied for the supervisory position. She began to receive notes from him at her desk and frequent calls at home. She continued to refuse to date him. Finally, he called her into his office, saying that he had been impressed by her work and viewed her as a strong candidate for promotion. However, this new position would require travel to out-of-town locations, and he questioned whether or not the plaintiff could handle the requirements of travel, because she had had no experience he could use in making this determination. He told her that he needed to go out of town on work-related business and suggested that she accompany him so that he could observe her away from the office. He also reminded her that such experience would be helpful and might strengthen her position to get the new job. She declined, and the position was subsequently awarded to another computer technician. The plaintiff then filed a sexual harassment charge against the director.

This case falls within the guidelines and parameters of sexual harassment laws and is an example of quid pro quo. The director was clearly told "no" on several occasions, and the case does not provide evidence that the director offered other applicants the opportunity to observe the nature of their work and behavior outside of the work setting.

Forensic psychologists may receive an increase in referrals from attorneys seeking damages for psychological trauma related to sexual harassment or from attorneys defending such suits. In accepting such referrals, forensic psychologists necessarily agree to thoroughly investigate these claims, as well as the claimant's pre-claim personality.

7

SEXUAL OFFENDERS

Consider the following case: The patient was a 47-year-old, divorced, White man who lived alone. His divorce became final three months before the evaluation. He had been married once before, which also ended in divorce. He said his first wife was on drugs, and he could not live like that. He presented himself as having high spiritual beliefs and showed the examiner a cross that he carried in his pocket.

He was housed in a residential program for molesting his daughter for one year. This activity consisted of fondling her breasts, vagina, and buttocks. He would kiss her, and she would masturbate him. He alleged, "Never intercourse." His wife caught him in bed with his daughter in a sexual act and turned him in to the police. He said, "I have not spent time in jail, might not have gone to jail, and they might go easy on me because of my suicide attempts, according to my lawyer." He was currently charged with felony child molestation and had a restraining order preventing him from contact with any of his minor children or his ex-wife.

He reported having molested other girls. He admitted to having sexual relations with his niece when she was age 9. He also admitted to having been arrested and convicted of child solicitation after attempting to pick up some young girls at their school.

He had attempted suicide twice in the previous seven months. His first attempt involved a medication overdose, and in the second attempt, two months previously, he put the barrel of a .22 rifle in his mouth and pulled the trigger. He was hospitalized for days and saw a psychologist and a psychiatrist. He was placed on Paxil and trazodone.

He had a long history of emotional abuse by his mother from age 3 to 11. She would ridicule him for wetting the bed and would hang his sheets out the window in the morning for the children to see on their way to school. He would then be teased and picked on at school. He began cross-dressing at age 13, wearing his mother's and sister's clothing without their knowledge and masturbating wearing their panties. He stated that he still liked to wear urinated pants. He said the urge came to him and occasionally he urinated on himself until he got cold, and then he would get turned off. He said this was erotic to him. He reported having serious back injuries and surgical repair, including a spinal implant to block the pain, and he said this caused erectile dysfunction. Later, however, he said he was able to achieve an erection with his daughter and to ejaculate on her stomach. He said that he was unable to achieve an erection or ejaculation with his ex-wife, and this was a source of distress in their marriage. When he tried to shoot himself, he was wearing women's underpants, and he ejaculated when he was shot.

The evaluating psychologist gave the following diagnoses:

- I Pedophilia, nonexclusive type
- Transvestic Fetishism
- Urophilia
- Sexual abuse of a child
- II Antisocial Personality Disorder
- III status/post (s/p) back surgeries with implant stimulator
- IV Problems with primary support group (family separation, divorce, sexual abuse of daughter)
- Occupational problems (job loss)
- Economic problems (hospital and legal bills)
- Problems related to interaction with the legal system (arrested and charged with felony child molestation)
- V Global Assessment Functioning (GAF): 35 (current)

Now consider the following statistics. In the United States, there are about 120,000 substantiated cases of child sexual abuse each year. Ten percent of these victims are under 4 years of age; 36% are age 12 or older. Girls represent 77% of all sexual abuse victims and boys, 23%. Sixty-five percent of all sexual abuse victims are White; 77% of the perpetrators are parents, and 11% are other relatives of the victims. Only 2% of the perpetrators are people in other caretaking roles for the child victim, and the other 10% are strangers (National Clearinghouse on Child Abuse and Neglect Information, 2002).

About 60% of sexual offenders were on probation or parole at the time of their most recent attempt. The typical sexual offender who molests unfamiliar victims molests an average of 117 children, most of whom do not report the offense. About 90% of the victims know their perpetrators. About 71% of child sexual offenders are under the age of 35, about 80% have normal intelligence scores, and about 59% gain access to their victims through seduction or excitement (National Clearinghouse on Child Abuse and Neglect Information, 2002).

Children often fail to disclose sexual abuse out of fear that the disclosure will result in consequences that are worse than revictimization, including fear of consequences for the perpetrator (often their father). Child victims are embarrassed to answer questions about sexual abuse allegations; they feel guilty and feel that something is wrong with them and that the abuse is their fault. They may feel anger toward the nonabusing parent for not protecting them, and many deny that any abuse took place. Particularly young victims may be unable to articulate abuse and may not recognize the behavior as sexual abuse.

Victims of child abuse tend to have later problems with interpersonal relations and with trusting other people, have feelings of guilt, and may experience delayed-onset posttraumatic stress disorder and various anxiety and depressive disorders. The abuse can profoundly affect later attitudes toward self, sexuality, and trusting relationships.

About 500,000 rapes and sexual assaults occur each year in the United States. About 67% of rape victims are under the age of 18. Twenty-nine percent of female victims report that the offender was a stranger. About 81% of rape victims are White, 18% Black, and 1% from other races. Women living in poverty are twice as likely to be raped as women with higher incomes. One in four African American women and one in five White women report having been raped.

Most child abusers are not strangers to the victim. The majority are known by the victim and are usually closely related. Most abusers live conventional, law-abiding lives, except for their occasional aberrant behavior. For the most part they are not mentally ill, and any defects in their functioning occur within the interpersonal realm and not in the cognitive or intellectual domains. In some cases the perpetrators were childhood victims of abuse, neglect, or abandonment. Child molesters are probably different than child rapists. The former try to lure the child into sex acts, reward them for their participation, and then threaten them if they tell anyone about it. The latter overpower and threaten to kill their victims and use force to achieve submission, and their victims succumb to save their lives.

Most rapes are not reported to the authorities, and most rapists commit multiple rapes before apprehension. Women view rape not as a sexual experience, but rather as a violent episode. Freudian interpretation of the female psyche focused on the alleged character trait of masochism, which led to beliefs that victims were responsible and provoked the attack by being seductive in word or dress and that they actually enjoyed it. Anachronistic attitudes in men who view women's bodies as men's property or only as a source of pleasure also feed rapist fantasies.

Rapists have reported that they planned to rape someone, and they rape women who are vulnerable (e.g., alone) rather than women who exhibit any personal characteristic that might encourage them. However, rapists differ in their definitions of who is vulnerable. They usually look for places that are isolated but that draw unsuspecting victims. Rapists threaten to kill their victims and brandish weapons to prove their point. Many use alcohol or drugs before the rape. The act is filled with terror and pain for the victim. Most allegations of rape are true; most false allegations of rape are made by teenagers who are under pressure from parents to explain behavior such as being out all night or getting pregnant.

Most rapists are young and unlikely to be psychotic or mentally defective, but they do show evidence of character pathology and low self-esteem. Motivation for rape involves hostility toward women, and there may be no other motivation. Rapists want to dominate, humiliate, degrade, and defile women.

ISSUES IN THE FORENSIC ASSESSMENT
OF SEXUAL OFFENDERS

The forensic assessment of suspected or known sexual offenders differs in two main ways from the clinical assessment of these same patients in nonforensic settings. First, there are usually legal issues that interact with clinical assessment, including determining danger to the community and risk of recidivism, assisting the courts in determining guilt or innocence, and even helping resolve custody disputes. There are also areas of overlap, such as in determining suitability for treatment or selecting targets of treatment.

Second, in forensic evaluations, the alleged perpetrator is a reluctant participant in the evaluation process. Generally, they deny all allegations and have little motivation to cooperate with the assessment other than to resist, deny, lie, underreport, and act in other ways to convince the psychologist that they are innocent. This type of reaction and defensive demeanor often persist even after they have been adjudicated guilty and have been ordered to participate in treatment programs for sexual offenders as part of their sentencing. They usually see nothing wrong with themselves and spend an inordinate amount of time complaining about the unfairness of the judicial system. Even when they admit to some sexual act, their admission is filled with justifications, rationalizations, and excuses (e.g., "I thought she was older," "She led me on").

This chapter reports on the main personality traits identified in sexual offenders, discusses ways of assessing these offenders, and highlights the major findings from assessment measures. The most common assessment measures for sexual offenders (other than the clinical interview) have been objective tests, primarily the Minnesota Multiphasic Personality Inventory (MMPI), and projective tests, primarily the Rorschach. Secondarily, there is a fairly large literature on the use of phallometric assessment, and there is vigorous interest in a new assessment technique—statement analysis— and I discuss these methods as well.

One problem in the assessment of sexual offenders is that the psychological characteristics that differentiate sexual offenders from other groups may not cause the behavior in question. Some characteristics may be putatively related to a given behavior (e.g., psychopathy), whereas others (e.g., dependency) may be a consequence of the behavior. The value in determining these classes of behaviors is that one may be able to identify them within an individual on demand. It would then be up to the court (and to theory builders) to use this information for their selected purposes.

Data presented in this chapter were derived from either institutionalized sexual offenders or those at other points in the criminal justice system. Little or no information is available about offenders who have not been apprehended or about persons who belong to groups who condone and practice pedophilia. There is no reason to believe that the available data would not be applicable to similar offenders, but this remains a researchable question.

PSYCHOLOGICAL PROFILING

Psychological profiling refers to the identification of a cluster of personality traits that differentiates one criterion group from another and that can be accurately assessed on psychological (personality) tests. The psychological profiling of sexual offenders relies on the assumption that the personalities of sexual offenders differ in degree or kind from those of other offenders and that the personalities of subgroups within the sexually abusing population (e.g., rapists, exhibitionists, voyeurs) are also different from each other (Levin & Stava, 1987). Psychologists may be asked whether there are identifiable personality characteristics or psychological test profiles of sexual abusers according to published scientific research. The next step is to ask whether or not the defendant has those traits or fits that profile.

The legal considerations concerning the admissibility of psychological testimony regarding the profiling of a child sexual abuser based on psychological tests has been reviewed (Peters & Murphy, 1992). Case law can be cited that favors both admitting and excluding such evidence. In *People v. Stoll* (1989), the California State Supreme Court allowed to stand a psychologist's expert testimony that concluded, based on an interpretation of the MMPI and the Millon Clinical Multiaxial Inventory (MCMI), that the defendant had normal personality functioning and showed no evidence of sexual deviancy in the personality profile. In *People v. Ruiz,* 1990, the California Circuit Court of Appeals allowed evidence to be admitted that the defendant was or was not likely to have committed the offense based on psychological testimony about character evidence obtained through psychological testing and interview.

On the other hand, in *Williams v. State* (1983), the defense proposed to call a psychologist as a witness who would testify that based on testing, which included the MMPI, the defendant did not have the character disorders almost always found in child molesters and therefore was statistically unlikely to have committed the offense. The court disallowed the proposal, arguing that such testimony was based on conjecture and not substantive fact. In *State v. Fitzgerald* (1986), a psychologist testified as to the typical traits of pedophiles and concluded that the defendant did not have these traits. The profile was rejected by the court as irrelevant, because it was not generally accepted in the scientific community and would be confusing to the jury.

Many forensic psychologists dispute the value of psychological profiling, and others consider it useful. The court, depending on the jurisdiction, may give such testimony scrutiny as to propriety, relevance, and possible prejudice. The psychologist should consult with an attorney as to the admissibility of anticipated testimony before deposition.

The use of psychological profiling remains controversial (W. L. Marshall, 1999). Conclusions are not definitive. Some authors find replicable MMPI profile types (Kalichman, 1989, 1990) and conclude that MMPI profiles are able to discriminate between child molesters and nonmolesters (Ridenour, Miller, Joy, & Dean, 1997). Others, however, do not, and therefore they argue that the MMPI is of little value in profiling sexual offenders as it applies to guilt or innocence (Duthie & McIvor, 1990; Goeke & Boyer, 1993; Hunter, Childers, Gerald, & Esmaili, 1990; McAnulty, Adams, & Wright, 1994; Valliant & Blasutti, 1992; Vaupel & Goeke, 1994; Yanagida & Ching, 1993). Most argue that empirical research does not substantiate the use of psychological tests to determine guilt or innocence (W. L. Marshall & Hall, 1995; W. D. Murphy & Peters, 1992), and some have concluded that "attempts to identify individuals as likely sexual offenders on the basis of their MMPI profiles are reprehensible. . . . This practice represents a serious misuse of the MMPI and is not supported [in the literature]" (Erickson, Luxenberg, Walbek, & Seely, 1987, p. 569).

Goeke and Boyer (1993) attempted to construct an MMPI-based incest perpetrator scale using the method of group comparisons or empirical criterion keying. However, item shrinkage on cross-validation led them to abandon this effort. Interestingly, the item "I have never been in trouble because of my sexual behavior" was retained in cross-validation, but, in my personal experience, this item has also been endorsed as false by nonsexual offenders. Drug addicts without a history of sexual offenses frequently endorse this item and, upon inquiry, report that they had contracted a sexually transmitted disease. Applicants for access to nuclear power plants have occasionally endorsed this item as well. When asked what kind of trouble they had been in, one said, "My wife doesn't like that I masturbate." Another told me, "My wife caught me cheating." Hence, endorsement of this item does not necessarily indicate that the respondent is a sexual offender.

In conclusion, despite opinions to the contrary, it would be difficult to ignore psychological test results that are commonly seen among sexual offenders, even if those results are not specific to that population. It certainly would call for greater scrutiny using other investigative and assessment tools.

ASSESSMENT OF THE SEXUAL OFFENDER

A comprehensive assessment of the sexual offender generally entails psychological assessment, a clinical interview, review of records (e.g., police reports, victim statements), and in some settings phallometric assessment. The latter is most often conducted in research settings or when evaluating risk of recidivism after a period of incarceration.

The clinical interview of sexual offenders is not substantially different than any other forensic interview. The clinician tries to ascertain what the alleged perpetrator can report about the alleged sexual behavior, but the clinical interview is not a rich source of valid information concerning criminal behavior. The offender usually lies, falsifies, and denies the allegations or, if the evidence is overwhelming, has problems recalling any of the significant details or justifies the behavior ("she led me on," "she looked older than her age," "I didn't know she was underage").

In any event, clinical interviews with sexual offenders should try to ascertain

- basic demographic information;
- childhood history of physical or sexual abuse;

- history of sexual behavior (both consenting and coercive);
- an exploration of fantasies associated with sexual behavior (including fantasies about any sexual behavior, whether or not the person admits to engaging in the behavior);
- history of any paraphilias (e.g., exhibitionism, fetishism, rape, frottage);
- social, employment, and medical history;
- substance abuse history;
- prior psychological or psychiatric treatment; and
- history of involvement with the criminal justice system, including legal charges and convictions.

The psychologist should try and confirm any obtained data with ancillary sources and collateral information.

Psychologists who assess alleged or adjudicated sexual offenders need to keep in check their normal responses to heinous behavior. Reviews of allegations and records are likely to engender strong emotions that could interfere with the needed objectivity of the assessment process. Suggestions for maintaining objectivity are to (a) focus on facts; (b) to keep in check any feelings of anger that are aroused, especially when faced with denial (or even admission) or refusal to consider treatment; and (c) to remember to place the sexual offender's personality within the context of other problems that may also be of clinical relevance.

Two types of test are often considered for use with sexual offenders: (a) a test of general psychopathology, usually the MMPI–2, and (b) a measure that assesses sexual history, attitudes, dysfunctions, and knowledge. Several of the latter kind of test have been published for use in research and assessment of sexual offenders; unfortunately, most have inadequate psychometric properties.

Psychologists may be called on to answer six assessment questions when evaluating a sexual offender. They may be asked to comment or testify on one, on any combination, or on all six questions. These questions involve general psychopathology, psychopathy, deviant sexual interests, risk of recidivism, and amenability to treatment and, to a lesser extent, whether the offender fits a certain profile. Throughout all assessments, the question of dissimulation needs to be routinely evaluated (Lanyon, 2001).

General Psychopathology

Psychological testing of a sexual offender almost always includes a general test of psychopathology. The MMPI has been the instrument of choice (for adults), but the Personality Assessment Inventory (Morey, 1991) may also be used for such screening, although little empirical research has addressed its use with a sexual offender population.

The MCMI, as revised, is a very good instrument for assessing personality disorders, but it has only a limited literature base on use with forensic populations, and even less so with sexual offenders. Bard and Knight (1986), using cluster analysis, found four distinct MCMI personality subtypes in sexual offenders: detached, antisocial-aggressive, antisocial-negativistic, and a subclinical profile with scales in the normal range. Barnett and McCormack (1988) gave the MCMI to 147 child molesters. The resulting profiling indicated the highest elevations on the Dependent Personality Disorder scale, suggesting that child molesters see themselves as inadequate and ineffectual and may seek acceptance from a partner whose capacity to reject is limited. Chantry and Craig (1994) gave the MCMI to 201 child molesters and 195 rapists in a correctional setting. The child molesters scored highest on the Dependent scale, suggesting traits of passivity, insecurity, docility, and lack of initiative and a tendency to acquiesce to a strong authority figure to gain affection, protection, and security. Child molesters also scored high in Anxiety and Depression. The (adult) victim attained normal value MCMI scores but appeared more egocentric, entitled, and independent and without psychic distress.

Based on the popularity of the MCMI–III with other populations, use of this instrument with sexual offenders can be expected to increase. The Minnesota Multiphasic Personality Inventory—Adolescent (MMPI–A; Butcher et al., 1992) has been most widely used with adolescents, including juvenile offenders, but data on the MMPI–A with sexual offenders are scarce. The MMPI–A can be helpful in screening for psychopathology and psychopathy and in assessing the juvenile's attitudes toward the evaluation; the psychologist can review the MMPI–A validity scales and check for dishonesty, defensiveness, malingering, or cooperativeness.

One study used the MCMI with juvenile sexual offenders against children ($N = 20$) and juvenile peer-age sexual offenders ($N = 16$). The child offenders scored significantly higher on Schizoid and Dependent compared with the peer-age group. Both groups scored in the clinically significant range on Antisocial. The child offender groups scored in the clinical range on Dependent, and the peer-age offenders also scored high on the Narcissistic scale (D. R. Carpenter, Peed, & Eastman, 1995).

Although little or no data are available on the use of the Millon Adolescent Clinical Inventory (MACI; Millon, 1993) with this population, this instrument is substantially shorter than the MMPI–A and, in my experience, has been more acceptable to adolescents. Also, the test has extremely useful content scales (Identity Diffusion, Self-Devaluation, Body

Disparagement, Sexual Discomfort, Peer Insecurity, Social Sensitivity, Family Discord, Childhood Abuse, Eating Dysfunction, Substance Abuse Proneness, Delinquent Predisposition, Impulsive Propensity, Anxious Feelings, Depressive Affect, and Suicidal Tendency) that address many, if not most, issues relevant to the assessment of juvenile sexual offenders.

However, many juvenile offenders do not have the requisite reading ability to validly respond to paper-and-pencil tests. In these instances, the Rorschach is the instrument of choice.

Juvenile sexual offenders often have other diagnoses from the *Diagnostic and Statistical Manual of Mental Disorders* (fourth edition; American Psychiatric Association, 1994), especially conduct disorders, attention deficit disorders with or without hyperactivity, learning disabilities, affective and anxiety disorders (e.g., posttraumatic stress disorder), and substance abuse, and they may even have personality disorders, especially antisocial and narcissistic personality disorders. It is incumbent on the psychologist to assess for these as well.

Many sexual abusers have a history of being sexually abused themselves. In such cases, they are trying to work through their own trauma of abuse and unresolved conflicts in a kind of displaced repetition compulsion. Sexual offenders with a history of prior child victimization appear more pathological on psychological tests (Hunter et al., 1990).

Psychopathy

The presence of psychopathy has been found to be a mediating variable in predicting sexual offending recidivism. Hare's (1991) Psychopathy Check List is the test most often used to screen for psychopathy. It has good reliability and validity for this population and shows good predictive validity for both sexual and violent recidivism. It shows a moderate relationship to phallometric testing, but it does not discriminate sexual offenders from nonsexual offenders. It does predict criminal recidivism (Quinsey & LaLumiere, 1996) and has been shown to be superior to other risk scale measures in predicting violent criminal behavior (Serin, 1996). There is also a version for juveniles.

Also, the MMPI–2 Psychopathic Deviate (Pd) clinical scale, along with the Antisocial Practices scale (and Anger scale), shows good convergent validity with antisocial personality disorder and psychopathy (Bosquet & Egeland, 2000; Lilienfeld, 1996; S. R. Smith, Hilsenroth, Castlebury, & Durham, 1999). The antisocial personality disorder scale of the MCMI–III is also relevant for such assessment. For example, violent offenders have been shown to be more impulsive and less empathic than nonviolent offenders (Nussbaum et al., 2002), and lack of empathy is a hallmark, pathognomonic trait of psychopaths.

Deviant Sexual Interests

Measures of sexual interest are often included in sexual offender evaluations. The two such measures most often mentioned in the literature are the Multiphasic Sex Inventory (Nichols & Molinder, 1996) and the Abel Assessment for Sexual Interests (Abel, Huffman, Warberg, & Holland, 1998). These measures are relatively recent and have not yet been fully supported by empirical data. However, the introduction of empirical, objective data for assessing sexual interests is a promising development.

The Multiphasic Sex Inventory is a 300-item, true–false self-report inventory. It assesses a wide range of psychosexual characteristics of sexual offenders. It has scales measuring Rape Fantasy, 11 sexual offense scales, five scales measuring atypical sexual behavior (Fetishes, Voyeurism, Obscene Phone Calling, Bondage, and Sadism), two sexual cognitive disturbance scales (Cognitive Distortion, Sexual Obsessions), and a Sexual Knowledge and Beliefs scale. The test has acceptable reliability, with test–retest reliabilities ranging from .64 to .92 over a three-week period (Nichols & Molinder, 1984, 1996) and acceptable internal consistency and convergent validity (Kalichman, Henderson, Shealy, & Dwyer, 1992), but this test may be susceptible to faking (Haywood, Grossman, Kravitz, & Wasyliw, 1994). There is a juvenile version of the Multiphasic Sex Inventory, but there is even less research with this instrument than on the adult version. Despite its weaknesses, this test may have some clinical utility for descriptive purposes.

The Abel Assessment for Sexual Interest includes a self-report inventory about sexual history and a second part consisting of 135 slides in which the person is asked to rate, on a scale of 1 to 7, whether the picture is disgusting or sexually arousing. A computer records the viewing time—actually reaction time—to potentially sexually evocative stimuli. This method is less invasive than phallometric assessment, but there is little validity information for this method, especially for juveniles. Abel and colleagues have also developed a Sexual Interest Card Sort (Abel, Lawry, Karlstrom, Osborn, & Gillespie, 1994), which is sometimes used as a measure of sexual interests when treating sexual offenders. However, a Maine court found this test inadmissible (personal communication, M. Fogel, September 17, 2003). Additional instruments for assessing various aspects of sexual abuse and of evaluating sexual abusers are contained in Beech, Fischer, and Thornton (2003).

Risk of Relapse, Reoffense, or Recidivism

Psychologists may be called on to evaluate risk of relapse prior to release from prison or as part of presentencing procedures. This type of evaluation is particularly important because at least 16 states have enacted so-called sexual predator laws, which provide for involuntary commitment of sexually violent offenders after they have served their prison terms if they are likely to engage in sexually predatory acts. The U.S. Supreme Court has ruled such laws constitutional (*Kansas v. Hendricks*, 1997). Most of the time, this process is done subjectively, taking into account all known facts. However, a few measures have been published for this phase of the evaluation.

The U.S. Supreme Court has upheld the constitutionality of the use of civil commitment procedures to confine sexually violent offenders who are a danger to others, even though they do not have a mental illness. Twelve states now require civil commitment of sexual offenders, and eligible offenders are locked up in a secure facility when it has been determined that they are substantially likely to engage in acts of sexual violence.

Predicting sexual recidivism is difficult, because it is a relatively rare event (i.e., the base rate is low), because abuse often goes unreported or undetected, and because the research tends to use too short a follow-up period to assess recidivism, which may occur but not necessarily during the follow-up period. On the other hand, the low base rate might be due to other factors, such as the effectiveness of treatment, rehabilitation, or continued monitoring, especially among juvenile sexual offenders.

It may also be useful to think of the sexual offender population as differing in probability of recidivism. For example, the situationally opportunistic offender has a lower risk of recidivism than the chronic offender, the extremely hard-core offender, and the mentally disturbed offender, even within other typologies. However, Quinsey and LaLumiere (1996) reported that having male victims and a biological relationship to the victim are two of the most powerful variables in assessing the likelihood of relapse among sexual offenders. In fact, they reported that about one third of the child molesters were homosexual, which is a rather high percentage given their relatively low percentage in the overall population (Levin & Stava, 1987).

The instrument that appears most often in the literature is the Sex Offender Appraisal Guide (Quinsey, Harris, Rice, & Cormier, 1998), which was developed on Canadian sexual offenders who were incarcerated or hospitalized. The test includes several items from the Psychopathy Checklist—Revised (Hare, 1991), and there are sections on substance abuse and criminal history.

The Sexual Violence Risk—20 (Boer, Hart, Kropp, & Webster, 2001) is a 20-item checklist of risk factors for sexual violence that were derived from a literature review on sexual offenders. The factors fall into three main categories: psychosocial adjustment, history of sexual offenses, and future plans. Data are easily coded, and the results are translated into a low, medium, or high level of risk. The test has limited psychometric data published to date.

The Static: 99 (R. K. Hanson & Thornton, 1999) is a test used to screen sexual offenders about to be released from prison. It has 10 items and relies on actuarial means to assess sex abusers. Items pertain to prior sex offenses, age when the offender will be released from prison (higher points if under age 25), history of male victims, crimes against related victims, prior nonsexual crimes, cohabitation status (more points if homeless), and victim characteristics. It is a static measure because it relies on variables that do not change.

Because the empirical literature does not provide a list of variables that are invariably predictive of recidivism, it is recommended that the psychologist use a two-step approach for the assessment. First, the clinician should use an actuarial approach and take into account the base rate of the behavior in the general population of offenders with this problem and at the particular setting or facility (if known). This should be the starting point. The best generalization is that, among child molesters, father–daughter incest offenders with no other victims have the lowest recidivism rates, heterosexual extrafamilial child molesters have an intermediate recidivism rate, and homosexual child molesters have the highest recidivism rate (Quinsey et al., 1998). However, when evaluating for recidivism, the number of past offenses and the frequency of molestation are probably two key variables to consider. Second, the psychologist would adjust this likelihood up or down on the basis of the totality of the assessment and clinical judgment.

The following are reasonable variables to be considered in most cases:

- number of prior offenses (first offense vs. chronicity);
- amount of prior criminal behavior of any kind;
- admission and acceptance of responsibility for the sexual offense;
- willingness to discuss the nature of the offense in detail;
- expressions of guilt and remorse for the offense;
- evidence of empathy for the victim;
- admission that the behavior is wrong;
- absence of major psychiatric syndromes, especially psychopathy, psychosis, and clinical depression with or without suicide;
- level of social adjustment or maladjustment;
- amount of family and social support; and
- willingness to change lifestyle and behavior to minimize reoccurrences (e.g., acceptance of psychological treatment).

Conroy (2003) offered the following variables as those most consistently related to recidivism among sexual predators: (a) a history of deviant sexual interests and prior criminal offenses, especially with victims who are strangers to the perpetrator; (b) failure to cooperate with law enforcement officials and with treatment providers; (c) history of substance abuse, especially when it is used to trigger the abuse; (d) presence of psychopathy; and (e) rape as the preferred method of offense.

Amenability to Treatment

Approaches to treatment of sexual offenders have generally relied on cognitive–behavioral interventions that seek to control deviant arousal; promote reconditioning, possibly through exercises that require prolonged masturbation while listening to or observing tapes or films of appropriate sexual behavior; and provide relapse prevention strategies. Group and family therapy may also be used as an ancillary technique (Crolley, Roys, Thyer, & Bordnick, 1998), and there are multiple suggestions on how to affect sexual offender motivations (Tierney & McCabe, 2002). More than 20 different methods or procedures have attempted to influence sexual preference (Kelly, 1982).

Although the literature is somewhat sparse in applying psychological data to predict response to treatment among sexual offenders, there is general agreement that psychological tests do play a role in treatment planning (Heersink & Strassberg, 1995; Herkov, Gynther, Thomas, & Myers, 1996; W. D. Murphy & Peters, 1992; Vaupel & Goeke, 1994). Although psychopathy is generally negatively correlated with successful treatment outcome, there is some evidence that scores decrease after treatment, suggesting that some psychological changes may result from treatment (G. L. Davis & Hoffman, 1991). There is a general belief that patients with differing personality types warrant different dispositions (G. C. Hall, Shepherd, & Mudrak, 1992). For example, offenders with lower MMPI scale scores were less likely to attend treatment sessions, whereas scores on F (degree of distress and level of psychopathology) and K (defensive responding) predicted attendance at treatment sessions and clinician ratings of treatment participation (Kalichman, Shealy, & Craig, 1990).

There also are treatment implications based on MMPI profile types. For example, groups with less psychopathology may be more responsive to psychotherapy. Groups that are more aggressive may need social skills training and instructions to differentiate aggressive from assertive responses. Patients who are in higher levels of distress may be more amenable to interventions (Kalichman, 1991), whereas groups with more severe psychopathology and more sociopathic traits may be refractory to treatment (Kalichman, Dwyer, Henderson, & Hoffman, 1992). Unfortunately, I found no study that showed that scores on the Psychopathic Deviate (Pd) scale decrease in response to treatment, and some studies have shown that they do not (Crolley et al., 1998; Davis & Hoffman, 1991). Characteristics associated with Pd elevations have been considered the defining characteristics of the sexual abuser.

Lanyon (2001) reported that the following factors should be considered when assessing amenability to treatment: heterosexual interests, skills, and experience; availability of personal and emotional support; availability of appropriate sexual partners; freedom from substance abuse; general absence of character disorders; and ability and willingness to work toward treatment goals. Among the most relevant factors are admission of guilt, acceptance of responsibility for the crime, desire for the behavior to stop, and positive motivation for treatment.

PHALLOMETRIC ASSESSMENT

The *Ethical Standards and Procedures for the Management of Sex Offenders* (Association for the Treatment of Sexual Abusers, 1997) states, "Physiological assessment data can be helpful in confronting a client who denies deviant sexual behavior, deviant sexual fantasies, and/or deviant sexual arousal" (p. 40). Phallometric testing involves monitoring penile tumescence while the patient is exposed to videos, films, or audiotapes depicting people engaging in various behaviors. It is sometimes referred to as plethysmography. In this assessment procedure, the patient is placed in a room in a comfortable chair, isolated from the examiner and from the measuring equipment. Verbal but not physical contact is maintained throughout the testing. The patient places a small transducer on his penis. Either penile circumference or penile volume is measured during the test. If volume is measured, then a small glass tube is placed over the penis that measures displacement of air by an erection. The stimuli include both neutral stimuli (e.g., walking in a park) and provocative stimuli (e.g., people in various sexual acts that are either coerced or consenting).

Audio stimuli eliminate possible ethical concerns that exist with films and videos of youths and may be the preferred method. Audiotape recordings can be simulated and even experimental variables introduced, such as varying the vocal intensity of violence and coercion. This methodology measures sexual arousal directly, as opposed to self-report measures. Generally, both visual slides and audiotapes are used with both neutral and violent stimuli. Because some men are apparently able to exert a degree of voluntary control over erection, patients are generally asked to perform some mental task, such as counting backward, between trials to preclude cognitive rehearsal strategies that may be used to try and beat the test. Even so, the detection of deviant arousal with phallometric testing is not 100% reliable, though it has produced very few false positives. It also does not confirm that an alleged perpetrator engaged in any particular behavior or crime and should not be used to determine whether a particular offender is guilty of a given charge. It does have relevance, though, in the assessment of future risk.

Regardless whether audio or visual stimuli are used, this research has demonstrated that penile responses are consistent with patients' sexual histories. That is, child sexual abusers show greater sexual arousal to pictures of children or descriptions of sexual practices involving children, compared with normal men. Both homosexual and heterosexual men show phallometric results that correspond to their sexual preferences and victims.

Phallometry is limited to male sexual offenders who molest or rape their victims. With other types of sexual offenders, such as exhibitionists, phallometry adds nothing to our understanding of this behavior. Also, there are other types of sexual crimes, such as bestiality, frottage, necrophilia, and voyeurism, but phallometry has not been used with these types of offender. Also, it has not been used to study paraphilias such as fetishism. And, of course, although women rarely are sexual offenders, phallometry would have no role in assessing female offenders (Marshall & Fernandez, 2000).

The data also show that although reliable group differences have appeared, the results may not be as useful in an individual case as would be required in a trial situation. There is also evidence that patients can fake or suppress erection responses when instructed to do so, and in actual clinical situations it is impossible to know whether or not the patient is faking. Hence, test results are not admissible in court. Still, the sensitivity of phallometric testing is generally good for stimuli that depict male and female prepubescents, pubescents, and adults. In fact, the more sexual content involving adult women is presented, the less likely phallometric tests are to identify the individual as a pedophile (R. Blanchard, Klassen, Dickey, Kuban, & Blak, 2001). A positive response to pedophilic stimuli (i.e., arousal) has been correlated with having multiple victims, having a male victim, having very young victims, and having extrafamilial victims (Seto, LaLumiere, & Blanchard, 2000). The reader is referred to more authoritative sources for a detailed review of this research (Blader & Marshall, 1989; Grossman, Martis, & Fichtner, 1999; W. L. Marshall, 1996; W. L. Marshall & Fernandez, 2000; W. L. Marshall, Jones, Ward, Johnston, & Barbaree, 1991; W. D. Murphy & Peters, 1992; Quinsey & LaLumiere, 1996). The MMPI has been found to correlate with penile plethysmography scores to a significant degree among child molesters (McAnulty et al., 1994).

In summary, a useful model for the assessment of sexual offenders includes (a) a functional analysis of how the offender's problems contributed to the offense, (b) actuarial methods to evaluate risk profiles, (c) identification of stable and dynamic risk factors that increase risk of reoffense, and (d) monitoring of acute factors that may suggest that reoffense is imminent (Beech et al., 2003).

STATEMENT ANALYSIS

The need for statement analysis derives from the fact that sexual offenders almost always deny the allegations. However, denial is not a dichotomous variable, and there may be degrees of denial. For example, some offenders may issue a complete denial, whereas others may admit the behavior but justify it (e.g., "I didn't know she was underage. She looked much older than her age"). Some will profess no memory of the event. Because denial and deception are such salient traits of most sexual offenders, there is a need for a triangulation of measures that assess for deception. All objective personality tests are vulnerable to dissimulation, and most have scales that assess for it. However, a confluence of objective tests, physiological measures, structured interviews, and statement analyses can lead to a more accurate assessment of denial.

Statement analysis is drawing increasing attention and can help the psychologist determine the veracity of both the victim's and the alleged perpetrator's guilt or innocence. For the most part, this domain more properly belongs to law enforcement officials and to triers of fact. However, to the extent that psychologists can develop and refine methods of investigation, this method can add to the overall evaluation of the offender and victim. Statement analysis can be fairly formal, looking for discrepancies, contradictions, and illogical occurrences in the statements of both victim and alleged perpetrator. Scientific Content Analysis (SCAN) is a more formal method of analyzing statements.

Statement analysis relies on the possibility that verbal cues may reveal more truthful information than nonverbal cues (Hall & Pritchard, 1996). The SCAN method was developed by Avinoam Sapir, a polygraph examiner in the Israeli police department (Sapir, 1987). SCAN has the examiner identify semantic elements of speech and changes in language during questioning to uncover information that the person is trying to conceal. With the SCAN method, eight criteria are used to assess a statement's validity: (a) pronouns, (b) connections, (c) first-person singular, (d) denial of allegations (indirect—"I couldn't have done it"—and direct—"I didn't do it"), (e) lack of memory (suggesting concealment of details), (f) time (percentage of the story pertaining to before and after the crime), (g) missing or unnecessary links (gaps in story), and (h) changes in language (suggesting an emotional response and possibly deception).

With SCAN, specific aspects of written statements are analyzed for their coherent structure. There are nine content areas to analyze:

- general characteristics (logical structure, unstructured productions, and quantity of details);

- specific content (contextual embedding, description of inter-actions, reproduction of the conversation, unexpected complications);
- peculiarities of content (unusual details, superfluous details, details not understood, external associations, subjective mental state, perpetrator's mental state);
- motivation-related content (spontaneous corrections, admitting lack of memory, doubting own testimony, self-depreciation, pardoning the perpetrator);
- offense-specific elements (characteristic details);
- psychological characteristics (inappropriate language and knowledge, inappropriate affect, susceptibility to suggestion);
- interview characteristics (suggestive, leading, or coercive questioning; inadequate interviewing techniques);
- motivation (questionable motives to report, questionable context of disclosure, pressure to report falsely); and
- investigative questions (contrary to laws of nature, contradictory statements, contradictory evidence).

The SCAN technique is interesting and should be considered by psychologists as one of the tools for possible use in sexual offender evaluations. Of course, one would have to be trained in this method. However, this technique is in its infancy, and there is very little published information on its reliability and validity, despite its increasing use among crime investigators (Driscoll, 1994; Ruby & Brigham, 1997, 1998). Similar techniques have also been applied in the assessment of statements from alleged abuse victims, including young children (M. L. Rogers, 1990).

The next section contains statements from both an alleged victim and an alleged perpetrator. Following these statements is a list of items to consider when analyzing the statements.

Victim's Statement

I don't know where to start. I'm nervous. My mom and me were living real good together a couple of years ago. Then Mom met C, and he was real nice. He would give me and Mom money so we could go shopping before we moved in with him. Then my mom was going to get married, and she was real nervous, and then she married him and right after that, I don't know, when we moved in, he would tell us how stupid we were, and he'd give me the worst jobs in the house and, I don't know, then him and my mom would be fighting and he would beat her up, throw her out. He had like 10 bolts on the door. He'd lock us in and lock us out. He'd go somewhere and leave us locked up 'til he got home. Then it just started that he'd throw my mother out and tell her to get out of here, and she'd run back and he'd say get out of here. Then he'd lock the door, and I couldn't get out. Then it started where he'd be, like, "Let me touch your butt," "Let me spank you." Then he'd start spanking me. He'd say I did something wrong. Then he'd start feeling and shaking. He shook real weird all of the time. And he'd want more each time. Every time he'd touch my boobs, "Let me fondle you," "Let me go down your pants and see what you have." My brother, J, he'd be there. He [C] had a gun. "If you don't let me do this, I'll hold the gun to J's head" . . . little black gun about this big [gestures].

Then one time I got scared. He was sleeping. I ran to one of my mother's friends [K]. I had to crawl out the window. Then I'd run and tell her what he wanted to do, how he wanted to touch me and stuff. And one day I slept overnight because I couldn't go back to him. My mother knew he wouldn't let her in. She was real scared. So one day I was over at K's house. My mother said I could because she didn't want to go back to him, that he would threaten me because I didn't know he was trying to molest me and stuff, because I was afraid to tell her, because I didn't know what she was going to say. So I spent the night there and he came over at 7:00 in the morning and told her to get this little whore out of there—she's coming back with me! And he even told K. She told him he was a molester and he said that he was going to try to molest her little granddaughter and "I'll fuck your brains out too, because you never had . . . ." I don't know, you're talking about so many different things now, I don't know what I was going to say. There was another person who heard that, because he said it to her on the phone.

Then one day when we were even staying there anymore—we were staying at _____ then I was coming out here to visit one of my friends and he was following us and tried to run us off the road. One of our friends ran to a police station, and they found a bat in C's car—like an axe handle, but they asked him what it was for, and he said, "I keep it for protection." He is real scary. His eyes get real big and he shakes, nervous. I just think my brother should be with my mother. C is sick, and I don't want to turn out like C. I been with my mother a long time. Nothing happened to me. She's always taken care of me, always shown me love. I guess that's about all.

[Examiner: Tell me about one specific time.] One time he said, "Let me undress you for a shower," because my brother got sick and vomited on me. I was afraid to be around him. Mom was not around then, because he had threatened her out the house that time, and he locked the door so she couldn't come in. He undressed me—tried to undress me. I told him to get away from me, and I guess he went to bed and left me alone. He was shaking all over. He took off my shorts. He was touching my boobs. I was crying.

Then he tried to take off my underwear and pants, and I told him to get away from me, and he went and left.

[Examiner: What did you let him do?] I didn't want to. I had to. He'd beat my little brother. I love my brother. I let him touch my boobs but not down there. He tried to. Then I kept asking him why he wanted more. Is it going to come to that you have to do it with me? And he said, yes, P, if it comes to that, I can make things better for you.

[Examiner: Ever intercourse?] No.

Alleged Perpetrator's Statement

You've got to realize P [the victim] is very mature physically, but not mature. She lay her face in the middle of my crotch. I was laying on the bed watching TV. She put her face in my crotch. She moved her chin up and down. "Hey, wait!" I grabbed her. I twisted her breast. I left her bruised for it. "I don't care whether you're kidding or not." Then I went up to the kitchen. I dragged her and told her mother what happened.

Me and M [P's mother] went somewhere, left P with the kids. I told her if somebody comes to the house, don't let them in. The transmission of the car started to slip. We went back. There was a bicycle laying against the garage. I pitched it out the door. I sent her to her room and told her, "Two weeks in your room." By Monday she was out of her room. M let her out. She short-circuited my authority. M's way to deal with it is, don't do it 'til you're 16, and I'll buy you a car.

I told you about the couch. P ran away. She had to be dragged back. It's verifiable. She's smart but wild—foul language and behavior. She put me in an abnormal situation—the things she asked me to do—you couldn't believe. I told you about the situation where she asked me if you want a blow job, asked what dick tastes like, do it with a Popsicle. She was trying to shock me. I told M about it every time something happened. The girl would drop her pants and shoot me the moon. I gather she meant to show me her rear, but she showed me her front. I said "uh-oh." She told me a blow job would keep her virginity.

[Examiner: When did she ask you about the blow job?] She laid her face right in my crotch and said, "Do you want a blow job?" I don't care if she was kidding or not. I was so mad. Pissed off.

[Examiner: When did she ask you what dick tastes like?] She was sitting on the couch. It might have been at the same time she was eating a Popsicle.

[Examiner: When did she expose herself to you?] She was exposing herself to me in front of her mother one day, her breasts in the living room.

[Examiner: Did she do it on purpose?] Yes, she was flaunting her body. There was some competition for my attention.

What to Look for When Analyzing Statements

The psychologist should look for the following when analyzing statements (Ostrov, 1993):

- whether the initial statement unambiguously indicates abuse;
- whether the child's statements appear to be escalating possibly to the point of absurdity, with qualitative changes, or whether the statement reflects increasing details that are remembered;
- whether there is appropriate affect associated with recounting the story;
- whether the story is eagerly told or told with embarrassment;
- whether a progression of activities is described;
- whether alternative explanations are available (e.g., appropriate touching, observed sexual behavior between others in the house besides the named perpetrator); and
- whether the child's revelations were reinforced, perhaps unwittingly, by the person who first heard about it or by others. Were these revelations shaped by asking leading questions?

PERSONALITY TRAITS OF SEXUAL OFFENDERS

The personality assessment of sexual offenders would be most useful if the results could be related to particular variables of interest. The variables of most interest with sexual offenders are establishing a common profile associated with sexual victimization, predicting recidivism, and selecting targets for treatment interventions.

The responses of recently apprehended sexual offenders or those assessed shortly before trial are likely to be affected by emotional reactions to the arrest or forthcoming trial. Their voluntary responses are most likely to include distortions (i.e., lies, underreporting) under such circumstances. Using projective tests mitigates this problem.

Most studies of personality in sexual offenders stress the heterogeneity of this population. This diversity has led researchers to develop various classification systems to see if there are meaningful personality differences among groups within the larger population. Cluster analysis has been the method of choice in this regard. Although many subtypes have been proposed, the literature often categorizes these groups by the preferred sex of the child, the nature of the offense (e.g., rape, indecent exposure), the relationship to the victim (e.g., incest vs. nonincest), and the degree of force or violence used in the behavior (e.g., rape, nonviolent coercion).

Prentky and Knight (1990) developed an increasingly popular model for classifying sexual offenders. They proposed looking at the degree of fixation (low vs. high) and degree of social competence (low vs. high) on one pole, and the amount of contact (high vs. low), the meaning of that contact (interpersonal vs. narcissistic), the degree of physical contact (low vs. high), and the kind of contact (sadistic vs. nonsadistic) on the other pole. The model was based on both theoretical and empirical data and has implications for assessment and treatment planning. For example, sexual offenders high in child fixation, low in social competence, high in amount of contact, high in self-indulgence, and high in aggressivity are at greater risk for recidivism and are more refractory to treatment. However, the model ignores personality factors in the offender that may mediate behavior.

Many attempts have been made to classify sexual offenders into "types." However, a continuum approach is probably more useful than dichotomous approaches. One methodological problem pertains to possible sampling bias. Much of the published literature reports data on sexual offenders who were evaluated while in prison, rather than in the presentencing stage in the legal process. Also, many offenders are recidivists, and the effects of imprisonment on behavior are confounded with any preexisting psychopathology. In addition, many variables need to be considered before drawing conclusions and generalizations. Among these are the gender of the victim, the age of the victim, the degree of force against the victim (e.g., fondling vs. rape), and the relationship to the victim (incest vs. acquaintance vs. stranger abuse and rape). Many studies used samples of convenience and small sample sizes.

The data seem to suggest that sexual offenders show more psychopathology on psychological tests, including greater shyness and introversion, a more guarded response to personality questionnaires, and lower self-esteem than normal respondents. Sexual offenders are socially and emotionally immature and tend to have poor social skills and poor impulse control, and the more disturbed sexual offender shows evidence of psychotic thinking. In fact, these personality characteristics of sex abusers seem to match the developmental period of their victims (Finkelhor & Araji, 1986).

MMPI Studies With Sex Abusers

Although MMPI-derived scales may be of value with sexual offenders (Langevin, Wright, & Handy, 1990; Lanyon, 1993), most reports in the literature have focused on clinical scales and code types. As a group, most sexual offenders deny the crime, even after adjudication. One can expect such minimization and defensive responding on self-report inventories (Grossman, Haywood, Ostrov, & Wasyliw, 1992). Table 7.1 presents an overview of MMPI studies that have published T score data on sexual abusers since 1975.

The modal profile is a 1-point code with elevations on Psychopathic Deviate (Pd) and subspikes on Depression (Dep) and Schizophrenia (Sc;

TABLE 7.1
Minnesota Multiphasic Personality Inventory (MMPI) Studies of Sexual Abusers

Scale	Study 1			Study 2		Study 3		Study 4		
	I	II	III	I	II	I	II	I	II	III
N	37	38	10	18	15	36	47	13	21	17
L	53	53	53	56	50	50	53	50	53	53
F	50	50	66	60	58	58	64	70	63	62
K	57	62	57	57	57	59	57	48	54	57
Hs	53	57	63	54	65	52	59	42	38	36
Dep	56	60	63	63	68	60	68	70	65	60
Hy	60	60	63	57	67	60	61	60	60	60
Pd	60	64	82	62	71	69	79	65	63	60
Mf	63	61	61	57	59	61	59	61	61	62
Pa	53	59	70	59	59	63	67	70	67	62
Pt	54	58	63	56	60	63	64	45	36	30
Sc	55	61	73	57	71	65	73	55	45	34
Ma	60	58	63	53	55	57	60	45	53	58
Si	49	51	50	46	55	53	52	58	58	53

(continued)

TABLE 7.1
Minnesota Multiphasic Personality Inventory (MMPI) Studies of Sexual Abusers *(Continued)*

Scale	Study 5			Study 6		Study 7		Study 8	Study 9		Study 10	Study 11
	I	II	III	I	II	I	II		I	II		
N	40	32	16	35	28	15	10	10	33	29	406	81
L	42	54	48	60	61	50	53	51	50	50	47	51
F	81	55	39	61	60	75	75	63	58	60	65	67
K	36	64	49	54	56	48	51	52	53	51	47	55
Hs	66	45	62	63	61	57	64	68	36	40	60	64
Dep	78	48	70	68	67	70	75	66	56	64	70	72
Hy	62	55	58	64	67	61	65	65	56	60	63	67
Pd	78	79	67	70	71	79	79	74	53	57	72	78
Mf	—	—	—	57	56	60	62	67	63	65	68	66
Pa	83	52	42	62	60	67	69	66	62	59	65	66
Pt	78	49	53	63	62	67	74	78	28	34	68	71
Sc	98	52	50	62	61	77	81	82	32	38	72	77
Ma	71	69	25	58	58	65	62	63	50	58	63	60
Si	63	41	54	67	53	58	59	60	52	53	62	60

(continued)

TABLE 7.1
Minnesota Multiphasic Personality Inventory (MMPI) Studies of Sexual Abusers *(Continued)*

Scale	Study 12					Study 13					Study 14	
	I	II	III	IV	V	I	II	III	IV	V	I	II
N	39	12	39	21	9	21	61	14	9	6	33	55
L	53	66	57	45	47	57	54	58	50	47	56	59
F	53	68	59	74	89	54	61	73	80	98	61	57
K	56	59	57	45	44	57	63	50	44	37	51	55
Hs	48	69	60	57	71	48	53	72	62	68	64	56
Dep	54	71	61	61	71	47	59	76	60	70	69	64
Hy	53	66	59	54	63	47	53	65	56	58	66	61
Pd	67	78	75	76	80	62	71	83	82	81	75	68
Mf	56	62	54	67	57	53	57	62	59	60	64	61
Pa	53	76	64	69	85	46	62	78	75	95	62	59
Pt	51	67	59	67	82	47	57	75	68	86	65	60
Sc	54	85	65	76	101	52	63	88	85	102	67	62
Ma	61	65	62	71	78	65	65	70	82	79	59	59
Si	49	54	53	55	59	50	52	59	57	65	56	55

(continued)

TABLE 7.1
Minnesota Multiphasic Personality Inventory (MMPI) Studies of Sexual Abusers *(Continued)*

Scale	Study 15								Study 16		
	I	II	III	IV	V	VI	VII	VIII	I	II	III
N	8	21	8	6	16	7	6	12	54	42	48
L	58	44	56	48	49	63	55	49	53	53	56
F	62	59	60	88	50	50	60	86	68	62	64
K	54	48	70	40	59	69	49	46	49	53	53
Hs	43	34	49	43	30	29	36	69	47	39	36
Dep	82	63	68	60	54	58	58	94	63	60	60
Hy	67	58	76	56	58	65	51	77	58	55	51
Pd	64	57	64	69	48	41	48	81	60	60	57
Mf	65	71	64	62	55	60	61	73	59	57	57
Pa	67	62	59	83	56	59	56	84	70	62	62
Pt	44	36	30	60	20	20	30	71	40	30	21
Sc	42	39	36	80	20	20	39	86	50	46	38
Ma	35	51	48	70	48	43	48	69	58	58	58
Si	69	55	50	58	46	47	64	66	56	54	50

(continued)

TABLE 7.1
Minnesota Multiphasic Personality Inventory (MMPI) Studies of Sexual Abusers *(Continued)*

Scale	Study 17	Study 18		Study 19							
		I	II	I	II	III	IV	V	VI	VII	VIII
N	61	123	138	27	9	7	4	4	20	21	9
L	52	48	45	45	48	50	52	48	51	52	51
F	60	57	69	65	56	72	56	72	61	52	62
K	55	53	46	43	64	40	57	53	52	60	50
Hs	58	51	65	46	60	62	58	70	53	50	53
Dep	66	57	78	51	62	78	66	82	70	53	80
Hy	63	57	66	50	73	60	66	73	58	54	70
Pd	74	72	80	62	84	70	70	90	70	52	75
Mf	62	66	71	63	72	60	66	72	67	65	68
Pa	63	57	70	58	68	62	65	78	62	55	72
Pt	63	56	76	57	62	78	66	88	63	50	74
Sc	66	61	82	63	65	80	66	92	62	52	75
Ma	60	62	64	62	58	60	65	50	50	51	62
Si	54	53	66	55	42	70	51	68	67	50	55

(continued)

TABLE 7.1
Minnesota Multiphasic Personality Inventory (MMPI) Studies of Sexual Abusers *(Continued)*

Scale	Study 20				Study 21			Study 22				
	I	II	III	IV	I	II	III	I	II	III	IV	V
N	45	17	16	12	47	42	18	15	17	29	38	11
L	57	59	48	48	55	51	46	48	46	48	53	44
F	57	61	71	90	59	64	80	55	68	59	51	71
K	56	55	45	44	53	52	44	51	48	57	63	50
Hs	51	67	58	80	51	64	73	45	70	54	47	58
Dep	53	67	67	74	56	74	83	59	92	70	51	63
Hy	51	68	57	68	55	66	72	51	67	63	62	64
Pd	65	68	80	80	66	81	89	58	88	74	58	83
Mf	57	61	59	66	59	62	67	64	76	71	64	73
Pa	55	70	75	90	61	70	84	56	72	66	57	69
Pt	53	59	69	84	54	77	83	56	80	59	44	70
Sc	58	63	77	103	57	75	96	53	79	60	45	78
Ma	63	58	69	76	65	65	76	53	55	52	55	76
Si	51	56	59	61	51	55	82	59	72	58	45	55

(continued)

TABLE 7.1
Minnesota Multiphasic Personality Inventory (MMPI) Studies of Sexual Abusers *(Continued)*

Scale	Study 23	Study 24			Study 25			Study 26		
		I	II		I	II		I	II	III
N	32	20	20		30	60		87	23	12
L	54	50	50		50	46		55	48	56
F	67	66	53		60	55		57	75	67
K	52	50	57		53	62		59	41	55
Hs	62	64	56		57	54		54	59	78
Dep	63	72	59		63	56		57	69	90
Hy	64	64	61		57	54		58	54	75
Pd	68	72	62		67	67		68	71	80
Mf	60	59	57		63	61		60	68	73
Pa	64	66	56		65	65		59	76	75
Pt	62	69	55		65	54		59	79	81
Sc	69	73	56		63	57		60	88	80
Ma	62	64	57		63	60		58	77	58
Si	55	56	52		54	50		56	65	63

(continued)

TABLE 7.1
Minnesota Multiphasic Personality Inventory (MMPI) Studies of Sexual Abusers (Continued)

Scale	Study 27 I	Study 27 II	Study 27 III	Study 28 I	Study 28 II	Study 28 III	Study 29	Study 30	Total N	Mean MMPI
N	9	99	22	19	18	16	29		2,697	
L	50	46	47	58	59	57	50			52
F	62	60	47	60	61	71	58			64
K	50	45	53	48	46	43	59			52
Hs	61	63	59	60	61	67	47			56
Dep	65	60	57	63	58	67	63			65
Hy	55	63	53	55	53	57	62			61
Pd	66	79	50	64	59	66	64			69
Mf	60	65	59	—	—	—	63			63
Pa	64	62	49	57	60	72	62			65
Pt	65	61	49	56	59	67	44			59
Sc	64	60	43	59	62	73	48			64
Ma	49	49	54	59	51	64	55			59
Si	57	55	46	—	—	—	53			53

Note. Dashes indicate no data for that score on variable. Study 1 is McCreary, 1975b. Study 2 is McCreary, 1975a. Study 3 is Rader, 1977. Study 4 is J. A. Armentrout and Hauer, 1978. Study 5 is Anderson, Kunce, and Rich, 1979. Study 6 is Panton, 1979. Study 7 is Quinsey, Arnold, and Pruesse, 1980. Study 8 is Kirkland and Bauer, 1982. Study 9 is Scott and Stone, 1986. Study 10 is G. C. Hall, Maiuro, Vitaliano, and Proctor, 1986. Study 11 is G. C. Hall, 1989. Study 12 is Kalichman, 1989. Study 13 is Kalichman, 1990. Study 14 is Hunter, Childers, Gerald, and Esmaili, 1990. Study 15 is Duthie and McIvor, 1990. Study 16 is Kalichman, 1991. Study 17 is G. L. Davis and Hoffman, 1991. Study 18 is G. C. Hall, Graham, and Shepherd, 1991. Study 19 is Kalichman, Henderson, Shealy, and Dwyer, 1992. Study 20 is Shealy, Kalichman, Syzmanowski, and McKee, 1991. Study 21 is G. C. Hall, Shepherd, and Mudrak, 1992. Study 22 is Kalichman, Henderson, Shealy, and Dwyer, 1992. Study 23 is Yanagida and Ching, 1993. Study 24 is Vaupel and Goeke, 1994. Study 25 is McAnulty, Adams, and Wright, 1994. Study 26 is Heersink and Strassberg, 1995. Study 27 is Roys and Timms, 1995. Study 28 is Herkov, Gynther, Thomas, and Myers, 1996. Study 29 is Crolley, Roys, Thyer, and Bordnick, 1998. Study 30 is Grossman, Wasyliw, Benn, and Gyoerkee, 2002.

TABLE 7.2
Minnesota Multiphasic Personality Inventory—2
Studies of Sexual Abusers

Scale	Study 1	Study 2		Study 3			Total N	Mean
		I	II	I	II	III		
N	91	13	43	60	24	25	256	57
L	55	—	—	60	53	59		55
F	58	—	—	55	54	52		51
K	48	—	—	48	55	54		53
Hs	54	48	52	59	55	51		55
Dep	56	57	48	58	56	54		53
Hy	55	50	53	52	56	52		62
Pd	64	64	56	61	64	64		51
Mf	50	55	51	46	57	47		54
Pa	49	56	50	55	59	53		55
Pt	56	57	56	55	56	51		57
Sc	59	58	53	57	60	55		50
Ma	53	50	46	53	47	52		50
Si	56	57	45	56	55	54		54
Code	[a]	'4	[a]	[a]	'4	'4		[a]

Note. Dashes indicate no data for that scale on variable. Study 1 is Mann, Stenning, and Borman, 1992. Study 2 is Ridenour, Miller, Joy, and Dean, 1997. Study 3 is Grossman, Wasyliw, Benn, and Gyoerkee, 2002.
[a]Within normal limits.

4'28). Elevations on Pd are associated with school, relational, and legal problems and often authority problems. Patients with high scores tend to be impulsive and irresponsible, have a low frustration tolerance, are manipulative and extroverted, and often have problems with substance abuse. The subspike on Dep probably represents some distress over their current situation. These patients were given a psychological evaluation after they were caught, charged, or convicted of a sexual crime. They were awaiting trial, were in prison, or were in a prison treatment program for sexual offenders. Their scores on Dep may represent not clinical depression, but sadness over being caught and being restricted through incarceration. The subspike on Sc does not, in general, represent traits associated with schizophrenia, as the name of the scale implies. The bulk of the sex-related items are keyed on this scale. The fact that Sc is mildly elevated probably suggests that the patient has endorsed those items. High scores on Sc may also suggest disturbance in cognition and thinking.

Table 7.2 presents MMPI–2 scores of sexual abusers. The MMPI results are interpreted with the principles of elevation, shape, and slope. Interpretation of profile shape can be improved with visualization, so the modal profile appearing in Tables 7.1 and 7.2 is also presented in Figure 7.1. Presenting only the modal profile of sexual abusers, however, may mask meaningful differences among different types of perpetrators (e.g., rapists, incest

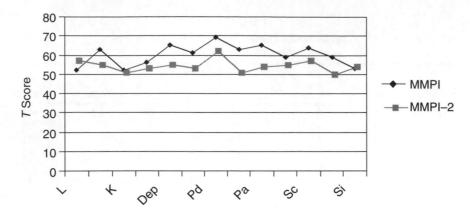

Figure 7.1. Modal Minnesota Multiphasic Personality Inventory profile of sexual abusers.

perpetrators, exhibitionists). Accordingly, Table 7.3 presents MMPI published data according to type of abuse.

The data in Table 7.1 represent the MMPI findings from the sexual abusing or offending populations of 30 separate studies and from 85 different samples ranging up to N = 406, with a median sample size of 21. The table presents aggregate scores for all types of sexual offenders as a class. This modal profile is coded as a 1-point code with peaks on Psychopathic Deviate (Pd) and subspikes on Depression (Dep), Paranoia (Pa), and Schizophrenia

TABLE 7.3
Minnesota Multiphasic Personality Inventory
T Scores for Specific Types of Sexual Abusers

Scale	Child abusers	Indecent exposure	Rapists	Incest	Miscellaneous sexual abusers	All studies
No. of studies	19	2	8	3	5	29
Total subjects	1,605	121	788	111	514	2,679
L	52	52	53	52	50	52
F	55	56	67	60	64	64
K	60	59	52	53	48	52
Hs	55	56	56	57	57	56
Dep	67	60	66	64	63	65
Hy	62	61	59	62	58	61
Pd	69	69	71	66	68	70
Mf	64	61	61	61	56	63
Pa	65	61	67	63	64	65
Pt	58	59	59	59	61	59
Sc	62	63	68	61	67	64
Ma	59	59	62	58	62	60
Si	57	51	56	57	55	55

(Sc)—4'268. The psychological and personality characteristics associated with this code type emphasize the antisocial characteristics associated with an elevated Pd scale and are so well-known that they need not be reported here. The mild spike on Dep is best interpreted as temporary distress over being caught and in a (legal) situation that also distresses them, rather than true guilt over the behavior or clinical depression. The mild elevation on Sc is probably because many of the sex-related items on the MMPI are scored on this scale, suggesting they have endorsed some of those items (e.g., responding *false* to "I've never been in trouble because of my sex behavior"). The mild elevation on Pa is probably related to the offender's need to be vigilant and suspicious of people to avoid getting caught, rather than clinical paranoia.

Pedophiles

Pedophilia is any sexual behavior, whether forced or unforced, between an adult and a minor (prepubertal) child. The word literally means "filial love for a child," but it has come to mean sex with a child. The personality characteristics of pedophiles may differ on the basis of whether they are first offenders or chronic recidivists (McCreary, 1975a) and whether they are homosexually or heterosexually fixated. Chronic abusers have been described as impulsive, unconventional, bizarre, confused, and alienated (Schizophrenia), with many psychosomatic complaints (Hypochondriasis, Hysteria; McCreary, 1975a; Panton, 1979). They seem to be more introverted, to lack self-confidence, and to be immature and distressed (Kalichman, 1991). Nonforceful molesters tend to endorse items pertaining to self-alienation and family discord, whereas child rapists tend to endorse items related to social alienation and authority conflicts (Levin & Stava, 1987). Rapists and pedophiles tend to score higher on needs for abasement and lower on needs for aggression compared with nonsexual offenders, suggesting that they are guilt ridden and try to suppress the expression of aggression (Levin & Stava, 1987). Pedophiles seem inept in interpersonal relationships, feel that they are helpless in an overpowering environment, and have little insight into their own behavior. Although physical damage to children can occur, more often pedophilia occurs without physical force.

Table 7.3 summarizes MMPI scores from 19 studies based on more than 1,600 child abusers. The modal profile was essentially indistinguishable from the modal profile of the sexual abuser, with elevations on Psychopathic Deviate (Pd), Depression (Dep), Paranoia (Pa), Schizophrenia (Sc), and Hysteria (Hy), coded '42 683.

However, MMPI studies with cluster analysis reveal several types based on different personality manifestations. A particularly dangerous type is the MMPI profile with significant elevations on the F validity scale and

Schizophrenia (Sc; with or without elevations on Psychopathic Deviate [Pd]) and suggests severe psychopathology. This type shows long-term social maladjustment, a poor work history, and frequent involvement with the law early in life and continuing into adulthood. Such people show evidence of more paraphilias and may exhibit both psychotic and aggressive behaviors (Anderson, Kunce, & Rich, 1979; Erickson et al., 1987; G. C. Hall, 1989; G. C. Hall, Graham, & Shepherd, 1991; G. C. Hall, Maiuro, Vitaliano, & Proctor, 1986; G. C. Hall et al., 1992; Kalichman, 1989, 1990; Kalichman et al., 1990; Kalichman, Henderson, Shealy, & Dwyer, 1992).

The MMPI type characterized by a 49' profile code type reflects a character disorder. Substance abuse is usually a prominent characteristic of this type, and it is the modal profile type of a criminal offender with a diagnosis of antisocial personality disorder (Anderson et al., 1979; Erickson et al., 1987; G. C. Hall et al., 1992; Kalichman, 1990).

The MMPI code types with elevations on Depression (Dep) and Psychopathic Deviate (Pd; 24/42) may make a good impression on the examiner, because they are manipulative and want to portray a demeanor of sadness and regret—probably not for committing the crime, but for being caught. Some actually do feel guilty about their behavior but seem unable to stop it. Offenders with these code types are described as passive and dependent, impulsive, uncomfortable in social situations, and shy and ineffectual and have problems with substance abuse (Anderson et al., 1979; Duthie & McIvor, 1990; Erickson et al., 1987; G. C. Hall et al., 1992; Kalichman & Henderson, 1991).

Rapists

Rape may be defined as sexual contact with children, adolescents, or adults in which force, threat of force, or coercion is used by the assailant against the victim. Rape is a crime of both sex and aggression, and there may be some important personality differences between those who rape children and those who rape adults (J. A. Armentrout & Hauer, 1978). The former have been shown to have more psychopathology, greater levels of emotional disturbance, and lower levels of self-esteem (Kalichman, 1991). The personalities of rapists reflect more denial, depression, anger, hostility, acting out, aggression, and suspiciousness than those of exposers. Compared to offenders convicted of physical assault, rapists were more hostile, anxious, and aggressive and had more bizarre mentation (Rader, 1977). They tended to endorse MMPI items such as delight in getting away with a crime (Erickson et al., 1987). However, some were able to produce normal MMPI code types, though even this group has subspikes on Psychopathic Deviate (Pd) usually around ½ standard deviation below the critical threshold for clinical significance, and up to five different MMPI profile codes have been identified with cluster analysis (Kalichman, 1988a, 1989, 1990).

The modal MMPI profile of the rapist, based on eight separate studies totaling just under 800 total participants, is a 1-point code characterized by clinical elevations on Psychopathic Deviate (Pd) and subspikes on Depression (Dep) and Schizophrenia (Sc). This modal code type appears isomorphic with the modal code type of all sexual offenders and with pedophiles and is coded 4'82. In general, rapists tend to be somewhat depressed and anxious, to use projection as a defense along with acting out, to fear emotional involvement, to be pleasure oriented, and to lack empathy, and they are poor in communication. They are angry, hostile, irritable, and resentful.

Indecent Exposure

Indecent exposure is a "pure sex" crime, because it usually involves no physical violence. The personality of offenders convicted of indecent exposure is usually described as passive, timid, and self-effacing and as showing a lack of assertion. They have feelings of inadequacy, especially in relation to their sexuality; they are immature and are prone to experience perceived threats to their masculinity. On the MMPI, first offenders tend to receive normal MMPI scores, whereas chronic offenders show impulsivity, irritability, estrangement, and sexual adjustment problems. They appear to be mildly nonconforming, as evidenced by minor run-ins with the law (McCreary, 1975b; Rader, 1977).

The modal MMPI profile, based on only two MMPI studies totaling 121 indecent exposure offenders, is a 1-point code with an elevated Psychopathic Deviate (Pd) scale with few subspikes on the remaining clinical scales.

Incest

One classification model categorizes child sexual abusers into two groups—*fixated* and *regressed*. Fixated abusers have permanent sexual interest in children, possibly suggesting an early arrested psychosexual development. The regressed type is more reflective of the incest perpetrator. This type has a primary sexual identification and orientation toward adults, but the person regresses in the face of overwhelming stress and turns to a child for sexual gratification (Hunter et al., 1990).

Fathers who commit incest have been described as socially immature with significant character (antisocial) pathology characterized by passive-dependent traits, fear of inadequacy in the traditional sexual role, feelings of inferiority, exaggerated needs for attention, and social withdrawal, but also as manipulative, as having problems with impulse control, and as resentful of authority. Many have significant problems with substance abuse, particularly alcohol (Kirkland & Bauer, 1982). Many are not demonstrably pathological, and much of their antisocial attitudes and behavior is covert. In fact, their MMPIs tend to be in the subclinical range (Scott & Stone, 1986).

Others show more characterological defects associated with chronic anger, a passive-aggressive personality, overcontrolled hostility, and marital problems (Erickson et al., 1987). They also seem to differ on whether they admit the offense. Those who admitted the offense were found to be socially isolated, dependent, regressing, and angry and had unresolved gender identity issues. Those who did not admit the offense were rigid and impulsive, externalized their anger, and showed more sociopathy, and they were more difficult to engage in therapy (Vaupel & Goeke, 1994).

The modal profile of incest perpetrators, based on only four MMPI studies with more than 500 participants, was a within normal limits profile (Kirkland & Bauer, 1982; Panton, 1976; Scott & Stone, 1986; Vaupel & Goeke, 1994). In other words, one would not suspect any pathology on the basis of MMPI scores. This seems to add credence to clinical reports that incestuous behaviors often continue for substantial periods of time without being noticed by others.

I have found only one study that looked at adult men who had been abused by their maternal caregivers ($N = 20$). These victims showed features of posttraumatic stress disorder. A smaller subgroup showed characteristics of depression and sociopathy and may correspond to known offenders with history of childhood abuse (by men). Both groups had much subjective distress and psychological disruption (Roys & Timms, 1995).

Miscellaneous Sex Abusers

Some MMPI studies aggregated miscellaneous sexual offenders without specifying the nature of the offense. Peaks on Psychopathic Deviate (Pd) and subspikes on Schizophrenia (Sc), Depression (Dep), and Paranoia (Pa) characterized the modal code type for this group.

In summary, the data reviewed here suggest that, whether or not the nature of the offense is specified, the modal code type of sexual offenders is a 1-point code peaking on Psychopathic Deviate (Pd) with mild elevations on Depression (Dep), Schizophrenia (Sc), and Paranoia (Pa). The MMPI results of incest perpetrators often peak on Pd without accompanying elevations.

Code Types

Modal profiles may mask meaningful subgroups among a heterogeneous population of abusers. One way to capture the more common types of abuser is to review the code types for each of the published samples. Many of the studies reported cluster analysis subgroups among the larger population of abusers, thereby attesting to the diversity of abuser types. Table 7.4 presents the various code types reported in the literature.

The findings in Tables 7.3 and 7.4 validate the findings from an array of other clinical sources and lead to the following conclusions:

- The sexual abusing and sexual offending population is heterogeneous.
- No one MMPI profile is commonly associated with sexual abuse.
- A common MMPI modal profile is often found among sexual offenders. This code type is characterized by peaks on Psychopathic Deviate (Pd) and subspikes on Depression (Dep), Paranoia (Pa), and Schizophrenia (Sc). These subspikes are usually one-half standard deviation below the Pd clinical scale.
- Incest perpetrators tend to have within normal limits MMPI profiles.
- Cluster analysis and a review of MMPI code types across a plethora of studies indicate that there is no one code type characteristic of a typical sexual offender, and many offenders do not even have the modal code type associated with the sexual offender group.
- The MMPI is best used as a measure of psychopathology and character pathology, and not as a measure to assign guilt or innocence.

Lanyon (1993) found that MMPI special scales suggestive of sexual deviance—Pedophile (Pe), Sexual Deviation (Sv), Aggravated Sex (ASX), and Sexual Morbidity (Sm)—differentiated sexual offenders from control participants, but these differences were largely attributed to offenders who admitted the crime. The differences were maintained even after groups were equated for degree of psychopathology. After controlling for defensive responding, these special scales were able to differentiate groups, including the offenders who did not admit the offense. These special scales held some promise but lost a substantial number of items in the MMPI–2 restandardization.

Rorschach Assessment

There have been few Rorschach studies with sexual abusers. Rorschach signs of defensive responding (high P, D, A, Lambda, and PER; low R, Blends, and ZF) did not distinguish between groups of alleged sexual offenders who did and did not admit to the charges. This suggests that the Rorschach may not be sensitive to response distortion indicative of defensiveness (Wasyliw, Zenn, Grossman, & Haywood, 1998). However, in a later study, the Rorschach responses of sexual abusers showed evidence of psycho-

TABLE 7.4
Minnesota Multiphasic Personality Inventory Code Types Among Sexual Abusers

Author(s)	Code type	Type of abuse	Size of sample	% of total
	Within normal limits		1,118	31
McCreary, 1975b		Indecent exposure	37	
McCreary, 1975a		Child abusers	18	
J. A. Armentrout and Hauer, 1978		Rapists and miscellaneous	17	
Scott and Stone, 1986		Incest	33	
		Incest	29	
Kalichman, 1989		Adult rapists	39	
Kalichman, 1990		Adult molesters	21	
Duthie and McIvor, 1990		Child abusers	16	
		Child abusers	7	
		Child abusers	8	
Kalichman, 1991		Child and adolescent rapists	42	
		Child and adolescent rapists	48	
Kalichman and Henderson, 1991		Child abusers	27	
		Child abusers	21	
G. C. Hall, Shepherd, and Mudrak, 1992		Child abusers	47	
Kalichman, Henderson, Shealy, and Dwyer, 1992		Child abusers	15	
		Child abusers	38	
Vaupel and Goeke, 1994		Incest	20	
Roys and Timms, 1995		Miscellaneous abusers	9	
Herkov, Gynther, Thomas, and Myers, 1996		Miscellaneous abusers	19	
Grossman, Wasyliw, Benn, and Gyoerkoe, 2002	'4 (T 64–69)	Miscellaneous abusers	416	12
McCreary, 1975b		Indecent exposure	38	
Rader, 1977		Exposure, rapists	36	
Hunter, Childers, Gerald, and Esmaili, 1990		Child abusers	55	
Shealy, Kalichman, Syzmanowski, and McKee, 1991		Child abusers	45	
McAnulty, Adams, and Wright, 1994		Child abusers	30	
		Child abusers	60	
Heersink and Strassberg, 1995		Child abusers	87	

(continued)

TABLE 7.4
Minnesota Multiphasic Personality Inventory Code Types Among Sexual Abusers (Continued)

Author(s)	Code type	Type of abuse	Size of sample	% of total
Roys and Timms, 1995		Miscellaneous abusers	9	
Herkov et al., 1996		Miscellaneous abusers	22	
		Miscellaneous abusers	18	
Crolley, Roys, Thyer, and Bordnick, 1998		Miscellaneous abusers	16	
	2'4		16	< 1
Anderson, Kunce, and Rich, 1979		Miscellaneous abusers	16	
	4'		393	11
Panton, 1979		Incest	35	
		Incest	28	
Kalichman, 1989		Adult rapists	39	
Kalichman, 1990		Adult molesters	61	
Hunter et al., 1990		Child abusers	33	
G. L. Davis and Hoffman, 1991		Child abusers	61	
G. C. Hall, Graham, and Shepherd, 1991		Miscellaneous abusers	123	
Kalichman and Henderson, 1991		Child abusers	4	
Roys and Timms, 1995		Child abusers	9	
	5'		21	< 1
Duthie and McIvor, 1990		Child abusers	21	
	6'		71	2
Kalichman, 1991		Child and adolescent rapists	54	
Shealy et al., 1991		Child abusers	17	
	'26, 2'6, 26'		42	1
J. A. Armentrout and Hauer, 1978	'26	Rapists and miscellaneous abusers	21	
Duthie and McIvor, 1990	2'6	Child abusers	8	
	26'	Rapists and miscellaneous abusers	13	
	28		18	< 1
Erickson, Luxenberg, Walbek, and Seely, 1987		Miscellaneous abusers	18	
	42'		93	2
Erickson et al., 1987		Miscellaneous abusers	36	
Kalichman and Henderson, 1991		Child abusers	20	

(continued)

TABLE 7.4
Minnesota Multiphasic Personality Inventory Code Types Among Sexual Abusers (Continued)

Author(s)	Code type	Type of abuse	Size of sample	% of total
Kalichman, Dwyer, Henderson, and Hoffman, 1992		Child abusers	29	
Grossman et al., 2002		Miscellaneous abusers	8	
	43'		28	1
Erickson et al., 1987		Miscellaneous abusers	19	
Kalichman and Henderson, 1991		Child abusers	9	
	45'		45	1
Erickson et al., 1987		Miscellaneous abusers	45	
	46'		30	1
Erickson et al., 1987		Miscellaneous abusers	30	
	47'		19	<1
Erickson et al., 1987		Miscellaneous abusers	19	
	48'		120	3
McCreary, 1975b		Child abusers	33	
Rader, 1977		Exposers, rapists	47	
Erickson et al., 1987		Miscellaneous abusers	58	
	4'9, 49		104	3
Anderson et al., 1979		Miscellaneous abusers	32	
Erickson et al., 1987		Miscellaneous abusers	40	
Yanagida and Ching, 1993		Child abusers	32	
	87		15	<1
Erickson et al., 1987		Miscellaneous abusers	15	
	89		9	<1
Erickson et al., 1987		Miscellaneous abusers	9	
	482, 428		441	12
Quinsey, Arnold, and Pruesse, 1980		Child molesters, rapists	15	
G. C. Hall, Maiuro, Vitaliano, and Proctor, 1986		Rapists	406	
Vaupel and Goeke, 1994		Incest	20	
	486		25	1
McCreary, 1975b		Indecent exposure	10	
Shealy et al., 1991		Child abusers	16	

(continued)

TABLE 7.4
Minnesota Multiphasic Personality Inventory Code Types Among Sexual Abusers *(Continued)*

Author(s)	Code type	Type of abuse	Size of sample	% of total
Kalichman, 1989	489, 849	Adult rapists	41	1
Kalichman, 1990		Adult molesters	21	
Kalichman, Dwyer, Henderson, and Hoffman, 1992		Child abusers	9	
			11	
Quinsey et al., 1980	874	Child molesters, rapists	20	<1
Kirkland and Bauer, 1982		Incest	10	
			10	
	High ranging codes 8427		518	15
			316	9
Quinsey et al., 1980		Child molesters, rapists	10	
G. C. Hall, 1989		Sexual assaulters	81	
G. C. Hall et al., 1991		Miscellaneous abusers	138	
Kalichman and Henderson, 1991		Child abusers	7	
		Child abusers	9	
G. C. Hall et al., 1992		Child abusers	42	
Kalichman, Dwyer, Henderson, and Hoffman, 1992		Child abusers	17	
Heersink and Strassberg, 1995		Child abusers	12	
			96	
Anderson et al., 1979	8624	Miscellaneous abusers	40	
Kalichman, 1989		Adult rapists	12	
Kalichman, 1990		Adult molesters	14	
Duthie and McIvor, 1990		Child abusers	12	
G. C. Hall et al., 1992		Child abusers	18	
Kalichman, 1990	8649	Adult molesters	67	2
			67	
Kalichman, 1989	8674	Adult rapists	12	<1
Shealy et al., 1991		Child abusers	120	
			12	
Kalichman and Henderson, 1991	8726	Child abusers	4	<1
			4	
Heersink and Strassberg, 1995	8697	Child abusers	23	1
			23	

pathology, even though many of the sexual abusers tended to minimize their psychopathology on the MMPI and MMPI–2 (Grossman, Wasyliw, Benn, & Gyoerkoe, 2002). Regarding the Rorschach variables indicative of Emotional Distress (D score, Adjusted D score), Impaired Judgment (Wsum6, X+%, X–%, and 2Ab+ Art + Ay), Interpersonal Dysfunction (H, M-, Sex), and the special indexes indicative of psychopathology (DEPI, SCZI, CDI, and S-Con), results have shown that all relevant indexes were higher in the sexual abuser groups than in the general population. Thus, as a group, even the minimizers of psychopathology on the MMPI or MMPI–2 were not able to conceal their psychopathology on the Rorschach.

One study looked at Rorschach signs suggestive of anxiety and hopelessness, painful introspection, and distorted views of others. They also assessed primitive dependency needs, poor self-esteem or excessive self-focus, tendency to fantasize about abuse, tendency to avoid emotionally tinged stimuli, and chronic oppositionality and hostility. The incarcerated pedophiles were significantly different than comparison groups on these variables, suggesting that the pedophiles had many core personality traits of a narcissistic personality disorder but were less well defended against feelings of vulnerability and painful introspection than other incarcerated men (Bridges, Wilson, & Gacono, 1998). This study has value in the theoretical understanding of the personality of the pedophile but is not useful for individual prediction or for detection of sexual deviation involving children.

The results of these studies suggest that the combination of the MMPI and the MCMI or the MACI combined with the Rorschach should be considered part of a basic assessment test battery with sexual abusers.

What do the empirical findings in the assessment literature tell us about the nature of sexual offenders? For the most part, the results suggest that these perpetrators have traits associated with either psychopathy or aggressive, passive-aggressive, or dependent disorders. Using Millon's theoretical conceptualization, researchers categorize the dependent as passive in mode of adaptation and dependent in interpersonal relationships. The antisocial is categorized as active in adaptation and independent in relationships. The aggressive style is imbalanced on the pain–pleasure continuum and independent in interpersonal relationships. The passive-aggressive style is active in adaptation and ambivalent in interpersonal relationships.

ETHICAL ISSUES

Ethical issues pervade the assessment and treatment of sexual offenders. Perhaps the most problematic issue pertains to testifying as to recidivism or the future sexual behavior of convicted felons. Current empirical data do not yet strongly support the validity of predictors for recidivism (Blau,

1998), although there are some productive lines of inquiry, as referenced earlier in this chapter. Yet psychologists may be asked to make generalizations about sexual offenders that are not tied to empirical data (Melton, Petrila, Poythress, & Slobogin, 1997).

Concerns have been raised about the invasive nature of phallometric assessment, particularly with juveniles. During the procedure they may be exposed to sexual stimuli beyond their experience, which may evoke curiosity and experimentation (possibly with subsequent victims). There is also limited evidence documenting the utility of these procedures with juvenile offenders.

CASE EXAMPLE

This section presents a case example that includes both history and psychological test results. Findings are presented with a focus on the critical thinking that led to the final conclusions.

Reason for Referral

The patient was a 17-year-old, single White man who was court-referred for a psychological evaluation following his arrest for sexual molestation (digital penetration). He had no prior psychiatric or criminal record and resided in a household with other siblings and both parents, who were engaged in professional careers. Neither parent had any prior history of behaviors requiring mental health services.

Circumstances of Arrest

Statements by both the victim and the perpetrator verified the following account: The patient was attending a group sleepover at a friend's house. Unable to sleep, the patient decided to go downstairs and get a glass of milk (the patient does not drink alcohol). On descending the stairs, he walked by an adolescent girl sleeping on the couch. Her nightgown was scrunched up and lying near the top of her thighs. He reached down and inserted his finger into her vagina. She awoke and screamed, waking up the others, who called the police, and the patient was arrested.

Referral Questions

The court wanted to know the following:

- Does a pattern of sexually deviant behavior seem to exist?
- What is the nature and history of this pattern of sexually deviant behavior?
- Given the nature and history of this pattern of sexually deviant behavior, is treatment appropriate for this individual, and if so, in what setting and under what conditions?
- Was the person honest with the evaluator during the course of the evaluation?

The court issued specific instructions stating that the purpose of the evaluation was to assess how similar or dissimilar, with regard to developmental history, personality profile, sexual interests, arousal, and honesty, this adolescent was compared with adolescent men known to have histories of being sexual with children (i.e., psychological profiling instructions). The court further stated that it was not within the scope of the evaluation to determine whether there was a sexual act or acts with a specific child as alleged. (This was not an issue, because the perpetrator admitted to the behavior as described).

Evaluation Components

The following measures were used in the evaluation:

- Millon Clinical Multiaxial Inventory,
- Thematic Apperception Test (TAT),
- sentence completion test,
- figure drawings (not presented here),
- clinical interviews,
- interviews with both parents, and
- court document review.

History

The family history was negative for mental illness and substance abuse. The parents had been married for over 30 years without incident. They reported no developmental problems or school-related problems with the perpetrator. He did have a history of marijuana abuse beginning at age 14 and continuing in escalating amounts over the next 3 years until he accepted his parents' admonitions and encouragements to attend a youth-oriented Alcoholics Anonymous meeting, where he continued to go regularly; he had been abstinent for 9 months. The patient said he started using marijuana because he was curious and because all his friends were doing it. He liked it and did not see any problems with it, until it began causing trouble between him and his parents. He also decided to stop drinking alcohol at the time he stopped marijuana use. He reported that neither alcohol nor marijuana were involved in the sexual crime, which was verified by physical tests following the arrest.

Sexual History

The patient reported no prior sexual history other than masturbation. He was embarrassed to discuss this area of his life with the examiner and refused to discuss any sexual fantasies, but he adamantly insisted that he had no prior sexual experience and that this was his first sexual episode with someone else.

The patient could not report why he did what he did. He did not know the girl very well; she was a friend of a friend, whom he had met at the party that night, which was parentally supervised. He did not even spend that much time with her at the party and spent most of the evening with his previous peer network of friends. There were no alcohol or drugs at the party (attested to by supervising parents in the police record). They played some games, watched videos, talked, and went to bed at around 2:30 a.m. He felt wound up and could not sleep, and after about a half hour he decided to go downstairs and get some milk. He thought that would help him relax and would put him to sleep.

As he approached the bottom of the stairs, he saw the girl sleeping on the couch. He had to pass by the couch to get into the kitchen. As he passed the couch, he inserted his finger into her vagina. He denied having sexual thoughts while he was lying in bed and as he was coming down the stairs. He was unable or unwilling to articulate what his thoughts were when he noticed her lying on the couch. He was unable to say exactly when he noticed her thighs, and he could not tell the evaluator if he had an erection, stating simply, "I don't know." He also was unable to tell the evaluator why he did it, and the evaluator became convinced that he really did not know why he did it. For this reason, the evaluator administered some projective tests, hoping to uncover a possible unconscious motivation.

Statements to the police essentially corroborated the story as told here and did not address any of the variables discussed above for statement validity. Hence, there is no need to present that material here.

Psychological Test Results

The patient was given the Millon Adolescent Clinical Inventory. Several of the MACI scales are relevant for this assessment, specifically the modifying indexes for test-taking attitudes, the Unruly and Forceful personality pattern scales for evidence of conduct-disordered behavior, the

Sexual Discomfort Expressed Concerns scale, and the Delinquency Predisposition and Impulsive Propensity clinical syndrome scales.

The modifying indexes suggested that the patient scored in the clinically significant range on disclosure. This indicates that he had a broad tendency to avoid self-disclosure and an unwillingness to divulge personal material. It may also indicate problems with introspection. This finding was consistent with his presentation in the clinical interview, but also was consistent with general denial among sexual offenders on objective psychological tests.

The personality pattern scales indicated that he scored in the clinically significant ranges on Dramatizing, Conforming, Submissive, and Egotistic, and his personality description would be a melding of the traits measured by those scales. Essentially, he seemed to have a need for both attention and security. Behaviorally, he probably engaged in behaviors to draw attention, being quite gregarious and perhaps socially facile. He seemed extroverted and outgoing and also perhaps uninhibited, at least at the surface level. People with this personality style tend to have lots of friends but can be impulsive. However, these impulsive behaviors are done within generally conforming social guidelines to ensure the satisfaction of approval and maintenance of desired attention. He tended to suppress or repress negative emotions, and thereby maintained self-discipline. He probably acted respectfully with authority but vented about authority figures with trusted friends. The egotistic part of his personality was probably related more to a general state of being an adolescent than to any ingrained traits.

The patient had neither significant expressed concerns nor any apparent clinical syndromes. His Delinquent Predisposition scores were in the normal range but were slightly higher than other scales because he endorsed past behaviors associated with marijuana use. However, he had a broad tendency to deny problems. Was this part of his developing a histrionic style, and hence unconscious, or was it an intentional masking of troublesome behaviors? To help answer this question, the evaluator turned to projective techniques.

The patient's figure drawings were consistent with the findings on the MACI. Human figures were characterized by large drawings and to some extent flamboyant details (especially on the male figure), consistent with his histrionic style.

Salient sentence completion responses appear in Exhibit 7.1. The patient tended to exhibit acceptance of personal responsibility for his behavior (1, 4) within the context of a developed superego and conscience (7, 8, 9, 10), repressed aggression (2, 3), and nonimpulsive behavior (5, 6). His responses were replete with dutiful and admiring responses toward his parents, with a lament that they were too restrictive. Overall, the Rorschach showed aspects of his basic personal style of primary histrionic and conforming traits

EXHIBIT 7.1
Patient's Psychological Test Results

Millon Clinical Multiaxial Inventory

Scale		Base rate score
	Modifying indexes	
X	Disclosure	10
Y	Desirability	72
Z	Debasement	35
	Personality patterns	
1	Introversive	44
2A	Inhibited	35
2B	Doleful	18
3	Submissive	80
4	Dramatizing	92
5	Egotistic	78
6A	Unruly	55
6B	Forceful	28
7	Conforming	55
8A	Oppositional	30
8B	Self-Demanding	26
9	Borderline Tendency	31
	Expressed concerns	
A	Identity Diffusion	41
B	Self-Devaluation	15
C	Body Disapproval	7
D	Sexual Discomfort	58
E	Peer Insecurity	26
F	Social Insensitivity	60
G	Family Discord	58
H	Childhood Abuse	14
	Clinical syndromes	
AA	Eating Dysfunctions	6
BB	Substance-Abuse Proneness	44
CC	Delinquent Predisposition	66
DD	Impulsive Propensity	39
EE	Anxious Feelings	60
FF	Depressive Affect	18
GG	Suicidal Tendency	11

(continued)

EXHIBIT 7.1
Patient's Psychological Test Results *(Continued)*

Thematic Apperception Test

Card 1

A kid looking at a violin. The kid is really frustrated with it because he's having trouble playing it. (?) He had to learn how to play something, and he couldn't figure it out. So he's taking a break. (?) He'll learn to play a song. He'll figure it out.

Card 2

(Long reaction time) I'm kind of stumped on this one. I guess it could be like a family on a farm. The guy with the horse is the father. The girl with the books is the daughter, and the lady by the tree is the mother. The dad's working. Looks like it would be really far out. What led up to this? The dad had to work and the mother came out to be near him, and the daughter just got back from school. (?) He finished the work, and they'll go inside and eat dinner.

Card 3BM

Is that a kid? The kid's really tired, and he just plopped like that. Maybe he's had a boring day, and he's, like, really tired and bored. He'll sleep, and then he wakes up later.

Card 4

The two people are, like, boyfriend/girlfriend, a couple. The guy is pissed because, like, some other guy who's not in the picture was saying real bad things to this women [*sic*], and the lady says, "Chill out! No big deal!" The guy doesn't do anything.

Card 6BM

The old lady is looking out the window 'cause that's what old ladies do. She's bored and alone. The old lady is getting old lady sickness—like forgetful. The guy is her son, and he's going to put her in this old lady house, but he's nervous about what he will say, so he's working himself to say it. He's, kind of feels guilty about it.

Card 7BM

The other guy is really sad—like someone from his family must have died. He could be at a funeral 'cause they're all dressed up and the older guy is like talking to him. Helping him feel better. He gets over it. He feels better.

Card 8BM

Looks like he died on the table—something really bad just happened to him, like a car accident, and they're doing emergency surgery on him. But it's too late. The guy in the picture in the center is the same guy on the table. He's not really there. It's like his spirit. (?) There's a light going across the picture so it's the light of a near death experience so he just goes towards the light and goes to heaven.

Card 9BM

Looks like something like World War II. All the people are in World War II. A whole bunch of people died and they just kind of stacked up the dead people. They are soldiers. They are remembered for serving and for dying for their country in the war.

(continued)

EXHIBIT 7.1
Patient's Psychological Test Results *(Continued)*

Card 10

The person towards the bottom is the kid. He or she—I can't tell—was away from home for a really long time and the person towards the top is the parent of the kid and the parent was really worried about the kid but now the kid is home again the parent is really grateful that the kid is OK.

Card 11

No idea what this is. (?) People climbing rocks. They do this for fun. They're rock climbers. They're climbing up the mountain. They finally get to the top and had a lot of fun.

Card 12M

A person laying down—like sick—about going to die on his death bed. Looks like the father is standing up. He's just praying for his daughter. The daughter gets better.

Card 13MF

The guy standing up—he's married, and he has to go to work. The girl in bed is the wife. She stays home and takes care of the kinds [*sic*]. He has to go to work. That's why he's got the shirt and tie on.

Card 14

That's a kid at night in his rom [*sic*]. He's sneaking out of the house because his friends are outside and they want to talk to him. He talks to them and he goes back up to his room and goes to sleep.

Card 15

Really crazy one—all these are creepy. Some Halloween thing is going on. He's in a graveyard and a ghost is in the graveyard. He's just hanging out there and he scares a bunch of people.

Card 16

For real? There's a guy playing his guitar. He's like in a band and a bunch of people are with him and like his music. He plays shows. The crowd likes it and eventually they all go home.

Card 17

Looks like a super hero. Like muscles and everything. Climbing down the rope to save the day. There's a bank being robbed and like he came to catch the bank robber. After that he catches the bank robber and saves the day.

Card 20

A guy. I think he's looking at the big bushes or flowers—but it's nighttime and I guess it's a light. Just checking out the flowers. After that he just goes for a walk and goes home.

(continued)

EXHIBIT 7.1
Patient's Psychological Test Results *(Continued)*

Some Relevant Sentence Completion Responses

Sentence stem	Response
1. Sentence stem	Response
2. He felt to blame when	he broke the plate.
3. When she refused him	hew [*sic*] said OK.
4. When she turned him down	I left the house.
5. His poor grades were due to	not listening in class.
6. When I have to make a decision	I ask other's [*sic*] opinions.
7. If I can't get what I want	I have to accept it.
8. He felt he had done wrong when he	felt guilty.
9. My worst failing is	when I don't treat people nice.
10. His conscience bothered him when he	did something bad.
11. If I were king I would	be nice to people.

Note. (?) indicates an examiner question.

similar to those observed on the MACI. Emotions were probably generally held in check but might occasionally erupt. There was material pertaining to absence of aggression, but no details pertaining to sexuality. This probably was a conscious suppression on his part when completing the sentence stems. To get at this material, the evaluator turned to the TAT.

The patient's TAT provides evidence of denial and repression of sexual impulses (1, unconscious fears of sexual inadequacy reflected in trouble with the violin—a sexually symbolic object; 2, did not notice the pregnant woman; 13MF, did not address the seminude figure in bed; and 20, "looks" at flowers—a symbol of virginity and sexuality). An additional defense is escape (2, 3BM, 6BM, 8BM, 9BM), correlating with his history of marijuana abuse. He may have had problematic object relations with women (his mother?), who are seen somewhat negatively (4, 6BM), and some impulses to act out (4, 14), but there was recognition of negative consequences for this behavior (17BM), so it was mostly controlled (4). Histrionic traits of acting to draw attention were evident (16, 17BM), with additional evidence of some problematic interpersonal relationships in his environment (4, 6BM, 8BM, 10). The TAT appeared quite consistent with the MACI test findings.

Psychologist's Conclusions

Although this patient showed evidence of some denial in responding to objective testing, this was probably associated with an underlying psychological character structure of a histrionic quality that used denial and repression as the main defense against undesired impulses, combined with some conscious embarrassment about his recent behavior. Given his character structure and age, his digital insertion was probably an unplanned, impulsive act that was unlikely to appear again. He tended to take responsibility for his behavior and expressed remorse and guilt for it. This patient showed little evidence of a sexual offending character structure. He showed no evidence of a pattern of sexually deviant behavior. He was in a caring, supportive, and loving family environment and was likely to benefit from short-term outpatient counseling.

In summary, this chapter presented some statistics on the extent of child abuse in America; addressed the controversial issue of psychological profiling of sexual offenders, which rests on the issue of personality traits in this group; discussed the forensic and psychological assessment of sexual offenders; presented commonly used tools for their assessment (clinical interview, personality tests, deviant interest tests) and additional assessment methods (e.g., statement analysis, phallometry); referenced data on risk of relapse, reoffense, and recidivism; and concluded by presenting a case and its analysis through to conclusions.

8

ASSESSMENT OF ABUSE, AGGRESSION, AND LETHAL VIOLENCE

Since the courts ruled in 1976 that psychologists may be held civilly liable for failure to warn potential victims of lethal violence (*Tarasoff v. Regents of the University of California*, 1976), the need to properly assess client dangerousness has become prominent in the training and practice of forensic psychologists. Questions pertaining to such issues as parent, child, or spouse physical abuse, involuntary commitment because of dangerousness, release of sexual predators from jail, orders of protection, and release of patients from mental hospitals who were deemed not guilty by reason of insanity are but a few areas in which a psychologist may be asked to perform a violence risk assessment.

This chapter presents research and clinical material on the assessment of abuse, aggression, and lethal violence. It focuses primarily on the psychometric assessment of personality factors and describes the instruments most often used with assaultive individuals and with murderers.

In addition, this chapter reviews the literature base with these instruments and describes their strengths, limitations, and continuing refinements. However, the reader should understand that a comprehensive psychological evaluation of an individual defendant recognizes and uses all sources of data (e.g., clinical interviews, collateral sources, patient records, and police reports), in addition to objective and projective personality test findings, and takes into account other kinds of testing such as cognitive and neuropsychological functioning. Thus, the content of this chapter is somewhat limited in comparison to actual practice, where psychometric findings are integrated with other sources of information.

In 1978 Thomas Barefoot was convicted of murdering a police officer. After hearing testimony from a psychiatrist that Barefoot was likely to commit violence again, the jury sentenced the defendant to death. The verdict was appealed, based in part on the question of whether a psychiatrist could predict future violence. In 1983 the American Psychiatric Association submitted an amicus curiae brief to the U.S. Supreme Court indicating that psychiatric predictions of future violence were wrong in two out of every three cases. The Court ruled that it was constitutional for psychiatrists to render such predictions for purposes of determining whom to execute, even when they were often inaccurate (*Barefoot v. Estelle*, 1983). Since then, the task has shifted from predicting future violence to evaluating future risk.

The Minnesota Multiphasic Personality Inventory (MMPI) has been the most frequently used psychological test with murderers and with violent and assaultive individuals. There is a substantial literature base on this test for this population, and several assessment refinements have been made, particularly in the area of developing homogeneous patient profiles and in developing special scales from the MMPI item pool. This chapter focuses on MMPI studies with this population. It also presents data from the Millon Clinical Multiaxial Inventory (MCMI) and the Rorschach when available.

OVERVIEW

There are six issues that need to be understood before discussing research findings with the MMPI (or any other assessment tool):

1. All available research has assessed patients and presented empirical group data after the crime has been committed and the perpetrator apprehended. The patient's psychological state before committing the offense is a matter of conjecture, interpolation, and judgment. The offender's psychological state at the time of the assessment is what is actually being measured. The psychological effects of imprisonment itself might also be reflected in test findings, depending on the length of incarceration prior to the assessment (Westermeyer, 1974).
2. Timing of the assessment may affect test results. An offender who is tested in conjunction with a hearing to determine competency to stand trial or while addressing other pretrial

evaluation issues in association with an insanity plea might show different test results than an offender who is tested as part of a research project after he or she has been sentenced and confined in prison for a determined length of time (Finney, Skeeters, Auvenshine, & Smith, 1973; Holcolm, Adams, Nicholas, Ponder, & Anderson, 1984; Panton, 1976).

3. Perpetrators of violence are a heterogeneous population. A political assassin or organized crime hit man would have different personality traits and motivations than an armed robber who, based on circumstances, goes too far and kills a store employee. The fired employee who returns to the scene of his former employment with a shotgun, killing those in his path, is certainly driven by different psychological forces than the chronically abused housewife who, after sustaining years of physical abuse, engages in a violent and lethal act out of desperation and hopelessness. The drug dealer who was cheated by a street addict and arranges for a substantial increase in the heroin content of a bag that, when injected, results in a lethal overdose is operating from a different psychological framework than a man who murders while drunk. These subtle differences must be addressed methodologically and understood psychologically to provide a full accounting of the personality and motives of those who commit murder. Yet these nuances are unlikely to be fully captured by a single assessment instrument. Psychological tests tell us what, but they do not tell us why.

4. Moderator variables such as race, gender, and educational level (and its correlates—IQ, social status, and occupational status) can also affect scores among offenders (Holcolm & Adams, 1982; Holcolm, Adams, & Ponder, 1984). For example, Mc-Donald and Paitich (1981) found that variables that differentiated murderers from nonmurderous felons disappeared when they were compared to people who were unemployed. This illustrates the importance of controlling to moderator variables in research. Researchers and psychologists evaluating an individual patient must consider these variables and how they may affect test scores (Sutker & Moan, 1973).

5. The context of the crime must always be considered, especially when conducting violence risk assessments.

6. Finally, there are problems with self-report methodology as a method of personality assessment. First, the patient has to have some self-understanding and self-awareness. Second, the patient must be willing to report that knowledge in an unbiased

and truthful manner. However, in forensic settings, a myriad of motivations might compel an offender to lie, exaggerate, fake illness, or underreport certain key problems that could be detrimental to the defendant at trial. Malingering may be common among murderers. In fact, a significant number of patients awaiting trial claim amnesia and attribute it to alcohol or drug use or to some emotional block related to the facts of the crime (Parwatikar, Holcolm, & Menninger, 1985). Although the MMPI has scales that screen for such tendencies, these matters need to be under continuous scrutiny during the evaluation.

ASSESSMENT OF VIOLENCE

The MacArthur violence risk assessment study (Monahan et al., 2001) is the most comprehensive study on violence risk assessment to date. In this study, 1,136 men and women between the ages of 18 and 40 were monitored and followed for 1 year after discharge from a psychiatric hospital. This sample was then compared with 519 patients also discharged from the psychiatric hospital who served as a comparison cohort. Both violence (i.e., battery with physical injury) toward others and aggressive acts (battery without physical injury) were studied. A total of 134 variables were associated with future violence at 20 weeks and at 1 year follow-up. These variables were divided into dispositional (i.e., demographic), historical, contextual, and clinical variables. History of violent behavior was perhaps the most significant variable, but presence of an antisocial or borderline personality disorder was also significant, even in the absence of a documented history of violence.

Test Signs of Violence and Aggression

The MMPI, the MCMI, and the Rorschach are the best indicators of aggression. Elevations on the F validity scale, Psychopathic Deviate (Pd), and Hypomania (Ma; Huesmann, Lefkowitz, & Eron, 1978); the 43, 48/84, and 49/94 2-point code types and selected MMPI types of the Megargee classification system; the Anger and Antisocial Practices content scales, and the Overcontrolled Hostility (OH) supplemental scale are the MMPI measures most likely to be associated with aggression.

The Antisocial, Aggressive-Sadistic, and to some extent Passive-Aggressive, Borderline, Paranoid, and possibly Delusional Disorder scales are the MCMI elevations most likely to reflect aggression (Craig, 1993b). A number of Rorschach variables have been proposed as measures of aggression.

The Aggressive Movement (Ag) response is scored whenever a movement response is clearly aggressive in nature (e.g., two bears fighting). The Aggressive Content (AgC) response is scored when the aggressive response is predatory, injurious, harmful, or dangerous (e.g., a shotgun), and the Morbid Content (MOR) special score is coded when objects are seen as destroyed, dead, spoiled, damaged, injured, or broken (e.g., a smashed, dead frog, a gloomy-looking willow tree). Gacono and Meloy (1994) published a list of objects that would meet the definition of AgC, and the reader can use this list as a guide for scoring responses that are similar to their published list.

Primary Aggression (A1) responses describe intense murder or sado-masochistic aggression (e.g., two killers stabbing a boy). Secondary aggression (A2) responses include hostility or aggression that is more socially tolerated and nonlethal (e.g., two bears fighting). Aggressive Potential (AgPot) responses indicate that an aggressive act is likely to occur or is imminent (e.g., two lions about to pounce on unsuspecting prey); this category of response is thought to reflect sadistic features in the examinee. Past Aggression (AgPast) responses indicate that the act has occurred or the object has been the target of aggression (e.g., a dead bug that someone stepped on and smashed its head) and implies possible masochistic features in the examinee; this score is frequently accompanied by a Morbid Content response (Meloy & Gacono, 1992). Finally, Gacono and Meloy (1994) recommended scoring Sado-Masochism (SM) when an aggressive response is accompanied by pleasurable affect.

These aggressive responses can be reliably scored and have been shown to be related to *Diagnostic and Statistical Manual of Mental Disorders* (DSM–IV; American Psychiatric Association, 1994) diagnoses of Antisocial and Borderline Personality Disorders. They were also related to a self-report measure of anger and antisocial practices (Baity & Hilsenroth, 1999; Baity, McDonald, & Hilsenroth, 2000), and the reader should consult this source for interpretive meanings of these scores, especially because psychopaths tend to produce fewer of these responses than other groups.

Table 8.1 displays the common indexes of aggression in frequently used psychological tests. Forensic groups are a very heterogeneous population, and samples are likely to contain inmates with primary personality disorders, especially antisocial personality disorders, but also substance abuse, transient psychotic symptoms, and even frank psychosis and secondary anxiety disorders. Thus, there is likely to be substantial comorbidity associated with any individual felon. Furthermore, psychologists use group base rate data to make inferences about an individual in violence risk assessments. Legal challenges to this practice can be expected, and arguments will be made that either the group data are erroneous or, more likely, the group data are inappropriately applied to the individual defendant, who may not match every feature on which the group data are based.

TABLE 8.1

Indexes of Aggression

Test	Indexes
Minnesota Multiphasic Personality Inventory—2	Scales F, 4, 8, 9 Code types 34/43, 48/84, 49/94 Content scales: Anger (ANG), Antisocial Practices (ASP) Supplemental scale: Overcontrolled Hostility (OH)
Millon Clinical Multiaxial Inventory (all versions)	Scales Antisocial, Aggressive-Sadistic, Passive-Aggressive, Possibly Borderline and Paranoid, and Delusional Disorder
Rorschach	Ag, AgC, AgPot, AgPast, Mor

Note. 4 = psychopathic deviant; 8 = schizophrenia; 9 = hypomania; Ag = aggression; AgC = aggression, cooperative; AgPot = aggression, potential; AgPast = aggression, past; MOR = morbid.

In forensic settings, clinical elevations have often been observed on the F validity scale, Psychopathic Deviate (Pd), Paranoia (Pa), Psychasthenia (Pt), and Schizophrenia (Sc), regardless of gender or diagnosis, in MMPI studies. In the clinical literature, this code type has been associated with mental illness diagnoses, but the correlates of the 678' 3-point code may be different in forensic than in clinical populations and may include personality-disordered inmates in addition to those with more severe forms of psychopathology. On the MMPI–2, female felons scored higher on Pt than male felons, suggesting the presence of greater reported anxiety in this group (P. Wright, Nussbaum, Lynett, & Buis, 1997).

Female offenders (N = 71) assessed prior to trial produced a 468' code type (Aderibigbe & Weston, 1996). This code type usually reflects severe emotional adjustment problems, with many paranoialike symptoms, expressed anger that is quickly rationalized, severe relationship difficulties, sexual maladjustment, and much alienation. This code type has also appeared in group profiles of battered women (Craig, 1999a). Male felons (N = 217) charged with both violent and nonviolent offenses and assessed prior to trial had a high-ranging code type (8674+), with elevations on the content scales of depression (DEP), bizarre mentations (BIZ), health concerns (HEA), and negative treatment indicators (TRT). The modal code type among the sample was 68/86', usually suggestive of a psychotic diagnosis (Shea, McKee, Shea, & Culley, 1996). Civilly committed patients scored highest on Schizophrenia (Sc) and Psychopathic Deviate (Pd) with subspikes on Depression (Dep) and Paranoia (Pa), whereas those judged not guilty by reason of insanity produced subclinical scores on most MMPI–2 scales (Moskowitz, Lewis, Ito, & Ehrmentraut, 1999). These base rate data may be used as comparison standards against which to compare individual felons. Also, forensic-specific data are available on specific MMPI scales (Fjordbak, 1985).

Violence Risk Assessment in Juvenile Offenders

The material in this chapter on the assessment of violence and violence risk in adults is also applicable to violence risk assessment in juveniles. As with adults, the ability of mental health professions to accurately predict dangerousness is problematic because of its low base rate (i.e., infrequent occurrence). The following risk factors have received some empirical support and have been associated with future violence in adolescents (Ackerman, 1999; Grisso, 2003):

- past violent behavior;
- truancy, school dropout, expulsion, failing grades, and other school disciplinary problems;
- substance abuse;
- diagnoses associated with mood disorders, posttraumatic stress disorder (PTSD; mostly from history of childhood abuse), and attention deficit disorders with or without hyperactivity;
- personality traits of anger, impulsiveness, lack of empathy, poor attachment to others, externalization of blame, perceived helplessness, and borderline personality traits;
- a preference for violent movies, films, and computer games; violent fantasies and dreams; revenge lists;
- family conflict, especially parental aggression, divorce, separation, or abandonment;
- association with peers who are aggressive (e.g., gangs) or social isolation; and
- childhood fire setting, enuresis, and cruelty to animals.

In addition to these factors, one also has to consider external factors, such as opportunistic and other environmental factors, that may instrumentally contribute to the risk of violence. No one risk factor is sufficient to warrant a prediction of dangerousness, but a higher number of these risk factors increases the risk of future violence.

DOMESTIC VIOLENCE AND PARTNER ABUSE

Abuse may be construed as physical, psychological (verbal or emotional), or sexual. Examples of psychological abuse include such behaviors as yelling, acts of intimidation, threats, acts of withholding, and limiting the partner's behavior. Domestic violence and partner abuse may be defined as a pattern of physical, psychological, or sexual threats or abusive behavior designed to exert power and control over another person. Statistics on the prevalence of spouse abuse vary depending on whether the victims were assessed in hospital emergency rooms, psychiatric clinics, or other settings. Between 20% and 35% of (primarily) women report that they have been abused at some point in their lifetime.

Domestic abuse starts out slowly and grows in intensity while the relationship develops. If abuse started early in a relationship, chances are the person would immediately end that relationship. However, domestic abuse intensifies gradually over time, and by then the victim feels unable to leave.

Theories of the causes of domestic violence include individual variables and sociocultural explanations. Social learning, attributional and feminist theories, and psychopathology diagnoses are most prominent in the literature. Most models incorporate psychological factors by way of explanation, because demographic and sociocultural explanations cannot explain all of the manifestations of abusive relationships. Interpersonal factors include family stress, financial problems, relational conflict, and power differentials, and more macro variables include a patriarchal society and social or subcultural tolerance of family violence. Similarly, although alcoholism is often associated with partner abuse, most alcoholics are not abusive. So personological explanations need to be considered to complete the explanatory matrix. Issues of low self-esteem and witnessing family violence between parents as a child are the two most frequently mentioned psychological variables associated with partner abuse.

Dutton (1994) argued that partner abuse is triggered by internal mood states rather than by external events. He viewed abusiveness as a deficit in attachment that generates rage. The origins of this deficit are traced to early developmental and frustrated attachment needs that reenact this perceived loss within the context of intimate relationships. It is a form of "protest anger" that follows perceived threats of separation and abandonment. The fearful attachment pattern, he argued, is strongly associated with intimacy anger, and this object relational template, in combination with attributions and projections, results in abusiveness. Thus, early developmental experiences result in an abusive personality.

A person is more likely to experience an episode of violence in the home than anywhere else. Surveys report that up to 33% of households report histories of conjugal violence (Hale, Zimostrad, Duckworth, & Nicholas, 1988). Surveys taken at hospital emergency rooms report that the prevalence of acute trauma from domestic abuse was 2.2%, rising to 14% among women who reported physical or sexual abuse during the past year and 37% for those reporting emotional or physical abuse at some time in their lives (Dearwater, 1998).

Explanations of abusive relationships have focused on such factors as poverty, unequal sex roles and pervasive cultural sexism in which women are deemed property, past history of abuse as a child, witnessing fathers who assaulted mothers, a lack of effective support systems, substance abuse comorbidities, delusional jealousy, and head injuries with or without dementia. The role of batterers' psychological characteristics has been emphasized (Else, Wonderlich, Beatty, Christie, & Straton, 1993; Hamberger & Hastings, 1988).

Although domestic violence transcends race, income, ethnicity, and religion, the following correlates have often been cited as leading to higher rates of domestic violence:

- relative youth (18–25 years of age), poverty, unemployment, and low-prestige jobs;
- a history of childhood abuse or witnessing parental violence;
- chronic alcoholism;
- attitudes, attributions, cognitions, and irrational beliefs that serve as intervening variables between emotional arousal and partner aggression;
- low self-esteem;
- previous violent episodes;
- domineering and overcontrolling relationship patterns;
- family stress (e.g., job loss, work stress);
- religious incompatibility; and
- diagnoses of antisocial or borderline personality disorder, intermittent explosive disorder, and alcoholism.

However, in a literature review of the correlates of domestic violence, only 10 of 42 correlates consistently discriminated between violent and nonviolent samples. In fact, the majority had too little empirical support to be reliable. It is also unclear whether these factors play a predisposing, precipitating, or a perpetuating role, or some combination, in partner violence.

I focus here on individual personality characteristics and personality disorders that have been associated with the perpetration of physical abuse. An understanding of the personality of the batterer can help psychologists both assess this population and design treatment intervention programs to change this behavior and break the cycle of violence.

Clinical Interview

Clinical descriptions of male batterers (Flourney & Wilson, 1991; Hale et al., 1988; Lohr, Hamberger, & Bonge, 1988; C. M. Murphy, Meyer, & O'Leary, 1993) have focused on their lack of assertiveness, a learned predisposition toward violence, social isolation, cultural norms that support marital violence, a denial of responsibility for their violent behavior, low ego strength, impulsive decision making without regard for future consequences, a desire to control their families and environment, rigid and self-serving styles of thinking, tendency toward moodiness, vindictiveness, over-sensitivity, emotional instability, hypervigilance, threat orientation, poor problem-solving skills, irrational beliefs, problems related to negative affect, and negative self-concept.

Evidence of these traits should be explored in the clinical interview. The acronym RADAR is a useful mnemonic device for routine assessment of domestic violence:

- **R**outinely ask questions about abuse. Although many women may be victims of abuse, they may not necessarily volunteer the information. Make sure you ask these questions without the presence of another person.
- **A**sk direct questions about abuse. If applicable, acknowledge the impact and severity of the abuse.
- **D**ocument your findings. Use the patient's own words. Use a body map (if available) to supplement your recordings, or document your findings in words.
- **A**ssess patient safety. Find out if it is safe for the person to go home.
- **R**eview the person's options and need for referrals.

Signs and symptoms of domestic violence depend, again, on the setting in which the evaluation occurs. In general, frequent medical visits with complaints of pain, especially with little physical evidence; reports of chronic headaches, sleep disturbances, fatigue, and decreased concentration; abdominal and gastrointestinal complaints; and reports of depression and suicidal ideation may indicate the possibility of spouse abuse. Frequent injuries to the head, neck, chest, abdomen, pelvis, and thighs and repeated contusions, abrasions, minor lacerations, and injuries can suggest physical abuse. There are also gynecological and obstetric manifestations that need not be reported here.

Physical abuse is easier to determine than emotional abuse. However, although bruises may go away in a few weeks, the emotional scars of abuse can last a lifetime. When forensic psychologists become involved in these cases, abuse has already been suspected, if not established.

TABLE 8.2
Minnesota Multiphasic Personality Inventory *T* Scores of Physical Abusers

Scale	Study 1		Study 2			Study 3	Mean *T* scores
	I	II	I	II	III		
L	54	50	53	51	48	48	51
F	56	63	90	54	66	59	66
K	53	52	50	51	46	50	50
Hs	49	66	83	50	60	55	60
Dep	56	71	89	55	72	61	67
Hy	53	65	80	65	64	57	62
Pd	59	76	90	62	75	67	71
Mf	56	64	66	55	63	65	61
Pa	56	67	90	50	69	60	65
Pt	52	69	91	50	70	61	65
Sc	53	69	95	49	70	62	66
Ma	57	61	79	58	62	63	63
Si	51	57	67	51	60	55	57

Note. Study 1 is Flourney and Wilson, 1991. Study 2 is Hale, Zimostrad, Duckworth, and Nicholas, 1988. Study 3 is Else, Wonderlich, Beatty, Christie, and Straton, 1993.

Although perpetrators of domestic violence are a heterogeneous population and may display different patterns of aggressive behavior stemming from different causes (C. M. Murphy et al., 1993), psychological studies of this population tend to find certain characteristics associated with abusive behavior. Table 8.2 displays MMPI results with male batterers that are visually depicted in Figure 8.1, and Table 8.3 lists MCMI studies with spouse abusers (Fraboni, Cooper, Reed, & Saltstone, 1990).

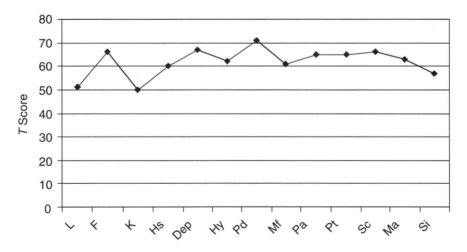

Figure 8.1. Modal Minnesota Multiphasic Personality Inventory profile of physical abusers.

TABLE 8.3
Millon Clinical Multiaxial Inventory Base Rate Scores for Physical Abusers

| | Study 1 | | | | | | | | | | | |
Scale	A	B	C	D	E	F	G	H	I	J	K	L
N	12	10	14	13	12	16	12	12	10	14	10	14
Schizoid	76	63	23	17	43	56	37	33	80	77	17	18
Avoidant	80	73	27	28	46	54	47	57	93	79	37	32
Depressed	—	—	—	—	—	—	—	—	—	—	—	—
Dependent	49	45	46	50	87	77	46	50	93	91	76	83
Histrionic	53	63	66	68	56	60	73	75	53	57	73	73
Narcissistic	63	73	80	83	55	63	85	85	55	59	75	79
Antisocial	76	78	76	83	36	66	86	87	63	53	56	57
Aggressive	—	—	—	—	—	—	—	—	—	—	—	—
Compulsive	37	38	66	70	70	35	35	37	45	44	66	73
Passive-Aggressive	77	80	43	47	25	33	77	73	95	83	36	37
Self-Defeating	—	—	—	—	—	—	—	—	—	—	—	—
Schizotypal	—	—	—	—	—	—	—	—	—	—	—	—
Borderline	—	—	—	—	—	—	—	—	—	—	—	—
Paranoid	—	—	—	—	—	—	—	—	—	—	—	—
Anxiety	—	—	—	—	—	—	—	—	—	—	—	—
Somatoform	—	—	—	—	—	—	—	—	—	—	—	—
Bipolar	—	—	—	—	—	—	—	—	—	—	—	—
Dysthymia	—	—	—	—	—	—	—	—	—	—	—	—
Alcohol	—	—	—	—	—	—	—	—	—	—	—	—
Drugs	—	—	—	—	—	—	—	—	—	—	—	—
Posttraumatic Stress Disorder	—	—	—	—	—	—	—	—	—	—	—	—
Thought Disorder	—	—	—	—	—	—	—	—	—	—	—	—
Major Depression	—	—	—	—	—	—	—	—	—	—	—	—
Delusional Disorder	—	—	—	—	—	—	—	—	—	—	—	—

(continued)

TABLE 8.3
Millon Clinical Multiaxial Inventory Base Rate Scores for Physical Abusers (Continued)

Scale	Study 2			Study 3		Study 4	Study 5		Study 6					
	A	B	C	A	B		A	B	A	B	C	D	E	F
N	68	52	76	77	57	49	24	24	48	23	20	12	33	66
Schizoid	70	32	31	40	60	—	58	57	34	34	34	24	34	51
Avoidant	78	44	33	52	62	—	68	44	41	55	41	46	41	58
Depressed	—	—	—	—	—	—	—	—	—	—	—	—	—	—
Dependent	74	41	62	55	61	52	43	58	55	47	55	47	61	47
Histrionic	53	73	63	68	65	65	75	57	61	65	68	71	65	65
Narcissistic	58	80	69	28	71	72	87	66	62	64	67	76	67	67
Antisocial	62	82	60	68	73	77	93	59	61	61	64	79	64	73
Aggressive	—	—	—	—	—	85	96	65	—	—	—	—	—	—
Compulsive	48	47	67	15	54	—	60	63	68	64	63	49	63	59
Passive-Aggressive	83	68	31	64	75	—	92	56	33	24	40	64	47	64
Self-Defeating	—	—	—	—	—	—	75	43	—	—	—	—	—	—
Schizotypal	—	—	—	52	61	61	70	54	47	44	47	47	47	56
Borderline	—	—	—	58	63	66	81	53	44	41	47	55	64	61
Paranoid	—	—	—	64	72	—	73	56	61	53	61	69	64	69
Anxiety	—	—	—	56	75	—	50	39	44	38	48	56	52	60
Somatoform	—	—	—	54	60	—	51	49	44	38	47	51	54	56
Bipolar	—	—	—	60	00	—	65	49	50	50	60	67	60	62
Dysthymia	—	—	—	52	69	—	56	45	41	33	44	48	48	56
Alcohol	—	—	—	70	75	—	72	46	45	55	66	70	68	72
Drugs	—	—	—	71	75	—	81	53	60	50	50	71	69	73
Posttraumatic Stress Disorder	—	—	—	—	—	—	—	—	—	—	—	—	—	—
Thought Disorder	—	—	—	58	64	—	55	36	54	44	49	54	54	60
Major Depression	—	—	—	52	61	—	58	39	43	34	43	52	52	59
Delusional Disorder	—	—	—	64	66	—	54	42	64	57	57	64	64	67

(continued)

TABLE 8.3
Millon Clinical Multiaxial Inventory Base Rate Scores for Physical Abusers (Continued)

Scale	Study 7		Study 8	Mean base rate scores
	A	B		
N	32	38	60	576 (total)
Schizoid	39	73	59	45
Avoidant	44	83	60	53
Depressed	—	—	57	57
Dependent	28	40	57	58
Histrionic	78	55	51	64
Narcissistic	86	68	61	69
Antisocial	89	84	44	69
Aggressive	90	82	49	78
Compulsive	51	54	56	55
Passive-Aggressive	89	87	48	59
Self-Defeating	56	77	51	60
Schizotypal	53	67	50	54
Borderline	68	82	35	54
Paranoid	61	62	58	59
Anxiety	30	63	52	51
Somatoform	47	52	46	50
Bipolar	62	55	55	54
Dysthymia	34	73	45	49
Alcohol	65	70	52	63
Drugs	76	70	41	65
Posttraumatic Stress Disorder	—	—	36	36
Thought Disorder	50	61	42	52
Major Depression	48	63	39	49
Delusional Disorder	47	51	55	58

Note. Dashes indicate no data for that scale on variable. Study 1 is Hamberger and Hastings, 1986. Study 2 is Lohr, Hamberger, and Bonge, 1988. Study 3 is Hamberger and Hastings, 1988. Study 4 is Beasley and Stoltenberg, 1992. Study 5 is C. M. Murphy, Meyer, and O'Leary, 1993. Study 6 is Hastings and Hamberger, 1994. Study 7 is Tweed and Dutton, 1999. Study 8 is Sugihara and Warner, 1999.

The appearance of the 43/34 MMPI code type has been associated with violence and assaultive behavior, as well as with parole violations within one year of prison release (K. R. Davis & Sines, 1971; Persons & Marks, 1971). This code type reflects problems with impulse control, emotional instability, substance abuse history, moodiness, hostility, immaturity, dependency, lack of assertion, irresponsibility, manipulativeness, and aggressive and assaultive behavior. Up to 85% of men with this code type have had histories of violence (Persons & Marks, 1971). However, not all studies have validated these findings (J. A. Buck & Graham, 1978; Gynther, Altman, & Warbin, 1973; Lothstein & Jones, 1978; Werner, Becker, & Yesavage, 1983). In the latest study, 94 men in a state prison were given the Buss Durkee Hostility Inventory and the Monroe Dyscontrol Scale. There were no significant differences between groups who had a 43/34 code type and those who did not. Groups did not differ in types of hostility, how they expressed their hostility, or crimes for which they were incarcerated. These offenders showed no greater proclivity for violence than other offenders with other MMPI code types. However, the Overcontrolled Hostility (OH) scale was elevated in the 43/34 group (O'Sullivan & Jenelha, 1993).

In conclusion, the presence of a 43/34 code type does not conclusively establish the presence of a violent past, nor does it predict a violent future. It does, however, warrant closer scrutiny from the clinician, especially if the patient has a 43' code type with an elevated Overcontrolled Hostility (OH) score (Walters, Solomon, & Greene, 1982; Walters, Greene, & Solomon, 1982), which suggests a tendency to deny anger and hostile intentions and problems in displaying emotions, especially anger. It is unlikely that a single MMPI code type would be present in violent offenders and that other code types would be absent. In fact, MMPI interpretive manuals report that aggression and violence are also associated with 48/84 and 46/64 code types.

Battered Wife Syndrome

Walker (1979) conceptualized the battered wife syndrome, and defense lawyers have used this syndrome to argue that a homicide was motivated by a woman's need for self-defense. Frequently there is little or no physical evidence that the woman was in imminent danger. Sometimes evidence of prior abuse, such as hospital or medical records or testimony from family or friends, is also lacking. Still, battered wife syndrome is a frequently used defense for a battered woman who has killed her partner, and this defense has been accepted as part of the evidence in both case and appellate law (Blowers & Bjerregaard, 1994). Additionally, the syndrome has been invoked as a defense in cases other than homicide, including drug running, child abuse, and child homicide (Follingstad, 2003).

The common characteristics and psychological sequelae of this disorder are low self-esteem, a tendency to underestimate one's abilities, traditional attitudes toward gender roles, acceptance of responsibility for the batterer's actions, guilt, denial of feeling terrified and angry, a passive approach displayed to others in an effort to prevent further violence, a belief that no one can help, and severe stress reactions with physiological complaints (Walker, 1979). Many of these characteristics are similar to the Self-Defeating Personality Disorder as conceptualized by Millon (Millon & Davis, 1997). However, caution is warranted when ascribing this diagnosis to battered women, because other explanations are possible. Women may remain in battering relationships not because of a personality disorder, but because they are socialized into helping relationships, because of learned helplessness, because they lack economic alternatives, or because of behaviors associated with the psychology of victimization. Furthermore, women react in different ways to the abuse experience, depending on the presence or absence of personal resources and social support, vulnerability factors (e.g., history of childhood abuse, witnessing parental violence), and concurrent stressors (Follingstad, 2003).

Battered wife syndrome is not an official diagnostic category and does not appear in the *DSM–IV*. However, the literature does support the diagnosis of PTSD in such cases, and the Pk or Ps scales from the MMPI–2 can be useful in making this diagnosis (as can an 82/28 code type). One difficulty is establishing whether the pattern of psychological symptoms occurred before the beatings or is the result of the beatings. A good clinical history is needed to help sort this out.

For example, a 41-year-old, remarried White man was screened for access to a nuclear power plant. His MMPI–2 code type was 4'-3, with *T* scores at 69 and 64 respectively. In a clinical interview, the patient reported a history of battery of his wife and a disorderly conduct charge, reduced from a battery charge, for which he spent two months in jail. He also had a history of attempted suicide about two years previously; he attempted to electrocute himself while in the bathtub. This case illustrates that close scrutiny and a thorough clinical interview are necessary whenever this code type appears in a client.

MMPI Studies

MMPI studies, though infrequent (see Table 8.2 and Figure 8.1), tend to support the clinical description associated with domestic violence. These men show impulsiveness; disrespect for social standards; frequent difficulties with the law and with their families; a tendency to minimize and to externalize blame for their (violent) behavior; a tendency toward substance abuse; elevations on Psychopathic Deviate (Pd); low ego strength (Es, K); a tendency toward dependency in interpersonal relations, especially an over-dependence on their spouse (Dependency [Dy] scale, if scored); and feelings of inadequacy and situational depression (42/24 or 4'2 code types). Evidence of mild thought disorder is also present (subspike on Schizophrenia [Sc]). Although the MMPI studies suggest serious psychological maladjustment in perpetrators of domestic abuse, the MCMI studies further refine this picture and suggest serious personality pathology and personality disorders among male batterers.

MCMI Studies

There have been many MCMI-based studies pertaining to the personality of domestic violence perpetrators (Craig, 2002). Hamberger and Hastings (1986) found several subtypes of personality styles among male batterers, but three styles tended to predominate. The first type was defined as schizoid/borderline. These patients were withdrawn, asocial, moody, emotionally volatile, and hypersensitive and overreactive to perceptions of interpersonal slights. The second type was narcissistic and antisocial (called "instrumental/antisocial"). These offenders were highly self-centered, had cognitive schemas in which they felt entitled to be treated according to their wishes and desires, used others to meet their own needs for dominance and compliance, and responded to aggravations with threats and aggression. The third type (overcontrolled and dependent) was seen as passive-dependent and compulsive. They saw themselves as weak, passive, placating, and submissive; lacked self-esteem; and acted out rebelliously when their needs were not met, although in general they tried to suppress their anger and hostility so they would not be rejected. Five other personality styles were determined with cluster analysis procedures, but these were variations of these three basic types that varied in degree and intensity. Most men in these groups had diagnosable personality disorders.

These initial findings have been partially replicated in subsequent studies. Lohr et al. (1988), also using cluster analysis with male batterers and the MCMI, found an antisocial/aggressive/narcissistic type, a narcissistic/compulsive type, and a passive-aggressive/avoidant type among a sample of batterers. Beasley and Stoltenberg (1992), using the MCMI–II, found physical abusers to be characterized by elevations on the Narcissistic, Antisocial, Schizotypal, Borderline, and Aggressive/Sadistic scales. Other investigators have reported similar findings (Dutton, 1994; Gondolf, 1999; S. D. Hart, Dutton, & Newlove, 1993; C. M. Murphy et al., 1993; Sugihara & Warner, 1999). These disorders significantly correlate with histories of severe childhood abuse (C. M. Murphy et al., 1993).

The literature is at an early stage in describing batterers and in identifying what differentiates batterers from offenders who do not batter. The initial picture that emerges from these data suggests that the batterer has needs for unconditional love, approval, and acceptance, especially from his spouse, yet they are overly sensitive to perceived threats of subtle and often misrepresented or misinterpreted signs of rejection. They are affectively labile and have irrational beliefs, up to and including mild thought disorders, that justify their behavior and actions and relieve them of blame and responsibility for their actions. This literature base further suggests that the role of psychopathology, and in particular personality pathology, must be considered as part of the clinical picture of the physical abuser. Personality-disordered batterers may all exhibit problematic anger and dyscontrol of emotion, but they do so for different internal psychological reasons. Though the final common pathway is an abusive relationship, the motivations behind this are different for each disorder.

For example, the narcissistic personality may experience an event as injurious to their psyche. Their feelings of entitlement and importance, now injured, are combined with their trait characteristics of aggression and hostility and are then manifested as anger and abuse. If certain other background characteristics are also present, such as prior history of childhood abuse or nonegalitarian attitudes toward women, then their risk of physically abusing a partner is increased.

The literature (Tweed & Dutton, 1999) has focused on three distinct types of spouse abusers. The first type is a person who is violent only with his wife, tends to use less severe forms of violence, usually is assaultive under the influence of alcohol, and is quite remorseful after the incident. The second type is similar to the first but has more anger and jealousy and may have a criminal record for other violent acts as well. The third type is severely violent both inside and outside the home, abuses drugs or alcohol or both, has an extensive criminal record, and was abused as a child. This schemata concentrates on patterns of abuse but ignores the individual variables that seem to permeate these types, which are best construed in terms of personality disorders, most commonly antisocial, aggressive, and passive-aggressive (negativistic) disorders.

As indicated in Table 8.3, the aggressive-sadistic personality style or disorder has been implicated in several studies with spouse abusers. Although clinical studies have reported that partner abusers tend to be overly dependent on their wives, psychological test findings show a general absence of problems with dependency. It is possible that what has been termed "dependency" in clinical reports is really insecure attachment. A dependent style is associated with passive and inhibited behavior, whereas insecure attachment is manifested by an active search for attachment objects and acting out when attachment to those objects is threatened with separation (S. D. Hart et al., 1993; Tweed & Dutton, 1999).

AGGRESSION

A review of Tables 8.2 and 8.3 indicates that the MCMI-derived aggressive, antisocial, and negativistic personality styles have been associated with physical abuse. Although the *DSM–IV* did not retain the aggressive-sadistic style as part of official nomenclature, the literature clearly shows that such a style is related to abusive behavior. In Millon's theory, the aggressive-sadistic personality is strong on the pain and active polarities, weak on the passive and other reinforcement polarities, and average on the pleasure and self-reinforcement polarities (see chap. 2, this volume).

Aggressive personality styles and disorders occur on a continuum of severity. At the lower end of the severity spectrum, these patients may not be publicly antisocial, but rather are verbally abusive and humiliating in relationships. They are aggressive, commanding, domineering, hardheaded, dominating, and intimidating. They are bossy and expect loved ones to comply with their demands, which they view as quite reasonable. They become argumentative and even combative when others object to their demands. Some are able to sublimate these traits into socially approved vocations and occupations. When stressed, they are prone toward marital problems and spouse abuse.

The more severe type is probably a pathological variant of the antisocial personality style. They are more of the explosive type of personality who show uncontrollable rage, usually at the expense of weaker people. They are quite opinionated, closed-minded, authoritarian, competitive, combative, and domineering. They are easily excitable, generally hostile, and belligerent. Clinically, they react with sudden outbursts that are unwarranted by the nature of the stimulus. They are interpersonally abusive and experience satisfaction when they inflict pain, whether psychological or physical. Hence, they behave in a humiliating, demeaning, and controlling manner. They erupt in violent, unpredictable behavior of near-ferocious intensity that often seems irrational to those around them. The effects of such behavior are to intimidate and control people. They become combative when they feel provoked and are seen as antagonistic and disagreeable people. They violate the rights of others and tend to be fearless, intimidating, destructive, and brutal. Psychodynamically, the motivation for their explosiveness may be to release anger and tension associated with feelings of humiliation and betrayal. In a psychoanalytic sense, they are sadists. They are prone toward antisocial acts and legal problems (Millon & Davis, 1997).

This profile represents the prototype aggressive personality style, which Millon called the "explosive sadist," represented by a 1-point code, peaking on MCMI–III scale 6B (Forceful). Millon further theorized that several subtypes of the basic style may also exist, referred to as the tyrannical sadist, the enforcing sadist, and the spineless sadist, and he provided initial descriptions.

The tyrannical sadist type is theorized to thoroughly enjoy menacing and brutalizing others. In fact, they seem to go out of their way to create suffering in others. They are intentionally abusive, frightening, and cruel to force others to submit to their demands as an exertion of their power. They act in an unmerciful and inhumane way until the object of their wrath is submissive. This type can engage in physical abuse or may use unrelenting criticism, constant demeaning, and emotional tirades without actual physical abuse. Millon believed that their motivation is to inspire terror and intimidation. Of course, one cannot be so sadistic without a relational partner who submits to these behaviors, so they seem to select weaker partners who may object but who ultimately tolerate their tirades. Millon further speculated that the underlying motivation of this personality type is the fear that others will discover their low self-esteem and insecurities. These people have learned that they can feel superior by overpowering others into submission, so their primary goal is subjugation. Remorse is generally absent. They are likely to have MCMI–III scale elevations peaking on the Aggressive-Sadistic and Passive-Aggressive (Negativistic) scales or in combination with the Paranoid (Pa) scale (6BP).

The enforcing sadist type has similar aggressive prototype traits but has learned to sublimate them into socially approved roles, such as police officers, career military personnel, judges, and academic deans. Their basic enjoyment is to seek out and punish rule breakers. Millon excluded from this type people who occupy these roles and act in a balanced and fair manner. This type abuse their power to discharge their aggression and hostility while occupying socially sanctioned roles. The old notion of the "hanging judge" seems to fit this type. These people have a proud and justified demeanor as they use their power to punish others. Their MCMI–III code type is likely to be a 6B7, with elevations on the Aggressive-Sadistic and Compulsive scales.

The spineless sadist type is said to be essentially insecure and acts in a counterphobic way through a dominant and cruel demeanor. People with this type of personality tend to pick on people weaker than themselves to ensure their victory. They publicly act in a self-assured manner, which belies their true feelings. Millon believed that they act brutally out of fear. In a counterphobic way, they demonstrate to others that they are neither anxious nor intimidated. He argued that they attack in others the very elements of their own psyche they wish to deny. The 6B2A MCMI–III code type, with scales peaking on Aggressive-Sadistic and Avoidant, might reflect this aggressive type.

The derivation of the sadistic personality style is a matter of conjecture. A history of childhood physical abuse may be one source of etiology, but not everyone who has been abused develops an aggressive-sadistic style. Millon believed that these types have learned to believe and expect that others will be hostile. To fend off this anticipated attack, they try and grab as much power and control as they can to prevent others from using it on them. Then they use this power against those who have been mean to them in the past, as well as to control others to prevent them from acting hostilely toward them. The aggressive-sadistic personality might resort to physical abuse to control their partners.

Antisocial Style

The antisocial personality style is well understood by most clinicians. In Millon's theory, the antisocial style is strong on the self and active polarities, weak on the pain and passive polarities, and average on the pleasure polarity. These patients are essentially fearless, aggressive, impulsive, irresponsible, dominating, and narcissistic. At less severe levels, they appear self-reliant, tough, and competitive. With more severe manifestations, they are ruthless, intimidating, pugnacious, victimizing, brutal, vindictive, and vengeful. They harbor grudges and resentments against people who disapprove of their behavior. They seem to be excessively touchy and jealous and brood over perceived slights. They provoke fear in those around them through their intimidating social demeanor. They seem to be chronically dissatisfied and often display an angry and hostile affect. They feel most comfortable when they have power and control over others, who they view as weak and who desire to control them. Thus, they maintain a fiercely independent stance and act in a self-reliant manner.

They often ascribe their own malicious motives to others. They are continuously on guard against anticipated ridicule and act out in a socially intimidating manner to provoke fear and control other people. They are driven by power and by malevolent projections, so they react to maintain their autonomy and independence. They believe that other people are malicious and devious, justifying to themselves a forceful counteraction. They are prone toward substance abuse, relationship difficulties, vocational deficits, and legal problems. Some are able to sublimate these traits into various businesses where these traits have instrumental value. Most, however, have a myriad of problems with societal institutions.

The antisocial personality type feels that others are out to control them. Therefore, they must control others at all costs. These malevolent projections and other irrational beliefs, combined with other antisocial traits, often impel them to act out their anger in a first strike attack, as well as to keep others in control and subservient to their needs. Millon speculated that this prototype style has five subtypes, referred to as covetous, reputation-defending, risk-taking, nomadic, and malevolent. All of these antisocial types have the basic features of the antisocial style but differ somewhat in the way they are expressed or in which traits of the basic style are salient.

The covetous type is the basic prototype described above (MCMI–III code type 6A). The reputation-defending type has a self-image of being unflawed and intransigent. Thus, they dislike to be questioned or challenged and display their toughness when their status or capabilities are demeaned. They react to perceived slights with vindictive behaviors. They defend their own self-image at all costs and are likely to act out when they feel disrespected. Their main motivation seems to be a need to guard against the possibility that others of the reputation-defending type will demean them or take away their power. Perhaps gang leaders and the violence between gangs over turf illustrate this concept (Millon & Davis, 1997). This type is generally not hostile; in fact, in quiescent moments when their sense of self is not challenged, they can be quite calm and charming. When aggrieved, however, they will react with violence to maintain their self-image as indomitable. This type is likely to have peaks on the Antisocial and Narcissistic scales of the MCMI–III (6A5 code type).

The risk-taking type is adventurous, pleasure seeking, bold, audacious, daring, and even reckless. Their impulsivity and love of danger can involve them in foolhardy and perilous activities. These activities are enjoyed for their own sake and not for any other purpose. More normal variations of this style might be personalities who enjoy hang gliding, parasailing, and bungee jumping, unlike the risk-taking psychopath, who engages in behaviors that most others view as extremely dangerous and normally want to avoid. This type engages in hazardous and even frightening activities. They are primarily thrill seekers, but they are also undependable and unreliable and disregard the effects of their behavior on others. Millon argued that this personality type feels trapped by routine and overburdened by responsibilities, feels empty inside, is unwilling to reduce a personal sense of autonomy, and acts to show others that they will do whatever they want to do (Millon & Davis, 1997). This type might have clinical elevations on the Antisocial and Histrionic scales of the MCMI–III (6A4 code type).

The nomadic antisocial type is considered a person who drifts in and out of peripheral roles in society. These are the bums, vagabonds, vagrants, dropouts, and misfits of society and the tramps and wanderers with no goals and a live-for-today attitude. They run away from society when they feel like unwanted misfits. They feel angry at perceived injustices, but they also feel sorry for the way they have been treated, and so they distance themselves from others. Compared with the other subtypes of the antisocial prototype, the nomadic type is relatively benign. Many develop substance abuse problems, avoid work, and engage in minor crimes to support themselves. They also avoid adult responsibilities. Many are homeless. MCMI–III code types of 6A1 (Antisocial and Schizoid) or 6A2A (Antisocial and Avoidant) might reflect this type.

The malevolent type feels that others deserve revenge and punishment and acts with brutality, belligerence, and maliciousness when the person feels they are called for. They anticipate betrayal and carry out a first strike with cold-blooded justifications and without guilt or remorse. Millon theorized that this type of person was victimized as a child and hence rejects feelings of tenderness or empathy. Many feel suspicious and have an intense sense of hostility. They are most dangerous when they feel rejected. They are likely to have peaks on the Antisocial and Aggressive scales (6A6B code type) or on the Antisocial and Paranoid scales (^AP code type).

Passive-Aggressive (Negativistic) Style

In Millon's theory, the passive-aggressive style is strong on the active polarity, weak on the enhancement (pleasure) and other reinforcement polarity, and average on the pain, passive, and self-reinforcement polarities. These people behave in a passive, compliant, and obedient manner at one moment and then show negativistic and oppositional behavior the next. They are moody, grumbling, disagreeable, irritable, pessimistic, and hostile. Erratically and even explosively angry and stubborn, they often feel guilty and contrite after their outbursts. Accordingly, they keep those around them on edge, because they never know how the person will react. These people feel misunderstood and unappreciated, believe they have been treated unfairly, and constantly complain. They seem persistently petulant, querulous, and discontented. They vacillate between passive dependency and stubborn contrariness. They expect disappointments in life and have unstable and conflicted interpersonal relationships. They often have problems with authority and, if employed, may have job difficulties. Elevations on this scale can be considered a good indication for psychiatric intervention. Millon theorized that there are four subtypes to this style—circuitous, abrasive, discontented, and vacillating.

The circuitous subtype is the traditional passive-aggressive style, where opposition is displayed through procrastination, stubbornness, neglect, forgetfulness, undependability, and other indirect ways of venting anger, resentments, and resistance. Many have dependent features to their personality. They tend to behave in an oppositional manner but in ways that are not clearly oppositional. That is, they seem to have legitimate excuses for their behavior and deny conscious intentions. In fact, they plead innocence when confronted or challenged, which tends to deflect criticism for their behavior, although most who know them well are exasperated by the repeated acts of resistance. These behaviors are strongly resistant to change. The MCMI–III code type 8A3, with elevations on the Passive-Aggressive (Negativistic) and Dependent scales, probably reflects this type.

The abrasive negativist is characterized by frequent quarrelsome, disputatious, and argumentative behavior, with frequent contradictions and consistently testy attitudes. They are seen as irritable, contentious, nagging, antagonistic, and oppositional. They never seem happy or content. They rarely show remorse for their behavior and feel justified in their continued fault finding. MCMI–III scores peaking on Passive-Aggressive (Negativistic) and Aggressive-Sadistic (8A6B) represent this style.

The discontented negativist is constantly grumbling, bitter, cranky, moody, pessimistic, vexed, ill humored, and, of course, discontented. Nothing seems to please them. They constantly gripe about something. Their attitudes seem petty. They rarely act in ways that result in retaliation. Rather, they are more subtle in their complaints. The MCMI–III scales of Passive-Aggressive (Negativistic) and Depressive (8A2B) might reflect this style.

Vacillating negativists are described as indecisive, bewildered, and perplexed and as having trouble articulating their feelings and understanding their own moods. They act in an apparent independent, disputatious manner on one occasion and in a dependent and clinging way on another occasion. Their intimate interpersonal relationships are kept on edge because others are never sure how they will react. At one moment they seem happy and content, and the next they are disgruntled. Thus, most people try to avoid close encounters with them, if possible. Their mood changes are usually unpredictable. An 8AC (Passive-Aggressive [Negativistic] and Borderline) code type seems to capture this subtype.

The passive-aggressive (negativistic) personality may batter because of deficits in emotional control. They keep others on edge with their moodiness, mercurial and quixotic emotionality, petulance, disagreeableness, and negativistic and disputatious demeanor and words, combined with seemingly sincere words of contrition following an emotional upheaval.

Millon and Davis (1997) reported on a domain-based description of personality disorders using clinical criteria to define each domain. Their behavioral criteria include expressive acts and interpersonal conduct. Phenomenological domains include cognitive style, object representations, and self-image. Intrapsychic domains include regulatory mechanisms and morphological organization. Finally, the biophysical domain is associated with mood or temperament. Each personality disorder can be described using each of these domains.

Behavioral criteria include expressive acts, defined as observable physical and verbal behavior, and interpersonal conduct, or the person's style of relating to others. Phenomenological domains include cognitive style, defined as how a person perceives events, processes information, organizes thoughts, and communicates reactions, and object (internalized) representations, which are attitudes based on particular experiences, memories, associated affect, and the like that form a substrate of how the person reacts to significant objects in his or her life. The self-image is the person's perception and sense of self—of who he or she is as a person. The regulatory dimensions in the intrapsychic domain are usually internal and unconscious processes that regulate behavior. The concepts of id, ego, and superego are examples of such regulatory processes. A person's morphological organization is an overall configuration of personal elements in a person's intrapsychic system that provide personality cohesion, balance, and structural strength to personality. Finally, a person's mood or temperament adds a biological component to personality functioning.

Each personality disorder can be described in these terms. I use this scheme to portray the disorders more frequently seen in abusive populations. Descriptions here are necessarily truncated, and the interested reader is referred to Millon and Davis (1997) for a more detailed presentation of these personality styles and disorders.

The aggressive-sadistic style is characterized by the following:

- *expressive acts:* fearless, attracted to challenge, undaunted by pain;
- *interpersonal conduct:* cruel, intimidating, humiliating, abusive;
- *cognitive style:* dogmatic, opinionated, closed-minded, authoritarian, intolerant;
- *object representations:* pernicious, driven by aggression and malicious attitudes;
- *self-image:* competitive, tough, powerful, domineering;
- *regulatory mechanisms:* isolated, detached from own destructive behaviors;
- *morphological organization:* eruptive, powerful, explosive, aggressive; and
- *mood or temperament:* hostile, pugnacious, argumentative, mean-spirited.

The antisocial style is characterized by the following:

- *expressive acts:* impulsive, manipulative, uses others for self-gain, does not plan ahead, callous;
- *interpersonal conduct:* unreliable, duplicitous, engages in illegal behaviors;
- *cognitive style:* deviant, immoral and amoral, rejects traditional values;

- *object representations:* rebellious, vengeful, malicious, controlling;
- *self-image:* independent; does not want limitations, restraints, or controls; displays no personal loyalties;
- *regulatory mechanisms:* acting out, little guilt, few constraints;
- *morphological organization:* unbounded, low frustration tolerance; and
- *mood or temperament:* callous, insensitive, ruthless, cold-blooded, indifferent.

The narcissistic style is characterized by the following:

- *expressive acts:* arrogant, indifferent to the rights of others;
- *interpersonal conduct:* feelings of entitlement, nonempathic, takes others for granted;
- *cognitive style:* expansive, preoccupied with own successes;
- *object representations:* contrived, rationalizes ideas and values to suit own purposes;
- *self-image:* admirable, self-assured;
- *regulatory mechanisms:* rationalization, self-deception, justification of own behavior;
- *morphological organization:* spurious, dismissive of conflicts, behavior seems obvious to others; and
- *mood or temperament:* nonchalant, imperturbable, optimistically buoyant.

The passive-aggressive (negativistic) style is characterized by the following:

- *expressive acts:* stubborn, contrary, resistant, undermines others, impetuous;
- *interpersonal conduct:* contrary, maintains unstable attitudes and positions that confuse others;
- *cognitive style:* negativistic, disdainful, cynical, and skeptical;
- *object representations:* oppositional, has a blend of conflicting ideas and impulses;
- *self-image:* discontented, feels misunderstood and unappreciated, pessimistic, disgruntled;
- *regulatory mechanisms:* displacement, acts perplexed or forgetful or even righteous;
- *morphological organization:* divergent, seems to have incompatible ideas and behaviors but justifies them defensively; and
- *mood or temperament:* irritable, touchy, resentful, easily annoyed and frustrated.

The interested reader is urged to consult Millon and Davis (1997) for a more thorough description of these prototypes and their theorized subtypes. Also, the material described in this section may have relevance to material discussed later in this chapter, which details the personality literature pertaining to murderers.

The MCMI–III should be an instrument of choice in the psychometric assessment of domestic violence. There is a good literature base for use of this instrument with this population, and the role of personality pathology among spouse abusers has clearly been established.

CASE EXAMPLE

The patient is a 33-year-old, married, unemployed African American man tested while hospitalized for treatment for drug dependence. The patient requested a psychological evaluation, which had been ordered by the court, to refute allegations of sexual abuse and molestation brought by his 13-year-old stepdaughter.

According to the patient, when he and his wife returned from out of town, they learned that his stepdaughter had filed sexual molestation charges against him. He also discovered that she had stolen some money from his jacket, so he immediately went to school, took her out of class, and pulled her by the arm, forcing her to open her locker to look for the money. He stated that she lied about the sexual abuse because she wanted to leave home. His cousin had been sexually abused, and he believed she talked to his stepdaughter about it, which is where she got the idea. He denied that the stolen money was for him to buy drugs, saying it was food money. He said doctors could not find any evidence of sexual abuse. He added that no charges were brought against him by the police, who felt there was insufficient evidence. The State Child Advocate Authority removed all his children from the home, who went to live with their grandmother. His spouse was 4 months pregnant, and he wanted his children returned home.

The patient reported having freebased cocaine for about 20 years, stating that he had been using cocaine daily at a cost of $100 per day. He insisted he used this much daily and said he supported his habit with illegal activities. He began snorting heroin about 2 months previously and had used alcohol since age 10, when he was involved with a group of people that participated in negative behaviors. He insisted he regularly drank beer for 23 years.

His substance abuse caused him financial, medical, and physical problems. He was currently unemployed but worked odd jobs and was a roofer by trade. He reported paranoid traits and thinking when freebasing cocaine, but no other psychiatric problems.

He had had one prior treatment episode for drug abuse, after which he remained abstinent for 1½ years, until he relapsed in the company of old friends. He began drinking alcohol, then using marijuana sprinkled with cocaine, and finally returning to freebasing cocaine. His family history was positive for substance abuse. His father was a heroin addict, and his mother was an alcoholic and beat him, ridiculed him, and chastised him for being "just like your father." His siblings all had a substance abuse problem as well. He left home at age 13 to live with an aunt to avoid the beatings and constant humiliation.

He had been involved with his wife for about 12 years, and they had been married for 4 years. He had five biological children and two stepchildren, all of whom he was raising. He admitted to frequent arguments with his wife, especially over raising the children. He stated he had been "hard" on his stepdaughter, in order to "teach her the right way," but she had been rebellious. He wanted his wife to discipline her more, but she tended to side more with her daughter. This had resulted in many arguments.

The mental status exam at the time of testing was normal, except for chronic feelings of anger, rage, and temper. He showed no evidence of delusions or hallucinations; no homicidal or suicidal thoughts; clear sensorium; intact relationship skills; normal appetite, energy, and sleep; good hygiene; and a somewhat anxious mood with mild pressured speech, probably situationally induced by the impending court case. There were no perceptual distortions, but the patient did experience some paranoia under the influence of freebased cocaine. Table 8.4 presents his MMPI–2 and MCMI–II test scores.

Test Results

The patient seemed to approach the MMPI–2 with a nondefensive and open manner, suggesting that he cooperated with the testing process. Test results reflected mild depression, along with feelings of inadequacy, moodiness, sensitivity to criticism, dissatisfaction with his life situation, low self-esteem, and many family problems. There was evidence of hostility, self-centeredness, and antisocial practices, along with addictive behaviors.

On the MCMI–II, the patient again showed evidence of a good level of disclosure and nondefensive responding. He scored high on the Passive-Aggressive (Negativistic), Antisocial, Aggressive, Self-Defeating, and Avoidant scales. These results suggest that the patient could be expected to be negativistic, querulous, demanding, resentful, irritable, and belligerent. He was conflicted between his desire to remain independent, so that others would not control him, and his desire to be accepted. He was sensitive to rejection and might act precipitously out of perceived rejection. Such results portray him as angry, aggressive, petulant, irritable, and moody and as having

TABLE 8.4

Minnesota Multiphasic Personality Inventory—2 (MMPI–2) and
Millon Clinical Multiaxial Inventory—II (MCMI–II) Test Scores
for a Case of Physical Abuse

MMPI–2		MCMI–II	
Scale	Score	Scale	Score
L	48 (R3)	Disclosure (X)	100
F	48 (R4)	Desirability (Y)	72
K	35 (R8)	Debasement (Z)	64
FB	R7		
TRIN	65 (T)	Schizoid (1)	60
VRIN	65	Avoidant (2)	97
		Dependent (3)	80
Hs	48	Histrionic (4)	79
Dep	66	Narcissistic (5)	85
Hy	40	Antisocial (6A)	107
Pd	62	Aggressive-Sadistic (6B)	110
Mf	52	Compulsive (7)	50
Pa	46	Passive-Aggressive (8A)	108
Pt	55	Self-Defeating (8B)	110
Sc	51	Schizotypal (S)	65
Ma	62	Borderline (C)	109
Si	57	Paranoid (P)	63
ANX	57	Anxiety (A)	66
FRS	56	Somatoform (H)	48
OBS	47	Bipolar: Manic (N)	79
DEP	59	Dysthymic (D)	70
HEA	62	Alcohol (B)	89
BIZ	63	Drug (T)	104
ANG	63	Thought Disorder (SS)	63
CYN	68	Major Depression (CC)	63
ASP	65	Delusional Disorder (PP)	64
TPA	68		
LSE	59		
SOD	49		
FAM	80		
WRK	59		
TRT	49		
MAC–R	36 (raw)		
APS	54		
AAS	80		
ES	40		
DO	30		
RE	30		
OH	55		

Critical item: At times I feel like smashing things. (T)

trouble controlling his behavior. He was likely to engage in antisocial acts, was quite narcissistic, and had erratic emotionality.

The patient was also given the Adjective Check List and scored high in needs for dependence, autonomy, and aggression and low in needs for nurturance, endurance, orderliness, understanding, affiliation, and deference. This need pattern suggests a conflict between dependence and independence (some of the adjectives checked were *argumentative, complaining, forceful, headstrong, touchy, hard-headed, hostile, aggressive,* and *irritable,* combined with *easygoing, meek, reasonable, weak,* and *withdrawn*). He was prone to engage in behaviors that hurt others, either emotionally or physically, and maintained a fiercely independent and controlling demeanor, yet he also leaned on others for support and care. He was quite critical of others, and his aggressiveness when slighted would make him difficult to live with. Also, he was unlikely to see a task (e.g., psychotherapy) through to its finish and was lacking in affiliation and nurturing behaviors. He lacked self-control, showed a discrepancy between the way he was and the way he would like to be, and scored low on a scale measuring personal adjustment. He did score high on the Counseling Readiness scale, interpreted as another example of his desire to put himself into dependent relationships rather than as a true desire for change.

Test Integration

The MMPI–2 and MCMI–II both suggest that the patient felt vulnerable and had few ego resources to control his impulses. All three tests indicate a personality pattern characterized by anger, hostility, and aggressiveness. The MMPI–2 and MCMI–II both suggest moodiness, sensitivity to criticism, low self-esteem, substance abuse, self-centeredness, and antisocial activities. Test results suggest that his essential conflict is between a desire for dependence and a desire to remain independent, most clearly seen in the MCMI–II and Adjective Check List. Treatment outcome was predicted to be poor, unless there was some external pressure compelling him to participate in treatment.

Dynamics

This patient was seen as at risk for perpetration of physical abuse, based on history of physical abuse as a child, chronic anger and rage, and a relationship with his spouse that duplicated, somewhat, the relationship he had had with his mother. His stepdaughter was trying to leave home at the same age that he left home, and for many of the same reasons. Repetition compulsion may be the central theme in his personality, and he may be using drugs to help control his anger, in addition to whatever positive feelings he derives from them.

Treatment Recommendations

The psychologist made five recommendations for the patient:

- drug-free aftercare counseling in an outpatient clinic for relapse prevention;
- outpatient marital therapy, if possible;
- joint outpatient parenting classes;
- referral for anger management classes; and
- continued court supervision until he completes the above programs.

After the test results were given to the client, he reported that his spouse currently was in a shelter for battered women. His motivation for treatment was good, as long as he was under court supervision with respect to the placement of his children. The court-appointed testing was subsequently conducted by a court-appointed psychologist.

LETHAL VIOLENCE

Three types of studies have used the MMPI on murderers. The first type compares the MMPI profiles of murderers with those of some other control group. An offshoot of this type of research is to use multivariate statistics and cluster analysis to discern meaningful subgroups within the larger population. The second type of study uses this subgroup methodology to find distinct cluster or group profile types, and then to determine external characteristics associated with each group profile. The Megargee classification system, discussed later in this chapter, is the most elegant and elaborated study of this type. Finally, special scales have been derived from the MMPI item pool that bear on the question of lethally aggressive behavior. The scale that has been given the most attention by researchers is the Overcontrolled Hostility (OH) scale, which will be discussed later in this chapter.

MMPI Group Profiles of Murderers

The literature discussed in this section focuses exclusively on psychological and psychometric test evidence as it pertains to personality traits of murderers. This is not to imply that other factors, such as social and demographic characteristics and family history, are unimportant in understanding lethal violence (H. V. Hall, 2000).

Tables 8.5 and 8.6 present an overview of studies that have reported MMPI scores for male, female, and adolescent murderers. For men there were 17 studies and 34 data sets. Sample sizes in these studies ranged from 12 to 135, with a median of 45. Inspection of the data reveals the following: First, the Psychopathic Deviate (Pd) scale is clinically elevated in almost all profiles. However, this sign is not pathognomonic of murderers; most people with elevated Pd scores do not commit murder. Second, the Schizophrenia (Sc) scale was clinically elevated in many studies. Only one study found a within normal limits mean profile. Finally, the average code type was 8462 based on a total sample size of 161.

The aggregate median profile of male murderers, based on a total sample size of 1,048, is a high-ranging code characterized by elevations in Schizophrenia (Sc), Psychopathic Deviate (Pd), Paranoia (Pa), and Depression (Dep) (8462) (see Figure 8.2). This profile suggests persons who are hostile, resentful, bitter, angry, argumentative, and irritable. Social maladjustment is likely to be present, and they make excessive demands on others for attention, although they resent others placing demands on them. They use projection, rationalization, and externalization as primary defenses and act out impulsively.

There are paranoid features, such as suspiciousness, a variety of sensitivities, and perhaps problematic thought processes. Aggressive outbursts, substance abuse, antisocial behavior, and authority problems may be present. They are likely to have a history of family and social problems. A personality disorder, either narcissistic or antisocial, or both, is often associated with this profile type. This personality description is considered characterological rather than situational and reflects the person's personality prior to the act of murder. (An individual murderer may or may not have this prototypic MMPI profile.)

There has been only one MMPI study on female murderers. The mean profile was a 46 code type, but at subclinical levels (Kalichman, 1988b). Only one MMPI–2 study has been published with female murderers (McKee, Shea, Mogy, & Holden, 2001). They found variations of the 486 code type in three separate groups of female murderers.

A number of variables can affect test scores (Fraboni, Cooper, Reed, & Saltstone, 1990). Studies that have addressed these variables are reviewed briefly in the next few sections.

Race

Holcolm and Adams (1982) reported that Black murderers scored higher than White murderers on Hypomania (Ma) and lower on Social Introversion (Si). However, when IQ was controlled, differences between Black and White murderers disappeared (Holcolm, Adams, & Ponder, 1984).

TABLE 8.5
Minnesota Multiphasic Personality Inventory *T* Scores of Violent Offenders Emphasizing Murderers

Scale	Study 1		Study 2	Study 3	Study 4		Study 5	Study 6		Study 7	Study 8	
	I	II			I	II		I	II		I	II
N	80	56	44	34	25	25	61	91	46	107	40	12
L	50	50	53	52	—	—	50	50	53	50	52	51
F	66	67	60	60	—	—	68	80	90	68	71	74
K	56	55	59	55	—	—	48	49	49	54	51	53
Hs	53	55	59	62	65	61	48	53	54	78	69	62
Dep	60	65	63	66	73	78	76	74	71	63	72	67
Hy	65	64	62	63	67	64	65	67	67	61	69	64
Pd	76	75	71	72	79	76	67	67	67	78	78	77
Mf	56	57	57	54	63	63	69	58	61	68	57	65
Pa	57	64	59	67	65	68	50	79	81	70	73	68
Pt	58	64	60	63	71	74	54	50	50	86	75	77
Sc	62	70	65	70	77	77	86	65	71	92	83	81
Ma	67	70	58	62	64	62	59	60	68	68	69	70
Si	52	53	50	52	57	61	55	62	58	58	58	58
Code	49'	489'	4'8	48'	482'	2846	824'	6243	428'	8746	8476	847
											(continued)	

TABLE 8.5
Minnesota Multiphasic Personality Inventory *T* Scores of Violent Offenders Emphasizing Murderers *(Continued)*

Scale	Study 9					Study 10	Study 11		Study 12	Study 13				
	I	II	III	IV	V		I	II		I	II	III	IV	V
N	17	26	21	25	21	137	111	49	96	20	13	18	14	15
L	46	53	53	50	64	50	50	53	53	45	53	56	50	60
F	96	120	53	68	80	83	85	86	83	100	115	58	66	76
K	40	45	60	49	56	50	52	53	49	40	46	62	48	55
Hs	72	90	52	54	77	54	53	49	52	58	80	31	39	52
Dep	80	95	58	65	80	75	74	68	62	77	96	64	65	75
Hy	65	82	56	55	73	66	67	65	65	64	86	60	56	69
Pd	78	90	67	74	81	68	68	65	65	79	80	50	60	67
Mf	61	68	51	59	61	61	60	62	60	61	71	60	57	61
Pa	94	105	55	70	83	83	83	80	79	100	108	59	70	85
Pt	85	97	52	66	77	50	53	45	48	71	79	21	40	44
Sc	101	130	55	75	88	67	69	67	65	96	117	23	50	55
Ma	70	81	58	69	63	63	60	65	60	75	75	50	58	58
Si	67	72	47	54	63	62	63	55	61	66	71	48	54	62
Code	8672	8672	4'	489	642	6248	8243	2843	643	6842	8623	a	6'	623

(continued)

TABLE 8.5

Minnesota Multiphasic Personality Inventory T Scores of Violent Offenders Emphasizing Murderers (Continued)

Scale	Study 14 I	Study 14 II	Study 15 I	Study 15 II	Study 16 I	Study 16 II	Study 16 III	Study 16 IV	Study 17	Total subjects	Mean profile	MMPI–2 mean profile (N = 135)
N	48	41	20	19	45	26	61	16	135	1,048		
L	53	53	57	55	56	52	58	63	56		53	56
F	78	78	55	55	50	57	56	61	76		74	76
K	49	53	59	57	56	53	65	62	45		53	45
Hs	49	49	55	52	47	50	55	68	46		58	46
Dep	70	72	57	54	52	55	56	72	67		69	67
Hy	64	65	58	53	53	50	62	67	62		63	62
Pd	61	62	69	67	58	70	72	77	55		70	55
Mf	62	59	55	53	56	57	61	60	48		62	48
Pa	76	76	55	55	51	56	56	63	75		70	75
Pt	43	46	56	55	48	57	56	68	42		60	42
Sc	61	57	56	58	49	60	57	70	53		74	53
Ma	63	58	55	64	57	68	58	64	49		65	49
Si	56	60	52	47	47	50	49	57	60		58	60
Code	62'	62'	4'	4'	a	49'	4'	4273	62'	8462		

Note. Dashes indicate no data for that scale on variable. Study 1 (Sutker & Moan, 1973) examined the profiles of White (I) and Black (II) murderers. Study 2 (Deiker, 1974) examined the profiles of male murderers. Study 3 (Panton, 1976) examined the profiles of death row inmates. Study 4 (Quinsey, Arnold, & Pruesse, 1980) examined the profiles of murderers of family members (I) and non–family members. Study 5 (McDonald & Paitich, 1981) examined the profiles of male and female murderers. Study 6 (Holcolm & Adams, 1982) examined the profiles of White (I) and Black (II) murderers. Study 7 (Langevin, Paitich, Orchard, Handy, & Russon, 1982) examined the profiles of a sample of murderers. Study 8 (R. Rogers & Seman, 1983) examined the profiles of sane (I) and insane (II) murderers. Study 9 (Anderson & Holcolm, 1983) examined the profiles of five cluster analysis types. Study 10 (Holcolm & Adams, 1983) examined the profiles of Black and White murderers. Study 11 (Holcolm, Adams, & Ponder, 1984) examined the profiles of White (I) and Black (II) murderers. Study 12 (Holcolm & Adams, 1985b) examined the profiles of a sample of murderers. Study 13 (Holcolm, Adams, & Ponder, 1984) examined the profiles of five cluster analysis types. Study 14 (Holcolm & Adams, 1985a) examined the profiles of murcerers while sober (I) and drunk (II). Study 15 (Kalichman, 1988b) examined the profiles of male murderers of domestic victims (I) and strangers (II). Study 16 (Kalichman, 1988a) examined the profiles of four cluster analysis types. Study 17 (Shea, McKee, Shea, & Culley, 1996) examined the profiles of male murderers using the MMPI–2.
aWithin normal limits.

TABLE 8.6
Minnesota Multiphasic Personality Inventory *T* Scores
for Female and Adolescent Murderers

Scale	Study 1	Study 2 I	Study 2 II	Study 2 III	Study 3
N	16	14	15	14	18
L	51	57	60	60	47
F	56	66	72	68	86
K	53	50	47	52	46
Hs	52	62	64	61	55
Dep	53	66	73	64	68
Hy	56	59	64	59	68
Pd	65	62	68	70	75
Mf	43	52	62	60	55
Pa	63	71	71	68	76
Pt	53	65	68	64	70
Sc	56	66	69	69	77
Ma	57	50	55	52	68
Si	55	59	59	53	60
Code	4'6	486	6847	486	8647

Note. Study 1 (Kalichman, 1988a) examined the profiles of female murderers. Study 2 (McKee, Shea, Mogy, & Holden, 2001) examined the profiles of female filicide (I), matricide (II), and homicide (III) cases. Study 3 (Cornell, Miller, & Benedek, 1988) examined the profiles of adolescent murderers.

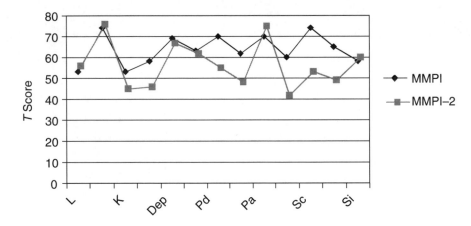

Figure 8.2. Modal Minnesota Multiphasic Personality Inventory (MMPI; *N* = 1,048) and MMPI–2 (*N* = 34) profiles of murderers.

Relationship to the Victim

There is some evidence that MMPI scores differ on the basis of the relationship of the murderer to the victim. Women who murdered their domestic partner scored higher on Paranoia (Pa) and Social Introversion (Si) compared with men who murdered either their partner or a stranger.

These results suggest that these women had more sensitivity and social withdrawal, perhaps as a result of chronic physical abuse. In fact, their MMPI profile was within normal limits. In contrast, men who murdered strangers, compared with men who murdered their domestic partner, had higher levels of social extroversion and impulsivity (low Si). They also had more evidence of sociopathy (Pd) than female murderers (Kalichman, 1988b).

Substance Abuse

Holcolm and Adams (1985a) compared four groups of murderers and the presence of substance abuse. Group I consisted of 41 men who murdered while intoxicated, Group II included 48 men who murdered while sober, Group III consisted of 130 male psychiatric patients without histories of substance abuse or violence, and Group IV consisted of 40 nonviolent patients in a detoxification program. The violent group scored higher on Paranoia (Pa) and lower on Hypomania (Ma), reflecting more suspiciousness and irritability. Men who murdered while sober scored lower on Masculinity/ Femininity (Mf), suggesting lower sensitivity, but higher on Psychopathic Deviate (Pd) compared with those who murdered while drunk. The latter group had higher L validity scores, suggesting psychological naïveté.

Amnesia

Inmates undergoing pretrial evaluation were divided into three groups: (a) those who confessed to their crime (*n* = 50), (b) those who denied their crime (*n* = 31), and (c) those who claimed amnesia (*n* = 24). Inmates claiming amnesia scored higher on Hypochondriasis (Hs), Depression (Dep), and Hysteria (Hy). These claims of more physical problems and depression were interpreted as signs of malingering (Parwatikar et al., 1985).

Death Row Status

Inmates on death row had higher elevations on Paranoia (Pa) and Schizophrenia (Sc). The elevation of these scores suggests hopelessness, frustration, alienation, and resentment, rather than psychotic processes, and may be attributed to the effects of possible death rather than to preexisting personality characteristics (Dahlstrom, Panton, Bain, & Dahlstrom, 1986).

In summary, the literature reviewed here suggests that there is no single MMPI profile code type specific to people who murder. There are code types that appear more frequently in groups of murderers, but they also appear in those who do not murder. However, any individual patient who has an MMPI profile similar to that of the modal types should receive a more thorough scrutiny and evaluation regarding violent tendencies, as-saultive behavior, and probability estimates for risk of lethal violence.

MMPI Group Classification of Murderers

The evidence suggests that murderers are not a homogeneous population and can be differentiated on a number of dimensions, including psychological ones. Megargee (1977) sought to develop a prisoner taxonomic system that was reliable, economical, valid, and dynamic; that possessed clear operational definitions; and that would have treatment implications. His classification system based on this taxonomy now meets the standards of the American Correctional Association and satisfies federal court mandates.

Using cluster analysis techniques, 10 MMPI "types" were found in a sample of 1,344 men ages 18 to 27 incarcerated at a Tallahassee federal medium security prison (Megargee & Dorhout, 1977; J. Meyer & Megargee, 1977). In addition to the MMPI, these prisoners were given the California Psychological Inventory, the State–Trait Anxiety Inventory, the Adjective Check List, the Personal Opinion Study, the Interpersonal Sensitivity Inventory, an attitudes toward parents scale, and a prisonization scale. This battery of tests was given along with a structured clinical interview that was tape-recorded and scored on 250 items by independent raters. Additional data included prison investigation reports and Bureau of Prisons demographic sheets.

Megargee's analysis indicated that these 10 MMPI-based types differed substantially in family and social history, lifestyle and personality patterns, prison adjustment, and recidivism. In fact, they differed on 140 of 164 variables tested. Modal characteristics of a typical member of each group were then established (Megargee, 1984a, 1984b; Megargee & Bohn, 1977). As of 1983, about 30,000 federal prisoners had been typed using the Megargee typology (Kennedy, 1986). When the Tallahassee Federal Correctional Institution assigned inmates to living arrangements based on the Megargee classification system, serious assaults dropped by 46% (Megargee, 1984a). Thus, the classification system provides a means of distinguishing potentially violent from nonviolent prisoners.

Megargee chose nondescriptive names for these 10 types in an alphabetized format as follows: Able, Baker, Charlie, Delta, Easy, Foxtrot, George, How, Item, and Jupiter, and the system has been ordered on a continuum from the most benign to the most pathological types (I, E, B, A, G, D, J, H, F, C) (Motiuk, Bonta, & Andrews, 1986). The types, along with their basic characteristics, are presented in Table 8.7.

The reliability of the Megargee typology has been established by studying the interrater reliability in terms of classifying individual MMPI profiles, by using test–retest methodology, and by determining the typology's replicability in other populations (Zager, 1988). Research has provided strong support for the validity of the original 10 types. These types have appeared in federal penitentiaries (Bohn, 1979; Edinger, 1979; Edinger & Auerbach,

1978; Edinger, Reuterfors, & Logue, 1982; R. W. Hanson, Moss, Hosford, & Johnson, 1983; Johnson, Simmons, & Gordon, 1983; Louscher, Hosford, & Moss, 1983; Megargee, 1986; Megargee & Bohn, 1977; Mrad, Kabacoff, & Cuckro, 1983; Simmons, Johnson, Gouvier, & Muzyczka, 1981; Van Voorhis, 1988; Walters, Mann, Miller, Hemphill, & Chlumsky, 1988), state penitentiaries (Booth & Howell, 1980; Carey, Garske, & Ginsberg, 1986; Edinger, 1979; K. N. Wright, 1988), medium-security facilities (Carey et al., 1986; Johnson et al., 1983), high-medium-security facilities (Van Voorhis, 1988; N. H. Wrobel, Wrobel, & McIntosh, 1988), high-security facilities (Louscher et al., 1983; Simmons et al., 1981), and maximum-security settings (Louscher et al., 1983; Motiuk et al., 1986; Walters, 1986; N. H. Wrobel et al., 1988). They also appear among death row inmates (Dahlstrom, Panton, et al., 1986), prison halfway house participants (Motiuk et al., 1986; Mrad et al., 1983), military prisons (Walters, 1986; Walters, Scrapamsky, & Marlow, 1986; Walters et al., 1988), forensic populations (DiFrancesca & Meloy, 1989; Hutton, Miner, & Langfeldt, 1993; N. H. Wrobel et al., 1988), presentencing psychiatric samples (T. A. Wrobel, Calovini, & Martin, 1991), and incarcerates who have threatened the U.S. president (Megargee, 1986).

The typology has been documented across a variety of geographic settings and states, other than in Florida, where it was developed, including Alabama (Edinger, 1979), California (DiFrancesca & Meloy, 1989; Hanson et al., 1983; Hutton et al., 1993; Louscher et al., 1983), Indiana (Van Voorhis, 1988), Kansas (Walters, 1986), Kentucky (Johnson et al., 1983), Louisiana (Schaffer, Pettigrew, Blovin, & Edwards, 1983), Missouri (Anderson & Holcolm, 1983; Megargee, 1986; Mrad et al., 1983), North Carolina (Dahlstrom, Panton, et al., 1986; Edinger, 1979; Edinger et al., 1982; Megargee, 1986), Ohio (Carey et al., 1986; Van Voorhis, 1988; T. A. Wrobel et al., 1991), Tennessee (Simmons et al., 1981; Veneziano & Veneziano, 1986), and Utah (Booth & Howell, 1980), as well as in Canada (Motiuk et al., 1986).

Although the system has been used with female prisoners (Edinger, 1979; Schaffer et al., 1983; T. A. Wrobel et al., 1991) and with adolescent incarcerates (Doren, Megargee, & Schreiber, 1980; Veneziano & Veneziano, 1986), research has not yet established the utility of the Megargee classification system with these groups. Use with adolescents may be particularly problematic, because their personality may not have solidified into its adult form. To date, there has been relatively little interest in Megargee's treatment recommendations associated with the typology (Kennedy, 1986).

Although not designed specifically as a classification system for murderers, Megargee reported that types Charlie, Foxtrot, and How—the more pathological types—were more prone toward violent behavior. Edinger (1979) independently replicated the typology and found that types Charlie and Jupiter had committed more violent crimes, including

TABLE 8.7
Capsule Characteristics of the Ten Types

Name and proportion	MMPI characteristics	
	Elevation	Pattern
Able (17%)	Moderate; peak score at 70 or less	Bimodal, with peaks on 4 and 9
Baker (4%)	Moderate; Pd c70, Dep c65	Peaks on 4 and 2; slopes down and to the right
Charlie (9%)	High; peak score > 80, several > 70	Peaks on 8, 6, and 4; slopes up and to the right
Delta (10%)	Moderate to high; Pd at least 70, often 80–90	Unimodal; prominent Pd spike; others < 70
Easy (7%)	Low; top scale often < 70	43 profile; slopes down and to the right
Foxtrot (8%)	High; Top scores > 80 and others > 70	Slopes up and to the right; 89 and 4 top scores
George (7%)	Moderate; Dep and Pd c70	Like Baker, but scales 1, 2, and 3 are more elevated
How (13%)	Very high; top scores 80–90	Elevated multimodal profile; no particular code pattern
Item (19%)	Very low; Scores usually < 70	No particular code pattern
Jupiter (3%)	Moderate to high; peak scores > 70	Slopes up and to the right, with top scores on 8, 9, and 7

Note. MMPI = Minnesota Multiphasic Personality Inventory. From "Derivation, Validation, and Application of an MMPI-Based System for Classifying Criminal Offenders," by E. I. Megargee, 1984, *Medicine and Law, 3,* p. 513. Copyright 1984, CRC Press. Reprinted with permission.

TABLE 8.7
(Continued)

Observed modal characteristics	Management and treatment recommendations
Charming, popular, impulsive, and manipulative. Middle-class, achievement-oriented, do well in institution but emerge relatively unaffected.	Need change agent with sense of humor and structured setting to deal with their manipulative games and confront them with outcomes of their behavior.
Inadequate, anxious, defensive, constricted, and dogmatic; tend to abuse alcohol but not other drugs.	Initial anxiety requires supportive help. Later, many benefit from alcohol treatment and educational programming. Need counseling to stop self-defeating patterns.
Hostile, misanthropic, and suspicious, with extensive histories of maladjustment, crime, and drug and alcohol abuse. Alienated, aggressive, antagonistic, and antisocial.	Require secure setting and extensive programming. Consistency, fairness, and perseverance needed to avoid further need to use drugs or act out when stressed.
Amoral, hedonistic, egocentric, bright, and manipulative. Poor relations with peers and authorities. Impulsive sensation seeking leads to frequent infractions.	Often have extensive records requiring incarceration. Separate from weaker, more easily exploited inmates. Challenging and confronting needed, but prognosis poor.
Bright, stable, well-educated, middle-class, with good adjustment and resources. Underachievers who take the easy path but have good interpersonal relationships.	Minimal needs for structure and treatment. Should be challenged to take advantage of assets. Respond well to educational programming.
Tough, streetwise, cynical, antisocial. Deprivation and deviance lead to extensive criminal histories, and poor prison adjustment. Deficits in all areas.	Require structure and strong change agent. Extensive changes needed; peer counseling and program with obvious contingencies required to make behavior more socialized.
Hardworking, submissive, anxious, and from deviant families. Learned criminal values. Do their time and take advantage of educational and vocational opportunities.	Need to learn alternatives to crime as livelihood. Supportive treatment at outset, followed by rational–cooperative approach and education and vocational programming.
Unstable, agitated, disturbed, mental health problems. Function ineffectively in all areas and have extensive needs.	Require further diagnosis and program aimed at overcoming mental health problems. Warm but structured therapeutic environment with mental health resources needed.
Stable, effectively functioning, well-adjusted with minimal problems and few authority conflicts.	Basically normal group with minimal needs for structure, support, or treatment beyond what is dictated by the legal situation.
Are overcoming deprived background fairly well but have conflicts with staff and other inmates. Work hard and do better than expected after release.	Change agent needed to support efforts to overcome deficits via educational or vocational programming. Counseling and tolerance of setbacks that occur required.

murder, and showed more aggressive behavior in prison compared to the other groups. Because type Charlie has been particularly implicated in violence and murder (Anderson & Holcolm, 1983; Edinger, 1979; Hanson et al., 1983; Motiuk et al., 1986), a more detailed discussion of this MMPI code type is presented.

Type Charlie's MMPI profile is characterized by elevations on Schizophrenia (Sc), Paranoia (Pa), and Psychopathic Deviate (Pd) (an 864 3-point code type) and an acting-out aggressive profile type. This profile suggests a personality style that is sensitive to perceived threats and insults, a hostile and bitter demeanor ready to strike at the slightest provocation, and antisocial traits. Individuals with this profile tend to have authority problems, considerable anxiety, a deviant value system, and poor ego strength. They lack empathy; are cognitively and emotionally constricted; and feel alienated, resentful, bitter, and hostile. Charlie types show poor adjustment histories and tend to have many criminal convictions. On the Adjective Check List, these men and women endorsed adjectives that included negative affect and described themselves as less stable and as irresponsible (Megargee, 1977, 1986). They also tend to have a formal thought disorder, substantial energy, and much anger and are quite defensive (DiFrancesca & Meloy, 1989). Table 8.8 presents studies that have published T score information on type Charlie.

TABLE 8.8
Minnesota Multiphasic Personality Inventory T Scores
on Type Charlie Profiles in Published Studies

| Scale | Study 1 | Study 2 | | Study 3 | | Study 4 | Study 5 |
		I	II	I	II		
L	50	50	48	52	47	49	52
F	80	76	76	77	76	79	79
K	46	44	49	50	48	46	49
Hs	60	60	57	60	59	57	59
Dep	65	65	61	64	65	63	68
Hy	59	58	52	61	58	53	59
Pd	77	75	74	79	78	70	76
Mf	61	61	51	61	64	62	67
Pa	81	78	80	79	75	73	78
Pt	72	75	74	70	71	70	73
Sc	84	89	88	84	85	86	88
Ma	75	74	68	75	70	74	69
Si	57	60	62	53	61	58	59

Note. Study 1 is Megargee, 1977. Study 2 is Edinger, 1979 (I, men; II, women). Study 3 is Edinger, Reuterfors, and Logue, 1982. Study 4 is Mrad, Kabacoff, and Cuckro, 1983. Study 5 is Hutton, Miner, and Langfeldt, 1993.

Case Example

A 20-year-old African American inmate had the following MMPI T scores: L (43), F (64), and K (35) validity scales; Hypochondriasis (Hs, 57), Depression (Dep, 76), Hysteria (Hy, 50), Psychopathic Deviate (Pd, 53), Masculinity/Femininity (Mf, 43), Paranoia (Pa, 77), Schizophrenia (Sc, 73), Hypomania (Ma, 74), and Social Introversion (Si, 60). He had been convicted of first-degree murder and attempted murder.

He began drinking alcohol in substantial quantities around eighth grade and drank to intoxication on special occasions he chose to celebrate. He denied using illicit drugs. Although he had had no serious illnesses, he had received a gunshot wound to the head a few years previously, resulting in a three-day hospitalization. Subsequent to this incident, he reported migraine headaches, jaw pain, and nonspecific memory problems, although he showed no apparent memory disorders.

This inmate had argued with his eventual victims on a previous occasion and, on seeing them again on the street, left the area to find a means to kill them. He returned to the area, shot and killed one of the victims, and shot the other victim with the intent to kill him, but the victim recovered from his wounds. The inmate would not provide any other details, but he stated that he was involved in a gang both before his arrest and during his imprisonment. He later received his general equivalency diploma in prison.

His profile suggests an individual who is angry, depressed, and sullen. He gets upset with people who he believes have harmed him and blames other people for his difficulties. He appears tense, irritable, pessimistic, and preoccupied with his problems. Projection and acting out are his major defenses, and he seems prone to misunderstand the motives of other people. Paranoid features to his personality are likely. He has numerous somatic complaints with much anxiety, worry, and ruminations. Thinking is likely to be permeated by an obsessive quality. He views the world as a threatening place, feels he is getting a raw deal out of life, and sees little wrong in violating societal rules and conventions because of the perceived injustices that have been perpetrated on him. He is high strung, reports some bizarre perceptions, has unusual thinking and a sense of alienation, and lacks warm relationships, especially because he views others as potentially threatening and harmful. This inmate shows suspicious attitudes and an ingrained hostility, combined with malevolent projections. Such a psychological state puts him at risk for lethal violence.

The Megargee System and the MMPI–2

Megargee has been studying the impact of the MMPI restandardization on his classification system. He determined that a new set of classification rules are required when using the MMPI–2 and is presently conducting research to determine if the empirical correlates for the MMPI will be similar to those found for the MMPI–2 (Megargee, 1993, 1994). The original Megargee typology, developed on male offenders, tended to work well with female prisoners, too, although a higher proportion of women than men classified with type Charlie, one of the more deviant types. Megargee developed new rules for the classification of MMPI–2 profiles, and 88% of male profiles and 99% of female profiles were able to be classified according to the new system (Megargee, 1994, 1997).

Prior research with the Megargee typology with adolescent offenders resulted in a relatively low number of unclassified protocols. Subsequent research has suggested that the revised rules improve the classification system with adolescent offenders and that modal characteristics and management and treatment implications were able to be obtained for the 10 types (Pena & Megargee, 1997).

Preliminary data suggest that the patterns and configurations of male and female prisoners on the MMPI–2 compared favorably with the original norms (Megargee, 1997). The most prominent elevated MMPI–2 scales were the F validity scale, Psychopathic Deviate (Pd), Paranoia (Pa), Hypomania (Ma), the MacAndrews Alcoholism Scale—Revised (MAC–R), and the Antisocial Practices (ASP) scale for both genders and Masculinity/Femininity (Mf) and the Addiction Admission scale for women inmates (Megargee, Mercer, & Carbonell, 1999). Readers interested in using the Megargee classification system for MMPI–2 profiles should contact the test's publisher, National Computer Systems, which can score the MMPI–2 and classify the profile according to the Megargee system (Megargee, Carbonell, Bohn, & Sliger, 2001) for a nominal fee.

In summary, the following conclusions, based on research on the Megargee classification system, are offered:

- An individual in the group code may not show all of the characteristics of the group itself and may show variability around the prototype characteristics.
- The system is dynamic, and an individual may change group membership over the course of his or her sentence.
- The 10 types have appeared across multiple prison settings, although the prevalence of types within each setting shows considerable variability. Types Able, Charlie, Foxtrot, and How show exceptional validity.
- It is possible that different sorting rules may be required for White and minority inmates. The system works well in classifying women offenders, but empirical correlates with female offenders have not been established.

- There is a paucity of research using the system with adolescent offenders.
- Although the types have been replicated in many settings, there is less research verifying the correlates associated with each type.
- Type Charlie is particularly associated with poor adjustment and violent behavior, but this type is not specific to murderers.
- Although the Megargee typology was originally developed using young adult male federal prisoners, it has been found to be reliable and useful in forensic psychiatric inpatient settings as well (Hutton et al., 1993).

MMPI Special Scales

Early research sought to develop scales derived from the MMPI item pool that might be able to detect meaningful differences between criminal classification groups. Results were mixed. For example, Panton (1958), using the Prison Adjustment Scale (PAS), reported that the PAS was unable to distinguish among six crime classification groups, whereas Christensen and LeUnes (1974) found that the PAS, along with scales L and Psychopathic Deviate (Pd), did differentiate among crime classification groups.

The MMPI-derived Overcontrolled Hostility (OH) scale was an outgrowth of previous attempts to measure differences on hostility and impulse control between assaultive and nonassaultive criminals (Megargee, 1966; Megargee, Cook, & Mendelsohn, 1967). Megargee and his colleagues reasoned that there may be at least two distinct personality types among assaultive individuals, which they labeled "overcontrolled" and "undercontrolled." The former is characterized by excessive inhibitions against the expression of aggression in any form. Individuals of this type are extremely frustrated because their anger and hostility build up over time, until suddenly they commit an aggressive act of homicidal intensity.

Megargee conducted an item analysis of MMPI test responses of four groups: extremely assaultive, moderately assaultive, and nonassaultive criminals and normal participants. He developed a 31-item scale that was able to differentiate successfully among groups. This scale was cross-validated using independent samples. It is surprising that the types of items that successfully differentiated between the overcontrolled and undercontrolled types were passive and nonaggressive in quality. The scale positively correlated with validity scales L and K and Hysteria (Hy), suggesting rigidity, repression of conflicts, and a self-presentation of positive adjustments. It correlated negatively with Psychasthenia (Pt), Psychopathic Deviate (Pd), Schizophrenia (Sc), and Hypomania (Ma) scales, suggesting inhibition of acting out rebelliousness and authority conflicts. Megargee suggested that the OH scale is measuring impulse control and hostile alienation. Megargee set a raw score of > 18 (*T* 70) on the OH scale as indicating people who are highly overcontrolled and a raw score of < 11 (*T* 40) as reflecting undercontrolled hostility. Scores in the midrange are not significant.

A substantial amount of research has been conducted on the OH scale (see Table 8.9.). Much of this research has studied the scale's construct validity and its ability to distinguish between highly, moderately, and infrequently assaultive or nonassaultive inmates. The scale has also been factored (Walters & Greene, 1983). Research has supported the construct validity of the OH scale (du Toit & Duckitt, 1990; Gudjonsson, Peturrson, Sigurdardottir, & Skulason, 1991; Quinsey, Maguire, & Varney, 1983; White, 1975; White, McAdoo, & Megargee, 1973). These studies demonstrated that patients with high OH scores, when given other tests, have personality dimensions reflecting higher degrees of control, inhibition of aggression, and social adjustment.

In general, most studies have validated the OH scale, with high scores on the scale reflecting rigid control of aggression (Deiker, 1974; Henderson, 1983b; Lane & Kling, 1979; Quinsey et al., 1983; Walters, Solomon, & Greene, 1982). Studies that failed to support the Megargee typology have typically administered it apart from the MMPI by removing the 31 items and giving the scale as a single test (Hoppe & Singer, 1977; Rawlings, 1973).

Most published studies, which are described below, have reported on OH scores with a criterion group who were not murderers. Many other studies using inmate populations included murderers in their assaultive group and also included nonlethal violent inmates.

Deiker (1974) studied a sample of 44 homicidal male inmates in Massachusetts. These inmates had an average OH score of 14.5, indicating a rating of moderately overcontrolled. Quinsey, Arnold, and Pruesse (1980) reported that 25 murderers of family members had a mean score of 13.5 on the OH scale, whereas nonfamily murderers had a mean score of 14.0. Once again, these scores were in the moderate range. Finally, Quinsey et al. (1983) found that inmates who were classified as overcontrolled murderers attained a mean score of 18.5 on the OH scale, whereas inmates classified as undercontrolled murderers had a mean score of 12.5.

Research has largely supported the construct and concurrent validity of the Megargee typology of the overcontrolled and undercontrolled hostility personality types. However, Megargee never asserted that these are the only two types of murderers and never developed the scale to distinguish murderers from nonviolent inmates. The OH scale was designed to detect one type of murderer—the overcontrolled type—and the scale seems to function well in this area. There certainly are many other types of murderers and motivations for murder, and the OH scale would not be appropriate for these types. For example, some murderers have been socialized into a deviant

TABLE 8.9

Overview of Studies on the Overcontrolled Hostility (OH) Scale

Authors	Year of publication	Population studied	Findings
Megargee, Cook, and Mendelsohn	1967	64 male criminals	This study described the development and validation of the OH scale.
Blackburn	1972	165 men in maximum security	OH scores were loaded on the negative pole of the aggression factor among multiple measures of hostility and aggression.
Mallory and Walker	1972	88 male inmates grouped by assaultive and nonassaultive first offenders and recidivists	The OH scale did not discriminate between groups.
White, McAdoo, and Megargee	1973	75 youthful offenders	16PF correlates of high- and low-scoring OH inmates were consistent with the theoretical nature of the overcontrolled construct.
Deiker	1974	40 nonassaultive inmates 40 physically violent inmates 40 murderers	Multiple scales measuring hostility were consistent with Megargee's OH items, suggesting control of aggression among groups of felons.
Megargee and Cook	1975	86 probation applicants 44 assaultive prisoners	OH scale validity was not dependent on a "nay-saying" response set.
White	1975	60 youthful offenders	Scores on a personality measure were consistent with the Megargee typology of personality differences between high- and low-scoring subjects on the OH scale.
Paulson, Schwemer, and Bendel	1976	21 female and 32 male abusive parents 67 women and 46 men with family problems	The OH scale did not differentiate groups.
Rada, Laws, and Kellner	1976	52 rapists 12 child molesters	OH scale scores did not correlate with testosterone levels.

(continued)

TABLE 8.9

Overview of Studies on the Overcontrolled Hostility (OH) Scale (*Continued*)

Authors	Year of publication	Population studied	Findings
Hoppe and Singer	1977	115 male criminal offenders in a psychiatric hospital, subdivided into 5 groups based on criminal offense	Violent patients did not score higher on the OH scale.
McCreary and Padilla	1977	337 male offenders convicted for misdemeanors (varying race)	Mexican Americans scored higher on the OH scale, perhaps because of cultural factors.
Arnold, Quinsey, and Velner	1977	69 inmates with not guilty by reason of insanity convictions 60 inmates in maximum security	Maximum security patients scored higher on the OH scale, and their scores increased over a 3-year period.
Sutker, Allain, and Geyer	1978	Violent and nonviolent female prisoners	No difference was found between groups in OH scores.
Arnold, Fleming, and Bell	1979	1 murderer	A case study was described.
Quinsey, Arnold, and Pruesse	1980	150 inmates in maximum security	OH scores were unrelated to offense type.
Lane and Spruill	1980	110 male forensic patients in a state hospital	Inmates with high OH scores also scored higher on scales measuring denial, repression, and inhibition of aggression.
McDonald and Paitich	1981	61 murderers 42 assaultive inmates 24 controls	The OH scale did not discriminate between groups.
Walters, Greene, and Solomon	1982	780 outpatient psychiatric patients 29 OH patients	OH patients were marked by rigid denial and overcontrol of hostility.
Walters, Solomon, and Greene	1982	200 male inmates	Inmates with the 43 MMPI code type had higher OH scores than matched controls; this relationship also held with state psychiatric patients.
Walters and Greene	1983	200 male incarcerates	A factor analytic study of the OH scale was presented.

Author	Year	Sample	Findings
Quinsey, Maguire, and Varney	1983	Male murderers	A high-scoring OH group was less assertive than other groups in a role-playing task and on a questionnaire measuring aggression.
Rice, Arnold, and Tate	1983	25 inmates in maximum security	OH scores were related to faking indexes, suggesting that high scores may reflect a desire to appear normal.
Werner, Becker, and Yesavage	1983	31 male inpatient psychotics	OH scores correlated negligibly with measures of expressed hostility and assaultiveness; results suggest that scale does not predict violence among male psychotics.
Henderson	1983a	105 violent prisoners 87 nonviolent male prisoners	The nonviolent group scored lower on the OH scale.
Biaggio, Godwin, and Baldwin	1984	24 college students judged dependent 26 college students judged overcontrolled	In this analogue study, neither group were more compliant.
Villanueva, Roman, and Tuley	1988	99 offenders in residential treatment	OH scores did not differentiate successful from unsuccessful treatment.
Schmaltz, Fehr, and Dalby	1989	120 inmates in medium security 60 psychiatric patients	Inmates scored higher than psychiatric patients on the OH scale.
du Toit and Duckitt	1990	20 undercontrolled violent prisoners 21 overcontrolled violent prisoners 20 nonviolent prisoners	The overcontrolled group scored higher on the OH scale and lower on measures of aggression and higher on inhibition of aggression.
Truscott	1990	72 young male offenders	OH scores did not differentiate between levels or severity of assaultive behavior in criminal adolescents; inmates deemed to have an overcontrolled personality did not score higher on the OH scale.
Gudjonsson, Petursson, Sigurdardottir, and Skulason	1991	74 prisoners in Iceland	Overcontrol was correlated with both self-description and other-description measures; scores on OH were difficult to fake.
Blake, Penk, Mori, Kleespies, Walsh, and Keane	1992	37 psychiatric inpatients	The OH scale correlated .57 between MMPI versions 1 and 2.
Hutton, Miner, Blades, and Langfeldt	1992	412 male forensic patients	Blacks scored higher on OH than Whites.

Note. MMPI = Minnesota Multiphasic Personality Inventory.

subculture with norms that approve and reward aggression and violence in certain circumstances because of its instrumental value to the subgroup (du Toit & Duckitt, 1990). Researchers have sought to extend the OH scale beyond its original intent, and some of its limitations have become apparent. Finally, no study has assessed its predictive validity. The focus has been on construct and concurrent validity.

The OH remains a viable scale for the MMPI–2. When used in conjunction with other MMPI scales and code types, it can provide incremental validity and refinements in assessments.

CASE EXAMPLE

History

The inmate was a 45-year-old Black man who was admitted to the medical clinic of a correctional facility for treatment of recurrent depression. He had an extensive psychiatric background since his early teens and had had 40 psychiatric admissions to public and private psychiatric hospitals. He had a history of self-mutilation and had made five suicide attempts since the age of 18. At age 7, he began swallowing marbles and rocks whenever he became angry at his parents.

In his most recent attempt, he tried to kill himself by swallowing wire and bedsprings. During his incarceration, he swallowed broken glass, wire, and bedsprings to cope with his anger. The precipitant to his most recent attempt was a threat from a correctional officer to transfer him from the psychiatric residential wing to the general population.

His diagnoses at the time of the evaluation were Major Depression, Recurrent; Opiate and Cocaine Dependence, by history; and Antisocial and Borderline Personality Disorders. Psychiatric medications included Lithium and Prozac. He had a period of opiate addiction and was treated with methadone maintenance. He was also HIV-positive and was taking AZT. He contracted the disease from a former girlfriend, who later committed suicide.

The inmate's mother had died when he was a young child, and his father died of a gunshot wound when the inmate was in his teens. He had never married but had fathered two children with two different women. Both his current girlfriend and their infant were HIV-positive.

The inmate had a long history of violence and was convicted of murder and armed robbery on five separate occasions. He was awaiting trial for charges of arson and murder. He became involved with gangs early in life and started selling drugs at age 14. He reported difficulty in controlling his anger since age 8, when he stabbed his grammar school teacher in the back with a pair of scissors. He admitted to having a nasty temper and problems

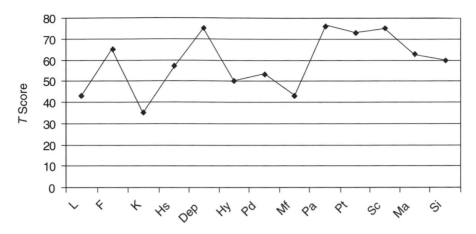

Figure 8.3. MMPI–2 scores for a man charged with murder.

with authority. His temper emerged whenever he believed that someone was trying to control him. During the elementary grades, he was placed in behavior-disordered programs. He didn't go to high school and supported himself by selling drugs and pimping. His IQ was in the average range.

Figure 8.3 presents this inmate's MMPI–2 profile. The Megargee classification of this profile is type Charlie.

Analysis

The profile suggests exaggeration; the inmate reported more symptoms than would be established by an objective review. This response set is understandable, given his motivation to remain in the psychiatric wing and his desire not to return to the general population. This circumstance nicely illustrates the effects of the context of testing as affecting test scores. However, by scrutinizing his current situation and his extensive psychiatric history, one can interpret a scaled-down version of the profile.

The profile suggests the presence of delusions, but not hallucinations (Paranoia [Pa] and Schizophrenia [Sc]), hyperactivity (Hypomania [Ma]), and antisocial behavior and traits (Psychopathic Deviate [Pd]). His content scales were not systematically elevated, as would be the case in a random response set, but were specifically elevated consistent with his history. He reported family problems (FAM), antisocial practices (ASP), anger (ANG), and bizarre mentations (BIZ). It is interesting that both the clinical scale and content scale suggesting depression were not significantly elevated. This may reflect a positive treatment response to the antidepressant drug Prozac.

This inmate has problems in controlling his anger, is hyperactive, tends to act out, has a low frustration tolerance, is emotionally labile, shows evidence of a thought disorder, is narcissistic, and is prone toward sexual acting out, lying, stealing, aggressive outbursts, and assaultive behaviors. His OH score is T 55, suggesting that he is not an overcontrolled hostility type. He has a number of persecutory ideas, lacks control, has problems with authority, and has a defensive structure characterized by projection and acting out. He is at extremely high risk for continued adjustment problems within the correctional facility. If this inmate is to receive psychological treatment, goals need to be directed at anger management. It seems that this person would not be able to function in society at the present time and that the long-term prognosis is poor. Confinement with humane care seems to be the appropriate treatment plan for him.

GROUP DIFFERENCES AND INDIVIDUAL PREDICTION

Until recently, the psychological literature has focused on group differences and has ignored the predictability of the criterion for any individual member of the group. The issue pertains to actuarial versus clinical prediction. Actuarial prediction tends to be accurate for the group but is unable to successfully predict which member of the group will demonstrate the criterion behavior—in this case, aggression and lethal violence. Clinical prediction from psychological tests relies on the test properties of sensitivity and specificity. Test sensitivity is defined as the probability that the person has the trait in question, given a test score that suggests the presence of the trait. Test specificity is the probability that the person does not have the trait if the test score suggests the absence of the trait.

In order for psychologists to make individual predictions from psychological tests, information must be available on the test's sensitivity and specificity. Statistically, these values should be above 70%, but base rates affect the accuracy of predictions. Base rates are the rate of occurrence of the criterion in the general population. If all patients with an affective disorder show depression, then the base rate for depression is 100%, and the evaluator does not need any other information to make a prediction about depression once he or she knows the patient has an affective disorder. If the rate of lethal violence in the general population is 1%, then the evaluator knows that 99% of the people he or she evaluates, in general, for lethal violence will not become violent. Of course, the rate of occurrence of violence in a forensic population is higher than 1%. Individual prediction is most reliable when the base rate of the behavior is 50%, but it becomes inordinately difficult when the base rate is less than 5%. Needless to say, there has been no information published to date on the sensitivity or specificity of any MMPI scale in the prediction of lethal violence, nor is this information available for the Megargee classification system or for the OH scale.

Relatively few studies have been reported on Rorschach findings with murderers. Adolescents who committed murder were divided into two groups, one who murdered in association with interpersonal conflict or dispute and the other who committed murder as part of another crime, such as a robbery or burglary. The Rorschach was used to study their object relations. The authors used Holt's (1975) scales to measure aggressive motives and scored aggressive Rorschach responses as attack responses, victim responses, and responses that depicted the results of aggression. Adolescents who murdered in the context of another crime had a pervasive deficit in their concepts of other people (i.e., object relations). For example, they had an immature and narcissistic conception of others and saw humans (on the Rorschach) as dehumanizing and frustrating, rather than as people deserving empathy. The authors suggested that the presence of victim responses on a Rorschach may indicate a particularly strong preoccupation with aggression (Greco & Cornell, 1992).

Meloy, Gacono, and Kenney (1994) studied Rorschach findings of sexual homicide offenders and nonsexual but violent psychopaths. Both groups had abnormalities in attachment (T responses), characterological anger (S responses), pathological narcissism (Reflection responses), borderline reality testing (X–%), and moderate and pervasive thought disorder (Wsum6). The sexual homicide group had more frequent affect hunger (T), more dysphoria ruminations (Vista responses), abnormal elevations of obsessional thoughts (FM), and greater interest in whole responses (W). The author concluded that abnormal bonding, characterological anger, formal thought disorder, and pathological narcissism are the psychological factors that seem to accompany sexual homicides.

The early memory technique may be able to distinguish criminally dangerous from nondangerous psychiatric patients. The Early Memory Aggressive Potential Score System uses the variables of memories of physical abuse and psychological abuse and number of aggressive memories, as well as severity ratings (Tobey & Bruhn, 1992). However, the technique needs replication and extension.

Guidelines for Assessment of Aggression and Violence Using Psychological Tests

Psychological tests were constructed to assess deficits and strengths in psychological functioning and to describe current psychological functioning. They were not developed to answer specific legal questions. These tests are of value in detecting substance abuse, psychiatric diagnoses, psychopathology, and malingering (Parwatikar et al., 1985). Although the studies detailed in this chapter indicate that no one profile is pathognomonic of violence, aggression, and murder, the presence of certain scale elevations does warrant additional scrutiny, evaluation, assessment, and concern.

The following guidelines are recommended to psychologists for use in assessing risk of aggression and violence using psychological tests:

1. Objective personality tests have their highest validity when used to determine present symptoms, traits, and disorders. Various degrees of inference are required to postdict psychological states retrospectively.

2. Consider the possible effects of the testing context on test scores. Also, evaluate whether certain moderator variables affected test scores.

3. Use both objective and projective psychological tests in the evaluation, and integrate test results with other sources of information, such as arrest records and collateral information, to produce a comprehensive report. Never use psychological tests alone to make final recommendations.

4. When selecting an objective personality test, the MMPI–2 has been the most frequently used and most frequently researched personality test with perpetrators of lethal violence and should be the instrument of choice. For evaluation of physical abuse, the MCMI has a good literature base and should be considered the instrument of choice.

5. Maintain an adequate level of knowledge about the professional literature regarding how physical abusers, assaultive patients, and murderers tend to score on psychological tests. Also, consider local base rates, or how particular patients tend to score on a test instrument in the particular setting.

6. Understand and appreciate the limitations of assessment instruments and of other sources of data.

7. Appreciate the social context in which the violence occurred, and not merely the personality traits that contributed to the violence.

8. Render a professional evaluation based on all known sources of information, adhering to data rather than speculations, hunches, intuition, guesses, or theoretical proclamations.

9. Make affirmative statements (either positive or negative), and don't be afraid to say, "I don't know." Others will afford the psychologist greater respect for such honesty.

10. Violence is a behavior with a low rate of occurrence. It is recommended that the psychologist render a violence risk assessment, and not make predictions of future violence.

11. Look especially for psychopathy and aggressive-sadistic and passive-aggressive (negativistic) personality disorders, which are commonly associated with violent behavior.

In summary, this chapter addressed the assessment of violence and aggression in both juveniles and adults. Included were the issues of domestic violence and partner abuse, the battered wife syndrome, and the assessment of lethal violence. The psychometric assessment of these behaviors emphasized MMPI studies, but Rorschach and MCMI studies were also presented. Millon's subtypes of personality disorders with the antisocial, aggressive, and passive-aggressive prototypes appear to be particularly helpful in understanding the empirical data. Guidelines for the assessment of lethal violence were offered, and several cases were interspersed throughout the chapter.

This chapter is an expanded version of "MMPI-Based Psychological Assessment of Lethal Violence," by R. J. Craig. Reprinted with permission from *Lethal Violence 2000: A Sourcebook on Fatal Domestic, Acquaintance, and Stranger Violence* (pp. 503–536), edited by H. V. Hall. Copyright 1998 by CRC Press, Boca Raton, Florida.

9

FUTURE DIRECTIONS

In this chapter I offer some ideas to improve the quality of the science and practice of forensic psychology. These ideas are derived from the literature base, and its lacunae, discussed throughout this book.

RESEARCH

Despite the clear-cut need to assess the validity of psychological assessment tools in forensic settings, there are a myriad of difficulties involved with such endeavors. Limited budgets constrain most agencies, which assign low priorities for this kind of research, and researchers are offered few incentives to conduct this research. Much of the research in this area emanates from dissertations, and most of these remain unpublished and lack the scrutiny of journal consulting editors. Despite these difficulties, continued research on the reliability and validity of psychological methods and tools in forensic practice remains among the highest priorities to advance the science of the psychology profession.

There is a critical need for extratest correlates of test signs in forensic populations. Many assessment tools have strong correlates coming from patients assessed in psychiatric and medical settings. Psychologists tend to extrapolate these correlates to patients assessed in forensic settings, but there is a need to determine if the correlates among forensic patients are similar to or different from those of clinical and medical populations.

Data on incremental validity are needed. Although psychologists continue to make decisions using multiple sources of data, the question remains as to how much additional data and information are needed before reaching a point of diminishing returns. Research studies of incremental validity, few and far between in most areas of psychology, are critically absent in forensic psychology.

The detection of malingering will continue to occupy the scrutiny of forensic psychologists. It is comforting that researchers continue to refine the assessment instruments to help with this task. The $F(p)$ and $F(b)$ scales of the Minnesota Multiphasic Personality Inventory—2 (MMPI–2) are excellent examples of these refinements, and these scales, as well as other MMPI–2 validity scales, operate reasonably well for these purposes. Still, they are not at 100% efficiency, and triangulation with other detection methods continues to be necessary in forensic evaluations. It is doubtful that any additional scales will emerge from the MMPI–2 item pool to add incremental validity in the detection of malingering in the foreseeable future. However, other assessment tools discussed in this volume could benefit from similar development and refinement.

In addition, psychologists need advances in research on all of the areas they are asked to evaluate in the forensic arena. In this way, psychological evaluation tools, be they record reviews, interviews, or testing, will be more precise and focused in terms of the target traits and behaviors.

It is encouraging to learn that psychologists in forensic practice do an excellent job of assessing psychopathy, especially in adults. There are several good instruments to choose from, and there is a strong empirical base supporting their findings and conclusions. One reason for this success is that the construct has clear-cut definitions and boundaries. Because psychopathy has well-defined criteria, the kappa scores for interrater reliability in the field trials for the *Diagnostic and Statistical Manual of Mental Disorders* (*DSM–IV*; American Psychiatric Association, 1994) were the highest of any personality disorder. This definitional distinction provides psychologists with better ways to conduct reliability and validity studies.

In the area of forensic practice, concurrent validity and predictive validity are most critical, and psychologists have a good knowledge base to use in assessing adult psychopathy. This is less true with the assessment of juvenile psychopathy, often confused with delinquency, which is more socially determined than affected by personality dynamics. Millon's theory of personality and personality pathology can be particularly useful in this distinction. Millon separated criteria that are more related to external, criminal behavior (e.g., truancy, arrests) from those more specific to internal, individual dynamics (e.g., lack of empathy). Thus, a person can have an antisocial personality style without the associated criminality often seen with this disorder.

Similarly, the theory is helpful in understanding Axis I disorders in the light of the person's underlying personality style. For example, whereas Major Depression may be the final common pathway, it can be derived from different personality dynamics. For a dependent personality, depression may be due to a perceived or actual loss of security; for an avoidant personality, it may be due to a recent episode of interpersonal rejection; for a narcissistic personality, it may be due to a narcissistic injury; and for a person with an antisocial personality, it may be due to an undesirable situation (e.g., facing criminal charges or sentencing).

TRAINING

Forensic psychologists require adequate training to properly interpret the test findings they will review in their work. They are likely to require specialized training and continuing postgraduate education, because graduate school training typically does not cover forensic practice in depth. Attendance at workshops and symposia that pertain to the forensic specialty are a necessity.

Ethical dilemmas in forensic assessment abound, yet there are few forums for forensic psychologists to discuss these dilemmas with others. Occasionally, the American Psychological Association (APA) produces a "casebook" that addresses ethical issues in psychology, but ethical dilemmas in forensic psychology are seldom discussed. This field has matured to the point where specialty-specific ethical issues can no longer be ignored. Ethical dilemmas in forensic assessment should now be included in any casebook on ethics. Similarly, a more organized and professional forum (other than Internet chat rooms) is needed for forensic psychologists to discuss and seek consultation from other forensic psychologists on problematic issues faced in the course of their professional responsibilities.

PERSONALITY

Psychologists will continue to use psychological tools that prove to be the most reliable and valid for the designated assessment purpose. Although newer instruments will certainly appear, and although currently available assessment tools will seek to improve their ability to accomplish their stated purpose, it is unlikely that there will be any advances in the process of test development, which is well understood and well codified in a series of clearly defined steps (Clark & Watson, 1995). Rather, what is needed are advances in explication of the constructs measured by current instruments.

For example, the diagnosis of Borderline Personality Disorder in the *DSM–IV* requires that the patient meet at least five of nine specified criteria. Mathematically, then, there are 45 ways for a patient to meet five of these criteria. Are there really 45 different types of borderlines? Obviously not! What is needed is improved theorizing on the nature of this construct and a greater explication of the criteria, with behavioral anchors, that define the disorder. Only then will psychological testing improve. The same comment holds for any number of constructs that psychologists are called on to assess.

Millon's theory of personality and personality pathology is currently the most comprehensive in explaining a variety of patient behaviors. Yet many psychologists continue to use the assessment instruments derived from the theory without invoking theory by way of explanation. Although this is acceptable for purposes of the court, the science of personology deserves more. Science advances by way of serendipitous findings, but also by developing and testing hypotheses derived from theory. More theory-derived research is needed in the forensic arena.

SCREENING FOR PUBLICLY SENSITIVE POSITIONS

The research on predictors of successful performance among police officers has established that many psychological measures do correlate with a number of objective job performance criteria one to three years after pre-employment screening. There is little research on predicting the long-term outcomes for police officers over longer periods of employment. Jurisdictions have been routinely screening police candidates for some time now, and those on the force have successfully passed this screening. Yet many police officers "go bad": abuse their power, commit felonies, and act in other ways to diminish public trust. Certainly exposure to life-changing events and opportunistic occasions while performing their duties could have an effect on a person. Research is needed to find predictors of these problematic behaviors over longer periods of time.

CHILD CUSTODY

Current assessment and evaluation instruments are quite good at determining current emotional states, but they are not as good when the task is to identify profiles that indicate parenting skills or deficits. Yet that is exactly what is asked of psychologists in custody evaluations. Continuing research is needed to identify external parenting correlates of test signs and test scores. In point of fact, there is not much evidence that associates parenting skills with particular test signs. Much of evaluating psychologists' conclusions and recommendations are based on clinical judgments and on extrapolations of the likely import of certain test findings.

This research task is not easy. It requires cooperation, from all parties, for longitudinal research that will determine outcomes of custody recommendations based on current assessment methodology, as well as the necessary funding to complete the task. Understandably, there is little or no motivation on the part of those awarded or denied custody to participate in such projects. Nevertheless, this is a necessary task waiting to be completed. One possibility in the interim would be to use a cross-sectional research design with available psychological assessment data collected for some other purpose. Researchers could seek to assess parenting skills from these alternate contexts and then correlate these skills with previous test scores. However, even this is a daunting task.

PERSONAL INJURY

Psychological assessment of personal injury litigants is good at determining whether the litigant's complaint of emotional distress is believable and whether the litigant has adjusted to the injury or remains in distress. In fact, such assessment is one of the strengths of personality-based forensic practice. What evaluating psychologists need are better methods of quickly and reliably determining preinjury personality to help determine the effects of the injury on the psyche. They also need long-term correlates of test scores postinjury, which would allow them to make more scientifically based predictions.

HARASSMENT

Harassment claims are likely to increase in the future. Public attention to this workplace problem is increasing, and employees may be more willing to come forward with allegations and suits. Forensic psychologists need more training and exposure to this area of litigation.

SEXUAL OFFENDERS

Despite efforts at rehabilitation, many sexual offenders released from prison continue to recidivate. There is a need for better tools to identify those individuals who are more likely to reoffend and those who are likely to benefit from treatment. Parenthetically, psychologists also need to design (and research) better interventions to reduce and eliminate sexual abuse behavior. Because of the public peril and psychological trauma resulting from sexual offenses, more money is needed in this arena to fund research.

ABUSE AND VIOLENCE

The Megargee clustering methodology with the MMPI and MMPI–2 has been useful in identifying inmates at risk for violent behavior in prison, and the MCMI-based clustering research has been useful in identifying profiles of spouse abusers. This research has been limited to concurrent validity research. No data have been presented on these typologies' predictive validities. Prospective studies are needed that identify individuals at risk for violence and then study them over time to determine the accuracy and validity of the hypothesized predictions.

In chapter 1 I identified the ever-expanding nature and content of forensic psychology. I mentioned that many of the content areas in forensic psychology overlap with the knowledge base in clinical and social psychology. Although this continues to be true, it is also true that forensic psychology has identified its own content and knowledge base, which are ever-expanding in a dynamic field. As new sources of litigation arise (often as a result of new laws or the application of existing laws to new areas of litigation), the content and knowledge base of forensic psychology will also expand.

In closing, I remind readers of the Preamble of APA's (2002a) Ethics Code:

> Psychologists are committed to increasing scientific and professional knowledge of behavior and people's understanding of themselves and others and to use such knowledge to improve the conditions of individuals, organizations, and society. . . . They strive to help the public in developing informed judgments and choices concerning human behavior. (p. 1062)

REFERENCES

Abel, G. G., Huffman, J., Warberg, B., & Holland, C. L. (1998). Visual reaction time and plethysmography as measures of sexual interest in child molesters. *Sexual Abuse: A Journal of Research & Treatment, 10*, 81–95.

Abel, G. G., Lawry, S. S., Karlstrom, E., Osborn, C. A., & Gillespie, C. F. (1994). Screening tests for pedophilia. *Criminal Justice and Behavior, 21*, 115–131.

Abidin, R. R. (1990). *Parenting Stress Index* (3rd ed.). Odessa, FL: Psychological Assessment Resources.

Achenbach, T. (1991). *Manual for the Child Behavior Check List 4-18 and 1991 profile*. Burlington: University of Vermont Department of Psychiatry.

Ackerman, M. J. (1995). *A clinician's guide to child custody evaluations*. New York: Wiley.

Ackerman, M. J. (1999). *Essentials of forensic psychological assessment*. New York: Wiley.

Ackerman, M. J., & Ackerman, M. C. (1997). Custody evaluation practices: A survey of experienced professionals (revisited). *Professional Psychology: Research and Practice, 28*, 137–145.

Ackerman, M. J., & Schoendorf, K. (1992). *Ackerman–Schoendorf Scales for Parent Evaluation for Custody (ASPECT)*. Los Angeles: Western Psychological Services.

Adams, K. M., Heilbronn, M., & Blumer, D. P. (1986). A multimethod evaluation of the MMPI in a chronic pain patient sample. *Journal of Clinical Psychology, 42*, 878–886.

Adams, K. M., Heilbronn, M., Silk, S. D., Reider, E., & Blumer, D. P. (1981). Use of the MMPI with patients who report chronic back pain. *Psychological Reports, 48*, 855–866.

Aderibigbe, Y., & Weston, A. (1996). Female offenders: A description of their pretrial MMPI evaluation. *American Journal of Forensic Psychiatry, 17*, 65–71.

Alterman, A. I., McDermitt, P. A., Mulvaney, F. D., Cacciola, J. S., Rutherford, M. J., Searles, J. S., et al. (2003). Comparison of embedded and isolated administration of the California Psychological Inventory socialization scale. *Psychological Assessment, 15*, 64–70.

American Academy of Child and Adolescent Psychiatry. (1997a). Practice parameters for child custody evaluation. *Journal of the American Academy of Child and Adolescent Psychiatry, 36*, 57S–68.

American Academy of Child and Adolescent Psychiatry. (1997b). Practice parameters for child custody evaluation. *Journal of the American Academy of Child and Adolescent Psychiatry, 36*, 423–444.

American Academy of Family Mediators. (1998). *Standards of practice for family and divorce mediation*. Retrieved March 17, 2004, from http://mediate.com/articles/afccstds.cfm

American Bar Association. (1989). *ABA criminal justice mental health status*. Washington, DC: Author.

American Law Institute. (1962). *Model penal code, proposed official draft*. Philadelphia: Author.

American Professional Society on the Abuse of Children. (1997). *Guidelines for psychological evaluation of suspected sexual abuse in young children*. Oklahoma City, OK: Author.

American Psychiatric Association. (1987). *Diagnostic and statistical manual of mental disorders* (3rd ed., rev.). Washington, DC: Author.

American Psychiatric Association. (1994). *Diagnostic and statistical manual of mental disorders* (4th ed.). Washington, DC: Author.

American Psychological Association. (1981). Specialty guidelines for the delivery of services by clinical psychologists. *American Psychologist, 36,* 640–651.

American Psychological Association. (1993a). *Record keeping guidelines*. Washington, DC: Author.

American Psychological Association. (1993b, February). Practice tip from the APA Insurance Trust: Liability for custody evaluation. *Monitor* pp. 34.

American Psychological Association. (1994). Guidelines for child custody evaluation in divorce proceedings. *American Psychologist, 49,* 677–680.

American Psychological Association. (2002a). Ethical principles of psychologists and code of conduct. *American Psychologist, 57,* 1060–1073.

American Psychological Association. (2002b). Report of the Ethics Committee, 2001. *American Psychologist, 57,* 646–653.

Americans With Disabilities Act of 1990, 42 U.S.C.A., § 12101 *et seq.*

Anderson, W. P., Kunce, J. T., & Rich, B. (1979). Sex offenders: Three personality types. *Journal of Clinical Psychology, 35,* 671–676.

Anderson, W. R., & Holcolm, W. R. (1983). Accused murderers: Five MMPI personality types. *Journal of Clinical Psychology, 39,* 761–768.

Arbisi, P. A., Ben-Porath, Y. S., & McNulty, J. L. (2003). Empirical correlates of common MMPI–2 two-point codes in male psychiatric inpatients. *Assessment, 10,* 237–247.

Arfice, P. A., & Ben-Porath, Y. S. (1998). The ability of the Minnesota Multiphasic Personality Inventory—2 validity scales to detect faked bad responses in psychiatric inpatients. *Psychological Assessment, 10,* 221–228.

Armentrout, D. P., Moore, J. E., Parker, J. C., Hewett, J. E., & Feltz, C. (1982). Pain-patient MMPI subgroups: The psychological dimensions of pain. *Journal of Behavioral Medicine, 3,* 201–211.

Armentrout, J. A., & Hauer, A. L. (1978). MMPIs of rapists of adults, rapists of children, and non-rapist sex offenders. *Journal of Clinical Psychology, 34,* 330–332.

Arnold, L., Fleming, R., & Bell, V. (1979). The man who became angry once: A study of overcontrolled hostility. *Canadian Journal of Psychiatry, 24,* 762–766.

Arnold, L. S., Quinsey, V. L., & Velner, I. (1977). Overcontrolled hostility among men found not guilty by reason of insanity. *Canadian Journal of Behavioral Science, 9,* 323–340.

Arrigo, B., & Claussen, N. (2003). Police corruption and psychological testing: A strategy for preemployment screening. *International Journal of Offender Therapy and Comparative Criminology, 47,* 272–290.

Association for the Treatment of Sexual Abusers. (1997). *Ethical standards and principles for the management of sexual abusers.* Beaverton, OR: Author.

Association of Family and Conciliation Courts. (n.d.). *Model standards of practice for child custody evaluations.* Milwaukee, WI: Author.

Atkinson, J. H., Ingram, R. E., Kremer, E. F., & Saccuzzo, D. P. (1986). MMPI subgroups and affective disorder in chronic pain patients. *Journal of Nervous and Mental Disease, 174,* 408–413.

Azen, S. D., Snibbe, H. M., & Montgomery, H. R. (1973). A longitudinal predictive study of success and performance of law enforcement officers. *Journal of Applied Psychology, 57,* 190–192.

Baer, R. A., & Miller, J. (2002). Underreporting of psychopathology on the MMPI–2: A meta-analytic review. *Psychological Assessment, 14,* 16–26.

Baer, R. A., & Sikirnjah, G. (1997). Detection of underreporting on the MMPI–2 in a clinical population: Effects of information about validity scales. *Journal of Personality Assessment, 69,* 555–567.

Baer, R. A., Wetter, M. W., & Berry, D. T. R. (1992). Detection of underreporting of psychopathology on the MMPI: A meta-analysis. *Clinical Psychology Review, 12,* 509–525.

Baer, R. A., Wetter, M. W., Nicholson, D. S., Greene, R., & Berry, D. T. (1995). Sensitivity of the MMPI–2 validity scales to underreporting of symptoms. *Psychological Assessment, 7,* 419–423.

Bagby, R. M., Nicholson, R. A., Bacchiochi, J. R., Rysler, A. G., & Bury, A. S. (2002). The predictive capacity of the MMPI–2 and PAI validity scales and indices to detect coached and uncoached feigning. *Journal of Personality Assessment, 78,* 69–86.

Bagby, R. M., Nicholson, R. A., Buis, T., & Bacchiochi, J. R. (2000). Can the MMPI–2 validity scales detect depression feigned by experts? *Assessment, 7,* 55–62.

Bagby, R. M., Rogers, R., Nicholson, R. A., Buis, T., Seeman, M. R., & Rector, N. A. (1997). Effectiveness of the MMPI–2 validity indicators in the detection of defensive responding in clinical and nonclinical samples. *Psychological Assessment, 9,* 406–413.

Baile, W. F., Gibertini, M., Scott, L., & Endicott, J. (1993). Prebiopsy assessment of patients with suspected head and neck cancer. *Journal of Psychosocial Oncology, 10,* 79–91.

Baity, M. R., & Hilsenroth, M. J. (1999). Rorschach aggression variables: A study of validity and reliability. *Journal of Personality Assessment, 72,* 93–110.

Baity, M. R., McDonald, P., & Hilsenroth, M. J. (2000). Further exploration of the Rorschach Aggressive Content (AgC) variable. *Journal of Personality Assessment, 74,* 231–241.

Bannatyne, L. A., Gacono, C. B., & Greene, R. L. (1999). Differential patterns of responding among three groups of chronic, psychotic, forensic outpatients. *Journal of Clinical Psychology, 12,* 1553–1565.

Bard, L., & Knight, R. (1986). Sex offender subtyping with the MCMI. In C. Green (Ed.), *Conference on the Millon Inventories (MCMI, MBHI, MAPI)* (pp. 133–137). Minneapolis, MN: National Computer Systems.

Barefoot v. Estelle, 463 U.S. 880 (1983).

Barnett, R. W., & McCormack, J. K. (1988). MCMI child molester profiles. *Corrective and Social Psychiatry and Journal of Behavior Technology Methods and Therapy, 34,* 14–16.

Barrington, W. W., Angle, C. R., Willcockson, N. K., Padula, M. A., & Korn, R. (1998). Autonomic function in manganese alloy workers. *Environmental Research, 78,* 50–58.

Barth, P. S. (1990). Worker's compensation for mental stress. *Behavioral Sciences and the Law, 8,* 349–360.

Bartol, C. B. (1982). Psychological characteristics of small town officers. *Journal of Police Science and Administration, 10,* 58–63.

Bathhurst, K., Gottfried, A. W., & Gottfried, A. E. (1997). Normative data for the MMPI–2 in child custody litigation. *Psychological Assessment, 9,* 205–216.

Beals, R. K., & Hickman, N. W. (1972). Industrial injuries of the back and extremities. *Journal of Bone and Joint Surgery, 54-A,* 1593–1611.

Beasley, R., & Stoltenberg, C. D. (1992). Personality characteristics of male spouse abusers. *Professional Psychology: Research and Practice, 23,* 310–317.

Beck, A. J., & Steen, R. A. (1993a). *Beck Depression Inventory manual.* San Antonio, TX: The Psychological Corporation.

Beck, A. J., & Steen, R. A. (1993b). *Beck Anxiety Inventory manual.* San Antonio, TX: The Psychological Corporation.

Beech, A. R., Fischer, D. D., & Thornton, D. (2003). Risk assessment of sex offenders. *Professional Psychology: Research and Practice, 34,* 339–352.

Ben-Porath, Y. S. (1995). *Case studies for interpreting the MMPI–A.* Minneapolis: University of Minnesota Press.

Ben-Porath, Y. S., Graham, J. R., Hall, G. L., Hirschman, R. D., & Zaragoza, M. S. (1995). *Forensic applications of the MMPI–2.* Thousand Oaks, CA: Sage.

Bernstein, I., & Garbin, C. (1983). Hierarchical clustering of pain patients: MMPI profiles: A replication note. *Journal of Personality Assessment, 47,* 171–172.

Berry, D. T. (1995). Detecting distortions in forensic evaluations with the MMPI–2. In Y. Ben-Porath, J. Graham, G. Hall, R. Hirschman, & M. Zaragoza (Eds.), *Forensic applications of the MMPI–2* (pp. 82–102). Thousand Oaks, CA: Sage.

Berry, D. T., Baer, R. A., & Harris, M. J. (1991). Detection of malingering on the MMPI: A meta-analysis. *Clinical Psychology Review, 11,* 585–598.

Berry, D. T., Wetter, M. W., Youngjohn, J. B., Gass, C. S., Lamb, D. G., Franzen, M. A., et al. (1995). Over-reporting of closed-head injury symptoms on the MMPI–2. *Psychological Assessment, 7,* 517–523.

Beutler, L. E., Nussbaum, P. D., & Meredith, K. E. (1988). Changing personality patterns of police officers. *Professional Psychology: Research and Practice, 19,* 503–507.

Beutler, L. E., Storm, A., Kirkish, P., Scogin, F., & Gaines, J. (1985). Parameters in the prediction of police officer performance. *Professional Psychology: Research and Practice, 16,* 321–335.

Biaggio, M. K., Godwin, W. H., & Baldwin, H. K. (1984). Response to the interpersonal request styles by dependent and overcontrolled hostility personalities. *Journal of Clinical Psychology, 40,* 833–836.

Binder, L. M., & Rohling, M. L. (1996). Money matters: A meta-analytic review of the effects of financial incentives on recovery after closed-head injury. *American Journal of Psychiatry, 153,* 7–10.

Binder, L. M., & Willis, S. C. (1991). Assessment of motivation after financially compensable minor head trauma. *Psychological Assessment, 3,* 175–181.

Blackburn, R. (1972). Dimensions of hostility and aggression in abnormal offenders. *Journal of Consulting and Clinical Psychology, 78,* 20–25.

Blader, J. C., & Marshall, W. L. (1989). Is assessment of sexual arousal in rapists worthwhile? A critique of current methods and the development of a response compatibility approach. *Clinical Psychology Review, 9,* 569–587.

Blain, G. H., Gerbner, R. M., Lewis, M. L., & Goldstein, M. A. (1981). The use of objectively scorable House–Tree–Person indicators to establish sexual abuse. *Journal of Clinical Psychology, 37,* 667–673.

Blake, D. D., Penk, W. E., Mori, D. L., Kleespies, P. M., Walsh, S. S., & Keane, T. M. (1992). Validity and clinical scale comparisons between the MMPI and MMPI–2 with psychiatric inpatients. *Psychological Reports, 70,* 323–332.

Blanchard, D. D., McGrath, R. E., Pogge, D. L., & Khadini, A. (2003). A comparison of the PAI and MMPI–2 as predictors of faking-bad in college students. *Journal of Personality Assessment, 80,* 197–200.

Blanchard, R., Klassen, P., Dickey, R., Kuban, M. E., & Blak, T. (2001). Sensitivity and specificity of the phallometric test for pedophiles in nonadmitting sex offenders. *Psychological Assessment, 13,* 118–126.

Blau, T. H. (1998). *The psychologist as expert witness* (2nd ed.). New York: Wiley.

Blau, T. H., Super, J. T., & Brady, L. (1993). The MMPI good cop/bad cop profile in identifying dysfunctional law enforcement personnel. *Journal of Police and Criminal Psychology, 9,* 2–4.

Block, J. (1995). A contrarian view of the Five-Factor approach to personality description. *Psychological Bulletin, 117,* 187–215.

Blowers, A. N., & Bjerregaard, B. (1994). The admissibility of expert testimony on the battered woman syndrome in homicide cases. *Journal of Psychiatry and Law*, *22*, 527–560.

Blum, R. H. (1964). *Police selection*. Springfield, IL: Charles C Thomas.

Boccaccini, M. T., & Brodsky, S. L. (1999). Diagnostic test usage by forensic psychologists in emotional injury cases. *Professional Psychology: Research and Practice*, *30*, 253–259.

Boer, D. R., Hart, S. D., Kropp, P. R., & Webster, C. D. (2001). *Sexual Violence Risk—20* (SVR–20). Odessa, FL: Psychological Assessment Resources.

Bohn, M. J. (1979). Management classification for young adult inmates. *Federal Probation*, *43*, 53–59.

Bonsignore v. City of New York. (1981). In *New York Law Journal*, 78-0240.

Booker, A. B., Hoffschmidt, S. J., & Ash, E. (2001). Personality features and characteristics of violent events committed by juvenile offenders. *Behavioral Sciences and the Law*, *19*, 81–96.

Boone, K. B., Savodnik, D., Ghaffarian, S., Lee, A., Freeman, D., & Verban, N. G. (1995). Rey 15-item memorization and dot counting scores in a "stress" claim worker's compensation population: Relationship to personality (MCMI) scores. *Journal of Clinical Psychology*, *51*, 457–463.

Booth, R. J., & Howell, R. J. (1980). Classification of prison inmates with the MMPI: An extension and validation of the Megargee typology. *Criminal Justice and Behavior*, *7*, 407–422.

Borchgrevnik, G. E., Stiles, T. C., Borchgrevnik, P. C., & Lereins, I. (1997). Personality profile among symptomatic and recovered patients with neck sprain injury measured by the MCMI–I acutely and 6 months after car accidents. *Journal of Psychosomatic Research*, *42*, 357–367.

Borum, R., & Grisso, T. (1995). Psychological test use in criminal forensic evaluations. *Professional Psychology: Research and Practice*, *26*, 465–473.

Borum, R., & Stock, H. V. (1993). Detection of deception in law enforcement applicants: A preliminary investigation. *Law & Human Behavior*, *17*, 157–166.

Bosquet, M., & Egeland, B. (2000). Predicting parenting behaviors from Antisocial Practices Content Scale scores of the MMPI–2 administered during pregnancy. *Journal of Personality Assessment*, *74*, 146–162.

Bovan, J., & Craig, R. J. (2002). Validity of projective drawing indices of male homosexuality. *Psychological Reports*, *90*, 175–183.

Bow, J. N., & Quinnell, F. A. (2001). Psychologists' current practices and procedures in child custody evaluations: Five years after American Psychological Association guidelines. *Professional Psychology: Research and Practice*, *32*, 261–268.

Bradley, L. A., Hopson, L., & Ven der Heide, L. (1984). Pain-related correlates of MMPI profile subgroups among back pain patients. *Health Psychology*, *3*, 157–174.

Bradley, L. A., Prokop, C. K., Margolis, R., & Gentry, W. D. (1978). Multivariate analysis of the MMPI profiles of low back pain patients. *Journal of Behavioral Medicine, 1*, 253–272.

Brandt, J. R., Kennedy, W. A., Patrick, C. J., & Curtin, J. J. (1997). Assessment of psychopathy in a population of incarcerated offenders. *Psychological Assessment, 9*, 429–435.

Bricklin, B. (1984). *Bricklin Perceptual Skills*. Furlong, PA: Village.

Bridges, M. P., Wilson, J. S., & Gacono, C. B. (1998). A Rorschach investigation of defensiveness, self-perception, interpersonal relations, and affective states in incarcerated pedophiles. *Journal of Personality Assessment, 70*, 365–385.

Briere, J. (1996). *Trauma Symptom Checklist for Children: Professional manual*. Odessa, FL: Psychological Assessment Resources.

Briere, J. (2004). *Trauma Symptom Inventory*. Odessa, FL: Psychological Assessment Resources.

Briner, W., Risey, J., Guth, P., & Norris, C. (1990). Use of the Millon Clinical Multiaxial Inventory in evaluating patients with severe tinnitus. *American Journal of Otology, 11*, 334–337.

Brodzinsky, D. M. (1993). On the use and misuse of psychological testing in child custody evaluations. *Professional Psychology: Research and Practice, 24*, 213–219.

Buchholz, D. (1984). Use of the MMPI with brain damaged psychiatric patients. *Clinical Psychology Review, 4*, 693–701.

Buck, J. A., & Graham, J. R. (1978). The 4-3 MMPI profile type: A failure to replicate. *Journal of Consulting and Clinical Psychology, 46*, 344.

Buck, J. N. (1992). *House–Tree–Person projective drawing technique: Manual and interpretive guide* (rev. W. L. Warren). Los Angeles: Western Psychological Services.

Burbeck, E., & Furnham, A. (1985). Police officer selection: A critical review of the literature. *Journal of Police Science and Administration, 13*, 58–68.

Bureau of National Affairs. (1994, July). Importance of dealings with psychologists in harassment cases is stressed by panel. *BNA's Employment Discriminant Report, 3*, 52–53.

Burns, R. C., & Kaufman, S. (1972). *Actions, styles and symbols in Kinetic Family Drawings (KFD): An interpretive manual*. New York: Brunner/Mazel.

Burnstein, I. H. (1980). Security guards' MMPI profiles: Some normative data. *Journal of Personality Assessment, 44*, 377–380.

Bury, A. S., & Bagby, R. M. (2002). The detection of feigned and coached posttraumatic stress disorder with the MMPI–2 in a sample of workplace accident victims. *Psychological Assessment, 14*, 472–484.

Butcher, J. N., Dahlstrom, W. G., Graham, J. R., Tellegen, A., & Kaemmer, B. (1989). *Minnesota Multiphasic Personality Inventory—2: Manual for administration and scoring*. Minneapolis, MN: National Computer Systems.

Butcher, J. N., & Miller, K. B. (1999). Personality assessment in personal injury litigation. In A. Hess & I. Weiner (Eds), *The handbook of forensic psychology* (pp. 104–126). New York: Wiley.

Butcher, J. N., & Pope, K. S. (1993). Seven issues in conducting forensic assessments: Ethical responsibilities in light of new standards and new tests. *Ethics and Behavior, 3*, 267–288.

Butcher, J. N., & Rouse, S. (1996). Clinical personality assessment. *Annual Review of Psychology, 47*, 87–111.

Butcher, J. N., Williams, C. L., Graham, J. R., Archer, R., Tellegen, A., Ben-Porath, Y. S., & Kaemmer, B. (1989). *Minnesota Multiphasic Personality Inventory— Adolescent manual*. Minneapolis, MN: Pearson.

Butcher, J. N., Williams, C. L., Graham, J. R., Archer, R., Tellegen, A., Ben-Porath, Y. S., et al. (1992). *MMPI–A manual for administration*. Minneapolis, MN: Pearson National Computer Systems.

Calsyn, D. A., Louks, J., & Freeman, C. W. (1976). The use of the MMPI with chronic low back pain patients with a mixed diagnosis. *Journal of Clinical Psychology, 32*, 532–536.

Campos, L. P. (1989). Adverse impact, unfairness, and bias in the psychological screening of Hispanic peace officers. *Hispanic Journal of Behavioral Sciences, 11*, 122–135.

Carey, R. J., Garske, J. P., & Ginsberg, J. (1986). The prediction of adjustment to prison by means of an MMPI-based classification. *Criminal Justice and Behavior, 13*, 347–365.

Carpenter, B., & Raza, S. (1987). Personality characteristics of police applicants: Comparisons across subgroups and with other populations. *Journal of Police Science and Administration, 15*, 10–17.

Carpenter, D. R., Peed, S. F., & Eastman, B. (1995). Personality characteristics of sexual offenders: A pilot study. *Sexual Abuse: A Journal of Research and Treatment, 7*, 195–203.

Cashel, M. L., Rogers, R., Sewell, K. W., & Holliman, N. B. (1998). Preliminary validation of the MMPI–A for a male delinquent sample: An investigation of clinical correlates and discriminant validity. *Journal of Personality Assessment, 71*, 49–69.

Cattell, R. B. (1989). *The 16PF: Personality in depth*. Champaign, IL: Institute for Personality and Ability Testing.

Cattell, R. B., Eber, H. W., & Tatsuoka, M. M. (1970a). *Handbook for the Sixteen Personality Factor Questionnaire*. Champaign, IL: Institute for Personality and Ability Testing.

Cattell, R. B., Eber, H. W., & Tatsuoka, M. M. (1970b). *Handbook for the Sixteen Personality Factor Questionnaire* (Tabular Supplement No. 1). Champaign, IL: Institute for Personality and Ability Testing.

Chandarana, P. C., Conlon, P., Holliday, R. L., Deslippe, T., & Field, V. A. (1990). A prospective study of psychosocial aspects of gastric stapling surgery. *Psychiatry Journal of University of Ottawa, 15*, 32–35.

Chandarana, P. C., Cooper, A. J., Goldbach, M. M., Coles, J. C., & Vesely, M. A. (1988). Perceptual and cognitive deficit following coronary artery bypass surgery. *Stress Medicine, 4*, 163–171.

Chandarana, P. C., Holliday, R., Conlon, P., & Deslippe, T. (1988). Psychosocial considerations in gastric stapling surgery. *Journal of Psychosomatic Research, 32*, 85–92.

Chantry, K., & Craig, R. J. (1994). Psychological screening of sexually violent offenders with the MCMI. *Journal of Clinical Psychology, 50*, 430–435.

Chen, W. J., Chen, H., Chen, C. C., Yu, W., & Chen, A. T. (2002). Cloninger's Tridimensional Personality Questionnaire: Psychometric properties and construct validity in Taiwanese adults. *Comprehensive Psychiatry, 43*, 158–166.

Choca, J. P., & Van Denburg, E. (1996). *Interpretive guide to the Millon Clinical Multiaxial Inventory* (2nd ed.). Washington, DC: American Psychological Association.

Christensen, L., & LeUnes, A. (1974). Discriminating criminal types and recidivism by means of the MMPI. *Journal of Clinical Psychology, 30*, 102–113.

Civil Rights Act of 1964, 42 U.S.C., § 2000d.

Clark, L. A., & Watson, D. (1995). Constructing validity: Basic issues in objective scale development. *Psychological Assessment, 7*, 309–319.

Cleckley, H. (1941). *The mask of sanity.* St. Louis, MO: Mosby.

Cloninger, C. R. (1987a, April 24). Neurogenetic adaptive mechanisms in alcoholics. *Science, 236*, 410–416.

Cloninger, C. R. (1987b). A systematic method for clinical description and classification of personality variants. *Archives of General Psychiatry, 44*, 573–588.

Cloninger, C. R. (1987c). *Tridimensional Personality Questionnaire* (Version 4). Unpublished manuscript, Washington University, Center for the Psychobiology of Personality, St. Louis, MO.

Cloninger, C. R. (2000). A practical way to diagnose personality disorder: A proposal. *Journal of Personality Disorders, 14*, 99–108.

Cloninger, C. R., Przybeck, T. R., & Svrakic, D. M. (1991). The Tridimensional Personality Questionnaire: U.S. normative data. *Psychological Reports, 69*, 1049–1057.

Cloninger, C. R., Przybeck, T. R., Svrakic, D. M., & Wetzel, R. R. (1997). *The Temperament and Character Inventory (TCI): A guide to its development and use.* St. Louis, MO: Washington University, Center for the Psychobiology of Personality.

Cloninger, C. R., & Svrakic, D. M. (1994). Differentiating normal and deviant personality by the seven-factor personality model. In S. Strack & M. Lorr (Eds.), *Differentiating normal and abnormal personality* (pp. 3–25). New York: Springer Publishing Company.

Cloninger, C. R., Svrakic, D. M., & Przybeck, T. R. (1993). A psychobiological model of temperament and character. *Archives of General Psychiatry, 50*, 975–990.

Cohen, J. (1988). *Statistical power analysis for the behavioral sciences* (2nd ed.). Hillsdale, NJ: Erlbaum.

Cohen, J. (1992). A power primer. *Psychological Bulletin, 112,* 155–159.

Colorado v. Connelly, 479 U.S. 157 (1986).

Colotla, V. A., Bowman, M. L., & Shercliffe, R. J. (2001). Test–retest stability of injured worker's MMPI–2 profile. *Psychological Assessment, 13,* 572–576.

Committee on Ethical Guidelines for Forensic Psychologists. (1991). Specialty guidelines for forensic psychologists. *Law and Human Behavior, 15,* 655–665.

Conn, S. R., & Rieke, M. L. (1994). *16PF technical manual.* Champaign, IL: Institute for Personality and Ability Testing.

Conroy, M. A. (2003). Evaluation of sexual predators. In I. B. Weiner (Series Ed.) & A. M. Goldstein (Vol. Ed.), *Handbook of psychology: Vol. 11. Forensic psychology* (pp. 463–484). New York: Wiley.

Conte v. Horcher, 50 Ill. App. 3rd 151 (1977).

Cooke, D. J., Kosson, D. S., & Michre, C. (2001). Psychopathy and ethnicity: Structural, item and test generalizability of the Psychopathy Check List—Revised (PCL–R) in Caucasian and African American psychopaths. *Psychological Assessment, 13,* 531–542.

Cornell, D. G. (2003). Psychopathy scores predict adolescent inpatient aggression. *Assessment, 10,* 102–112.

Cornell, D. G., Miller, C., & Benedek, E. P. (1988). MMPI profiles of adolescents charged with homicide. *Behavioral Sciences and the Law, 6,* 401–407.

Cortina, J. M., Doherty, M. L., Schmitt, N., & Kaufman, G. (1992). The "Big Five" personality factors in the IPI and MMPI: Predictors of police performance. *Personnel Psychology, 45,* 119–140.

Costa, P. T., & McCrae, R. R. (1992). *Revised NEO Personality Inventory (NEO–PI–R) and NEO Five-Factor Inventory (NEO–FFI) professional manual.* Odessa, FL: Psychological Assessment Resources.

Costa, P. T., & Widiger, T. A. (Eds.). (2000). *Personality disorders and the five-factor model of personality.* Washington, DC: American Psychological Association.

Costello, R. M., Hulsey, T. L., Schoenfeld, L. S., & Ramamurthy, S. (1987). P–A–I–N: A four-cluster MMPI typology for chronic pain. *Pain, 30,* 199–209.

Costello, R. M., Schneider, S. L., & Schoenfeld, L. S. (1981). Time-related effects on MMPI profiles of police academy recruits. *Journal of Clinical Psychology, 37,* 518–522.

Costello, R. M., Schoenfeld, L., & Kobos, J. (1982). Police applicant screening: An analogue study. *Journal of Clinical Psychology, 11,* 121–129.

Cox, G. B., Chapman, C. R., & Black, R. G. (1978). The MMPI and chronic pain: The diagnosis of psychogenic pain. *Journal of Behavioral Medicine, 1,* 437–443.

Craig, R. J. (Ed.). (1993a). *The Millon Clinical Multiaxial Inventory: A clinical research information synthesis.* Hillsdale, NJ: Erlbaum.

Craig, R. J. (1993b). *Psychological assessment with the Millon Clinical Multiaxial Inventory (II): An interpretive guide*. Odessa, FL: Psychological Assessment Resources.

Craig, R. J. (1994). *MCMI–II/III interpretive system*. Odessa, FL: Psychological Assessment Resources.

Craig, R. J. (1995). Clinical diagnosis and MCMI codetypes. *Journal of Clinical Psychology, 51*, 352–360.

Craig, R. J. (1997). A selected review of the MCMI empirical literature. In T. Millon (Ed.), *The Millon inventories* (pp. 303–326). New York: Guilford Press.

Craig, R. J. (1998). MMPI-based psychological assessment of lethal violence. In H. V. Hall (Ed.), *Lethal violence 2000: A sourcebook on fatal domestic, acquaintance and stranger violence* (pp. 503–526). Boca Raton, FL: CRC Press.

Craig, R. J. (1999a). *Interpreting personality tests: A clinical manual for the MMPI–2, MCMI–III, CPI–R, and 16PF*. New York: Wiley.

Craig, R. J. (1999b). Testimony based on the Millon Clinical Multiaxial Inventory: Review, commentary, and guidelines. *Journal of Personality Assessment, 73*, 290–304.

Craig, R. J. (2002). Use of the Millon Clinical Multiaxial Inventory in the psychological assessment of domestic violence: A review. *Aggression and Violent Behavior, 7*, 1–9.

Craig, R. J., & Bivens, A. (1998). Factor structure of the MCMI–III. *Journal of Personality Assessment, 70*, 190–196.

Craig, R. J., & Horowitz, M. (1990). Current utilization of psychological tests at diagnostic practicum sites. *Clinical Psychologist, 43*, 29–36.

Craig, R. J., & Olson, R. (1997). Assessing PTSD with the Millon Clinical Multiaxial Inventory–III. *Journal of Clinical Psychology, 53*, 943–952.

Crolley, J., Roys, D., Thyer, B. A., & Bordnick, P. S. (1998). Evaluating outpatient behavior therapy of sex offenders: A pretest–posttest study. *Behavioral Modification, 22*, 485–501.

Crosby, A. (1979). The psychological examination in police selection. *Journal of Police Science and Administration, 7*, 215–229.

Curren, S. F. (1998). Revised IACP guidelines: Pre-employment psychological evaluation of law enforcement applicants. *Police Chief, 65*, 88–95.

Dagan, Y., Sela, H., Omer, H., Haller, D., & Dar, P. (1996). High prevalence of personality disorders among circadian rhythm sleep disorders (CRSD) patients. *Journal of Psychosomatic Research, 41*, 357–363.

Dahlstrom, W. G., Lachar, D., & Dahlstrom, L. E. (1986). Overview and conclusions. In *MMPI patterns of American minorities* (pp. 188–205). Minneapolis: University of Minnesota Press.

Dahlstrom, W. G., Panton, J. H., Bain, K. P., & Dahlstrom, L. E. (1986). Utility of the Megargee–Bohn MMPI typological assignments: Study with a sample of death row inmates. *Criminal Justice and Behavior, 13*, 5–17.

Dana, R. H. (1993). *Multicultural assessment perspectives for professional psychology*. Boston: Allyn & Bacon.

Dana, R. H. (1995). Culturally competent MMPI assessment of Hispanic populations. *Journal of Hispanic Psychology, 17*, 305–319.

Daubert v. Merrell Dow Pharmaceuticals, Inc., 113 S. Ct. 2786 (1993).

Davis, G. L., & Hoffman, R. G. (1991). MMPI and CPI scores of child molesters before and after incarceration-for-treatment. *Journal of Offender Rehabilitation, 17*, 77–85.

Davis, K. R., & Sines, J. O. (1971). An antisocial behavior pattern associated with a specific MMPI profile. *Journal of Consulting and Psychological Psychology, 36*, 229–234.

Dearwater, S. R. (1998). Prevalence of intimate partner abuse in women treated at community hospital emergency departments. *Journal of the American Medical Association, 280*, 433–438.

Deiker, T. E. (1974). A cross-validation of MMPI scales of aggression on male criminal criterion groups. *Journal of Consulting and Clinical Psychology, 42*, 196–202.

Detrick, P., & Chibnall, J. T. (2003). Prediction of police officer performance with the Inwald Personality Inventory. *Journal of Police & Criminal Psychology, 17*, 9–17.

Detrick, P., Chibnall, J. T., & Rosso, M. (2001). Minnesota Multiphasic Personality Inventory—2 in police officer selection: Normative data and relation to the Inwald Personality Inventory. *Professional Psychology: Research and Practice, 32*, 484–490.

Devan, J. L., Hungersford, L., Wood, H., & Greene, R. (2001, March 17). *Utilization of the MMPI/MMPI–2 as a personnel screening device for police officers: A meta-analysis.* Paper presented at the annual meeting of the Society for Personality Assessment, Philadelphia.

Diamond, R., Barth, J. T., & Zillmer, E. A. (1988). Emotional correlates of mild closed-head trauma: The role of the MMPI. *International Journal of Clinical Neuropsychology, 10*, 35–40.

DiFrancesca, K. R., & Meloy, J. R. (1989). A comparative clinical investigation of the "How" and "Charlie" MMPI subtypes. *Journal of Personality Assessment, 53*, 396–403.

Digman, J. M. (1990). Personality structure: Emergence of the five-factor model. *Annual Review of Psychology, 41*, 417–440.

Doren, D. M., Megargee, E. I., & Schreiber, H. A. (1980). The MMPI criminal classifications applicability to a juvenile population. *Differential View: A Publication of the International Differential Treatment Association, 9*, 42–47.

Driscoll, L. N. (1994). A validity assessment of written statements from suspects in criminal investigations using the SCAN technique. *Journal of Police Studies, 17*, 1–15.

Durham v. United States, 214 F.2d 862 (D.C. Cir., 1954).

Duthie, B., & McIvor, D. L. (1990). A new system for cluster-coding child molester MMPI profile types. *Criminal Justice and Behavior, 17,* 199–214.

du Toit, L., & Duckitt, J. (1990). Psychological characteristics of over- and under-controlled violent offenders. *Journal of Psychology, 124,* 125–141.

Dutton, D. G. (1994). The origin and structure of the abusive personality. *Journal of Personality Disorders, 8,* 181–191.

Dyer, F. J., & McCann, J. T. (2000). The Millon clinical inventories, research critical of their forensic application, and Daubert criteria. *Law and Human Behavior, 24,* 487–497.

Eber, H. W. (1991, October). *Good cop includes bad cop: A supplementary concept of police brutality.* Paper presented at the annual meeting of the Society of Multivariate Experimental Psychology, Albuquerque, NM.

Edens, J. F., Hart, S. D., Johnson, D. W., Johnson, J. K., & Oliver, M. E. (2000). Use of the Personality Assessment Inventory to assess psychopathy in offender population. *Psychological Assessment, 12,* 132–139.

Edinger, J. D. (1979). Cross-validation of the Megargee MMPI typology for prisoners. *Journal of Consulting and Clinical Psychology, 47,* 234–242.

Edinger, J. D., & Auerbach, S. M. (1978). Development and validation of a multidimensional multivariate model for accounting for infractionary behavior in a correctional setting. *Journal of Personality and Social Psychology, 36,* 1472–1489.

Edinger, J. D., Reuterfors, D., & Logue, P. (1982). Cross validation of the Megargee MMPI typology. *Criminal Justice and Behavior, 9,* 184–203.

Egeland, B., Erickson, N., Butcher, J. N., & Ben-Porath, Y. S. (1991). MMPI–2 profiles of women at risk for child abuse. *Journal of Personality Assessment, 57,* 254–263.

Elhai, J. D., Gold, S. N., Freuh, B. C., & Gold, S. N. (2000). Cross-validation of the MMPI–2 in detecting malingering posttraumatic stress disorder. *Journal of Personality Assessment, 75,* 449–463.

Elhai, J. D., Gold, S. N., Sellers, A. H., & Dorfman, W. I. (2001). The detection of malingering posttraumatic stress disorder with MMPI–2 faked bad indices. *Assessment, 8,* 221–226.

Ellwood, R. W. (1993). Psychological tests and clinical discriminations: Beginning to address the base rate problem. *Clinical Psychology Review, 13,* 409–419.

Else, L., Wonderlich, S. A., Beatty, W. W., Christie, D. W., & Straton, R. D. (1993). Personality characteristics of men who physically abuse women. *Hospital and Community Psychiatry, 44,* 54–58.

Equal Employment Opportunity Commission. (1987). *Guide to rights and responsibilities in resolving disputes in the federal government.* Washington, DC: EEOC.

Erickson, W. D., Luxenberg, M. G., Walbek, N. H., & Seely, R. K. (1987). Frequency of MMPI two-point code types among sex offenders. *Journal of Consulting and Clinical Psychology, 55,* 566–570.

Exner, J. E., Jr. (1993). *The Rorschach: A comprehensive system: Vol. I. Basic foundations* (3rd ed.). New York: Wiley.

Exner, J. E., Jr. (2002). A new nonpatient sample for the Rorschach comprehensive system: A progress report. *Journal of Personality Assessment, 78,* 391–404.

Faller, K. C., Froning, M. L., & Lipovsky, J. (1991). The parent–child interview: Use in evaluating child allegations of sexual abuse by the parent. *American Journal of Orthopsychiatry, 61,* 552–557.

Federal Insanity Defense Reform Act of 1984, 18 U.S.C. § 4241.

Federal Rules of Evidence. (1992). Boston: Little, Brown.

Feldman-Schorrig, S. (1996). Factitious sexual harrassment. *Bulletin of the American Academy of Psychiatry and Law, 24,* 387–392.

Finkelhor, D. (1990). Early and long-term effects of child abuse: An update. *Professional Psychology: Research and Practice, 21,* 325–330.

Finkelhor, D., & Araji, S. (1986). Explanations of pedophilia: A four factor model. *Journal of Sex Research, 22,* 1345–1361.

Finney, J. C., Skeeters, D. E., Auvenshine, C. D., & Smith, D. F. (1973). Phases of psychopathology after assassination. *American Journal of Psychiatry, 130,* 1379–1380.

Fjordbak, T. (1985). Clinical correlates of high Lie scale elevations among forensic patients. *Journal of Personality Assessment, 49,* 252–261.

Fletcher, K. (1991). *When Bad Things Happen scale.* (Available from the author, University of Massachusetts Medical Center, Department of Psychiatry, 55 Lake Avenue, North, Worcester, MA 01655)

Flourney, P. S., & Wilson, G. L. (1991). Assessment of MMPI profiles of male batterers. *Violence and Victims, 6,* 309–320.

Foa, E. (2003). *Post Traumatic Diagnostic Scale for PTSD.* Los Angeles: Western Psychological Services.

Follingstad, D. R. (2003). Battered woman syndrome in the courts. In I. B. Weiner (Series Ed.) & A. M. Goldstein (Vol. Ed.), *Handbook of psychology: Vol. 11. Forensic psychology* (pp. 485–507). New York: Wiley.

Foote, W. E. (2003). Forensic evaluation in Americans With Disabilities Act cases. In I. B. Weiner (Series Ed.) & A. M. Goldstein (Vol. Ed.), *Handbook of psychology: Vol. 11. Forensic psychology* (pp. 279–300). New York: Wiley.

Forth, A. E., Kosson, D. S., & Hare, R. D. (2003). *The Psychopathy Checklist: Youth version.* Toronto, Ontario, Canada: Multi-Health Systems.

Fow, N. R., Dorris, G., Sittig, M., & Smith-Seemiller, L. (2002). An analysis of the influence of sponsorship on MMPI changes among patients with chronic pain. *Journal of Clinical Psychology, 58,* 827–832.

Fox, D. D., Gerson, A., & Lees-Haley, P. R. (1995). Interrelationship of MMPI–2 validity scales in personal injury litigants. *Journal of Clinical Psychology, 51,* 42–47.

Fraboni, M., Cooper, D., Reed, T. L., & Saltstone, R. (1990). Offense type and two-point MMPI code profiles: Discriminating between violent and non-violent offenders. *Journal of Clinical Psychology, 46,* 774–777.

Franz, C., Paul, R., Bautz, M., Choroba, B., & Hildebrandt, J. (1986). Psychosomatic aspects of chronic pain: A new way of description based on MMPI item analysis. *Pain, 26,* 33–43.

Frederich, C., Pynoos, R., & Nader, K. (1992). *Childhood PTSD Reaction Index.* (Available from Frederich & Pynoos, 760 Westwood Plaza, Los Angeles, CA, 90024)

Freeman, C., Calsyn, D., & Louks, J. (1976). The use of the Minnesota Multiphasic Personality Inventory with low-back pain patients. *Journal of Clinical Psychology, 32,* 294–298.

Freuh, B. C., & Kinder, B. N. (1994). The susceptibility of the Rorschach inkblot test to malingering of combat-related PTSD. *Journal of Personality Assessment, 62,* 280–298.

Friedrich, C., Pynoos, R., & Nader, K. (1992). *Childhood PTSD Reaction Index.* Unpublished manuscript.

Friedrich, W. N. (1998). *Child social behavior interests manual.* Odessa, FL: Psychological Assessment Resources.

Friedrich, W. N., Grambasch, P., Dawson, L., Hewitt, S. K., Koverola, C., Lang, R., & Wolfe, V. (1992). Child Sexual Behavior Inventory: Normative and clinical comparisons. *Psychological Assessment, 4,* 303–311.

Gacono, C. B., Evans, F. B., & Viglione, D. J. (2002). The Rorschach in forensic practice. *Journal of Forensic Psychology Practice, 2,* 33–53.

Gacono, C. B., Loving, J. L., & Bodholt, R. H. (2001). The Rorschach and psychopathology: Toward a more accurate understanding of the Rorschach findings. *Journal of Personality Assessment, 77,* 16–38.

Gacono, C. B., Loving, J. L., Evans, F. B., & Jumes, M. T. (2002). The Psychopathy Check List—Revised: PCL–R testimony and forensic practice. *Journal of Forensic Psychology Practice, 2,* 11–32.

Gacono, C. B., & Meloy, J. R. (1994). *The Rorschach assessment of aggression and psychopathic personalities.* Hillsdale, NJ: Erlbaum.

Gallucci, N. T. (1997). On the identification of patterns of substance abuse with the MMPI–A. *Psychological Assessment, 9,* 224–232.

Gandolfo, R. (1995). MMPI–2 profiles of worker's compensation claimants who present with complaints of harassment. *Journal of Clinical Psychology, 51,* 711–715.

Ganellen, R. J. (1994). Attempting to conceal psychological disturbance: MMPI defensive response sets and the Rorschach. *Journal of Personality Assessment, 63,* 423–437.

Ganellen, R. J. (2001). Weighing evidence for the Rorschach's validity: A response to Wood et al. (1999). *Journal of Personality Assessment, 77,* 1–15.

Garb, H. N. (1999). Call for a moratorium on the use of the Rorschach Inkblot Test in clinical and forensic settings. *Assessment, 6,* 313–318.

Garb, H. N., Wood, J. M., & Nezworski, M. T. (2000). Projective techniques and the detection of child sexual abuse. *Child Maltreatment, 5,* 161–168.

Garb, H. N., Wood, J. M., Nezworski, M. T., Grove, W. M., & Stejskal, W. J. (2001). Toward a resolution of the Rorschach controversy. *Psychological Assessment, 11*, 433–448.

Garron, D. C., & Leavitt, F. (1983). Chronic low back pain and depression. *Journal of Clinical Psychology, 39*, 486–493.

Gaston, L., Brunet, A., Koszycki, D., & Bradwejn, J. (1996). MMPI profile of acute and chronic PTSD in a civilian sample. *Journal of Traumatic Stress, 9*, 817–832.

Geisinger, K. F. (Ed.). (1992). *Psychological testing of Hispanics*. Washington, DC: American Psychological Association.

General Electric v. Joiner, 118 S. Ct. 512 (1997).

Gentry, W. D., Shaw, W. D., & Thomas, M. (1974). Chronic low back pain: A psychological profile. *Psychosomatics, 15*, 164–177.

Gerard, A. B. (1994). *Parent–Child Relationship Inventory (PCRI): Manual*. Los Angeles: Western Psychological Services.

Gindes, M. (1995). Guidelines for child custody evaluations for psychologists: A review and commentary. *Family Law Quarterly, 29*, 39–50.

Glaser, B. A., Calhoun, G. B., & Petrocelli, J. V. (2002). Personality characteristics of male juvenile offenders by adjudicated offenses as indicated by the MMPI–A. *Criminal Justice & Behavior, 29*, 183–201.

Goeke, J. M., & Boyer, M. C. (1993). The failure to construct an MMPI-based incest perpetrator scale. *International Journal of Offender Therapy and Comparative Criminology, 37*, 271–277.

Goldberg, L. R. (1981). Language and individual differences: The search for universals in personality lexicons. In L. Wheeler (Ed.), *Review of personality and social psychology* (Vol. 2, pp. 141–165). Beverly Hills, CA: Sage.

Goldstein, A. M., Morse, S. J., & Shapiro, D. L. (2003). Evaluation of criminal responsibility. In I. B. Weiner (Series Ed.) & A. M. Goldstein (Vol. Ed.), *Handbook of psychology: Vol. 11. Forensic psychology* (pp. 381–406). New York: Wiley.

Gondolf, E. W. (1999). MCMI–III results for batterer program participants in four cities: Less "pathological" than expected. *Journal of Family Violence, 14*, 1–17.

Goodman-Delahunty, J., & Foote, W. E. (1995). Compensation for pain, suffering, and other psychological injuries: The impact of *Daubert* on employment discrimination claims. *Behavioral Sciences and the Law, 13*, 183–206.

Goodwin, J. (1982). The use of drawings in incest cases. In J. Goodwin (with contributions), *Sexual abuse: Incest victims and their families* (pp. 47–56). Boston: John Wright PSG.

Gottlieb, M. C., & Baker, C. F. (1974, May). *Predicting police officer effectiveness*. Paper presented at the annual meeting of the Southeastern Psychological Association, El Paso, TX.

Gottsman, J. (1969). *Personality patterns of urban police applicants as measured by the MMPI*. Hoboken, NJ: Stevens Institute of Psychology, Laboratory of psychological studies.

Gough, H. G. (1969). *Manual for the California Psychological Inventory*. Palo Alto, CA: Consulting Psychologists Press.

Gough, H. G. (1987). *The California Psychological Inventory: Administrator's guide*. Palo Alto, CA: Consulting Psychologists Press.

Gough, H. G. (1994). Theory, development, and interpretation of the CPI Socialization scale [Monograph Supplement 1-V75]. *Psychological Reports, 75*, 651–700.

Gough, H. G. (with Bradley, P.). (1996). *CPI manual* (3rd ed.). Palo Alto, CA: Consulting Psychologists Press.

Graham, J. R., Ben-Porath, Y. S., & McNulty, J. L. (1999). *MMPI–2 correlates for outpatient community mental health settings*. Minneapolis: University of Minnesota Press.

Greco, C. M., & Cornell, D. G. (1992). Rorschach object relations of adolescents who committed homicide. *Journal of Personality Assessment, 59*, 574–583.

Greenberg, S. A., & Shuman, D. W. (1997). Irreconcilable conflict between therapeutic and forensic roles. *Professional Psychology: Research and Practice, 28*, 50–57.

Greene, R. L. (1987). Ethnicity and MMPI performance: A review. *Journal of Consulting and Clinical Psychology, 55*, 497–512.

Greiffenstein, M. F., & Baker, W. J. (2001). Comparison of premorbid and postinjury MMPI–2 profiles in late postconcussion claimants. *Clinical Neuropsychologist, 15*, 162–170.

Grilo, C. M., Sanislow, C., Fehon, D. C., Martino, S., & McGlashan, T. H. (1999). Psychological and behavioral functioning in adolescent psychiatric inpatients who report histories of childhood abuse. *American Journal of Psychiatry, 156*, 501–503.

Grisso, T. (1998). *Forensic evaluation of juveniles*. Sarasota, FL: Professional Resource Press.

Grisso, T. (2003). Forensic evaluation in delinquency cases. In I. B. Weiner (Series Ed.) & A. M. Goldstein (Vol. Ed.), *Handbook of psychology: Vol. 11. Forensic psychology* (pp. 315–334). New York: Wiley.

Grossman, L. S., Haywood, T. W., Ostrov, E., & Wasyliw, O. E. (1992). The evaluation of truthfulness in alleged sex offenders' self-reports: 16PF and MMPI validity scales. *Journal of Personality Assessment, 59*, 264–271.

Grossman, L. S., Haywood, T. W., Ostrov, E., Wasyliw, O. E., & Cavanaugh, J. L. (1990). Sensitivity of the MMPI validity scales to motivational factors in psychological evaluations of police officers. *Journal of Personality Assessment, 55*, 549–561.

Grossman, L. S., Martis, B., & Fichtner, C. G. (1999). Are sex offenders treatable? A research overview. *Psychiatric Services, 50*, 349–361.

Grossman, L. S., Wasyliw, O. E., Benn, A. F., & Gyoerkoe, K. L. (2002). Can sex offenders who minimize on the MMPI conceal psychopathology on the Rorschach? *Journal of Personality Assessment, 78*, 484–501.

Guck, T. P., Meilman, P. W., Skultety, F. M., & Poloni, L. D. (1988). Pain-patient Minnesota Multiphasic Personality Inventory (MMPI) subgroups: Evaluation of long-term treatment outcome. *Journal of Behavioral Medicine, 11*, 159–169.

Gudjonsson, D. H., Petursson, H., Sigurdardottir, H., & Skulason, S. (1991). Over-controlled hostility among prisoners and its relationship with denial and personality scores. *Personality and Individual Differences, 12*, 17–20.

Guisado, J. A., Vaz, F. J., Alarcon, J., Lopez-Ibor, Rubio, M. A., & Gaite, L. (2002). Psychopathological status and interpersonal functioning following weight loss in morbidly obese patients undergoing bariatric surgery. *Obesity Surgery, 12*, 835–840.

Gynther, M. (1972). White norms and Black MMPIs: A prescription for discrimination? *Psychological Bulletin, 78*, 386–402.

Gynther, M. D., Altman, H., & Warbin, R. W. (1973). A new actuarial-empirical automated MMPI interpretive program: The 4-3/34 code type. *Journal of Clinical Psychology, 29*, 229–231.

Hackney, G. R., & Ribordy, S. C. (1980). An empirical investigation of emotional reactions to divorce. *Journal of Clinical Psychology, 36*, 105–110.

Hagen, M. A., & Castagna, N. (2001). The real numbers: Psychological testing in custody evaluations. *Professional Psychology: Research and Practice, 32*, 269–271.

Hale, G., Zimostrad, S., Duckworth, J., & Nicholas, D. (1988). Abusive partners: MMPI profiles of male batterers. *Journal of Mental Health Counseling, 10*, 214–224.

Hall, G. C. (1989). WAIS–R and MMPI profiles of men who have sexually assaulted children: Evidence of limited utility. *Journal of Personality Assessment, 53*, 404–412.

Hall, G. C., Bansal, A., & Lopez, I. R. (1999). Ethnicity and psychopathology: A meta-analytic review of 31 years of comparative MMPI/MMPI–2 research. *Psychological Assessment, 11*, 186–197.

Hall, G. C., Graham, J. R., & Shepherd, J. B. (1991). Three methods of developing MMPI taxonomies of sexual offenders. *Journal of Personality Assessment, 56*, 2–13.

Hall, G. C., Maiuro, R. D., Vitaliano, P. P., & Proctor, W. C. (1986). The utility of the MMPI with men who have sexually assaulted children. *Journal of Consulting and Clinical Psychology, 54*, 493–496.

Hall, G. C., & Phung, A. H. (2001). Minnesota Multiphasic Personality Inventory and Millon Clinical Multiaxial Inventory. In L. A. Suzuki & G. Pontero (Eds.), *Handbook of multicultural assessment* (pp. 307–330). New York: Wiley.

Hall, G. C., Shepherd, J. B., & Mudrak, P. (1992). MMPI taxonomies of child sexual and non-sexual offenders: A cross-validation and extension. *Journal of Personality Assessment, 58*, 127–137.

Hall, H. V. (Ed.). (2000). *Lethal violence 2000: A sourcebook on fatal domestic, acquaintance and stranger violence*. Boca Raton, FL: CRC Press.

Hall, H. V., & Pritchard, D. A. (1996). *Detecting malingering and deception: Forensic distortion analysis (FDA)*. Delray Beach, FL: St. Lucie Press.

Halon, R. L. (2001). The Millon Clinical Multiaxial Inventory—III: The normal quartet in child custody cases. *American Journal of Forensic Psychology, 19*, 57–75.

Hamberger, L. K., & Hastings, J. E. (1986). Personality correlates of men who abuse their partners: A cross-validation study. *Journal of Family Violence, 1*, 323–341.

Hamberger, L. K., & Hastings, J. E. (1988). Characteristics of male spouse abusers consistent with personality disorders. *Hospital and Community Psychiatry, 39*, 763–770.

Hammer, E. F. (1963). *The clinical application of projective drawings*. Springfield, IL: Charles C Thomas.

Hammer, E. F. (1999). *Advances in projective drawing interpretations*. Springfield, IL: Charles C Thomas.

Handler, L., & Habenicht, D. (1999). The Kinetic Family Drawing technique: A review of the literature. *Journal of Personality Assessment, 62*, 440–464.

Handler, L., & Riethmiller, R. (1999). Teaching and learning the administration and interpretation of graphic techniques. In L. Handler & M. J. Hilsenroth (Eds.), *Teaching and learning personality assessment* (pp. 267–294). Mahwah, NJ: Erlbaum.

Hanson, R. K., & Thornton, D. (1999). Static 99: Improving actuarial risk assessment for sex offenders. In *User Report 1999–2002* (pp. 1–30). Ottawa, Ontario: Department of the Solicitor General of Canada.

Hanson, R. W., Moss, C. S., Hosford, R. E., & Johnson, M. E. (1983). Predicting inmate penitentiary adjustment: An assessment of four classificatory methods. *Criminal Justice and Behavior, 10*, 293–309.

Hanvik, L. J. (1951). MMPI profiles in patients with low back pain. *Journal of Consulting Psychology, 15*, 350–353.

Hare, R. D. (1991). *Manual for the revised Psychopathy Checklist*. Toronto, Ontario, Canada: Multihealth Systems.

Hargrave, G. E. (1985). Using the MMPI and CPI to screen law enforcement applicants: A study of reliability and validity of clinicians' decisions. *Journal of Police Science and Administration, 13*, 221–224.

Hargrave, G. E., & Hiatt, D. (1989). Use of the California Psychological Inventory in law enforcement officer selection. *Journal of Personality Assessment, 53*, 267–277.

Hargrave, G. E., Hiatt, D., & Gaffney, J. (1986). A comparison of MMPI and CPI test profiles for traffic officers and deputy sheriff. *Journal of Police Science and Administration, 14*, 250–258.

Hargrave, G. E., Hiatt, D., Ogard, E. M., & Karr, C. (1994). Comparison of the MMPI and MMPI-2 for a sample of peace officers. *Psychological Assessment, 6*, 27–32.

Harkness, A. R., & McNulty, J. L. (1994). The personality psychopathology five (Psy-5): Issue from the pages of a diagnostic manual instead of a dictionary. In S. Strack & M. Lorr (Eds.), *Differentiating normal and abnormal personality* (pp. 291–315). New York: Springer Publishing Company

Harris v. Forklift Systems, Inc., 114 S. Ct. 367, 510 U.S. 17, 126 L.Ed.2d 295 (1993).

Hart, R. (1984). Chronic pain: Replicated multivariate clustering of personality profiles. *Journal of Clinical Psychology, 40,* 129–133.

Hart, S. D., Dutton, D. G., & Newlove, T. (1993). The prevalence of personality disorder among wife assaulters. *Journal of Personality Disorders, 7,* 329–341.

Hartman, B. J. (1987). Psychological screening of law enforcement candidates. *American Journal of Forensic Psychology, 1,* 5–10.

Hastings, J. E., & Hamberger, L. K. (1994). Psychological modifiers of psychopathology for domestically violent and nonviolent men. *Psychological Reports, 74,* 112–114.

Hathaway, S. R., & McKinley, J. C. (1943). *Minnesota Multiphasic Personality Inventory.* Minneapolis: University of Minnesota Press.

Haynes, J. P., & Poltran, J. (1985). Patterns of practice with the TAT in juvenile forensic settings. *Journal of Personality Assessment, 49,* 26–29.

Haywood, T. W., Grossman, L. S., Kravitz, H. M., & Wasyliw, O. E. (1994). Profiling psychological distortion in alleged child molesters. *Psychological Reports, 75,* 915–927.

Heaton, R. K., Getto, C. J., Lehman, R. A., Fordyce, W. E., Brauer, E., & Groban, S. E. (1982). A standardized evaluation of psychosocial factors in chronic pain. *Pain, 12,* 165–174.

Heersink, N., & Strassberg, D. S. (1995). A normative and descriptive study of the MMPI with acknowledged child molesters. *Journal of Psychopathology and Behavioral Assessment, 17,* 377–391.

Heilbrun, K. (1992). The role of psychological testing in forensic assessment. *Law and Human Behavior, 16,* 257–272.

Heinze, M. C., & Grisso, T. (1996). Review of instruments assessing capacities used in child custody evaluations. *Behavioral Science and the Law, 14,* 293–313.

Hemphill, J. F., & Hart, S. D. (2003). Forensic and clinical issues in the assessment of psychopathy. In I. B. Weiner (Series Ed.) & A. M. Goldstein (Vol. Ed.), *Handbook of psychology: Vol. 11. Forensic psychology* (pp. 87–108). New York: Wiley.

Henderson, M. (1983a). An empirical classification of non-violent offenders using the MMPI. *Personality and Individual Differences, 4,* 671–677.

Henderson, M. (1983b). Self-reported assertion and aggression among violent offenders with high or low levels of over-controlled hostility. *Personality and Individual Differences, 4,* 113–115.

Herkov, M. J., Gynther, M. D., Thomas, S., & Myers, W. C. (1996). MMPI differences among adolescent inpatients, rapists, sodomists, and sexual abusers. *Journal of Personality Assessment, 66,* 81–90.

Herron, L., Turner, J., & Weiner, P. (1986). A comparison of the Millon Clinical Multiaxial Inventory and the Minnesota Multiphasic Personality Inventory as predictors of successful treatment by lumbar laminectomy. *Clinical Orthopaedics, 302*, 232–238.

Hersch, P. D., & Alexander, R. W. (1990). MMPI profile patterns of emotional disability claimants. *Journal of Clinical Psychology, 46*, 798–799.

Hess, K. D., & Brinson, A. (1999). Mediating domestic law issues. In A. K. Kess & I. B. Weiner (Eds.), *The handbook of forensic psychology* (pp. 63–101). New York: Wiley.

Hiatt, D., & Hargrave, G. E. (1988). MMPI profiles of problem police officers. *Journal of Personality Assessment, 52*, 722–736.

Hibbard, R. A., & Hartman, G. I. (1990). Emotional indicators in human figure drawings of sexually victimized and nonabused children. *Journal of Clinical Psychology, 46*, 211–219.

Hibbard, R. A., Roghmann, K., & Hoekelman, R. A. (1987). Genitalia in children's drawings: An association with sexual abuse. *Pediatrics, 79*, 129–137.

Hibbard, S. (2003). A critique of Lilienfeld et al.'s (2000) "The scientific status of projective techniques." *Journal of Personality Assessment, 80*, 260–271.

Hoffman, R. G., Scott, J. G., Emrick, M. A., & Adams, R. L. (1999). The MMPI–2 and closed-head injury: Effects of litigation and head injury severity. *Journal of Forensic Neuropsychology, 1*, 3–13.

Hogan, R. (1971). Personality characteristics of highly rated policemen. *Personnel Psychology, 24*, 679–686.

Hoge, R. D. (2002). Standardized instruments for assessing risk and need in youthful offenders. *Criminal Justice and Behavior, 29*, 280–296.

Hoge, R. D., & Andrews, D. A. (1996). *Assessing the youthful offender: Issues and techniques.* New York: Plenum Press.

Holcolm, W. R., & Adams, N. A. (1982). Racial influences on intelligence and personality of people who commit murder. *Journal of Clinical Psychology, 38*, 793–796.

Holcolm, W. R., & Adams, N. A. (1983). The inner-domain among personality and cognition variables in people who commit murder. *Journal of Personality Assessment, 47*, 524–530.

Holcolm, W. R., & Adams, N. A. (1985a). Personality mechanisms of alcohol-related violence. *Journal of Clinical Psychology, 41*, 714–722.

Holcolm, W. R., & Adams, N. A. (1985b). The development and cross-validation of an MMPI typology of murderers. *Journal of Personality Assessment, 49*, 240–244.

Holcolm, W. R., Adams, N. A., Nicholas, A., Ponder, H. M., & Anderson, W. (1984). Cognitive and behavioral practices of MMPI scores in pretrial psychological evaluations of murderers. *Journal of Clinical Psychology, 40*, 592–597.

Holcolm, W. R., Adams, N. A., & Ponder, H. M. (1984). Are separate Black and White norms needed? An IQ-controlled comparison of accused murderers. *Journal of Clinical Psychology, 40*, 189–193.

Holland, T. R., Heim, R. B., & Holt, N. (1976). Personality patterns among correctional officer applicants. *Journal of Clinical Psychology, 32,* 786–789.

Holt, R. D. (1975). Measuring libidinal and aggressive motives and their controls by means of the Rorschach test. In P. M. Lerner (Ed.), *Handbook of Rorschach scales.* New York: International Universities Press.

Hoppe, C. M., & Singer, R. D. (1977). Interpersonal violence and its relationship to some personality measures. *Aggressive Behavior, 3,* 261–270.

Huesmann, L. R., Lefkowitz, M. M., & Eron, L. D. (1978). Sum of MMPI scales F, 4, and 9 as a measure of aggression. *Journal of Consulting and Clinical Psychology, 46,* 1071–1078.

Hume, M. P., Kennedy, W. A., Patrick, C. J., & Partyka, D. J. (1996). Examination of the MMPI–A for the assessment of psychopathy in incarcerated adolescent male offenders. *International Journal of Offender Therapy and Comparative Criminology, 40,* 224–233.

Hunsley, J., & Bailey, J. M. (1999). The clinical utility of the Rorschach: Unfulfilled promises and an uncertain future. *Psychological Assessment, 11,* 266–277.

Hunter, J. A., Childers, J. A., Gerald, R., & Esmaili, H. (1990). An examination of variables differentiating clinical subtypes of incestuous child molesters. *International Journal of Offender Therapy and Comparative Criminology, 34,* 95–104.

Hutton, H. E., Miner, M. H., Blades, J. R., & Langfeldt, V. C. (1992). Ethnic differences on the MMPI Overcontrolled-Hostility Scale. *Journal of Personality Assessment, 58,* 260–268.

Hutton, H. E., Miner, M. H., & Langfeldt, V. C. (1993). The utility of the Megargee–Bohn typology in a forensic psychiatric hospital. *Journal of Personality Assessment, 60,* 572–587.

Hyer, L., Brandsma, J., & Boyd, S. (1997). The MCMIs and posttraumatic stress disorder. In T. Millon (Ed.), *The Millon Inventories* (pp. 217–244). New York: Guilford Press.

In re Gault, 387 U.S. 1 (1967).

International Association for the Study of Pain, Subcommittee on Classification. (1986). Pain terms: A current list with definitions and notes on usage. *Pain,* Suppl. 3, 215–221.

Inwald, R. E. (1988). Five-year follow-up of departmental terminations as predicted by 167 pre-employment psychological indicators. *Journal of Applied Psychology, 73,* 703–710.

Inwald, R. E., & Brockwell, A. L. (1991). Predicting the performance of government security personnel with the IPI and MMPI. *Journal of Personality Assessment, 56,* 522–535.

Inwald, R. E., Hurwitz, H., & Kaufman, J. C. (1991). Uncertainty reduction in retail and public safety–private security screening. *Forensic Reports, 4,* 171–212.

Inwald, R. E., Knatz, H., & Shusman, E. (1983). *Inwald Personality Inventory manual*. New York: Hilson Research.

Janson, H., & Stattin, H. (2003). Prediction of adolescent and adult delinquency from childhood Rorschach ratings. *Journal of Personality Assessment, 81*, 51–63.

Jay, G. W., Grove, R. N., & Grove, K. S. (1987). Differentiation of chronic headache from non-headache pain patients using the Millon Clinical Multiaxial Inventory (MCMI). *Headache, 27*, 124–129.

Jenkins v. U.S., 307 F.2d 637 (1962).

Johnson, D. A., Simmons, J. D., & Gordon, D. C. (1983). Temporal consistency of the Meyer–Megargee inmate typology. *Criminal Justice and Behavior, 10*, 263–268.

Jones, R. T. (1994). *Child's Reaction to Traumatic Events Scale (CRTES): A self-report traumatic events measure*. Blacksburg, VA: Virginia Polytechnic Institute and State University, Department of Psychology.

Jung, C. G. (1990). *Psychological types* (H. G. Baynes, Trans., R.F.C. Hull, rev.). Princeton, NJ: University of Princeton Press.

Kahill, S. C. (1984). Human figure drawings in adults: An update of the empirical evidence, 1967–1982. *Canadian Psychology, 25*, 269–292.

Kalichman, S. C. (1988a). Empirically derived MMPI profile subgroups of incarcerated homicide offenders. *Journal of Clinical Psychology, 44*, 733–738.

Kalichman, S. C. (1988b). MMPI profiles of women and men convicted of domestic homicide. *Journal of Clinical Psychology, 44*, 847–853.

Kalichman, S. C. (1989). Cluster analytically-derived MMPI profile subgroups of incarcerated adult rapists. *Journal of Clinical Psychology, 45*, 149–155.

Kalichman, S. C. (1990). Affective and personality characteristics of MMPI profile subgroups of incarcerated rapists. *Archives of Sexual Behavior, 19*, 443–459.

Kalichman, S. C. (1991). Psychopathology and personality characteristics of criminal sexual offenders as a function of victim age. *Archives of Sexual Behavior, 20*, 187–197.

Kalichman, S. C., Dwyer, M., Henderson, M. C., & Hoffman, L. (1992). Psychological and sexual functioning among outpatient sexual offenders against children: A Minnesota Multiphasic Personality Inventory (MMPI) cluster analytic study. *Journal of Psychopathology and Behavioral Assessment, 14*, 259–276.

Kalichman, S. C., & Henderson, M. C. (1991). MMPI profile subtypes of non-incarcerated child molesters. *Criminal Justice and Behavior, 18*, 379–396.

Kalichman, S. C., Henderson, M. C., Shealy, L., & Dwyer, M. (1992). Psychometric properties of the Multiphasic Sex Inventory in assessing sex offenders. *Criminal Justice and Behavior, 19*, 384–396.

Kalichman, S. C., Shealy, L., & Craig, M. E. (1990). The use of the MMPI in predicting treatment participation among incarcerated adult rapists. *Journal of Psychology and Human Sexuality, 3*, 105–119.

Kamphus, J. H., Kirgeares, S. L., & Finn, S. E. (2000). Rorschach correlates of sexual abuse: Trauma content and aggression indices. *Journal of Personality Assessment, 75,* 212–224.

Kansas v. Hendricks, 521 U.S. 346 (1997).

Karson, M., Karson, S., & O'Dell, J. (1997). *16PF interpretation in clinical practice: A guide to the fifth edition.* Champaign, IL: Institute for Personality and Ability Testing.

Keane, T., Malloy, P., & Fairbank, J. (1984). Empirical development of an MMPI subscale for the assessment of combat related posttraumatic stress disorder. *Journal of Consulting and Clinical Psychology, 52,* 888–891.

Keilin, W. G., & Bloom, L. J. (1986). Child custody evaluation practices: A survey of experienced professionals. *Professional Psychology: Research and Practice, 17,* 338–346.

Keller, L. S., & Butcher, J. N. (1991). *Assessment of chronic pain patients with the MMPI–2.* Minneapolis, MN: University of Minnesota Press.

Kelly, R. J. (1982). Behavioral reorientation of pedophiliacs: Can it be done? *Clinical Psychology Review, 2,* 387–408.

Kendall-Tackitt, K. A., Williams, L. M., & Finkelhor, D. (1993). Impact of sexual abuse in children: A review and synthesis of recent empirical studies. *Psychological Bulletin, 113,* 164–180.

Kennedy, T. D. (1986). Trends in inmate classification: A status report on two computerized psychometric approaches. *Criminal Justice and Behavior, 13,* 165–184.

Kirkland, K. D., & Bauer, C. A. (1982). MMPI traits of incestuous fathers. *Journal of Clinical Psychology, 38,* 645–649.

Kirkland, K. D., & Kirkland, K. L. (2001). Frequency of child custody evaluation complaints and related disciplinary action: A survey of state and professional psychology boards. *Professional Psychology: Research and Practice, 32,* 171–174.

Knapp, S., & Vendercreek, L. (2001). Ethical issues in personality assessment in forensic psychology. *Journal of Personality Assessment, 77,* 245–251.

Knatz, H. F., Inwald, R. E., Brockwell, A. L., & Tran, L. N. (1993). IPI and MMPI predictions of counterproductive job behaviors by racial group. *Journal of Business & Psychology, 7,* 189–201.

Koppitz, E. (1968). *Psychological evaluation of children's human figure drawings.* New York: Grune & Stratton.

Koretsky, M. B., & Peck, A. H. (1990). Validation and cross-validation of the MMPI with civilian trauma reactions. *Journal of Clinical Psychology, 46,* 296–300.

Kornfeld, A. D. (1995). Police officer candidate MMPI–2 performance: Gender, ethnic, and normative factors. *Journal of Clinical Psychology, 51,* 536–540.

Kornfeld, A. D. (2000). Harris–Lingoes MMPI–2 Pd subscales and the assessment of law enforcement candidates. *Psychological Reports, 86,* 339–343.

Kosson, D. S., Cyterski, T. D., Steuerwald, B. L., Neumann, C. S., & Walker-Matthews, S. (2002). The reliability and validity of the Psychopathy Checklist:

Youth Version (PCL–YV) in non-incarcerated adolescent males. *Psychological Assessment, 14,* 97–109.

Kuehnle, K. (1996). *Assessing allegations of child sexual abuse.* Sarasota, FL: Professional Resource Press.

Kuehnle, K. (2003). Child sexual abuse evaluations. In I. B. Weiner (Series Ed.) & A. M. Goldstein (Vol. Ed.), *Handbook of psychology: Vol. 11. Forensic psychology* (pp. 437–460). New York: Wiley.

Kumho Tire Company Ltd. et al. v. Carmichael et al., 526 U.S. 137 (1999).

Lally, S. J. (2001). Should human figure drawings be admitted into court? *Journal of Personality Assessment, 76,* 135–149.

Lampel, A. K. (1999). Use of the Millon Clinical Multiaxial Inventory—III in evaluating child custody litigants. *Journal of Forensic Psychology, 17,* 19–31.

Lane, P. J., & Kling, J. S. (1979). Construct validation of the Overcontrolled Hostility scale of the MMPI. *Journal of Consulting and Clinical Psychology, 47,* 781–782.

Lane, P. J., & Spruill, J. (1980). Validity of the overcontrolled/undercontrolled typology: Usage on criminal psychiatric patients. *Criminal Justice and Behavior, 7,* 215–228.

Langevin, R., Paitich, D., Orchard, B., Handy, L., & Russon, A. (1982). Diagnosis of killers seen for psychiatric assessment: A controlled study. *Acta Psychiatrica Scandinavica, 66,* 216–228.

Langevin, R., Wright, P., & Handy, L. (1990). Use of the MMPI and its derived scales with sex offenders. *Annals of Sex Research, 3,* 453–486.

Lanyon, R. I. (1993). Validity of the MMPI sex offenders scales with admitters and non-admitters. *Psychological Assessment, 5,* 302–306.

Lanyon, R. I. (2001). Psychological assessment procedures in sex offending. *Professional Psychology: Research and Practice, 32,* 253–260.

Larrabee, G. J. (1998). Somatic malingering on the MMPI and MMPI–2 in personal injury litigants. *Clinical Neuropsychologist, 12,* 179–188.

Leavitt, F., & Garron, D. C. (1982). Rorschach and pain characteristics of patients with low back pain and "conversion V" MMPI profiles. *Journal of Personality Assessment, 46,* 18–25.

Lees-Haley, P. R. (1997a). Attorney's influence on expert evidence in forensic psychological and neuropsychological cases. *Assessment, 4,* 321–326.

Lees-Haley, P. R. (1997b). MMPI–2 base rates for 492 personal injury plaintiffs: Implications and challenges for forensic assessment. *Journal of Clinical Psychology, 53,* 745–755.

Lees-Haley, P. R., English, L. T., & Glenn, W. J. (1991). A Fake Bad scale on the MMPI–2 for personal injury claimants. *Psychological Reports, 68,* 203–210.

Lefkowitz, J. (1977). Industrial-organizational psychology and the police. *American Psychologist, 32,* 346–363.

Leifer, M., Shapiro, J. P., Martone, M. W., & Kassem, L. (1991). Rorschach assessment of psychological functioning in sexually abused girls. *Journal of Personality Assessment, 56,* 14–28.

Levenson, H., Glenn, N., & Hirshfield, M. (1988). Duration of chronic pain with the Minnesota Multiphasic Personality Inventory: Profiles of industrially injured workers. *Journal of Occupational Medicine, 30,* 809–812.

Levin, S. M., & Stava, L. (1987). Personality characteristics of sex offenders: A review. *Archives of Sexual Behavior, 16,* 57–79.

Lewis, J. L., Simcox, A. M., & Berry, D. T. (2002). Screening for feigned psychiatric symptoms in a forensic sample by using the MMPI–2 and the Structured Inventory of Malingered Symptomatology. *Psychological Assessment, 14,* 170–176.

Lilienfeld, S. O. (1996). The MMPI–2 Antisocial Practices content scale: Construct validity and comparison with the Psychopathic Deviate scale. *Psychological Assessment, 8,* 281–293.

Lilienfeld, S. O., Wood, J. M., & Garb, H. M. (2000). The scientific status of projective techniques. *Psychological Science in the Public Interest, 1,* 27–66.

Logan, N. (in press). The diagnostic assessment of children. In R. J. Craig (Ed.), *Clinical and diagnostic interviewing* (2nd ed.). Northvale, NJ: Jason Aronson.

Lohr, J. M., Hamberger, L. K., & Bonge, D. (1988). The nature of irrational beliefs in different personality clusters of spouse abusers. *Journal of Rational-Emotive and Cognitive Behavior Therapy, 6,* 273–285.

Long, B. I. (1994). Psychiatric diagnoses in sexual harrassment cases. *Bulletin of the American Academy of Psychiatry and Law, 22,* 195–203.

Long, C. J. (1981). The relationship between surgical outcome and MMPI profiles in chronic pain patients. *Journal of Clinical Psychology, 81,* 744–749.

Lorr, M., & Strack, S. (1994). Personality profiles of police candidates. *Journal of Clinical Psychology, 50,* 200–207.

Losada-Paisey, G. (1998). Use of the MMPI–A to assess personality of juvenile male delinquents who are sex offenders and nonsex offenders. *Psychological Reports, 83,* 115–122.

Lothstein, L. M., & Jones, P. (1978). Discriminating violent individuals by means of various psychological tests. *Journal of Personality Assessment, 42,* 237–243.

Louscher, P. K., Hosford, R. E., & Moss, C. S. (1983). Predicting dangerous behavior in a penitentiary using the Megargee typology. *Criminal Justice and Behavior, 10,* 269–284.

Love, A. W., & Peck, C. L. (1987). The MMPI and psychological factors in chronic low back pain: A review. *Pain, 28,* 1–12.

Loving, J. L., & Russell, W. F. (2000). Selected Rorschach variables of psychopathic juvenile offenders. *Journal of Personality Assessment, 75,* 126–142.

Lubin, B., Larsen, R. M., & Matarazzo, J. D. (1984). Patterns of psychological test usage in the United States: 1935–1982. *American Psychologist, 39,* 451–454.

Lucio, E., Reyes-Lagunes, I., & Scott, R. L. (1994). MMPI–2 for Mexico: Translation and adaptation. *Journal of Personality Assessment, 63,* 105–116.

Machover, K. (1949). *Personality projection in the drawing of the human figure.* Springfield, IL: Charles C Thomas.

Malec, J. F., Romsaas, E., & Trump, D. (1985). Psychological and personality disturbance among patients with testicular cancer. *Journal of Psychosocial Oncology, 3,* 55–64.

Malec, J., Wolberg, W., Romsaas, E., Trump, D., & Tanner, M. (1988). Millon Clinical Multiaxial Inventory (MCMI) findings among breast cancer clinic patients after initial evaluation and at 4- or 8-month follow-up. *Journal of Clinical Psychology, 44,* 175–182.

Mallory, C. H., & Walker, C. E. (1972). MMPI O-H scale responses of assaultive and nonassaultive prisoners and associated life history variables. *Educational and Psychological Measurement, 32,* 1125–1128.

Mann, J., Stenning, W., & Borman, C. (1992). The utility of the MMPI–2 with pedophiles. *Journal of Offender Rehabilitation, 18,* 59–74.

Mannis, M. J., Morrison, T. L., Holland, E. J., & Krachmer, J. H. (1987). Personality trends in keratoconus: An analysis. *Archives of Ophthalmology, 105,* 798–800.

Marsh, S. (1962). Validating the selection of deputy sheriffs. *Public Personnel Review, 23,* 41–44.

Marshall, M., Helmes, E., & Deathe, A. B. (1992). A comparison of psychosocial functions and personality in amputee and chronic pain populations. *Clinical Journal of Pain, 8,* 351–357.

Marshall, W. L. (1996). Assessment, treatment, and theorizing about sex offenders: Developments during the past 20 years and future directions. *Criminal Justice and Behavior, 23,* 162–199.

Marshall, W. L. (1999). Diagnosing and treating sexual offenders. In A. K. Hess & I. B. Weiner (Eds.), *The handbook of forensic psychology* (2nd ed., pp. 640–670). New York: Wiley.

Marshall, W. L., & Fernandez, Y. M. (2000). Phallometric testing with sexual offenders: Limits to its value. *Clinical Psychology Review, 20,* 807–822.

Marshall, W. L., & Hall, G. C. (1995). The value of the MMPI in deciding forensic issues in accused sexual offenders. *Sexual Abuse: A Journal of Research and Treatment, 7,* 205–219.

Marshall, W. L., Jones, R., Ward, T., Johnston, P., & Barbaree, H. E. (1991). Treatment outcome with sex offenders. *Clinical Psychology Review, 11,* 465–485.

Matarazzo, J. D., Allen, B. V., Saslow, W., & Wiens, A. (1964). Characteristics of successful policemen and firemen applicants. *Journal of Applied Psychology, 48,* 123–133.

McAdams, D. P. (1992). The Five-Factor model in personality: A critical appraisal. *Journal of Personality, 60,* 329–361.

McAnulty, R. D., Adams, H. E., & Wright, L. W. (1994). Relationship between MMPI and penile plethysmography in accused child molesters. *Journal of Sex Research, 31,* 179–184.

McCabe v. Hoberman, 33 A.D.2nd 547 (1st Dept. 1969).

McCaffrey, R. J., Kirkling, E. J., & Marrazo, M. J. (1989). Civilian-rated posttraumatic stress disorder: Assessment-related issues. *Journal of Clinical Psychology, 45,* 72–76.

McCann, J. T. (1998). Defending the Rorschach in court: Admissibility using legal and professional standards. *Journal of Personality Assessment, 70,* 125–144.

McCann, J. T. (2002). Guidelines for forensic application of the MCMI–III. *Journal of Forensic Psychology Practice, 2,* 55–69.

McCann, J. T., & Dyer, F. J. (1996). *Forensic assessment with the Millon inventories.* New York: Guilford Press.

McCann, J. T., Flens, J. R., Campagna, V., Collman, P., Lazarro, T., & Connors, E. (2001). The MCMI–III in child custody evaluations: A normative study. *Journal of Forensic Psychology Practice, 1,* 27–44.

McCrae, R. R. (1991). The Five Factor model and its assessment in clinical settings. *Journal of Personality Assessment, 57,* 399–414.

McCreary, C. P. (1975a). Personality differences among child molesters. *Journal of Personality Assessment, 39,* 591–593.

McCreary, C. P. (1975b). Personality profiles of persons convicted of indecent exposure. *Journal of Clinical Psychology, 31,* 260–262.

McCreary, C., & Padilla, E. (1977). MMPI differences among black, Mexican-American, and white male offenders. *Journal of Clinical Psychology, 3,* 171–177.

McCreary, C. P., Turner, J., & Dawson, E. (1980). Emotional disturbance and chronic low back pain. *Journal of Clinical Psychology, 36,* 709–715.

McDonald v. United States, 312 F.2nd 844 (D.C. Cir. 1962).

McDonald, A., & Paitich, D. (1981). A study of homicide: The validity of predictive test factors. *Canadian Journal of Psychiatry, 26,* 549–554.

McGill, J. C., Lawlis, G. F., Selby, D., Mooney, V., & McCoy, C. E. (1983). The relationship of Minnesota Multiphasic Personality Inventory (MMPI) profile clusters to pain behaviors. *Journal of Behavioral Medicine, 6,* 77–92.

McGrath, R. E., & O'Malley, W. B. (1986). The assessment of denial and physical complaints: The validity of the Hy scale and associated MMPI signs. *Journal of Clinical Psychology, 42,* 754–760.

McGrath, R. E., Sweeney, M., O'Malley, W. B., & Carelton, T. K. (1998). Identifying psychological contributions of chronic pain complaints with the MMPI–2: The role of the K scale. *Journal of Personality Assessment, 70,* 448–459.

McKee, G. R., Shea, S. J., Mogy, R. B., & Holden, C. E. (2001). MMPI–2 profiles of filicidal, matricidal, and homicidal women. *Journal of Clinical Psychology, 57,* 367–374.

McKenna v. Fargo, 451 F. Supp. 1355 (U.S. District Courts, NJ, May 25, 1978).

McNulty, J. L., Graham, J. R., Ben-Porath, Y. S., & Stein, L. A. (1997). Comparative validity of MMPI–2 scores of African American and Caucasian mental health center clients. *Psychological Assessment, 9,* 464–470.

Medalia, A., Merriam, A., & Sandberg, M. (1989). Neuropsychological deficits in choreoacanthocytosis. *Archives of Neurology, 46,* 573–575.

Medoff, D. (1999). MMPI–2 validity scales in child custody evaluations: Clinical versus statistical significance. *Behavioral Sciences and the Law, 17,* 409–411.

Megargee, E. I. (1966). Undercontrolled and over-controlled personality types in extreme antisocial aggression. *Psychological Monographs, 80* (Whole No. 611).

Megargee, E. I. (1977). A new classification system for criminal offenders: I. The need for a new classification system. *Criminal Justice and Behavior, 4,* 107–114.

Megargee, E. I. (1984a). Derivation, validation and application of an MMPI-based system for classifying criminal offenders. *Medicine and Law, 3,* 109–118.

Megargee, E. I. (1984b). A new classification system for criminal offenders: VI. Differences among the types on the Adjective Checklist. *Criminal Justice and Behavior, 11,* 349–376.

Megargee, E. I. (1986). A psychometric study of incarcerated presidential threateners. *Criminal Justice and Behavior, 13,* 243–260.

Megargee, E. I. (1993). Using the MMPI–2 with criminal offenders: A progress report. *MMPI–2 & MMPI–A News & Profiles, 4,* 2–3.

Megargee, E. I. (1994). Using the Megargee MMPI-based classification system with MMPI–2s of male prison inmates. *Psychological Assessment, 6,* 337–344.

Megargee, E. I. (1997). Using the Megargee MMPI-based classification system with the MMPI–2s of female prison inmates. *Psychological Assessment, 9,* 75–82.

Megargee, E. I., & Bohn, M. J. (1977). A new classification system for criminal offenders: IV. Empirically determined characteristics of the ten types. *Criminal Justice and Behavior, 4,* 149–210.

Megargee, E. I., & Carbonell, J. L. (1995). Use of the MMPI–2 in correctional settings. In Y. Ben-Porath, J. Graham, G. Hall, R. Hirschman, & M. Zaragoza (Eds.), *Forensic applications of the MMPI–2* (pp. 127–159). Thousand Oaks, CA: Sage.

Megargee, E. I., Carbonell, J. L., Bohn, M. J., & Sliger, G. I. (2001). *Classifying criminal offenders with the MMPI–2: The Megargee system.* Minneapolis: National Computer System.

Megargee, E. I., & Cook, P. E. (1975). Negative response bias and the MMPI Overcontrolled-Hostility scale: A response to Deiker. *Journal of Consulting and Clinical Psychology, 43,* 725–729.

Megargee, E. I., Cook, P. E., & Mendelsohn, G. A. (1967). Development and validation of an MMPI scale of assaultiveness in overcontrolled individuals. *Journal of Abnormal Psychology, 72,* 519–528.

Megargee, E. I., & Dorhout, B. (1977). A new classification system for criminal offenders: III. Revision and refinement of the classificatory rules. *Criminal Justice and Behavior, 4,* 125–148.

Megargee, E. I., Mercer, S. J., & Carbonell, J. L. (1999). MMPI–2 with male and female state and federal prison inmates. *Psychological Assessment, 11*, 177–185.

Meloy, J. R. (1988). *The psychopathic mind: Origins, dynamics and treatment.* Northvale, NJ: Jason Aronson.

Meloy, J. R. (1991, Fall–Winter). Rorschach testimony. *Journal of Psychiatry and Law,* 221–235.

Meloy, J. R., & Gacono, C. B. (1992). The aggressive response and the Rorschach. *Journal of Clinical Psychology, 48*, 104–117.

Meloy, J. R., Gacono, C. B., & Kenney, L. (1994). A Rorschach investigation of sexual homicide. *Journal of Personality Assessment, 62*, 58–67.

Meloy, J. R., Hansen, T. L., & Weiner, I. B. (1997). The authority of the Rorschach: Legal citations during the past 50 years. *Journal of Personality Assessment, 69*, 53–62.

Melton, G., Petrila, J., Poythress, N., & Slobogin, C. (1997). *Psychological evaluations for the courts* (2nd ed). New York: Guilford Press.

Melzak, R., & Wall, P. D. (1965). Pain mechanisms: A new theory. *Science, 150*, 971–979.

Meritor Savings Bank v. Vinson, 106 S. Ct. 2399, 91 L.Ed.2d 49 (1986).

Meyer, G. J. (2001). Evidence to correct misrepresentations about Rorschach norms. *Clinical Psychology: Science and Practice, 8*, 389–396.

Meyer, G. J. (2002). Exploring possible ethnic differences in the Rorschach comprehensive system. *Journal of Personality Assessment, 78*, 104–125.

Meyer, G. J., Hilsenroth, M. J., Baxter, D., Exner, J. E., Fowler, J. C., & Resnick, J. (2002). An examination of interrater reliability for scoring the Rorschach comprehensive system in eight data sets. *Journal of Personality Assessment, 78*, 219–274.

Meyer, J., & Megargee, E. I. (1977). A new classification system for criminal offenders: II. Initial development of the system. *Criminal Justice and Behavior, 4*, 115–124.

Millon, C., Salvati, F., Blaney, M., Morgan, R., Mantero-Atrinza, E., Mlimas, N., et al. (1989). A psychological assessment of chronic fatigue syndrome/chronic Epstein–Barr virus patients. *Psychology and Health, 3*, 131–141.

Millon, T. (1983). *Millon Clinical Multiaxial Inventory manual.* New York: Holt, Rinehart & Winston.

Millon, T. (1987). *Millon Clinical Multiaxial Inventory—II: Manual for the MCMI–II.* Minneapolis, MN: National Computer Systems.

Millon, T. (1990). *Toward a new personology: An evolutionary model.* New York: Wiley.

Millon, T. (1993). *Millon Clinical Adolescent Inventory manual.* Minneapolis, MN: National Computer Systems.

Millon, T. (1994a). *Millon Clinical Multiaxial Inventory—III: Manual.* Minneapolis, MN: National Computer Systems.

Millon, T. (1994b). *Millon Index of Personality Styles manual*. San Antonio, TX: Psychological Corporation.

Millon, T. (Ed.). (1997). *The Millon inventories: Clinical and personality assessment*. New York: Guilford Press.

Millon, T., Antoni, M., Millon, C., Meagher, S., & Grossman, S. (2001). *MBMD manual*. Minneapolis, MN: National Computer Systems.

Millon, T., & Davis, R. (1997). *Disorders of personality*. New York: Guilford Press.

Millon, T., Meagher, S. E., & Grossman, S. D. (2001). Theoretical perspectives. In W. J. Livesley (Ed.), *Handbook of personality disorder: Theory, research, and treatment* (pp. 39–59). New York: Guilford Press.

Millon, T., Weiss, L., Millon, C., & Davis, R. (1994). *Millon Index of Personality Styles manual*. San Antonio, TX: Psychological Corporation.

Milner, J. S. (1990). *An interpretive manual for the Child Abuse Potential Inventory*. Webster, NC: Psytec.

Miranda v. Arizona, 384 U.S. 436 (1966).

M'Naughton, 10 CC. & F. 200, 8 Eng. Rep. 718 (1843).

Monahan, J., Steadman, H., Silver, E., Applebaum, P., Robbins, P., Mulvey, E., et al. (2001). *Rethinking risk assessment: The MacArthur study of mental disorder and violence*. New York: Oxford University Press.

Moore, J. M., Thompson-Pope, S. K., & Whited, R. M. (1996). MMPI–A profiles of adolescent boys with a history of firesetting. *Journal of Personality Assessment, 67,* 116–126.

Moos, R., & Moos, B. (1986). *The Family Environment scale manual* (2nd ed.). Palo Alto, CA: Consulting Psychologists Press.

Morey, L. C. (1991). *Personality Assessment Inventory*. Odessa, FL: Psychological Assessment Resources.

Morgan, C. D., Schoenberg, M. R., Dorr, D., & Burke, M. J. (2002). Overreport on the MCMI–III: Concurrent validation with the MMPI–2 using a psychiatric sample. *Journal of Personality Assessment, 78,* 288–300.

Morton, T. L., Farras, K. L., & Brenowitz, L. H. (2002). MMPI–A scores and high point of male juvenile delinquents: Scales 4, 5, and 6 as markers of juvenile delinquency. *Psychological Assessment, 14,* 311–319.

Moskowitz, J. L., Lewis, R. J., Ito, M. S., & Ehrmentraut, J. (1999). MMPI–2 profiles of NGRI and civil patients. *Journal of Clinical Psychology, 55,* 659–668.

Motiuk, L. L., Bonta, J., & Andrews, D. A. (1986). Classification in correctional halfway houses: The relative and incremental predictive criterion validities of the Megargee MMPI and LSI systems. *Criminal Justice and Behavior, 13,* 33–46.

Mrad, D. F., Kabacoff, R. A., & Cuckro, P. (1983). Validation of the Megargee typology in a halfway house setting. *Criminal Justice and Behavior, 10,* 252–262.

Mufson, D., & Mufson, A. (1997). Predicting police officer performance using the Inwald Personality Inventory: An illustration from Appalachia. *Professional Psychology: Research and Practice, 29,* 59–62.

Muller, B. P. (1990, June). *Twenty years of police selection with the MMPI and MMPI–2*. Paper presented at the 25th Annual MMPI–2 Workshop and Symposium, Minneapolis, MN.

Muller, B. P., & Bruno, L. N. (1986). *The MMPI and Inwald Personality Inventory (IPI) in the psychological screening of police candidates*. Paper presented at the 21st Annual Symposium on Recent Developments in the Use of the MMPI, Clearwater, FL.

Muller, B. P., & Bruno, L. N. (1990, August). *The myth of ethnic effects on MMPI*. Paper presented at the annual meeting of the American Psychological Association, Boston, MA.

Munley, P. H., Morris, J. R., McMurray, D. A., & Baines, T. C. (2001). A comparison of African American and White American veteran MMPI–2 profiles. *Assessment, 8*, 1–10.

Munsterberg, H. (1908). *On the witness stand*. New York: Doubleday.

Murphy, C. M., Meyer, S. L., & O'Leary, D. (1993). Family of origin violence and MCMI–II psychopathology among partner assaultive men. *Violence and Victim, 8*, 165–176.

Murphy, W. D., & Peters, J. M. (1992). Profiling child sexual abusers: Psychological considerations. *Criminal Justice and Behavior, 19*, 24–37.

Murray, H. A. (1943). *Thematic Apperception Test manual*. Cambridge, MA: Harvard University Press.

Murray, J. B. (1982). Psychological aspects of low back pain: Summary. *Psychological Reports, 50*, 343–351.

Murrie, D. C., & Cornell, D. G. (2002). Psychopathy screening of incarcerated juveniles: A comparison of measures. *Psychological Assessment, 14*, 390–396.

Myers, I. B., & McCaulley, M. H. (1992). *Manual: A guide to the development and use of the Myers–Briggs Type Indicator*. Palo Alto, CA: Consulting Psychologists Press.

Nader, K. O. (1997). Assessing traumatic experiences in children. In J. P. Wilson & T. M. Keane (Eds.), *Assessing psychological trauma and PTSD*. New York: Guilford Press.

Nader, K. O., Kriegler, J. A., Blake, D. D., & Pynoos, R. S. (1994). *Clinician-administered PTSD scale: Child and adolescent version (CAPS–C)*. White River Junction, VT: National Center for PTSD.

Naglieri, J. A., McNeish, T. J., & Baidos, A. N. (1991). *Draw-A-Person: Screening procedure for emotional disturbance*. Austin, TX: Pro-Ed.

Naliboff, B. D., & Cohen, M. J. (1983). Frequency of MMPI profile types in three chronic illness populations. *Journal of Clinical Psychology, 39*, 843–847.

Naliboff, B. D., Cohen, M. J., & Yellen, A. N. (1982). Does the MMPI differentiate chronic illness from chronic pain? *Pain, 13*, 333–341.

National Clearinghouse on Child Abuse and Neglect Information. (2002). *Statistics*. Washington, DC: Author.

Netter, B. E., & Viglione, D. J. (1994). An empirical study of malingering schizo-phrenia on the Rorschach. *Journal of Personality Assessment, 62,* 45–57.

Nichols, H., & Molinder, I. (1984). *Manual for the Multiphasic Sex Inventory.* Tacoma, WA: Criminal and Victim Psychology Specialists.

Nichols, H., & Molinder, I. (1996). *Multiphasic Sex Inventory—II.* Tacoma, WA: Nichols and Molinder Assessments.

Nicholson, R. A., Mouton, G. J., Bagby, R. M., Buis, T., Peterson, S. A., & Buigas, R. A. (1997). Validity of MMPI–2 indicators of response dissimulation: Receiver operator characteristic analysis. *Psychological Assessment, 7,* 471–479.

Noblitt, J. R. (1995). Psychometric measures of trauma among psychiatric patients reporting ritual abuse. *Psychological Reports, 77,* 743–747.

Nussbaum, D., Collins, M., Cather, J., Zimmerman, W., Fargusen, B., & Jacques, I. (2002). Crime type and specific personality indicia: Cloninger's TCI Impulsiv-ity, Empathy and Attachment subscales in non-violent, violent, and sexual offenders. *American Journal of Forensic Psychology, 20,* 23–56.

O'Connor, B. P., & Dyce, J. A. (1998). A test of models of personality disorder configuration. *Journal of Abnormal Psychology, 107,* 3–16.

Ollendick, D. G., & Otto, B. J. (1984). MMPI characteristics of parents referred for child-custody studies. *Journal of Psychology, 117,* 227–232.

Ollendick, D. G., Otto, B. J., & Heider, S. M. (1983). Marital MMPI characteristics: A test of Arnold's signs. *Journal of Clinical Psychology, 39,* 240–245.

Organista, P. B., & Miranda, J. (1991). Psychosomatic symptoms in medical out-patients: An investigation of self-handicapping theory. *Health Psychology, 10,* 427–431.

Ornduff, S. R., Centeno, L., & Kelsey, R. M. (1999). Rorschach assessment of malevolence in sexually abused girls. *Journal of Personality Assessment, 73,* 100–109.

Ornduff, S. R., Freedenfeld, R. N., Kelsey, R. M., & Critelli, J. W. (1994). Object relations of sexually abused female subjects: A TAT analysis. *Journal of Personal-ity Assessment, 63,* 223–238.

Ostrov, E. (1985, August). *Validation of police officer recruit candidates' self-reported drug use on the Inwald Personality Inventory Drug scale.* Paper presented at the meeting of the American Psychological Association, Los Angeles, CA.

Ostrov, E. (1993, November). *Sexual abuse allegations in child custody disputes.* Work-shop presented at the annual meeting of the Illinois Psychological Associa-tion, Chicago.

O'Sullivan, M. J., & Jenelha, R. P. (1993). The 3-4/4-3 MMPI code type in an offender population: An update on levels of hostility and violence. *Psychological Assessment, 5,* 493–498.

Otto, R. K. (2002). Use of the MMPI–2 in forensic settings. *Journal of Forensic Psychology Practice, 2,* 71–92.

Otto, R. K., Buffington-Vollum, J. K., & Edens, J. F. (2003). Child custody evaluations. In I. B. Weiner (Series Ed.) & A. M. Goldstein (Vol. Ed.), *Handbook of psychology: Vol. 11. Forensic psychology* (pp. 179–208). New York: Wiley.

Otto, R. K., & Butcher, J. N. (1995). Computer-assisted psychological assessment in child custody evaluations. *Family Law Quarterly, 29,* 79–96.

Otto, R. K., & Heilbrun, K. (2002). The practice of forensic psychology: A look toward the future in light of the past. *American Psychologist, 57,* 5–19.

Packer, I. K., & Borum, R. (2003). Forensic training and practice. In I. B. Weiner (Series Ed.) & A. M. Goldstein, *Handbook of psychology: Vol. 11. Forensic psychology* (pp. 21–32). New York: Wiley.

Pallone, N. J. (1992). The MMPI in police officer selection: Legal constraints, case law, empirical data. *Journal of Offender Rehabilitation, 17,* 171–188.

Palmer, L., Farrar, A. R., Valle, M., Ghahary, N., Panella, M., & DeGraw, D. (2000). An investigation of the clinical use of the House-Tree-Person projective drawings in the psychological evaluation of child sexual abuse. *Child Maltreatment, 5,* 169–175.

Panton, J. H. (1958). MMPI profile configurations among crime classification groups. *Journal of Clinical Psychology, 14,* 308–312.

Panton, J. H. (1976). Personality characteristics of death-row inmates. *Journal of Clinical Psychology, 32,* 306–309.

Panton, J. H. (1979). MMPI profile configurations associated with incestuous and non-incestuous child molesting. *Psychological Reports, 45,* 335–338.

Papciak, A. S., & Feurerstein, M. (1991). Psychological factors affecting isokinetic trunk strength testing in patients with work-related chronic low-back pain. *Journal of Occupational Rehabilitation, 1,* 95–104.

Parker, K. A. (1983). A meta-analysis of the reliability and validity of the Rorschach. *Journal of Personality Assessment, 47,* 227–231.

Parry, B. L., Ehlers, C. L., Mostofi, N., & Phillips, E. (1996). Personality traits in LLPDD and normal controls during follicular and luteal menstrual-cycle phases. *Psychological Medicine, 26,* 197–200.

Parwatikar, S. D., Holcolm, W. R., & Menninger, K. A. (1985). The detection of malingered amnesia in accused murderers. *Bulletin of the American Academy of Psychiatry and Law, 13,* 97–103.

Paulson, M. J., Schwemer, G. T., & Bendel, R. B. (1976). Clinical application of the Pd, Ma, and (OH) experimental MMPI scales to further understanding of abusive parents. *Journal of Clinical Psychology, 32,* 558–564.

Pena, L., & Megargee, E. (1997, June). *Application of the Megargee typology for criminal offenders to adolescents with the MMPI–A.* Paper presented at the 32nd Annual Symposium on Recent Developments in the Use of the MMPI–2 and MMPI–A, Minneapolis, MN.

Pena, L. M., Megargee, E. I., & Brody, E. (1996). MMPI–A patterns of male juvenile delinquents. *Psychological Assessment, 8,* 388–397.

Penk, W., Keane, T., Rabinowitz, R., Fowler, D., Bell, W., & Finkelstein, A. (1988). Post-traumatic stress disorder. In R. Greene (Ed.), *The MMPI: Use with specific populations* (pp. 198–213). Philadelphia: Grune & Stratton.

Penk, W., Rabinowitz, R., Black, J., Dolan, M., Bell, W., Roberts, W., et al. (1989). Comorbidity: Lessons learned about PTSD from developing PTSD scales for the MMPI. *Journal of Clinical Psychology, 45*, 709–717.

People v. Ruiz, 272 Cal. Rptr. 368 (1990).

People v. Stoll, 783 P.2d 698 (Cal. 1989).

Perrin, S., Van Hasselt, V. B., & Hersen, M. (1997). Validation of the MMPI PTSD scale against *DSM–III–R* criteria in a sample of battered women. *Violence and Victims, 12*, 99–103.

Perry, G. C., & Kinder, B. N. (1990). The susceptibility of the Rorschach to malingering: A critical review. *Journal of Personality Assessment, 54*, 47–57.

Persons, R. W., & Marks, P. A. (1971). The violent 4-3 MMPI personality type. *Journal of Consulting and Clinical Psychology, 36*, 189–196.

Peters, J. M., & Murphy, W. D. (1992). Profiling child sexual abusers: Legal considerations. *Criminal Justice and Behavior, 19*, 38–52.

Pistole, D. R., & Ornduff, S. R. (1994). TAT assessment of sexually abused girls: An analysis of manifest content. *Journal of Personality Assessment, 63*, 211–222.

Podrygula, S. (1997, June). *MMPI use in child custody evaluations: Ethical and professional issues.* Paper presented at the 32nd Annual MMPI–2 Symposium, Minneapolis, MN.

Pollach, D. R., & Grainey, T. F. (1984). A comparison of MMPI profiles for state and private disability insurance applicants. *Journal of Personality Assessment, 48*, 121–125.

Pope, K. S., Butcher, J. N., & Seelen, J. (1993). *The MMPI, MMPI–2, & MMPI–A in court: A practical guide for expert witnesses and attorneys.* Washington, DC: American Psychological Association.

Posthuma, A. B., & Harper, J. F. (1998). Comparison of MMPI–2 responses of child custody and personal injury litigants. *Professional Psychology: Research and Practice, 29*, 437–443.

Praver, F. (1994). *Child rating scales: Exposure to interpersonal abuse.* Unpublished copyrighted material. (Available from the author, 6 Marseilles Drive, Locust Valley, NY 11560)

Prentky, R. A., & Knight, R. A. (1990). Classifying sexual offenders: The development and corroboration of taxonomic models. In W. L. Marshall, D. R. Laws, & H. E. Barbaree (Eds.), *Handbook of sexual assault: Issues, theories, and treatment of the offenders.* New York: Plenum Press.

Pritchard, D. A., & Rosenblatt, A. (1980). Racial bias in the MMPI: A methodological review. *Journal of Consulting and Clinical Psychology, 48*, 263–267.

Prokop, C. K., Bradley, L. A., Margolis, R., & Gentry, W. D. (1980). Multivariate analysis of the MMPI profiles of low back pain patients. *Journal of Personality Assessment, 44*, 246–252.

Pugh, G. (1985). CPI and police selection. *Journal of Police Science and Administration, 4*, 419–425.

Putnam, F. W. (1990). *Child Dissociation Checklist* (Version 3.0-2/90). Bethesda, MD: National Institute of Mental Health, Laboratory of Developmental Psychology.

Quinsey, V. L., Arnold, L. S., & Pruesse, M. G. (1980). MMPI profiles of men referred for a pretrial psychiatric assessment as a function of offense type. *Journal of Clinical Psychology, 36*, 410–417.

Quinsey, V. L., Harris, G. T., Rice, M. E., & Cormier, C. A. (1998). *Violent offenders: Appraising and managing risk*. Washington, DC: American Psychological Association.

Quinsey, V. L., & LaLumiere, M. L. (1996). *Assessment of sexual offenders against children*. Thousand Oaks, CA: Sage.

Quinsey, V. L., Maguire, A., & Varney, G. W. (1983). Assertion and overcontrolled hostility among mentally disordered murderers. *Journal of Consulting and Clinical Psychology, 51*, 550–556.

Rada, R., Laws, D. R., & Kellner, R. (1976). Plasma testosterone levels in the rapist. *Psychosomatic Medicine, 38*, 257–268.

Rader, C. M. (1977). MMPI profile types of exposers, rapists, and assaulters in a court services population. *Journal of Consulting and Clinical Psychology, 45*, 61–69.

Rawlings, M. D. (1973). Self-controlled and interpersonal violence. *Criminology, 11*, 23–48.

Redlick, A. D., & Goodman, G. S. (2003). Taking responsibility for an act not committed: The influence of age and suggestibility. *Law and Human Behavior, 27*, 141–156.

Reed, M. K., Walker, B., Williams, G., McLeod, S., & Jones, S. (1996). MMPI–2 patterns of African-American females. *Journal of Clinical Psychology, 52*, 437–441.

Repko, G. R., & Cooper, R. (1985). The diagnosis of personality disorders: A comparison of MMPI profiles, Millon Inventory, and clinical judgment in a worker's compensation population. *Journal of Clinical Psychology, 41*, 867–881.

Retzlaff, P. D. (2000). Comment on the validity of the MCMI–III. *Law and Human Behavior, 24*, 499–500.

Reynolds, W. M., & Kobak, K. A. (1995). *Hamilton Depression Inventory: A self-report version of the Hamilton Depression Rating Scale*. Odessa, FL: Psychological Assessment Resources.

Rice, M. E., Arnold, L. S., & Tate, D. L. (1983). Faking good and bad adjustments on the MMPI and Overcontrolled Hostility in maximum security psychiatric patients. *Canadian Journal of Behavioural Science, 15*, 43–51.

Ridenour, T. A., Miller, A. R., Joy, K. L., & Dean, R. S. (1997). "Profile" analysis of the personality characteristics of child molesters using the MMPI–2. *Journal of Clinical Psychology, 53*, 575–586.

Riethmiller, R. J., & Handler, L. (1997). The great figure drawing controversy: The integration of research and clinical practice. *Journal of Personality Assessment, 69,* 488–496.

Roback, H. B. (1968). Human figure drawings: Their utility in the clinical psychologist's armamentarium for personality assessment. *Psychological Bulletin, 70,* 1–19.

Roberts, M., Thompson, J., & Johnson, M. (1999). *PAI Law Enforcement, Corrections, and Public Safety Selection Report module.* Odessa, FL: Psychological Assessment Resources.

Rogers, M. L. (1990). Coping with alleged false sexual molestation: Examination and statement analysis. *Issues in Child Abuse Accusations, 2,* 57–68.

Rogers, R. (Ed.). (1987; 1995). *Clinical assessment of malingering and deception.* New York: Guilford Press.

Rogers, R., Bagby, R. M., & Chakraparty, D. (1993). Feigning schizophrenic disorders on the MMPI–2: Detection of coached simulation. *Journal of Personality Assessment, 60,* 215–226.

Rogers, R., Bagby, R. M., & Dickens, S. E. (1992). *SIRS: Structured Interview of Reported Symptoms: A professional manual.* Odessa, FL: Psychological Assessment Resources.

Rogers, R., & Bender, S. D. (2003). Evaluation of malingering and deception. In I. B. Weiner (Series Ed.) & A. M. Goldstein (Vol. Ed.), *Handbook of psychology: Vol. 11. Forensic psychology* (pp. 109–129). New York: Wiley.

Rogers, R., Salekin, R. T., & Sewell, K. W. (1999). Validation of the Millon Clinical Multiaxial Inventory for Axis II disorders: Does it meet the *Daubert* standard? *Law and Human Behavior, 23,* 425–443.

Rogers, R., Salekin, R. T., & Sewell, K. W. (2000). The MCMI–III and the *Daubert* standard: Separating rhetoric from reality. *Law and Human Behavior, 24,* 501–506.

Rogers, R., & Seman, W. (1983). Murder and criminal responsibility: An examination of MMPI profiles. *Behavioral Sciences and the Law, 1,* 89–95.

Rohling, M. L., Binder, L. M., & Langhinrichsen-Rohling, J. (1995). Money matters: A meta-analytic review of the association between financial compensation and the experience and treatment of chronic pain. *Health Psychology, 14,* 537–547.

Rorschach, H. (1942). *Rorschach Inkblot Test.* Los Angeles: Western Psychological Services.

Roseby, V. (1995). Uses of psychological testing in a child-focused approach to child custody evaluations. *Family Law Quarterly, 29,* 97–110.

Rosen, J. C., Grubman, J. A., Bevins, T., & Frymoyer, J. W. (1987). Musculoskeletal status and disability of MMPI profile subgroups among patients with low back pain. *Health Psychology, 6,* 581–598.

Rosman, J. P., & McDonald, J. J. (1999). Forensic aspects of sexual harrassment. *Psychiatric Clinics of North America, 22,* 129–145.

Rothke, S. E., Friedman, A. F., Greene, R. L., Jaffe, A. M., Wetter, M. W., Cole, P., et al. (2000). Normative data for the F(p) scale of the MMPI–2: Implications for clinical and forensic assessment of malingering. *Psychological Assessment, 12,* 335–340.

Roys, D. T., & Timms, R. J. (1995). Personality profiles of adult males sexually molested by their maternal caregivers: Preliminary findings. *Journal of Child Sexual Abuse, 4,* 63–77.

Rubino, I. A., Sornino, A., Pezzarossa, B., Ciani, N., & Bassi, R. (1995). Personality disorders and psychiatric symptoms in psoriasis. *Psychological Reports, 77,* 547–553.

Ruby, C. L., & Brigham, J. C. (1997). The usefulness of criteria-based content analysis technique in distinguishing between truthful and fabricated allegations: A critical review. *Psychology, Public Policy, and the Law, 3,* 705–737.

Ruby, C. L., & Brigham, J. C. (1998). Can criteria-based content analysis distinguish between true and false statements of African-American speakers? *Law and Human Behavior, 22,* 369–388.

Russell, M., Karol, D., Cattell, R. B., Cattell, A. K., & Cattell, H. E. (1994). *16 PF: Fifth edition administrator's manual.* Champaign, IL: Institute for Personality and Ability Testing.

Saigh, P. A. (1997). *The Children's Posttraumatic Stress Disorder Inventory.* New York: University of New York Graduate School.

Salekin, R. T., Larrea, M. A., & Ziegler, T. (2002). Relationships between the MACI and the BASC in the assessment of child and adolescent offenders. *Journal of Forensic Psychology Practice, 2,* 35–50.

Salekin, R. T., Rogers, R., & Sewell, K. W. (1996). A review and meta-analysis of the Psychopathy Checklist and Psychopathy Checklist—Revised. *Clinical Psychology: Science & Practice, 3,* 203–215.

Salekin, R. T., Ziegler, T. A., Larrea, M. A., Anthony, V. L., & Bennet, A. (2003). Predicting dangerousness with two Millon Adolescent Clinical Inventory scales: The importance of egocentric and callous traits. *Journal of Personality Assessment, 80,* 154–163.

Sapir, A. (1987). *The LSI course on scientific content analysis (SCAN).* Phoenix, AZ: Laboratory for Scientific Interrogation.

Saxe, S. J., & Reiser, M. (1976). A comparison of three police applicant groups using the MMPI. *Journal of Police Science and Administration, 4,* 419–425.

Sbraga, T. P., & O'Donohue, W. (2003). Post hoc reasoning in possible cases of child sexual abuse: Symptoms of inconclusive origins. *Clinical Psychology: Science & Practice, 10,* 320–334.

Schaffer, C. E., Pettigrew, C. G., Blouin, D., & Edwards, D. W. (1983). Multivariate classification of female offender MMPIs. *Journal of Crime and Justice, 6,* 57–66.

Scheibe, S., Bagby, R. M., Miller, L. S., & Dorian, B. J. (2001). Assessing posttraumatic stress disorder with the MMPI–2 in a sample of workplace accident victims. *Psychological Assessment, 13,* 369–374.

Schlenger, W., & Kulka, R. (1987, August). *Performance of the Keane–Fairbank and other self-report measures in identifying posttraumatic stress disorder*. Paper presented at the annual meeting of the American Psychological Association, New York.

Schmaltz, B. J., Fehr, R. C., & Dalby, J. T. (1989). Distinguishing forensic psychiatric and inmate groups with the MMPI. *American Journal of Forensic Psychology, 7*, 37–47.

Schoenfeld, L. S., Kobos, J. L., & Phinney, I. N. (1980). Screening of police applicants: A study of reliability with the MMPI. *Psychological Reports, 47*, 419–425.

Schretland, D. (1988). The use of psychological tests to identify malingered symptoms of mental disorder. *Clinical Psychology Review, 8*, 451–476.

Schutte, J. W. (2001). Using the MCMI–III in forensic evaluations. *American Journal of Forensic Psychology, 19*, 5–20.

Scogin, F., Schumaker, J., Gardner, J., & Chaplin, W. (1995). Predictive validity of psychological testing in law enforcement settings. *Professional Psychology: Research and Practice, 26*, 68–71.

Scott, R. L., & Stone, D. A. (1986). MMPI profile constellations in incest families. *Journal of Consulting and Clinical Psychology, 54*, 364–368.

Scribner, C. M., & Handler, L. (1987). The interpreter's personality in Draw-A-Person interpretation: A study of interpersonal style. *Journal of Personality Assessment, 51*, 112–122.

Scrivner, E. M. (1994). *The role of police psychology in controlling excessive force*. Washington, DC: National Institute of Justice.

Segal, H. G., Westen, D., Lohr, N. E., & Silk, K. R. (1993). Clinical assessment of object relations and social cognition using stories told to the Picture Arrangement subtest of the WAIS–R. *Journal of Personality Assessment, 61*, 58–80.

Segal, J. (1996). Traditional MMPI–2 validity indicators and initial presentation of custody evaluations. *American Journal of Forensic Psychology, 14*, 55–63.

Serin, R. C. (1996). Violent recidivism in criminal psychopaths. *Law and Human Behavior, 20*, 207–217.

Seto, M. C., LaLumiere, M. L., & Blanchard, R. (2000). The discriminant validity of a phallometric test for pedophilic interests among adolescent sex offenders against children. *Psychological Assessment, 12*, 319–327.

Shaffer, J. W., Nussbaum, K., & Little, J. M. (1972). MMPI profiles of disability insurance claimants. *American Journal of Psychology, 129*, 64–67.

Shapiro, J. P., Leifer, M., Martone, M. W., & Kassem, L. (1990). Multimodal assessment of depression in sexually abused girls. *Journal of Personality Assessment, 55*, 234–248.

Shea, S. J., McKee, G. R., Shea, M. E., & Culley, D. C. (1996). MMPI–2 profiles of male pre-trial defendants. *Behavioral Sciences and the Law, 14*, 331–338.

Shealy, L., Kalichman, S. C., Syzmanowski, D., & McKee, G. (1991). MMPI profile subtypes of incarcerated sex offenders against children. *Violence and Victims*, *6*, 201–212.

Sherman, R. A., Camfield, M. R., & Arena, J. G. (1995). The effect of presence or absence of low back pain on the MMPI's conversion V. *Military Psychology*, *7*, 29–38.

Sheshkin, D. J. (2000). *Handbook of parametric and nonparametric statistical procedures*. Boca Raton, FL: Chapman & Hall/CRC Press.

Shusman, E. (1987). A redundancy analysis for the Inwald Personality Inventory and the MMPI. *Journal of Personality Assessment*, *51*, 433–440.

Shusman, E., Inwald, R., & Knatz, H. (1987). A cross-validation study of police recruit performance as predicted by the IPI and MMPI. *Journal of Police Science and Administration*, *15*, 162–169.

Shusman, E., Inwald, R., & Landa, B. (1984). Correction officer job performance as predicted by the IPI and MMPI. *Criminal Justice and Behavior*, *2*, 309–329.

Sidun, N. M., & Rosenthal, R. H. (1987). Graphic indicators of sexual abuse in Draw-A-Person tests of psychiatrically hospitalized adolescents. *Arts in Psychotherapy*, *14*, 25–33.

Siegel, J. C. (1996). Traditional MMPI–2 validity indicators and initial presentation in custody evaluations. *American Journal of Forensic Psychology*, *14*, 55–63.

Siegel, J. C., & Langford, J. S. (1998). MMPI–2 validity scales and suspected parental alienation syndrome. *American Journal of Forensic Psychology*, *16*, 5–14.

Simmons, J. G., Johnson, J. L., Gouvier, W. D., & Muzyczka, M. J. (1981). The Meyer–Megargee inmate typology: Dynamic or unstable? *Criminal Justice and Behavior*, *15*, 49–55.

Slesinger, D., Archer, R. P., & Duane, W. (2002). MMPI–2 characteristics in a chronic pain population. *Assessment*, *9*, 401–414.

Smith v. United States, 36 F.2d 548, 549 (D.C. Cir. 1929).

Smith, D., & Dumont, F. (1995). A cautionary study: Unwarranted interpretations of the Draw-A-Person test. *Professional Psychology: Research and Practice*, *26*, 298–303.

Smith, G. P., & Burger, G. K. (1997). Detection of malingering: Validation of the Structured Inventory of Malingered Symptomatology (SIMS). *Journal of the American Academy of Psychiatry and the Law*, *25*, 183–189.

Smith, S. R., Hilsenroth, M. J., Castlebury, F. D., & Durham, T. W. (1999). The clinical utility of the MMPI–2 Antisocial Practices Content Scale. *Journal of Personality Disorders*, *13*, 385–393.

Snibbe, H. M., Fabricatore, J., & Azen, S. P. (1975). Personality patterns of White, Black, and Mexican-American patrolmen as measured by the Sixteen Personality Factor Questionnaire. *American Journal of Community Psychology*, *3*, 221–226.

Snibbe, J. R., Peterson, P. J., & Sosner, B. (1980). Study of psychological characteristics of a worker's compensation sample using the MMPI and Millon Clinical Multiaxial Inventory. *Psychological Reports, 47,* 959–966.

Snyder, D. K., & Power, D. G. (1981). Empirical descriptors of unelevated MMPI profiles among chronic pain patients: A typological approach. *Journal of Clinical Psychology, 37,* 602–607.

Sparta, S. N. (2003). Assessment of childhood trauma. In I. B. Weiner (Series Ed.) & A. M. Goldstein (Vol. Ed.), *Handbook of psychology: Vol. 11. Forensic psychology* (pp. 209–231). New York: Wiley.

Spitzer, R. L., Williams, J. B., Gibbon, M., & First, M. B. (1994). *Structured interview for DSM—IV (SCID).* Washington, DC: American Psychiatric Press.

State v. Fitzgerald, 382 N.W. 2d 892 (Minn. App. 1986).

Stern, L. A., & Graham, J. R. (1999). Detecting faked-good profiles in a correctional facility. *Psychological Assessment, 11,* 386–395.

Sternbach, R. A., & Timmermans, G. (1975). Personality changes associated with reduction of pain. *Pain, 1,* 177–181.

Sternbach, R. A., Wolf, S. R., Murphy, R. W., & Akeson, W. H. (1973). Traits of pain patients: The low-back loser. *Psychosomatics, 14,* 226–229.

Storm, J., & Graham, J. R. (2000). Detection of coached general malingering on the MMPI–2. *Psychological Assessment, 12,* 158–164.

Stovall, G., & Craig, R. J. (1990). Mental representations of physically abused latency-aged females. *Child Abuse and Neglect, 14,* 233–242.

Strack, S., & Lorr, M. (1997). Invited essay: The challenge of differentiating normal and disordered personality. *Journal of Personality Disorders, 11,* 105–122.

Strassberg, D. S., Reimherr, F., Ward, M., Russell, S., & Cole, A. (1981). The MMPI and chronic pain. *Journal of Consulting and Clinical Psychology, 49,* 220–226.

Strong, D. R., Greene, R. L., Hoppe, C., Johnston, T., & Olesin, N. (1999). Taxometric analysis of impression management and self-deception on the MMPI–2 in child custody litigants. *Journal of Personality Assessment, 73,* 1–18.

Stukenberg, K., Brady, C., & Klinetob, N. (2000). Psychiatric inpatients and the MMPI–2: Providing benchmarks. *Journal of Clinical Psychology, 56,* 747–756.

Sugihara, Y., & Warner, J. A. (1999). Mexican-American male batterers on the MCMI–III. *Psychological Reports, 85,* 163–169.

Sutker, P. B., Allain, A. N., & Geyer, S. (1978). Female criminal violence and differential MMPI characteristics. *Journal of Consulting and Clinical Psychology, 46,* 1141–1143.

Sutker, P., & Moan, C. E. (1973). A psychosocial description of penitentiary inmates. *Archives of General Psychiatry, 29,* 663–667.

Swanson, D. W., Swenson, W. M., Maruto, T., & Floreen, A. C. (1978). The dissatisfied patient with chronic pain. *Pain, 4,* 367–378.

Swenson, C. H. (1957). Empirical evaluations of human figure drawings. *Psychological Bulletin, 54,* 431–466.

Swenson, C. H. (1968). Empirical evaluations of human figure drawings: 1957–1966. *Psychological Bulletin, 70,* 20–44.

Tarasoff v. Regents of the University of California, Supp. 131 Cal. Rep. 14 (1976).

Tharinger, D. J., & Stark, K. (1990). A qualitative versus quantitative approach to evaluating the Draw-A-Person and Kinetic Family Drawing: A study of mood-and-anxiety-disorder children. *Psychological Assessment, 2,* 365–375.

Tierney, D. W., & McCabe, M. P. (2002). Motivation for behavior change among sex offenders: A review of the literature. *Clinical Psychology Review, 22,* 113–129.

Timbrook, R. E., & Graham, J. R. (1994). Ethnic differences on the MMPI–2? *Psychological Assessment, 6,* 212–217.

Timbrook, R. E., Graham, J. R., Keiller, S. W., & Watts, D. (1993). Comparison of the Weiner–Harmon subtle–obvious scales and the standard validity scales in detecting valid and invalid MMPI–2 profiles. *Psychological Assessment, 5,* 53–61.

Tobey, L. H., & Bruhn, A. R. (1992). Early memories and the criminally dangerous. *Journal of Personality Assessment, 59,* 137–152.

Toyer, E. A., & Weed, N. C. (1998). Concurrent validity of the MMPI–A in a counseling program for juvenile offenders. *Journal of Clinical Psychology, 54,* 395–399.

Trowbridge, B. C. (2003). Suggestibility and confessions. *American Journal of Forensic Psychology, 21,* 5–23.

Truscott, D. (1990). Assessment of overcontrolled hostility in adolescents. *Psychological Assessment, 2,* 145–148.

Tsai, D. C., & Pike, P. L. (2000). Effects of acculturation on the MMPI–2 scores of Asian American students. *Journal of Personality Assessment, 74,* 216–230.

Tsushima, W. T., & Tsushima, V. G. (2001). Comparison of the fake bad scale and other MMPI–2 validity scales with personal injury litigants. *Assessment, 8,* 205–212.

Tuoko, H., Vernon-Wilkinson, R., & Robinson, E. (1991). The use of the MCMI in the personality assessment of head-injured adults. *Brain Injury, 5,* 287–293.

Turner, S. M., DeMers, S. T., Fox, H. R., & Reed, G. M. (2001). APA's guidelines for test user qualifications: An executive summary. *American Psychologist, 56,* 1099–1113.

Tweed, R. G., & Dutton, D. G. (1999). A comparison of impulsive and instrumental subgroups of batterers. *Violence and Victims, 13,* 217–230.

Uniform Marriage and Divorce Act, § 402, 9A U.L.A. 561 (1987).

United States v. Frye, 293 F. 1013 (D.C. Cir. 1923).

Uomoto, J. M., Turner, J. A., & Herron, L. D. (1988). Use of the MMPI and MCMI in predicting outcome of lumbar laminectomy. *Journal of Clinical Psychology, 44,* 191–197.

U.S. Equal Employment Opportunity Commission, U.S. Civil Service Commission, U.S. Department of Labor, and U.S. Department of Justice. (1978). Uniform guidelines on employee selection procedures. *Federal Register, 43*(166), 38295–38309.

Valliant, P. M., & Blasutti, B. (1992). Personality differences of sex offenders referred for treatment. *Psychological Reports, 71,* 1067–1074.

Van Der Velde, R. J. (1999). Accessing legal literature. In A. K. Hess & I. B. Weiner (Eds.), *The handbook of forensic psychology* (pp. 48–59). New York: Wiley.

Van Voorhis, P. (1988). A cross classification of five offender typologies: Issues of construct and predictive validity. *Criminal Justice and Behavior, 15,* 109–124.

Varela, J. G., Scogin, F. R., & Vipperman, R. K. (1999). Development and preliminary validation of a semi-structured interview for the screening of law enforcement candidates. *Behavioral Sciences and the Law, 17,* 467–481.

Vaupel, S., G., & Goeke, J. M. (1994). Incest perpetrator MMPI profiles and the variable of offense admission status. *International Journal of Offender Therapy and Comparative Criminology, 38,* 69–77.

Velasquez, R. J., Callahan, W. J., & Young, R. (1993). Hispanic–White MMPI comparisons: Does psychiatric diagnosis make a difference? *Journal of Clinical Psychology, 49,* 528–534.

Vendrig, A. A. (2000). The Minnesota Multiphasic Personality Inventory and chronic pain: A conceptual analysis of a long-standing but complicated relationship. *Clinical Psychology Review, 20,* 533–559.

Vendrig, A. A., Deckson, J. L., & Meg, H. R. (1999). Utility of selected MMPI–2 scales on the outcome prediction for patients with chronic back pain. *Psychological Assessment, 11,* 381–385.

Veneziano, C. A., & Veneziano, L. (1986). Classification of adolescent offenders with the MMPI: An extension and cross-validation of the Megargee typology. *International Journal of Offender Therapy and Comparative Criminology, 30,* 11–23.

Viglione, D. J. (1999). A review of recent research addressing the utility of the Rorschach. *Psychological Assessment, 11,* 251–265.

Viglione, D. J., Wright, D. M., Dizon, N. T., Moynihan, J. E., DuPuis, S., & Pizite, T. (2001). Evading detection on the MMPI–2: Does caution produce more reported patterns of responding? *Assessment, 3,* 237–250.

Villanueva, M. R., Roman, D. D., & Tuley, M. R. (1988). Determining forensic rehabilitation potential with the MMPI: Practical implications for residential treatment populations. *American Journal of Forensic Psychology, 6,* 27–35.

Wakefield, H., & Underwager, R. (1990). Personality characteristics of parents making false accusations of sexual abuse in custody disputes. *Child Abuse Accusations, 2,* 121–136.

Wakefield, H., & Underwager, R. (1991). Sexual abuse allegations in divorce and custody disputes. *Behavioral Sciences and the Law, 9,* 451–468.

Waldman, T. L., Silber, D. E., Holmstrom, R. W., & Karp, S. A. (1994). Personality characteristics of incest survivors on the Draw-A-Person questionnaire. *Journal of Personality Assessment, 63,* 97–104.

Walker, L. (1979). *The battered woman.* New York: Harper & Row.

Walters, G. D. (1986). Correlates of the Megargee criminal classification system: A military correctional setting. *Criminal Justice and Behavior, 13,* 19–32.

Walters, G. D., & Greene, R. L. (1983). Factor structure of the Overcontrolled-Hostility scale of the MMPI. *Journal of Clinical Psychology, 39,* 560–562.

Walters, G. D., Greene, R. L., & Solomon, G. S. (1982). Empirical correlates of the Overcontrolled-Hostility Scale and the MMPI 4-3 high-point pair. *Journal of Consulting and Clinical Psychology, 50,* 213–218.

Walters, G. D., Mann, M. F., Miller, M. P., Hemphill, L., & Chlumsky, M. L. (1988). Emotional disorder among offenders: Inter- and intrasetting comparisons. *Criminal Justice and Behavior, 15,* 433–453.

Walters, G. D., Scrapansky, T. A., & Marlow, G. A. (1986). The emotionally disturbed military offender: Identification, background and institutional adjustment. *Criminal Justice and Behavior, 13,* 261–285.

Walters, G. D., Solomon, G. S., & Greene, R. J. (1982). The relationship between the Overcontrolled Hostility scale and the MMPI 4-3 high point pair. *Journal of Clinical Psychology, 38,* 613–615.

Walters, G. L., & Clopton, J. R. (2000). Effect of symptom information and validity scale information on the malingering of depression on the MMPI–2. *Journal of Personality Assessment, 75,* 183–195.

Wasyliw, O. E., Zenn, A. F., Grossman, L. S., & Haywood, T. W. (1998). Detection of minimization of psychopathology in the Rorschach in cleric and noncleric alleged sex offenders. *Assessment, 5,* 389–397.

Watkins, C. E., Campbell, V. L., Nieberding, R., & Hallmark, R. (1995). Contemporary practice of psychological assessment by clinical psychologists. *Professional Psychology: Research and Practice, 26,* 54–60.

Watson, C. G. (1990). Psychometric posttraumatic stress disorder measurement techniques: A review. *Journal of Consulting and Clinical Psychology, 2,* 460–469.

Wechsler, D. (1997). *Wechsler Adult Intelligence Scale—Third Edition.* San Antonio, TX: The Psychological Corporation.

Wechsler, D. (2004) *Wechsler Intelligence Scale for Children—Fourth Edition.* San Antonio, TX: The Psychological Corporation.

Weiner, I. B. (2001). Assessment advocacy—Report of the SPA coordinator. *SPA Exchange, 12,* 7.

Weiner, I. B. (2003). Prediction and postdiction in clinical decision making. *Clinical Psychology: Science & Practice, 10,* 335–338.

Weiner, I. B., Exner, J. E., & Sciara, A. (1996). Is the Rorschach welcome in the courtroom? *Journal of Personality Assessment, 67,* 422–424.

Weiss, W. U., & Buehler, K. (1995). The Psychopathic Deviate scale of the MMPI in police selection. *Journal of Police and Criminal Psychology, 10,* 57–60.

Weissman, H. N., & DeBow, D. M. (2003). Ethical principles and professional competencies. In I. B. Weiner (Series Ed.) & A. M. Goldstein (Vol. Ed.), *Handbook of psychology: Vol. 11. Forensic psychology* (pp. 33–53). New York: Wiley.

Werner, P., Becker, J. M., & Yesavage, J. A. (1983). Concurrent validity of the overcontrolled hostility scale for psychosis. *Psychological Reports, 52,* 93–94.

West, M. M. (1998). Meta-analysis of studies assessing the efficacy of projective techniques in discriminating child sexual abuse. *Child Abuse and Neglect, 22,* 1151–1166.

Westen, D. (1991). Clinical assessment of object relations using the TAT. *Journal of Personality Assessment, 56,* 56–74.

Westen, D. (1997). Differences between clinical and research methods for assessing personality disorders: Implications for research and the evolution of axis II. *American Journal of Psychiatry, 154,* 895–903.

Westen, D., Lohr, N., Silk, K., Kerber, K., & Goodrich, S. (1985). *Object relations and social cognition TAT scoring manual.* Ann Arbor: University of Michigan.

Westermeyer, J. (1974). Caveats on diagnosing assassins. *American Journal of Psychiatry, 131,* 722–723.

Wetter, M. W., Baer, R. A., Berry, D. T., Robinson, L. H., & Sumpter, J. (1993). MMPI–2 profiles of motivated faking given specific symptom information: A comparison. *Psychological Assessment, 5,* 317–323.

Wetter, M. W., & Corrigan, S. K. (1995). Providing information to clients about psychological tests: A survey of attorney and law student attitudes. *Professional Psychology: Research and Practice, 26,* 474–477.

Wetter, M. W., & Deutsch, S. E. (1996). Faking specific disorders and temporal response consistency on the MMPI–2. *Psychological Assessment, 8,* 39–47.

White, W. C. (1975). Validity of the Overcontrolled-Hostility scale: A brief report. *Journal of Personality Assessment, 39,* 587–590.

White, W. C., McAdoo, W. G., & Megargee, E. I. (1973). Personality factors associated with over-and undercontrolled offenders. *Journal of Personality Assessment, 37,* 473–478.

Widiger, T. (in press). Interviewing for personality disorders. In R. J. Craig (Ed.), *Clinical and diagnostic interviewing* (2nd ed.). Northvale, NJ: Jason Aronson.

Wilfling, F. J., Klonoff, H., & Kokan, P. (1973). Psychological demographics and orthopaedic factors associated with predictions of outcome of spinal fusion. *Clinical Orthopaedics and Related Disorders, 90,* 153–160.

Williams v. State, 649 S.W.2d 693 (Tex. Ct. App. 1983).

Williams, C. W., Lees-Haley, P. R., & Djanogly, S. E. (1999). Clinical scrutiny of litigants' self-reports. *Professional Psychology: Research and Practice, 30,* 361–367.

Wilson, J., & Walker, A. (1990). Toward an MMPI trauma profile. *Journal of Traumatic Stress, 3,* 151–168.

Wise, E. A. (1996). Diagnosing posttraumatic stress disorder with the MMPI clinical scales: A review of the literature. *Journal of Psychopathology and Behavioral Assessment, 18*, 71–82.

Wolfe, V. V., Wolfe, D. A., Gentile, C., & Larose, L. (1986). *Children's Impact of Traumatic Events Scale*. London, Ontario, Canada: London Health Service Center, Department of Psychology.

Wood, J. M., & Lilienfeld, S. O. (1999). The Rorschach Inkblot test: A case of overstatement? *Assessment, 6*, 341–352.

Wood, J. M., Lilienfeld, S. O., Nezworski, M. T., & Garb, H. M. (2001). Coming to grips with negative evidence for the comprehensive system for the Rorschach: A comment on Gacono, Loving, and Bodholt; Ganellen; and Bornstein. *Journal of Personality Assessment, 77*, 48–70.

Wood, J. M., Nezworski, M. T., Garb, H. N., & Lilienfeld, S. O. (2001). The misrepresentation of psychopathology: Problems with the norms of the comprehensive system for the Rorschach. *Clinical Psychology: Science and Practice, 8*, 350–373.

Wood, J. M., Nezworski, M. T., & Stejskal, W. J. (1996). The comprehensive system and the Rorschach: A critical examination. *Psychological Science, 7*, 3–10.

Wright, K. N. (1988). The relationship of risk, needs, and personality classification systems and prison adjustment. *Criminal Justice and Behavior, 15*, 454–471.

Wright, P., Nussbaum, D., Lynett, E., & Buis, T. (1997). Forensic MMPI–2 profiles: Normative limitations impose interpretive restrictions with both males and females. *American Journal of Forensic Psychology, 15*, 19–37.

Wrobel, N. H., Wrobel, T. A., & McIntosh, J. W. (1988). Application of the Megargee typology to a forensic psychiatric population. *Criminal Justice and Behavior, 15*, 247–254.

Wrobel, T. A., Calovini, P. K., & Martin, T. O. (1991). Application of the Megargee MMPI typology to a population of defendants referred for psychiatric evaluation. *Criminal Justice and Behavior, 18*, 397–405.

Yanagida, E. H., & Ching, J. W. (1993). MMPI profiles of child abusers. *Journal of Clinical Psychology, 49*, 569–576.

Youngjohn, J. R. (1995). Confirmed attorney coaching prior to neuropsychological evaluation. *Assessment, 2*, 279–284.

Youngjohn, J. R., Davis, D., & Wolf, I. (1997). Head injury and the MMPI–2: Paradoxical severity effects and the influence of litigation. *Psychological Assessment, 7*, 177–184.

Zacker, J. (1997). Rorschach responses of police applicants. *Psychological Reports, 80*, 523–528.

Zager, L. D. (1988). The MMPI-based criminal classification system: A review, current status, and future directions. *Criminal Justice and Behavior, 15*, 39–57.

Zalewski, C., & Greene, R. L. (1996). Multicultural usage of the MMPI–2. In R. H. Dana (Ed.), *Handbook of multicultural assessment: Clinical, psychological, and educational applications* (pp. 77–114). San Francisco: Jossey-Bass.

Zeidhlach, D. (2003). *Critical thinking ability and personality dispositions*. Unpublished doctoral dissertation, Argosy University, Illinois School of Professional Psychology, Chicago.

Zivney, O. A., Nash, M. R., & Hulsey, T. L. (1988). Sexual abuse in early versus late childhood: Differing patterns of pathology as revealed on the Rorschach. *Psychotherapy, 25*, 99–106.

AUTHOR INDEX

Abel, G. G., 179
Abidin, R. R., 88
Achenbach, T., 34
Ackerman, M. C., 16, 84, 85, 87, 98, 100
Ackerman, M. J., 16, 30, 83, 84, 85, 87,
    88, 98, 100, 227
Adams, H. E., 174, 198, 206
Adams, K. M., 112, 127, 134, 140
Adams, N. A., 223, 252, 255, 257
Adams, R. L., 113, 136
Aderibigbe, Y., 226
Akeson, W. H., 112, 126
Alexander, R. W., 141
Allain, A. N., 268
Allen, B. V., 60, 66
Alterman, A. I., 24
Altman, H., 235
American Academy of Child and Adoles-
    cent Psychiatry, 83, 92
American Academy of Family Mediators,
    83
American Bar Association, 11
American Law Institute (ALI), 11
American Professional Society on the
    Abuse of Children, 83
American Psychiatric Association, 22,
    39, 52, 225, 278
American Psychological Association
    (APA), 7, 25, 28, 34, 36, 57, 82,
    83, 88, 101, 282
Americans With Disabilities Act (ADA),
    78
Anderson, W., 223
Anderson, W. P., 198, 202, 207, 208,
    209
Anderson, W. R., 255, 259, 262
Andrews, D. A., 34, 258
Angle, C. R., 139
Anthony, V. L., 33
Antoni, M., 137
Araji, S., 190
Arbisi, P. A., 132
Archer, R. P., 132
Arena, J. G., 113
Arfice, P. A., 20

Armentrout, D. P., 127, 134
Armentrout, J. A., 198, 202, 206, 207
Arnold, L. S., 198, 208, 255, 266, 268,
    269
Arrigo, B., 72
Ash, E., 33
Association of Family and Conciliation
    Courts, 83
Association for the Treatment of Sex
    Abusers, 183
Atkinson, J. H., 127, 134
Auerbach, S. M., 258–259
Auvenshine, C. D., 223
Azen, S. D., 60
Azen, S. P., 56, 71

Bacchiochi, J. R., 20
Baer, R. A., 18, 19, 20, 21, 85, 110, 146
Bagby, R. M., 19, 20, 144, 146, 161
Baidos, A. N., 17
Baile, W. F., 138
Bailey, J. M., 16
Bain, K. P., 257
Baines, T. C., 76
Baity, M. R., 225
Baker, C. F., 61, 66
Baker, W. J., 135, 136
Baldwin, H. K., 269
Bannatyne, L. A., 36
Bansal, A., 76
Barbaree, H. E., 184
Bard, L., 177
Barefoot v. Estelle, 222
Barnett, R. W., 177
Barrington, W. W., 139
Barth, J. T., 127
Barth, P. S., 109
Bartol, C. B., 62, 64, 66
Bassi, R., 139
Bathhurst, K., 85
Bauer, C. A., 198, 203, 204, 209
Bautz, M., 127, 133
Beals, R. K., 113, 126
Beasley, R., 234, 237

Beatty, W. W., 229, 231
Beck, A. J., 161
Becker, J. M., 235, 269
Beech, A. R., 179, 184
Bell, V., 268
Bendel, R. B., 267
Bender, S. D., 18
Benedek, E. P., 256
Benn, A. F., 198, 199, 206, 210
Bennet, A., 33
Ben-Porath, Y. S., 14, 20, 76, 86, 99, 132
Bernstein, I., 127, 134
Berry, D. T., 19, 20, 21, 85, 110, 135, 136, 146
Beutler, L. E., 62, 63, 66
Bevins, T., 127, 134
Biaggio, M. K., 269
Binder, L. M., 133, 135
Bivens, A., 145
Bjerregaard, B., 235
Black, R. G., 113, 126
Blackburn, R., 267
Blader, J. C., 184
Blades, J. R., 269
Blain, G. H., 17, 93
Blak, T., 184
Blake, D. D., 92, 269
Blanchard, D. D., 20
Blanchard, R., 184
Blasutti, B., 174
Blau, T. H., 4, 60–61, 210–211
Block, J., 49
Bloom, L. J., 16, 84, 85, 100
Blovin, D., 259
Blowers, A. N., 235
Blum, R. H., 61
Blumer, D. P., 112, 127, 134
Boccaccini, M. T., 161
Bodholt, R. H., 16
Boer, D. R., 180
Bohn, M. J., 258, 259, 264
Bone, 142
Bonge, D., 230, 234
Bonsignore v. City of New York, 56
Bonta, J., 258
Booker, A. B., 33
Boone, K. B, 139
Booth, R. J., 259
Borchgrevnik, G. E., 139, 140
Borchgrevnik, P. C., 139
Bordnick, P. S., 182, 198, 207

Borman, C., 199
Borum, R., 13, 14, 60, 70
Bosquet, M., 178
Bovan, J., 17
Bow, J. N., 84, 101
Bowman, M. L., 109
Boyd, S., 145
Boyer, M. C., 174, 175
Bradley, L. A., 126, 127, 134
Bradley, P., 68, 161
Bradwejn, J., 144
Brady, C., 36
Brady, L., 60–61
Brandsma, J., 145
Brandt, J. R., 31
Brenowitz, L. H., 32
Bricklin, B., 88
Bridges, M. P., 210
Briere, J., 91, 92, 161
Brigham, J. C., 186
Briner, W., 139
Brinson, A., 84, 99
Brockwell, A. L., 60, 62, 66, 72
Brodsky, S. L., 161
Brody, E., 32
Brodzinsky, D. M., 90
Bruhn, A. R., 273
Brunet, A., 144
Bruno, L. N., 57, 76
Buchholz, D., 137
Buck, J. A., 235
Buck, J. N., 16
Buehler, K., 64
Buffington-Vollum, J. K., 102
Buis, T., 20, 226
Burbeck, E., 56, 59
Bureau of National Affairs, 155
Burger, G. K., 146
Burke, M. J., 21
Burns, R. C., 16
Burnstein, I. H., 56
Bury, A. S., 20
Butcher, J. N., 13, 14, 21, 36, 87, 90, 99, 111, 112, 114, 131, 133, 140, 160, 177

Calhoun, G. B., 32
Callahan, W. J., 77
Calovini, P. K., 259
Calsyn, D. A., 126

Kalichman, S. C., 174, 179, 182, 198, 201, 202, 206, 207, 208, 209, 252, 255, 256, 257
Kamphus, J. H., 94
Kansas v. Hendricks, 180
Karlstrom, E., 179
Karol, D., 45, 161
Karp, S. A., 92
Karr, C., 60, 66, 67, 68
Karson, M., 45
Karson, S., 45
Kassem, L., 94
Kaufman, G., 72
Kaufman, J. C., 70
Kaufman, S., 16
Keane, T., 144
Keane, T. M., 269
Keilin, W. G., 16, 84, 85, 100
Keiller, S. W., 20
Keller, L. S., 111, 112, 114, 131, 133, 140
Kellner, R., 267
Kelly, R. J., 182
Kelsey, R. M., 93, 94
Kendall-Tackitt, K. A., 97
Kennedy, T. D., 258, 259
Kennedy, W. A., 31, 32
Kenney, L., 273
Kerber, K., 84
Khadini, A., 20
Kinder, B. N., 15, 20, 21
Kirgeares, S. L., 94
Kirkish, P., 62, 66
Kirkland, E. J., 144
Kirkland, K. D., 82, 198, 203, 204, 209
Kirkland, K. L., 82
Klassen, P., 184
Kleespies, P. M., 269
Klinetob, N., 36
Kling, J. S., 266
Klonoff, H., 113, 126
Knapp, S., 25
Knatz, H. F., 56, 57, 60, 71
Knight, R. A., 177, 189
Kobak, K. A., 161
Kobos, J. L., 61, 62, 66
Kokan, P., 113, 126
Koppitz, E., 16
Koretsky, M. B., 144
Korn, R., 139
Kornfeld, A. D., 63, 67, 68
Kosson, D. S., 23, 31

Koszycki, D., 144
Krachmer, J. H., 139
Kremer, E. F., 127, 134
Kriegler, J. A., 92
Kropp, P. R., 180
Kuban, M. E., 184
Kuehnle, K., 91, 92
Kulka, R., 144
Kunce, J. T., 198, 202, 207

Lachar, D., 75
Lally, S. J., 17
LaLumiere, M. L., 178, 180, 184
Lampel, A. K, 87
Landa, B., 57
Lane, P. J., 266, 268
Langevin, R., 190, 255
Langfeldt, V. C., 259, 262, 269
Langford, J. S., 86
Langhinrichsen-Rohling, J., 133
Lanyon, R. I., 176, 183, 190, 205
Larose, L., 92
Larrabee, G. J., 110
Larrea, M. A., 31, 33
Larsen, R. M., 13
Lawlis, G. F., 127, 134
Lawry, S. S., 179
Laws, D. R., 267
Leavitt, F., 127, 134
Lees-Haley, P. R., 12, 18, 110, 131, 132, 136
Lefkowitz, J., 59
Lefkowitz, M. M., 224
Lereins, I., 139
LeUnes, A., 265
Levenson, H., 127
Levin, S. M., 173, 180, 201
Lewis, J. L., 20, 146
Lewis, M. L., 17, 93
Lewis, R. J., 226
Lilienfeld, S. O., 15, 16, 23, 178
Lipovsky, J., 98
Little, J. M., 126
Logue, P., 259, 262
Lohr, J. M., 230, 234, 237
Lohr, N. E., 84, 93
Long, B. I., 160
Long, C. J., 126
Lopez, I. R., 76
Lorr, M., 50, 69

M'Naughton Case, 10
Moan, C. E., 223, 255
Mogy, R. B., 252, 256
Molinder, I., 179
Monahan, J., 224
Montgomery, H. R., 60
Mooney, V., 127, 134
Moore, J. E., 127, 134
Moore, J. M., 32
Moos, B., 34
Moos, R., 34
Morey, L. C., 56, 160, 177
Morgan, C. D., 21
Mori, D. L., 269
Morris, J. R., 76
Morrison, T. L., 139
Morse, S. J., 9
Morton, T. L., 32
Moskowitz, J. L., 226
Moss, C. S., 259, 259
Mostofi, N., 139
Motiuk, L. L., 258, 259, 262
Mrad, D. F., 259, 262
Mudrak, P., 182, 198, 206
Mufson, A., 71
Mufson, D., 71
Muller, B. P., 57, 66, 67, 68, 76
Munley, P. H., 76
Murphy, C. M., 230, 231, 234, 237
Murphy, R. W., 112, 126
Murphy, W. D., 174, 182, 184
Murray, H. A., 16
Murray, J. B., 112, 140
Murrie, D. C., 31, 33
Muzyczka, M. J., 259
Myers, I. B., 44
Myers, W. C., 182, 198, 206

Nader, K. O., 92
Naglieri, J. A., 17
Naliboff, B. D., 127, 133
Nash, M. R., 94
National Clearinghouse on Child Abuse
    and Neglect Information, 170, 171
Netter, B. E., 21
Neumann, C. S., 31
Newlove, T., 237
Nezworski, M. T., 15, 16, 84
Nicholas, D., 228–229, 231
Nicholas, N. A., 223

Nichols, H., 179
Nicholson, D. S., 20
Nicholson, R. A., 20
Nieberding, R., 13
Noblitt, J. R., 144
Norris, C., 139
Nussbaum, D., 48, 178, 226
Nussbaum, K., 126
Nussbaum, P. D., 63, 66

O'Connor, B. P., 53
O'Dell, J., 45
O'Donohue, W., 90
Ogard, E. M., 60, 66, 67, 68
O'Leary, D., 230, 234
Olesin, N., 85
Oliver, M. E., 24
Ollendick, D. G., 86, 87
Olson, R., 145
O'Malley, W. B., 113, 132
Omer, H., 139
Orchard, B., 255
Organista, P. B., 139
Ornduff, S. R., 93, 94
Osborn, C. A., 179
Ostrov, E., 57, 63, 189, 190
O'Sullivan, M. J., 235
Otto, B. J., 86, 87
Otto, R. K., 5, 13, 14, 90, 102

Packer, I. K., 13
Padilla, E., 268
Padula, M. A., 139
Paitich, D., 223, 255, 268
Pallone, N. J., 64, 65, 67
Palmer, L., 93, 94
Panella, M., 93, 94
Panton, J. H., 198, 201, 204, 207, 223,
    255, 257, 259, 265
Papciak, A. S., 138
Parker, J. C., 127, 134
Parker, K. A., 15
Parry, B. L., 139
Partyka, D. J., 32
Parwatikar, S. D., 224, 257, 273
Patrick, C. J., 31, 32
Paul, R., 127, 133
Paulson, M. J., 267
Peck, A. H., 144

Salekin, R., 14
Salekin, R. T., 15, 23, 31, 33
Saltstone, R., 231, 252
Sandberg, M., 138
Sanislow, C., 88
Sapir, A., 185
Saslaw, W., 66
Saslow, W., 60
Saxe, S. J., 61, 66
Sbraga, T. P., 90
Schaffer, C. E., 259
Scheibe, S., 144
Schlenger, W., 144
Schmaltz, B. J., 14, 269
Schmitt, N., 72
Schneider, S. L., 62, 66
Schoenberg, M. R., 21
Schoendorf, K., 88
Schoenfeld, L. S., 61, 62, 66, 127, 134
Schreiber, H. A., 259
Schretland, D., 110
Schumaker, J., 62
Schutte, J. W., 88
Schwemer, G. T., 267
Sciara, A., 15
Scogin, F. R., 62, 65, 66, 71
Scott, J. G., 113, 136
Scott, L., 138
Scott, R. L., 76, 198, 204, 206
Scrapansky, T. A., 259
Scribner, C. M., 17
Scrivner, E. M., 55
Seelen, J., 14
Seely, R. K., 175, 207
Segal, H. G., 93
Segal, J., 85
Sela, H., 139
Selby, D., 127, 134
Sellers, A. H., 20
Seman, W., 255
Serin, R. C., 178
Seto, M. C., 184
Sewell, K. W., 14, 15, 23, 32
Shaffer, J. W., 126
Shapiro, D. L., 9
Shapiro, J. P., 94
Shaw, W. D., 126
Shea, M. E., 226, 255
Shea, S. J., 226, 252, 255, 256
Shealy, L., 179, 182, 198, 202, 206, 207, 208, 209

Shepherd, J. B., 182, 198, 202, 206, 207
Shercliff, R. J., 109
Sherman, R. A., 113
Sheshkin, D. J., 70
Shuman, D. W., 12, 25
Shusman, E., 56, 57, 71, 72
Sidun, N. M., 93
Siegel, J. C., 85, 86
Sigurdardottir, H., 266, 269
Sikimjah, G., 20
Silber, D. E., 92
Silk, K. R., 84, 93
Silk, S. D., 112
Simcox, A. M., 20, 146
Simmons, J. D., 259
Simmons, J. G., 259
Sines, J. O., 235
Singer, R. D., 266, 268
Sittig, M., 112–113, 127
Skeeters, D. E., 223
Skulason, S., 266, 269
Skultety, F. M., 127, 134
Slesinger, D., 132
Sliger, G. I., 264
Slobogin, C., 8, 211
Smith, D., 17
Smith, D. F., 223
Smith, G. P., 146
Smith, S. R., 178
Smith v. United States, 10
Smith-Seemiller, 112–113, 127
Snibbe, H. M., 56, 60, 69, 71
Snibbe, J. R., 126, 139, 141, 142
Snyder, D. K., 127
Solomon, G. S., 235, 266, 268
Sornino, A., 139
Sosner, B., 126, 139, 140, 142
Sparta, S. N., 92
Spitzer, R. L., 161
Spruell, J., 268
Stark, K., 17
Stattin, H., 33, 34
Stava, L., 173, 180, 201
Steen, R. A., 161
Stein, L. A., 76
Stejskal, W. J., 16
Stenning, W., 199
Stern, L. A., 21
Sternbach, R. A., 109, 112, 113, 126
Steuerwald, B. L., 31

SUBJECT INDEX

345

Conjoint interviews, for sexual-abuse
allegations, 97–98
Consent, informed, 83
Consent, and sexual harassment allega-
tions, 162–163
Constructive knowledge standard, 157
Context
and test scores, 36, 274
of violence, 274
Contingency fees, 35
"Contract," on evaluation process, 36
Contributory negligence, 165
Court appearances, and data, xii
Covetous personality type, 242
CPI–R
in police psychology, 68
See also California Psychological
Inventory
Criminal defenses, 9–11
Cultural bias, in selection measures, 74

Data, base rate, xii, 36. See also Base
rate(s)
Daubert v. Merrell Dow Pharmaceuticals,
6–7
Daubert standard, 8, 14, 17
Death row status, and lethal-violence risk
assessment, 257
Delinquency, juvenile. See Juvenile
Depression, faking of, 20
Detection, of malingering and minimization, 18–19
Deviant sexual interests, assessment of,
179
Diagnostic and Statistical Manual of Mental
Disorders. See DSM–III; DSM–IV
Diminished capacity (insanity plea),
10–11
Discontented negativist personality type,
244
Dispositional theories of personality, 40
Divorce, and child custody evaluation, 84
Domestic violence and partner abuse,
227–235
and battered wife syndrome,
235–236
and MCMI studies, 231–234, 237–
238, 282
and MMPI studies, 231, 235,
236–237

Dominant function (Jung), 51
Draw-A-Person test, 16
and law enforcement screening, 56
DSM–III (Diagnostic and Statistical Manual
of Mental Disorders, 3rd ed.), and
avoidant personality disorder, 52
DSM–IV (Diagnostic and Statistical Manual
of Mental Disorders, 4th ed.)
and aggressive-sadistic style, 239
and battered wife syndrome, 236
criteria for antisocial personality in,
22
and diagnoses of Antisocial and
Borderline Personality Disorders,
225
and juvenile sexual offenders, 178
on personality disorders, 39–40
and psychodynamic categories, 42
and psychopathy, 278
Dual roles and relationships, 13, 25, 36
Duress, 9
Durham rule (insanity plea), 10
Durham v. United States, 10

Early Memory Aggressive Potential Score
System, 273
Ecological validity, xi
Education, and waiving of Miranda
rights, 29
Edwards Personal Preference Test, and
law enforcement screening, 56
Electra complex, 41
Emotional disturbance, as defense, 9
Employment decisions
and adverse impact, 73–78
and race norming, 78–79
Enforcing sadist personality type, 240
Equal Employment Opportunity Commis-
sion (EEOC), 73, 155–156, 163
Ethical Standards and Procedures for the
Management of Sex Offenders
(Association for the Treatment
of Sex Abusers), 183
Ethics in forensic psychological practice,
25, 35–37
and backward reasoning, 90
and child-custody evaluation, 101
and juvenile assessment, 34
need for discussions of, 279

and sexual-offender assessment or
treatment, 210–211
Evaluation process, for police force candi-
dates, 64–67
Evidence, rules of, 6–8
Evolution, and Millon's model, 50
"Explosive sadist," 239
Eysenck Personality Inventory, and law
enforcement screening, 56

Factor model, of Cattell, 45–46
Factors (Cattell), 45
Faking
detection of, 19–22
and IPI, 57
and MMPI, 110
and personal-injury litigation, 131
in phallometric assessment, 184
See also Malingering
False allegations of child abuse, 94–98
False confessions, 30
Falsifiability of scientific theories, 7
Federal Insanity Defense Reform Act
(insanity plea), 11
Federal Rules of Evidence (FRE), 6,
7, 8
Fifth Amendment protection, 36
Figure drawings, 16–17
in assessing child-abuse allegations,
92–93
case examples on, 17–18
in child custody evaluations, 84
for sexual offender (case history),
214
Five factor model of personality, 48–49
Forensically relevant instruments, 13.
See also Assessment instruments
Forensic assessment instruments, 13.
See also Assessment instruments
Forensic psychological practice
ethics in, 25, 35–37
and child-custody evaluation, 101
and juvenile offenders, 34
need for discussions of, 279
main functions and areas of, 4
preparation for, 4–8
Forensic psychology, 3–4
areas for improvement in, 277–282
and clinical psychology, 4, 12–13
as dynamic field, 282

interest and opportunities in, xi
and personality, xi
FRE (Federal Rules of Evidence), 6, 7, 8
Freud's psychoanalytic model of personality, 40–42
and rape victims, 172
Frye standard, 6, 8, 15

Gender bias, in *DSM–IV* criteria for per-
sonality disorders, 40
General Aptitude Test Battery (GATB),
78
General Electic v. Joiner, 7
Goldberg Index, 61
*Guidelines for Psychosocial Evaluation of
Suspected Sexual Abuse in Young
Children* (American Professional
Society on the Abuse of
Children), 83
Guilty but mentally ill (insanity plea), 11

Hamilton Depression Inventory, and
sexual harassment, 161
"Hanging judge," 240
Harassment, 164
need for increased training and
exposure in, 281
and significance of test data, 164
See also Racial harassment; Sexual
harassment
Harris v. Forklift Systems, Inc., 158, 161
Head injury, closed, 134–137
Heilbrun guidelines on psychological
tests, 7–8
"High stakes" testing, 13
Hippocrates, 39
Hispanics, and adverse impact, 76–77
Hostility
overcontrolled (OH scale), 235, 251,
265–270, 272
undercontrolled, 265, 266
House–Tree–Person test, 16, 18
Hypochondriasis, 111
Hysteria, 111

Impression management, 85
Imprisonment, psychological effects of,
222

MCMI (Millon Clinical Multiaxial
    Inventory), 14–15, 53
    in child custody evaluation, 87–88
    and medical settings, 137–140, 141,
        143
    and PTSD, 145
    and response distortion, 21
    and sexual harassment, 161
    and sexual offenders, 177, 210
        in case example, 215
    and treatment outcome, 140
    and violence risk assessment, 222,
        224, 226
        domestic violence, 231–234,
            237–238, 282
        lethal violence, 274
    and workers' compensation claims,
        141–142
MCMI–I, 14–15, 139
MCMI–II, 14–15, 23
    and domestic violence, 237
        case example of, 248–250
    and medical settings, 139
MCMI–III, 15, 52
    in assessment of psychopathy, 23–24
    in child custody evaluation, 87–88
    in personal-injury case study, 152
    and PTSD, 145
    with sexual offenders, 177, 178
    in violence risk assessment
        aggression, 240, 242, 242–243,
            244
        domestic violence, 247
McNaughton rule (insanity plea), 10
Megargee classification system, 251, 258–
        262, 259, 264–265, 282
    in case example, 271
    and MMPI–2, 263–264
    and OH scale, 265–266
    and test sensitivity or specificity, 272
Mental or emotional disturbance, as
        defense, 9
Mental health models, and medical
        populations, 141
Mental-physical problem, 108
Meritor Savings Bank v. Vinson, 156,
        162
Millon Adolescent Clinical Inventory.
    See MACI
Millon Behavioral Medicine Diagnostic
    (MBMD), 137

Millon Clinical Multiaxial Inventory.
    See MCMI
Millon Index of Personality Styles
    (MIPS), 72–73, 161
Millon's bioevolutionary theory of
    personality, 40, 49–53, 58, 278–
        279, 280
Minimization, detection of, 18–19
Minnesota Multiphasic Personality
    Inventory. See MMPI; MMPI–2
MIPS (Millon Index of Personality
    Styles), 72–73, 161
Miranda v. Arizona, 29
Miranda rights, youths' waiving of, 28
MMPI, 13
    in child custody evaluation, 85–87
    and chronic pain patients, 112–113,
        115–129, 131, 132–133
        in case study, 152, 153
    and closed head injuries, 135
    and IPI, 57
    for juveniles, 32
    and law enforcement screening, 56
    and personal injury, 141–142
        PTSD, 143–144
    and police psychology, 60–64, 65,
        66, 68
    and sexual offenders, 173, 174–175,
        176–177, 182, 190–201, 201–
        202, 204, 205, 210
        and code types, 205, 206–209
        incest, 204
        indecent exposure, 203
        pedophiles, 200, 201, 210
        rapists, 202–203
    and test bias, 75, 76
    and test sensitivity or specificity,
        272
    and treatment outcome, 140
    and violence risk assessment, 222,
        224, 226–227
        case example of, 248, 249
        domestic violence, 231, 235,
            236–237
        murderers, 252–263
        among prisoners, 282
        special scales for, 265–270
    and workers' compensation, 110
MMPI–2, 13, 14, 18, 56
    in assessment of psychopathy, 23
    and child custody evaluation, 85, 86

Regression to the mean, and police
screening, 73
Repetition compulsion
of childhood sexual abuse victims,
160
of sexual offenders, 178
in violence-risk case, 250
Research in forensic psychology, 4
future directions for, 277–279
in child custody evaluations,
280–281
in screening for police positions,
280
on sexual abuse, 282
and theory, 280
on violence risks, 282
Respondent superior dictum, 107
Risk management, in child-custody
evaluations, 101–102
Risk-taking personality type, 242
Rokeach Value Survey, and law
enforcement screening, 56
Rorschach test, 13, 15–16
in assessment of child-abuse
allegations, 93–94
in assessment of psychopathy, 24–
25, 26–27
attacks on, 16
in child custody evaluations, 84
for chronic pain patients, 134
and juvenile offenders, 33–34
and law enforcement screening, 56
and police psychology, 72
and response distortion, 21
and sexual harassment, 161
and sexual offenders, 173, 205, 210
in case example, 214, 218
juvenile, 178
and violence risk assessment, 222,
224–225, 226
murderers, 273
Rules of evidence, 6–8

Sadistic style, 245
Sadist personality types, 240–241
Sampling bias, for sexual offenders, 190
Sapir, Avinoam, 185
Schizophrenia, faking of, 20, 21
Scientific Content Analysis (SCAN),
185–186

Screening
and adverse impact, 73–78
of law enforcement personnel, 55–
57, 79, 280
and race norming, 78–79
Selection bias, 73–74
Self-deception, vs. impression management, 85
Self-Defeating Personality Disorder, 236
Self-report, in personal-injury case study,
149–152
Self-report measures
MCMI as, 53
in personality assessment, 223–224
Sensitivity of test, 272
Sentence completion tests
in child custody evaluations, 84
for sexual offender (case history),
214, 218
Sex Offender Appraisal Guide, 180
Sex offenders. *See* Sexual offenders
Sexual abuse. *See* Child sexual abuse
Sexual harassment, 155–157
case example on, 166–167
damages for, 159
and employer responsibilities,
157–158
examples of, 158–159
psychologist's role in examinations
for, 159–164, 167
Sexual Interest Card Sort, 179
Sexual offenders
assessment of, 172–173, 175–183,
184
ethical issues in, 210–211
and heterogeneity of population,
189
and personality traits, 189–210
phallometric, 183–184
through statement analysis,
185–189
case examples of, 169–170, 186–189,
211–219
and child sexual abuse statistics,
170–171
need for better identification of,
281–282
and psychological profiling,
173–175
Sexual orientation, and sexual harassment, 158

ABOUT THE AUTHOR

Robert J. Craig, PhD, ABPP, is a diplomate in clinical psychology and in administrative psychology. He is a fellow of the American Psychological Association in Division 50 (Addictions) and a fellow in the Society for Personality Assessment. He serves as a consulting editor to the *Journal of Personality Assessment* and is the recipient of the Martin Mayman Award for outstanding contributions to the literature of personality assessment. He directs the Drug Abuse Program at Chicago VA Health Care System and is adjunct professor at the Chicago School of Professional Psychology and at Roosevelt University. He has written 7 books and has over 100 publications in peer-reviewed journals. Dr. Craig has also conducted many forensic evaluations in a private practice setting.